Great Praise for *Great Heart*

"What does it feel like to starve to death? You wouldn't expect a victim to write a detailed account of the experience, but such was the indomitable character of Leonidas Hubbard. Though stranded in a merciless wilderness, he recorded his impressions to the very end. The story of his astonishing adventure is . . . a narrative that combines the grace of fiction with the power of history. . . . In a suspenseful narrative style *Great Heart* captures the excitement of bold trekking into the unknown. . . . These people were extraordinary individuals . . . dramatizing it all is the untamed magnificence of Labrador . . . the legacy of these adventures is an amazing tale—a campfire story well told."

—Peter M. Leschak, *New York Times Book Review*

"The story surprises and delights. The book is a solid joy."

—Annie Dillard, author of *Pilgrim at Tinker Creek*

"Davidson and Rugge are known and admired by many as authors of the enduringly valuable *The Complete Wilderness Paddler*. Now they have another book, this one a narrative of one of the great, if forgotten, wilderness epics. They have, remarkably, mastered another form of writing and told a story that is just about irresistible. All of this might have been lost if the authors had not recovered the documents, retraced the routes, and spent years putting together this first-rate book, one of the best of its kind in many years."

—*Outside*

"Historian James West Davidson and physician John Rugge . . . canoed the various routes themselves . . . and wrote a tale that combines scrupulous adherence to the evidence with a cross-cutting narrative Hitchcock would have admired. *Great Heart* is a prose epic of Labrador, George Elson its Odysseus."

—Dennis Drabelle, *Washington Post*

"What a movie this book would make. . . . It's the kind of book that will make anyone studying North American history look at Labrador with intense interest. . . . It's also the kind of book, written so fluidly, that captures a reader's imagination. . . . Davidson and Rugge are obviously passionate about the land. . . . Besides giving readers a literary adventure like no other, they pass on immense respect for the small band of history-makers who burned their hearts out mapping Labrador's barrens."

—Margaret Mironowicz, *Toronto Globe and Mail*

"The poetry of Service and Kipling, Jack London's *Call of the Wild*, the exploits of Peary . . . are the backdrops to *Great Heart*. . . . Two remarkable writers . . . have written a compelling story of robust, hearty adventure—and also of rivalry, suspense, romance, and fierce loyalty. Well-written, this book easily deserves a place on the shelves next to other great adventure books such as "Kon-Tiki" and perhaps even *Call of the Wild*."

—William Breyfogle, *Milwaukee Journal*

"The story of these four unlikely explorers . . . [is] to be remembered long after the pages of this book are closed. Hurrah for authors Davidson and Rugge for alchemizing the scattered diaries, letters, and printed accounts of these fatebound four into that most welcome of literary adventures: a good read."

—Ivan Doig, author of *This House of Sky*

GREAT HEART

Also by James West Davidson and John Rugge

THE COMPLETE WILDERNESS PADDLER

Great Heart

THE HISTORY OF A LABRADOR ADVENTURE

James West Davidson

and

John Rugge

With a New Introduction by
Howard Frank Mosher and
A New Afterword by the Authors

KODANSHA INTERNATIONAL

New York • Tokyo • London

Kodansha America, Inc.
114 Fifth Avenue, New York, New York 10011, U.S.A.

Kodansha International Ltd.
17-14 Otowa 1-chome, Bunkyo-ku, Tokyo 112, Japan

Published in 1997 by Kodansha America, Inc.
by arrangement with the authors.
Published simultaneously in Canada by
McGill-Queen's University Press.
First published in 1988 by Viking Penguin Inc.

This is a Kodansha Globe book.

Grateful acknowledgment is made for permission to reproduce photographs from the following sources: Mrs. Margaret Russell, of Mina Hubbard in 1908; Mr. Rudy Mauro, of Dillon Wallace III in 1973; the Canadian Public Archives, of Hubbard's final journal entry; Stephen Loring, of William Cabot, from the Cabot collection in the Museum of Anthropological Archives, the Smithsonian; and Dillon Wallace III, for many prints made from the original negatives in his collection. Photographs have also been reprinted from Dillon Wallace, *The Lure of the Labrador Wild*, and Mina Hubbard, *A Woman's Way Through Unknown Labrador*, when original negatives have not been found.

Extracts from the writings of Dillon Wallace are reprinted by permission of Dillon Wallace III.

Library of Congress Cataloging-in-Publication Data
Davidson, James West.
Great heart : the history of a Labrador adventure / James West Davidson and John Rugge ; with a new introduction by Howard Frank Mosher and a new afterword by the authors.
p. cm.
ISBN 1-56836-168-8 (pb)
1. Labrador (Nfld.)—Discovery and exploration. 2. Hubbard, Leonidas, 1872–1903—Journeys—Newfoundland—Labrador. 3. Wallace, Dillon, 1863–1939—Journeys—Newfoundland—Labrador. 4. Hubbard, Mina. 5. Elson, George—Journeys—Newfoundland—Labrador.
I. Rugge, John. II. Title.
F1136.D27 1996
971.8'201—dc20 96-30843

Book design by Ann Gold
Maps by James West Davidson

Printed in the United States of America

97 98 99 00 Q/FF 10 9 8 7 6 5 4 3 2

For S. Wilson Davidson and
John K. Rugge

Contents

BOOK TWO: ELSON'S RAINBOW

Acknowledgments

THE TWO OF US undertook this book more than ten years ago, which puts us more years over budget than we like to admit. Along the way, we have run up many debts, some of which can never be repaid.

Jim's father, S. Wilson Davidson, proved that a keen wit and generous humor can spring from the Calvinism of the Scots and a good Canadian heritage. Rug's father, John K. Rugge, inculcated not only a rich store of family lore but also a shoes-off approach to canoeing and an abiding respect for the outdoors. Their pride in this project helped to keep us going; regrettably, neither lived to see it finished.

Our research included a number of canoe trips to Labrador and other points north. Our companions on these expeditions have been our collaborators, readers, critics, and friends—true fellow travelers. We tip our paddles to Jesse Grunblatt, Dave Peach, Brad Prozeller, Pat Strohmeyer, and especially Joe Hardy, Ron Turbayne, and Sam Kauffmann, who followed the expedition routes with us and cheerfully endured diary readings, speculative musings, and photo opportunities even in the midst of the black-fly season. Greater love hath no man.

In Labrador, many people offered hospitality and assistance. John Montague and Johnny Michelin provided a host of stories and came to personify for us the best of the fur-trading life and heritage. Jon and Sue Garvin always made their home in Northwest River a welcome place. Doris Saunders, editor and moving spirit of *Them Days*, guides a dedicated staff in rounding up and publishing a library of oral histories that vividly portray life on "the Labrador."

Stephen Loring, an anthropologist and remarkably versatile

wanderer of the outdoors, has shared with us the journals, notes, and photographs of William Cabot, deep knowledge of the country, and boundless enthusiasm for northern studies. Eleanor Wheeler, another Labrador authority and longtime northern traveler, has given us the use of her fine library and the notes of her husband, E. P. Wheeler, as well as critical readings of an early draft. Richard Preston, an anthropologist at McMaster University, kindly supplied an unusual oral history of George Elson.

Several libraries have given indispensable assistance. The Public Archives of Canada lent us microfilms of the diaries of Leonidas Hubbard, George Elson, and Mina Hubbard. The Explorers Club in New York, at the behest of Donald Easton and archivist George Duck, provided Clifford Easton's diary. The North Adams (Massachusetts) Public Library wins two prizes—best microfilm of a local daily and most ancient microfilm reader. Sterling Memorial Library at Yale University made available materials ranging from correspondence of Mina Hubbard to the train schedules of the Montreal Express, circa 1903. Our candidate for best hometown library is Crandall Library of Glens Falls, New York; Bill Crawshaw and the late Betty McAndrew became our correspondents to some pretty obscure corners of North American history.

We will always be grateful to the descendants of those whose story this is. Our appreciation for Mina Hubbard's verve was much increased by our interviews with her daughter, Margaret Russell, and granddaughter, Niki Russell, as well as her friend, the late Selma Riza. Donald Easton proved right in describing his father's diary as packed with detail; he was wrong in hinting that we might find it slow going. Rudy Mauro, a lifelong authority on the Hubbard expeditions, shared sources and photographs with us. Dillon Wallace III allowed us generous access to his father's journals, letters, and photographs; time and again, he and his wife Loretta opened their hearth to us.

Many friends have been called upon to read our narrative in its various versions. Their criticisms and enthusiasm have helped in equal measure. We owe thanks to Kit and Bonnie Collier, John and Peter Davidson, Tom Dowling, Neil Gerdes, Esther Holley, Jean Kames, Charlotte Lee, Mark and Gretchen Lytle, Marie Morgan, Arnold Pritchard, Carolyn Reiners, Joe Reiners, Jr., Irene Solet, Michael Stoff, and Juris and Norine Vancans. Eleanor Davidson cheerfully investigated Hubbard's Michigan connections. Sam Kauffmann, Ken Ludwig, and Adrienne George provided especially detailed and suggestive readings. We also deeply appreciate the unfailing encouragement and generosity of two friends from a previous outing, Angus Cameron and Barbara Bristol.

Some writers are privileged to receive grants to support them during the fallow days of research and draft. Rug was fortunate instead to have Shirley J. Anderson to pick up the reins of the Hudson Headwaters Health Network—difficult work that only she could have done. Pam Smith signed on as a volunteer to type a few pages for us and, before she was done, had transcribed three book-length diaries in their entirety. We are grateful and amazed. Jim and Kay Henry of Mad River Canoes outfitted our several expeditions with Kevlar Explorers—canoes that proved to be the best all-around wilderness craft we have paddled. *Canoe* magazine afforded us the opportunity to test and eventually wear out many pieces of wilderness gear. And Joseph Untalan took time out of a busy schedule to make sharp, professional photographic prints and copy negatives from the originals of the Hubbard and Wallace expeditions.

Finally, Dan Frank, our editor, could not have been more supportive of this project, and his sharp eye and sharper pencil materially improved the final result. To his wife, Patricia Lowy, we owe the striking design of our book jacket.

Paul Tenan, the operator of our library shuttle service, once presented Rug with a fortune cookie that contained the message: "He who suffers remembers." Rug's wife, JoAnne, and the Rugges of the next generation, Bruin and Maile, have had to suffer the absence and the inevitable absentmindedness that commitment to this labor demanded. Our hope is that—some number of fortune cookies later—that commitment and that labor will be remembered as worthwhile.

As George Elson would say—"All aboard!"

—J. W. D. / J. R.
Smith's Restaurant
North Creek, New York

Introduction

A THOUSAND MILES northeast of Montreal, in the wild heart of some of the most forbidding territory on the face of the earth, the faint remains of a man's name are chiseled into a granite boulder. On this spot, Leonidas Hubbard, Jr., perished of starvation in the fall of 1903. His sensational fate as the leader of one of the most star-crossed explorations of this century made headline news throughout the United States and Canada. Yet, over the following decades, the details of his astonishing journey lapsed into the same mysterious obscurity that still shrouds the Labrador wilderness where he died.

The tale begins in New York City, just after the turn of the century. Hubbard, a recently married outdoor writer, was on the lookout for the kind of material all young authors would sell their souls for—a story that hadn't been told before. Though his own experience in the wilderness was limited, Hubbard wangled an assignment from *Outing* magazine to explore the little-known interior highlands of the Labrador-Ungava peninsula: more than half a million square miles of virtually uninhabited taiga and barren lands, stretching from the Gulf of St. Lawrence north to Ungava Bay, and from Hudson Bay east to the icy North Atlantic—a domain of thundering whitewater rivers, vast windswept lakes, and unbroken evergreen forests. To this day, it is a region inhabited by wolves, caribou, and little else.

With him, Hubbard took his close friend and fellow outdoorsman, a forty-year-old widowed attorney named Dillon Wallace, and George Elson, a young Scots-Cree guide and woodsman from Hudson Bay. In the late spring, the trio embarked in a single 18-foot canvas canoe, planning to cross "the last blank spot on the map of North America."

Hubbard's party entered this *terra incognita* with great enthusiasm. Almost immediately, however, they made a fatal error, mistaking an all-but-unnavigable stream for their intended route up the much larger Naskapi River. Blunder followed blunder until, on their last legs after months of fighting impassable rapids and impenetrable swamps, they were obliged to turn back before reaching their halfway point. During their forced retreat, the explorers abandoned their canoe, ran out of food, and were overtaken by the early onset of the fierce Canadian winter. Thirty miles from safety, Leonidas Hubbard collapsed and died. Miraculously, Wallace and Elson escaped with their lives, though not without further heroics rarely surpassed in the annals of true wilderness adventures.

Dillon Wallace chronicled the tragic saga of the 1903 odyssey in one of the most popular books of the day, *The Lure of the Labrador Wild*. Although Wallace as yet had no way of knowing this, Labrador would continue to exert a critical influence on his life for years to come. In 1905, Mina Hubbard, Leonidas's strong-willed widow, outraged over certain passages in Wallace's book that suggested Hubbard may have made serious mistakes in strategy, and deeply suspicious that Wallace may not have done all he could to save her husband, returned to Labrador with George Elson to retrace and complete her husband's journey, and to vindicate his name. At the same time, Wallace mounted his own hell-for-leather rival expedition. And in the early summer of that year, amidst a sensational media flap, the great race across interior Labrador was on.

Both of the 1905 trips were remarkably arduous, and full of adventure, as the competing expeditionaries desperately attempted to leap-frog one another across the alien landscape of the country that explorer Jacques Cartier called "the land God gave to Cain." More books were subsequently written: Mina Hubbard's *A Woman's Way Through Unknown Labrador*, Dillon Wallace's *The Long Labrador Trail*. Yet the tale of the race itself, the fierce jealousies and recriminations that fueled it, and the secret love story that emerged from it, cutting passionately across contemporary barriers of class and race, would remain untold for more than three quarters of this century.

It is the summer of 1975. Two upstate New Yorkers, John Rugge, a physician, and James West Davidson, a professional historian, both veteran canoeists and coauthors of *The Complete Wilderness Paddler*, are making their way into central Labrador, retracing a segment of Leonidas Hubbard's 1903 trip. At the south end of Hope Lake, they are astonished to see exactly the same scene that was photographed by the Hubbard party, right down to the identical three fir trees in the foreground, framing the sheer rock walls of mountains soaring straight up out of the lake—a scene of nearly preternatural desolation and immutability. Already, Davidson and Rugge are captivated by the allure of this primeval land, from which the last glacier retreated only 6,000 years ago. How many places, after all, have remained so totally unchanged and unspoiled seventy-five years into the most rapacious century in the history of mankind? Yet when they attempt to forge overland to the site of Hubbard's final resting place, through a jumbled maze of uncharted mountains, ponds, streams, and string bogs, they are driven back by pestilential hordes of mosquitoes and blackflies. The two travelers withdraw—but not before vowing to return and penetrate the mysteries surrounding Hubbard's expedition and the follow-up journeys, two years later, of his widow and Dillon Wallace.

The story of Davidson's and Rugge's explorations—both into Labrador and into the archives of libraries, newspaper files, and long-forgotten family papers—is in its way as compelling as Hubbard's own tale, which John Rugge, a bred-in-the-bone country boy, grew up hearing from his father. Deeply intrigued, Rugge scouted up copies of Dillon Wallace's *The Lure of the Labrador Wild* and *The Long Labrador Trail,* as well as Mina Hubbard's *A Woman's Way Through Unknown Labrador.* Years later, Dr. Rugge briefly cited the 1903 and 1905 Labrador expeditions, with a passing reference to Mina's conviction that Wallace was somehow to blame for her husband's death, in the wilderness canoeing guide he coauthored with Jim Davidson. Davidson's instincts as a historian were immediately aroused when, upon reading the turn-of-the-century Labrador books himself, he found no reference to any rivalry or bad feelings in either *A Woman's Way* or *The Long Trail.* Where, then, had his partner come by his information about the trouble between Mina and Wallace? Presumably from the oral history passed down through Rugge's family.

Suspecting that beneath the recorded stories of the three expeditions lay another story, one of human drama and emotions, Davidson and Rugge launched into a search of the newspapers of Hubbard's era. In files dating from the late spring to the early summer of 1905, they hit pay dirt. Headlines from New York to Halifax crackled with sensational innuendos about the "rival Labrador expeditions" and "Mrs. Hubbard's suspicions." With the game now afoot, the historian and the doctor began an intensive investigation to unearth whatever primary source material they could find for Wallace's and Mina Hubbard's books. A blind phone call, the longest of long shots, resulted in the location of Dillon Wallace's grandson, who, sometime later, discovered his grandfather's Labrador journals, long thought to have been lost, in the bottom of a dusty trunk. A speaking engagement led to an equally fortuitous meeting with Mina Hubbard's granddaughter, and the bonanza discovery, in the Canadian Public Archives in Ottawa, of the microfilmed diaries, not only those of Leonidas and Mina Hubbard, but of the Cree guide, George Elson, as well. By degrees, with the invaluable help of these "scrawled letters, waterspotted journals, [and] photograph negatives with black faces and white-coaled eyes," Davidson and Rugge were able to retrace the day-by-day course of all three Labrador expeditions.

The result of their decade-long research, which included several more canoe expeditions into the Labrador outback, was the publication, in 1988, of *Great Heart: The History of a Labrador Adventure*—a book that would quickly come to be regarded as a landmark in the literature of the Far North and literary adventure writing in general. Acclaimed by the *New York Times Book Review* as "an astonishing adventure . . . a narrative that combines the grace of fiction with the power of history," and by the *Washington Post Book World* as "an artfully told prose epic of Labrador," *Great Heart* has acquired over the years an impressive coterie of knowing devotees, from Annie Dillard to Ivan Doig, who hailed the book as "that most welcome of literary adventures: a good read." In fact, *Great Heart* is no more a mere adventure tale than, say, *A River Runs Through It* is just a fishing story. Rather, as Dillard, Doig, and numerous other writers and critics have suggested, it is a profound character-driven work of history and biography that reads like a first-rate novel. Yet until now, with its reissue by Kodansha America, coinciding with the scheduled filming in Newfoundland of a dramatic feature film based on Mina Hubbard's 1905 trip, *Great Heart* has remained nearly as well-kept a secret as the moving love story at its center and the harshly gorgeous land where it took place—a land whose very name, Labrador, remains a mystery to this day.

Coauthoring a book—any book—is a tricky undertaking. For starters, who'll write which sections? Having already collaborated successfully on their wilderness canoeing book, Rugge and Davidson had a solid working relationship; but *Great Heart* was no guide book.

How could two different authors, with entirely different styles and sensibilities, write an action-adventure story with a single unbroken tone and narrative voice throughout? As Rugge and Davidson considered their options, they hit upon a brilliant idea—one that would solve these technical problems at the same time that it enabled them to maintain the suspense of all three expeditions. Eschewing an "olympian perspective," they decided to retell the story not from their own viewpoint but, relying heavily upon the diaries of the four principals—Leonidas, Mina, George Elson, and Dillon Wallace—"to narrate the tale through the eyes of those who lived it." This decision not only enabled the authors to subsume their own personalities and voices in those of their characters, but to impart to the true story the engaging novelistic qualities that give *Great Heart* a uniquely powerful immediacy in the annals of exploration writing, without diminishing its accuracy as historical reportage.

The book is structured in two parts. Book One, "Hubbard's Lure," focuses on the fateful 1903 expedition, and exemplifies full-throttle action writing at its best, from the party's failure to locate their correct route to their hellish forced retreat from the bush, one short step ahead of winter. One might well expect Book Two, "Elson's Rainbow," to be a tad anticlimactic after the hideous death march of Book One. Not a bit of it. If anything, the drama intensifies as human issues come to the fore in the 1905 expeditions, with the bitter falling-out between Mina Hubbard and Dillon Wallace, and the surprising emergence of George Elson as the real hero and "great heart" of Mina's trip.

More wonderful still is the unexpected romance at the heart of Book Two, unguessed-at for decades. As George leads Mina confidently through a wilderness that to this very hour, in many places, has never seen a human footprint, he begins to fall in love with the attractive, high-spirited young widow. Elson's running journal of the 1905 trip is full of thinly veiled references to this growing romatic attachment, despite his almost certain knowledge that nothing can ever come of his feelings. His most telling revelation, partly crossed out but still legible, appears in the back of the diary: "If I was tould [*sic*] to go around the world and pick one out I would come back and still have you for sure." Elsewhere, just as he seems to teeter on the brink of an outright profession of love, he refers to "another book"—a private journal he seems to be keeping separately: "She is so bright and smart and I am glad that she does trust me. See other book." Unfortunately, no "other book" has ever been found—leaving the love story something of a mystery, and *Great Heart* the richer for it.

What, then, of these enduring enigmas at the heart of the book? Why did Hubbard perish in 1903, just thirty miles from safety? Was any part of George Elson's love for Mina, on the 1905 trip, reciprocated? And exactly who was this tremendously independent-minded woman who endeavored to complete the wilderness trek that had destroyed her husband two years earlier?

In their carefully considered epilogue, James West Davidson and John Rugge reflect on these conundrums, drawing measured conclusions where the facts will support them, and acknowledging the ultimately inscrutable nature of other matters.

As something of a Labrador hand myself, whose interest in the Hubbard story, like John Rugge's, dates back to my boyhood discovery of a battered copy of Dillon Wallace's *The Lure of the Labrador Wild* in my grandparents' farmhouse attic, I believe that, to one degree or another, the four main participants of this unforgettable tale achieved some approximation of what they were seeking. Adventurer and indefatigable romantic that he was, Leonidas Hubbard had the adventure of a lifetime, which, sadly, resulted in his death.

Dillon Wallace, for his part, discovered in Labrador a new career for himself—as a writer, and a good one. To this day, *The Lure of the Labrador Wild* is widely recognized as a classic of Far North literature; and after finishing *The Long Labrador Trail,* Wallace went on to write a total of twenty-five books of adventure and exploration for both children and adults.

George Elson, looking for little more than seasonal employment as a guide and a chance to see a new country, found in himself the qualities of a born leader. The portrait of Elson that emerges from *Great Heart* is that of a man of rare courage, judgment, and character. And while Mina almost certainly failed to return his love, she held George in such high regard that thirty years later, after a long, ultimately unsuccessful second marriage in England, she returned to Canada once again, met George, and went canoeing with him.

As for Mina, she not only became the first woman and the first non-native to venture across "the last blank spot on the map of North America," but did so with great good humor and élan.

Just two days away from her arrival at Ungava Bay, she wrote in her diary, "Though I dread going back, I think that I should like to spend the summer like this always. . . . Was thinking today how strange it is. I have not wanted to see anyone, I have been lonely for no one, etc., have come these two months to this deserted wilderness and have never felt as if I were far from home." In addition to realizing Leonidas's vision, she had found something more precious still: a measure of peace with herself. This was the great gift to Mina Hubbard of the wondrous and perilous land that had touched her life so deeply.

In the annals of Far North literature, *Great Heart* ranks with Dillon Wallace's *Lure,* Elliott Merrick's *True North,* and Lawrence Millman's *Last Places,* as a classic of the genre. In addition to its widely acknowledged literary merits, the Davidson-Rugge book is important because, do what we may, the great wilderness where its story took place is now shrinking fast, and treasuring the book may well be one of the best ways to preserve what is still left unspoiled of the land itself. Much of Labrador has already been ruined by open-pit mining, overrun by "sport hunters" out of luxury fly-in camps and, worst of all, flooded by man-made inland seas dammed up to fuel power plants, which light, among other places, the Montreal and New York boardrooms where such shortsighted decisions as drowning our last primordial wilderness and letting extraordinary books like *Great Heart* lapse out of print are made.

That Labrador, of all places, is a land worth preserving is a truism. Yet until you've stood in the midst of a migrating reindeer herd, as George Elson and Mina Hubbard did, or seen a great white wolf trot unconcernedly across your path, or fished a river never before fished by man for trout as colorful as the northern lights that illuminate the Labrador night sky, it's hard to imagine the splendors of this last boreal fastness.

"He's a beautiful place, Labrador is," an Inuit friend told me the last time I was there. "But so delicate, eh? So vulnerable. Once he's gone, the only place you'll ever find him again is in the pages of books like *Great Heart.*"

Howard Frank Mosher
July 1996

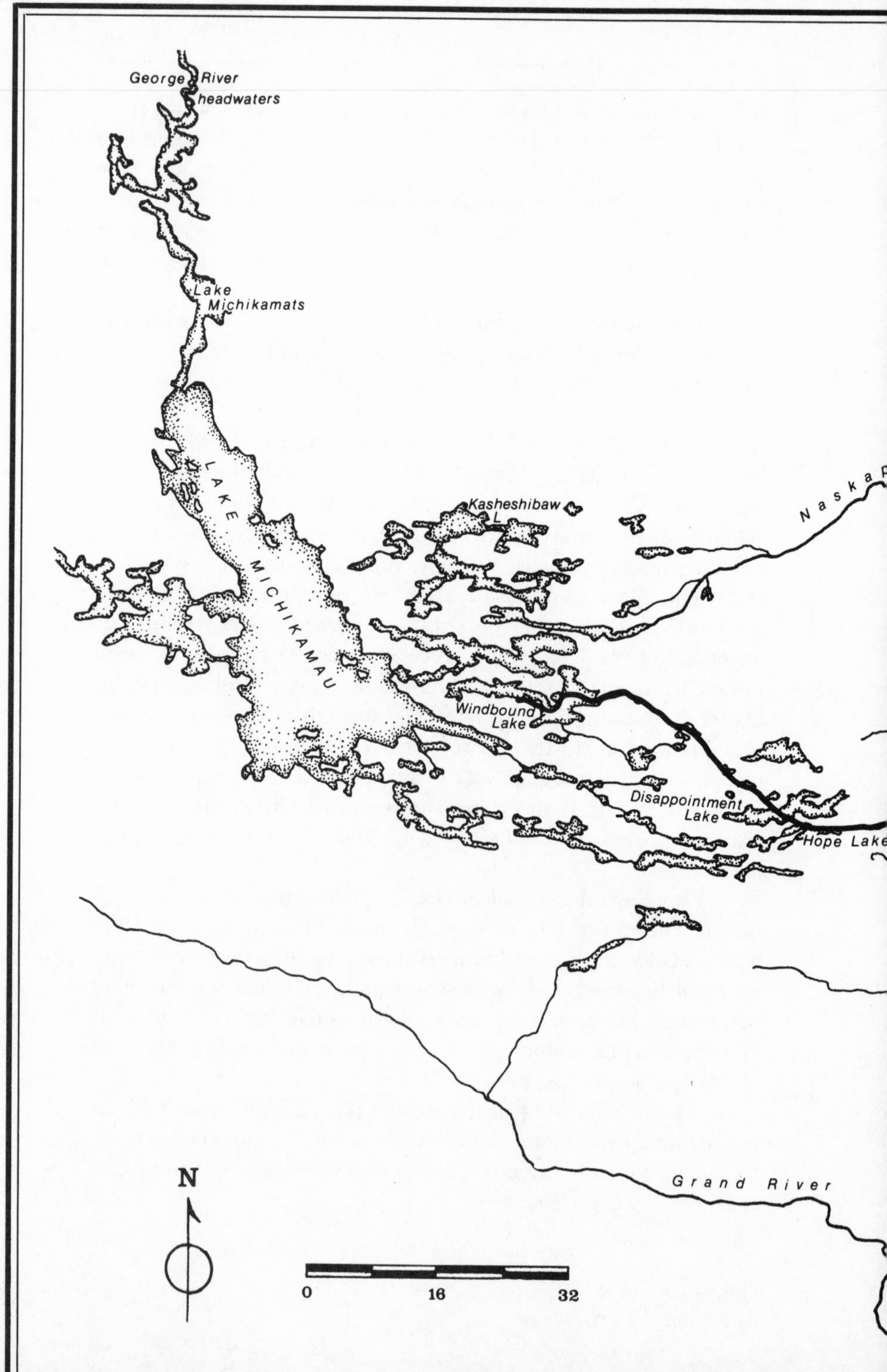
George River
headwaters
Lake
Michikamats
LAKE MICHIKAMAU
Kasheshibaw
L
Naskap
Windbound
Lake
Disappointment
Lake
Hope Lake
Grand River
N
0
16
32

The Route of 1903

HUBBARD

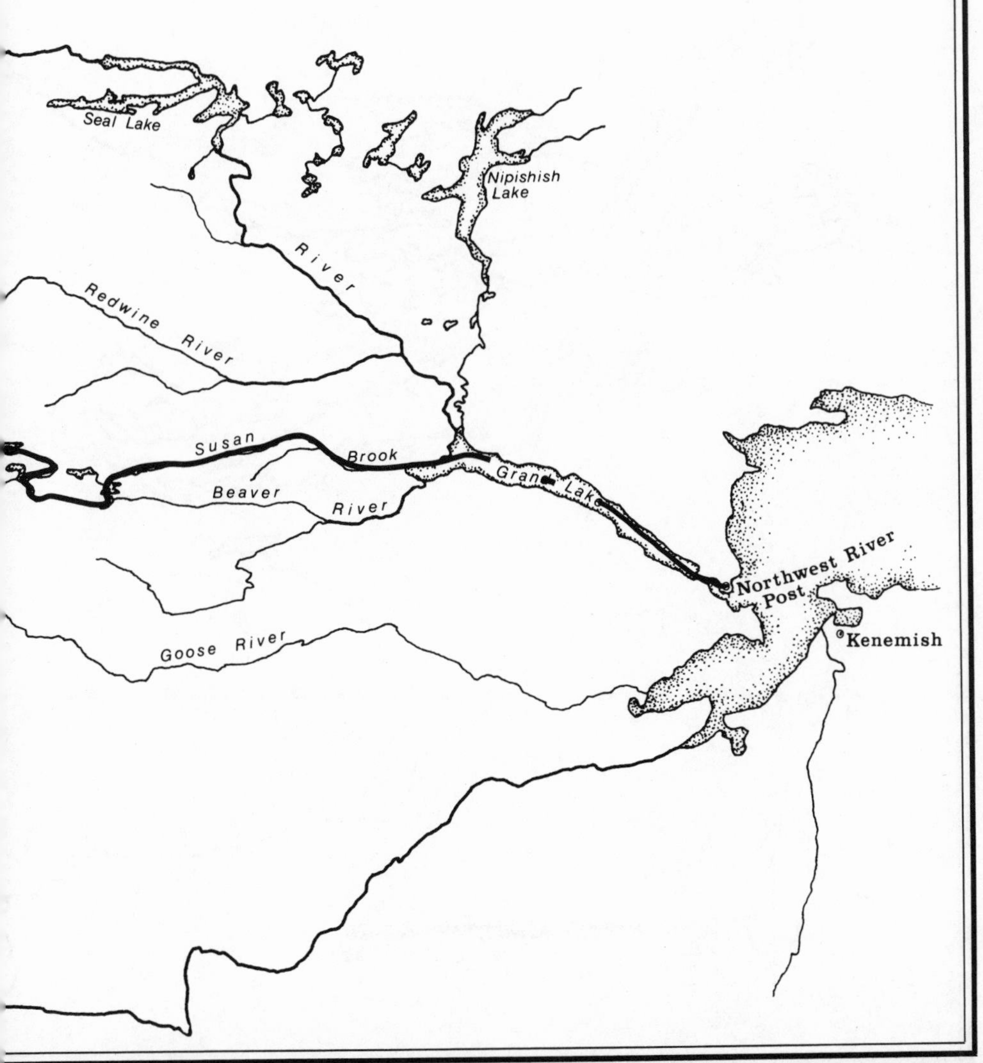

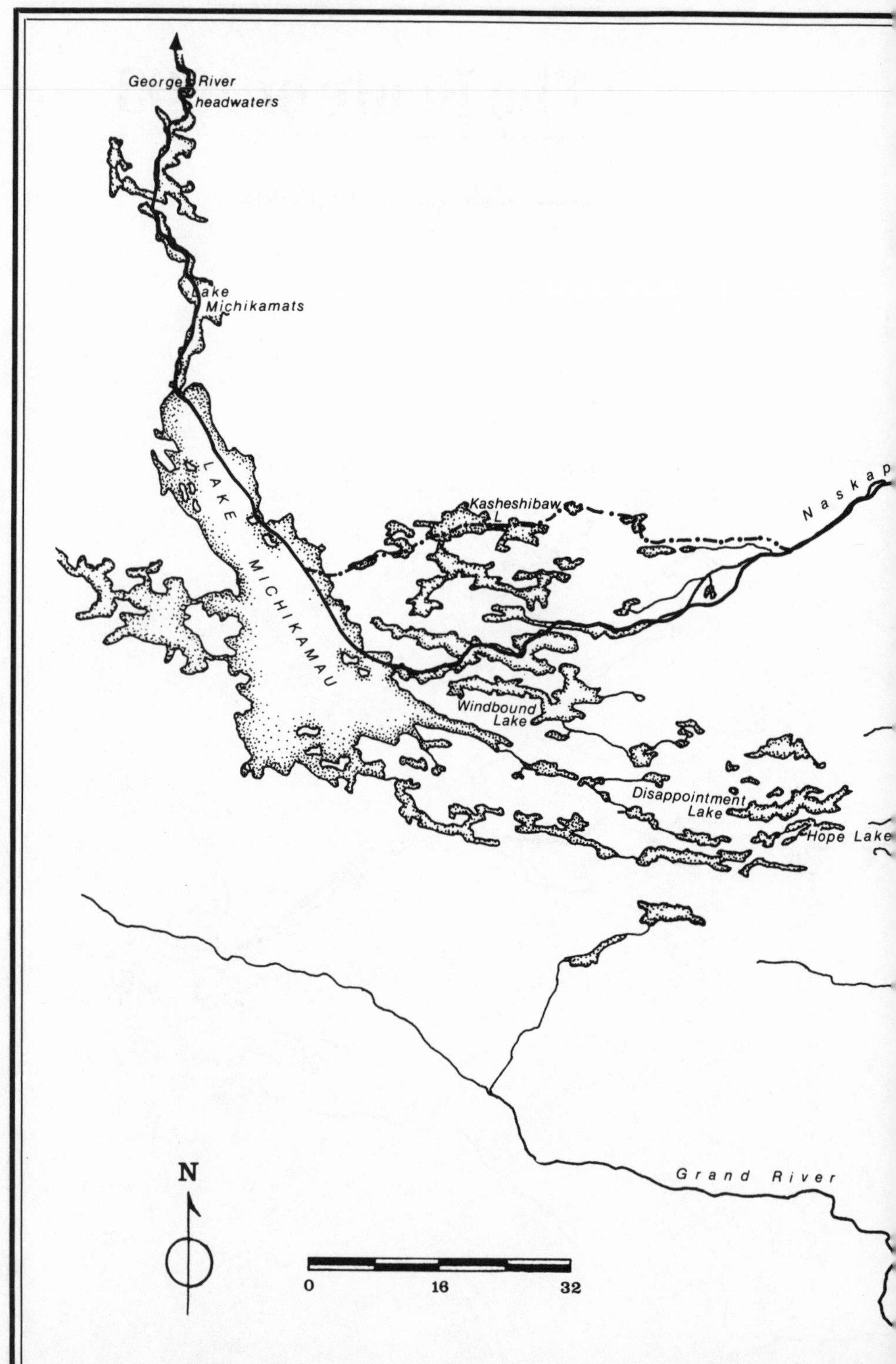
George River
headwaters
Lake
Michikamats
LAKE MICHIKAMAU
Kasheshibaw
L
Naskap
Windbound
Lake
Disappointment
Lake
Hope Lake
Grand River
N
0
16
32

The Routes of 1905

MINA HUBBARD

DILLON WALLACE

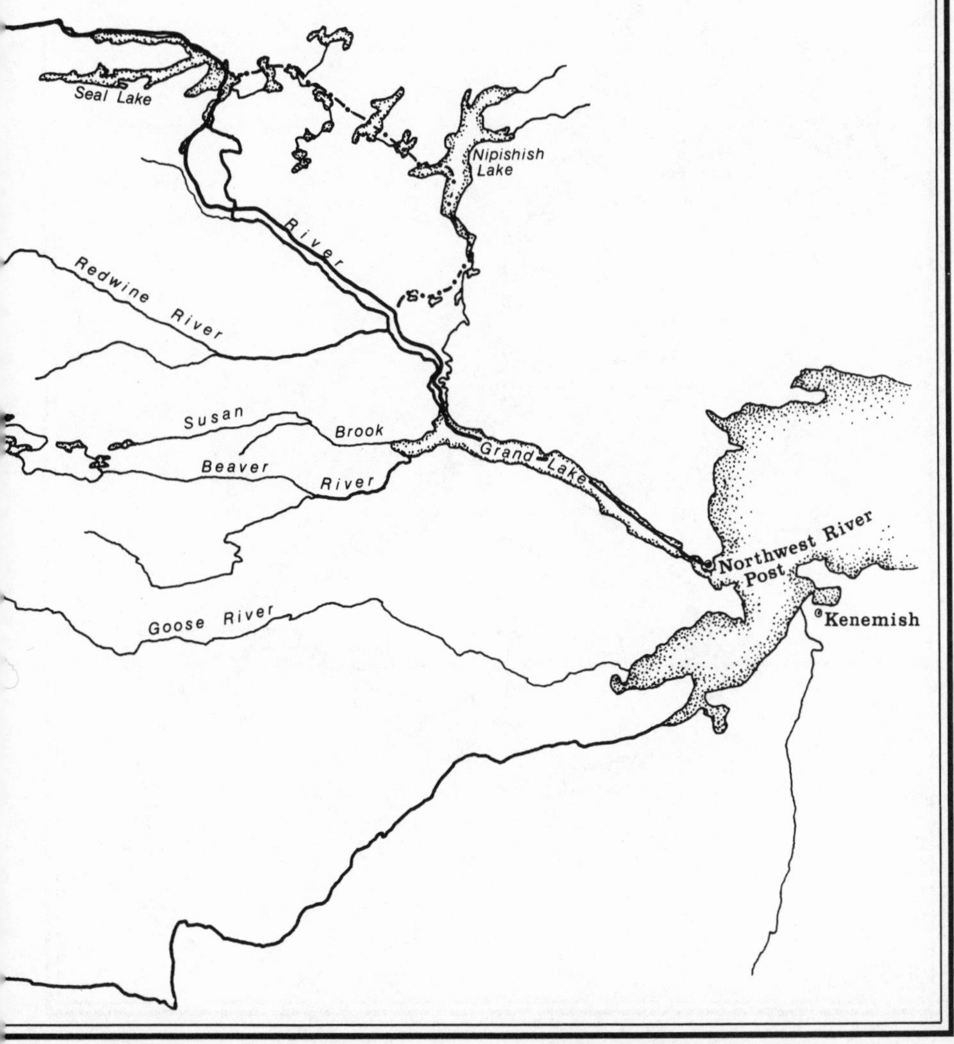

Labrador

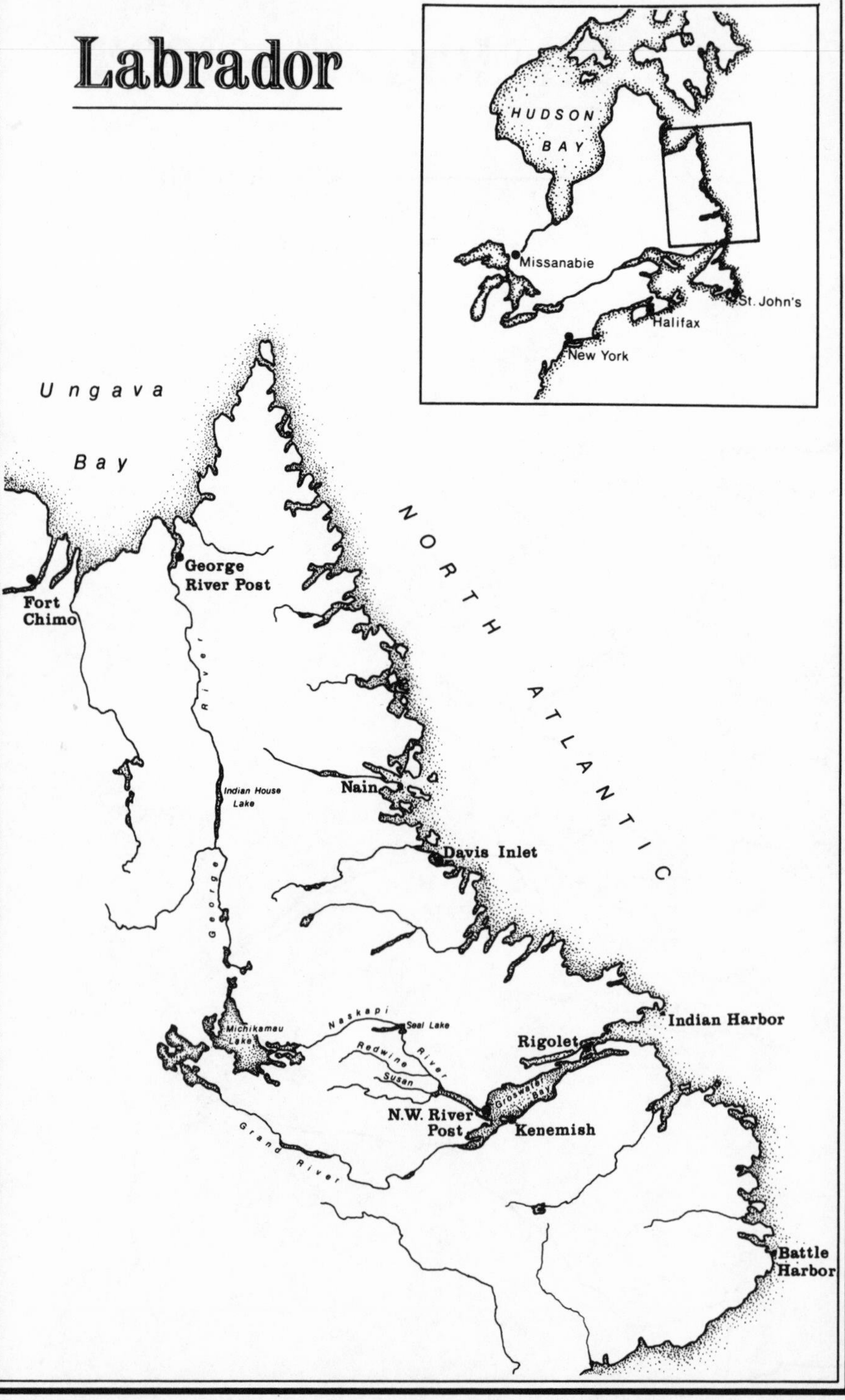

HUDSON BAY
Missanabie
St. John's
Halifax
New York
Ungava Bay
NORTH ATLANTIC
George River Post
Fort Chimo
George River
Indian House Lake
Nain
Davis Inlet
Indian Harbor
Rigolet
Michikamau Lake
Naskapi
Seal Lake
Redwine River
Susan
Groswater Bay
N.W. River Post
Kenemish
Grand River
Battle Harbor

Prologue

The Last Blank Spot on the Map of North America

THE MAN IS ALONE. He lies in a tent, pitched near a small stream amid a field of boulders and stunted spruce trees. Everywhere the ground is covered with a spongy, damp moss: pale and drained of color, like the man himself.

The moss and the spruce stretch on beyond the horizon without end. In low places, the land is broken by swamps and quaking bogs and pitcher plants; on higher hills, the scouring of wind, rain, and snow leaves only the boulders heaped across the fields.

Carefully the man props himself up so he can see his fire, then pulls his blanket closer. The tent, of old-fashioned balloon silk, stands with its front open to the flames. Their reds and oranges are the only warmth in the entire landscape—the only warmth left to him.

The man feels gently for the canvas bag at his side. He manages to pull out a notebook and stubby pencil. With his knife, he whittles a new point. It takes time; his hands are not working just right.

> Sunday, October 18th, 1903
>
> Alone—in camp . . .

It is an effort, now, even to write.

> Alone—in camp—junction of Nascaupee and some other stream—estimated (overestimated, I hope) distance above head of Grand Lake, 33 miles. . . .

> Our past two days have been trying ones. I have not written my diary because so very weak. Day before yesterday we caught sight of a caribou but it was on our lee, and winding us, got away before a shot could be fired. Yesterday at an old camp, we found the end we had cut from a flour bag. It had a bit of flour sticking to it. We boiled it with our old caribou bones and it thickened the broth a little.

Flour gone. Peameal gone. Sugar, coffee, cocoa—long gone. Canoe abandoned. Rifle, sextant, films—left along the trail. He has little now to sustain him; only his memories.

> We also found a can of mustard—Mina gave it to me—which we had thrown away. I sat and held it in my hand a long time, thinking how it came from Congers and our home, and what a happy home it was, and what a dear, dear girl presided. . . .
>
> Last night I fell asleep while the boys were reading to me. This morning I was very, very sleepy. After the boys left, I drank a cup of strong tea and some bone broth. I also ate some of the really delicious rawhide, boiled with the bones, and it made me stronger—strong to write this.

The rain, coming hard again, makes the fire hiss. Calmly the man studies the diminishing source of heat.

> My tent is pitched in open-tent style in front of a big rock. The rock reflects the fire, but now it is going out because of the rain. I think I shall let it go and close the tent, till rain is over, thus keeping out wind and saving wood. Tonight or tomorrow, perhaps, the weather will improve so I can build a fire, eat the rest of my moccasins, and have some more bone broth.
>
> I am not suffering. The acute pangs of hunger have given way to indifference. I am sleepy. I think death from starvation is not so bad. But let no one suppose I expect it. I am prepared—that is all. I think the boys will be able, with the Lord's help, to save me.

AFTER MONTHS, EVEN years, of dreaming, planning, and hard trekking, Leonidas Hubbard found himself finally at this camp, with its one remaining thread of hope. As the historical record makes clear, his tent was pitched by a stream known as the Susan, not far from where one of its tributaries joins it. The exact spot has since been marked by a small plaque.

The world is fairly littered with commemorative plaques, but this one is unusual. At least we have never seen any historical marker quite so far off the beaten track. There is no road leading to the site of Hubbard's camp—not even the faintest trail. Even now, after more than eighty years, no one hikes here. Around the spot, there is still only the white caribou moss and the scrub pine and the empty swamps. The nearest human dwelling is a trapper's cabin, itself deserted most of the year, some twenty miles distant. The closest settlement remains the outpost that Hubbard had been trying to reach. It is fifty miles away, with only forest and open water intervening.

Indeed, the entire Ungava-Labrador peninsula remains a vast roadless wilderness of mosquito-infested bogs, windswept barrens, and lakes without names. In its 550,000 square miles, Labrador has but one highway leading to the Outside, a track of gravel and mud that is passable only in certain seasons. Rough as it is, the road doesn't actually join any others; it just comes to an end at a railhead deep inside the northern forest. There, flatcars can be had to convey trucks and autos two hundred miles south to the macadam world.

For more than a decade, the harsh beauty of Labrador has attracted the two of us, a historian and a physician. In the spare months of our summers, we have paddled a number of rivers that work their way from the lakes of Labrador's high plateau through canyons to the sea, while the odd hours of our winters have been taken up reading about the land's history. It was by these routes, in ways sometimes oblique and roundabout, that we came to hear about Hubbard's camp by the stream and the story behind it.

This book is that history. It recounts the attempts of three expeditions to cross the barrens of Labrador, in 1903 and 1905. The mainspring of the tale—the man who drove it—was Leonidas Hubbard, Jr., a young journalist almost innocently in search of a reputation and eager to explore one of the last blank spots on the map of North America. But the story is not so much about Hubbard as about the way his dreams touched those closest to him: his wife, Mina; his companion, Dillon Wallace; and a remarkable half-Scottish, half-Cree woodsman from Hudson Bay, George Elson.

At the time, the Hubbard expeditions aroused intense public

interest, for the popular press was eager for tales of the far north. The first installment of Jack London's *Call of the Wild* appeared in the *Saturday Evening Post* the day Hubbard departed for Labrador, in June 1903, and Robert Peary was raising money for yet another assault on the North Pole. Hubbard's expedition was not exactly in the same league as Peary's; still, when the last ship of the Labrador run returned south with no word from the interior, the newspapers scented a story. FEAR EXPLORERS ARE LOST speculated the *New York Times* on November 1. MR. HUBBARD STILL MISSING reported the *Tribune* two weeks later. It was only in January that the first dispatches, relayed hundreds of miles by dogsled, began to hint at what had actually befallen Hubbard and his companions.

Those familiar with the outcome will understand the fell fascination of the tale. In any such drama, there are innumerable *what if's*, rehearsed over and over in the conviction that one decision or another might have made the difference between safety and success or failure and slow starvation. But, in truth, human fate seldom depends on the cast of a single die. It is the sum of many incremental steps, each shaped by the set of personal character. This is what makes the records of the Hubbard expeditions so compelling in the end: They show how the dearest of friends, pushed to the limits of human endurance, were forced to make decisions about each other's lives that would haunt them to the end of their days. For indeed, the matter did not rest in 1903. There proved to be not one but two sequels to the original expedition. Of these the press also took note; but because of the extraordinary passions and animosities aroused, the diaries of the participants were never made public and the complete story never told.

This is an attempt to recount the tale in full, based on our own retracing of the Labrador routes by canoe, as well as the first complete reading of the diaries, from both 1903 and 1905. While our narrative is history, the quality of the evidence that has been left behind is so detailed and rich it invites the historian to tell the story using techniques traditionally thought to belong to the province of fiction. We have done so but with the goal of reconstructing the past, not inventing a world of our own. Readers interested in our sources, reflections on points of controversy, and a few details of our own Labrador trips will find them in the epilogue and the chapter notes gathered at the end of the book.

Like the landscape of Labrador itself, Hubbard's tale is given to extremes. Few journals in the annals of exploration record a more selfless devotion in the face of privation, nor a fiercer rivalry in the wake of tragedy. The relation between extremes is hardly coincidental—for the depth of devotion is what gives the rivalry its sharpness, just as the beauty of the barrens arises out of their severity. The Hubbard expeditions attact us not so much as a long-neglected chapter in the history of exploration—they are that—but simply as a revelation of the human heart.

BOOK ONE
Hubbard's
Lure

1

Too Soon to Die

It was just getting light finally, early light before the sun come up. Now, for the first time, he could see the river. Hudson's River.

Even out the dusty window of the train it looked fine—big water and broad, with blue hills rising up the far side. Close to shore where the river cut near the track was a family of ducks, the mother teaching the little ones to dunk. George wished he could be down by the water's edge calling them. They were small ducks—little birds with a bit of white on their necks. He didn't know their name in English, but he could remember going out on the marshes as a boy and calling them; then watching as they circled round, looking down to see who had spoken so sweet and charmed them over with a cry like theirs. When he got older and his voice got too deep, the ducks wouldn't come anymore. But any time he heard them now—oh, he loved to sit and listen!

He pulled out his timetable with its list of stops and the mileage set out by each one. It had been a long ways to come. A couple-hundred-miles' upstream paddle from Hudson's Bay to Missanabie, even before boarding the train. Then at Missanabie, catch the Canadian Pacific, sit back, and tote up the miles. Missanabie, Ontario to New York City: 1,059. Two days' ride and exactly a thousand miles farther than Jerry had come.

Jerry was Mr. Hubbard's first guide. He'd been given an envelope of money and put on the train, like George. But after fifty-nine miles—only the first stop—he'd got off and turned back. It made George kind of uneasy.

On the back of the timetable was the menu of the New York Central buffet car—"buffay," they called it. Once in the city, putting up his meals was Mr. Hubbard's job—Mr. Hubbard would know that, wouldn't he? Still, that menu made George think. Maybe he better try the buffet.

The buffet car had lots of little tables, a long counter, and a man with a white jacket and black skin—George hoped he spoke English. He sure wouldn't speak Cree.

"Yes, suh," said the black fellow.

George was a bit taken aback. Nobody had ever called him sir before. He pulled the menu from his pocket.

Griddle cakes and maple syrup, that was no problem. But what were "graham gems"? Could you have graham gems for breakfast?

The black man was waiting.

"Please, some griddle cakes and maple syrup. Oatmeal and cream. Eggs and ham. A cup of coffee."

He wished he knew the real reason why Jerry had turned back. The whole village knew *what* had happened, but near as George could tell, only Mr. King and Jerry knew why. It had all started when Mr. Hubbard came to Missanabie on a fishing trip the year before and met Mr. King. A lot of sports came up to Missanabie to fish. Then, in late spring, a letter had come down the tracks from this Hubbard. He'd decided to do some exploring in Labrador and needed an Indian guide—maybe that fella Jerry he liked so much.

Jerry was a good trapper and in the woods a lot. He was honest and clever, spoke English, and had a family that could use the money. Three days after climbing aboard the CP he'd showed up back at Missanabie, looking fancy in a new suit but hardly able to walk. His head was full of liquor, and all that money gone.

The boys had never seen Mr. King so hot, but he settled down to a mild note to Mr. Hubbard. Jerry, he regrets to say, has decided not to make the trip. He's got no fear of Labrador, but he's heard about New York City and he won't come because he doesn't want to die so soon. Another man, name of George Elson, is on his way in Jerry's place.

George had to wonder, though. What was that business about dying so soon?

Jerry was a good man and no coward. Turning back like that—George didn't like the set of it. Why should Jerry worry about New York?

The thing was, Jerry knew Mr. Hubbard. Not too well, but he knew him. Had something about this Hubbard scared him off?

Maybe he should have talked to Jerry. He could've wandered

over to the Indian tents and sat at Jerry's fire one night; talked and poked sticks in the embers and finally worked around to asking about Hubbard. What would Jerry have said—anything much? Would he have been embarrassed about his drunk and not want to talk? Jerry didn't owe George anything, and, of course, George wasn't a full-blood. Jerry might've figured—George being part white and all—anything bad he said might get back to Mr. King.

How little Jerry knew. If it had been George's father—Scotch, a trader, and a Company employee—it might have been different. For George's father, Mr. King would have put his arm around his shoulder and talked to him low and quiet. But for the son of a country wife—the son by a Cree woman—that was something else. No matter how light that son looks; no matter if he could read and write; no matter, even, if somebody who didn't know better might call him sir—those things didn't stand. Any talk with Mr. King at Missanabie was kept straight and to business; and anything about a white man come up—why, you wouldn't even want to raise an eyebrow. Mr. Hubbard was a fine young man, Mr. King said. He was offering good money for a season's work. Did George care to undertake the job or not?

George Elson would undertake it. And having said so, would keep his course.

New York came up fast. One minute they were passing through little towns and green land, then the next they were over a bridge and coming into the city. The train stopped at a place called 125th Street, hardly more than a village, then dipped into its own cutting and down a tunnel so thick with soot the walls disappeared. After a while, it rolled into daylight and the conductor was calling out "Grand Central" and everybody was getting up.

George wandered out onto the platform with the others, toting his bag. Everyone seemed to be walking fast; it was like jumping into a river. He found himself moving along with the current.

Where would Mr. Hubbard be? George had not thought to ask this question. At Missanabie, a stranger gets off the train and everybody knows right away. The stationmaster comes up, and everything gets set right. At Grand Central no one looked to be in charge.

Mr. King had written Mr. Hubbard all the particulars—the time, the date, the train number. Had he sent along a description of George?

He moved along looking at everybody, nobody giving him a second glance. He circled back to his platform, waited for his train to empty the last of its passengers, rejoined the crowd, and finally passed out of the marble hall onto the street.

Hubbard had not come.

George fished inside his coat and pulled out a paper he was carrying. Outing—239 Fifth Ave.—NYC.

The street where he stood, number 42, made him nearly deaf with the noise. Gongs and whistles on the wagons, the iron wheels clanking over the cobbles, the horses whinnying, the small boys calling out with their papers. After watching a while, George began to sort things out. At the side of the street was a long line of two-wheel carriages, each with the driver sitting high in the back. Men coming out of the station got into these buggies and the drivers were their servants. Then he noticed that the men always went to the first buggy in line. If the men owned these buggies, wouldn't they be spread out here and there? The rides must be for hire.

He took a deep breath and stepped up to the first buggy. "239 Fifth Avenue, please?"

The driver nodded, moved a lever by his seat, and the passenger door swung open. George pitched his bag in and climbed aboard.

2

Everything on the Line

CASPAR WHITNEY, editor of *Outing* magazine, was informed that Hubbard's half-breed had arrived in the front room and deposited himself matter-of-factly in a chair near the door.

Whitney had a look for himself. The breed was tall and had a thick brown mustache. His complexion was light enough to pass for white. Not that it mattered; if anything, the half-breeds of Whitney's acquaintance were a worse lot of tatterdemalions than the full bloods. Hubbard had best lay down the law at the outset.

But where Hubbard was, nobody seemed to know. He had never bothered to take Whitney into his confidence about his arrangements, and Whitney was inclined to give him his head, even if Hubbard was sometimes a little too generous for his own good.

Yet Whitney had a legitimate pecuniary interest in the affair. His junior editor was leaving the *Outing* offices for five months or more. When Hubbard had first presented the proposal to cross Labrador in search of barren-ground caribou and the Naskapi Indians, he had the temerity to suggest being kept on salary during his absence. Whitney had cleared that point quickly. The pay would be for any articles written *and* accepted. In return, Whitney agreed to let *Outing* act as nominal sponsor, although even that concession made him uncomfortable. He was not entirely convinced Hubbard's expedition would be big enough to satisfy *Outing*'s rigorous standards. This would be a trip undertaken by canoe in the middle of summer, when fish and game were plentiful. Almost a picnic, by Whitney's reckoning. Admittedly, it would not do to have the assistant editor overshadowing the chief. But *Outing* oughtn't to be made to look like a Sunday-school operation either.

Now, the Northwest barrens in the dead of winter—*that* was hungry country. When Whitney had snowshoed two thousand miles across the Northwest Territories in '95, the sled dogs had been so ravenous they attacked and devoured a young bitch's litter as soon as she delivered. The Indian guides had been so famished, Whitney had to hold them at knife point—seven of them—to keep the emergency rations from being eaten. And then he had deliberately left behind the rations and trekked across the most desolate part of the barrens, knowing his party would return that way even more desperately in need of sustenance. Thanks to his foresight, he had gone home a man of reputation, able to write proudly that he had *not* yielded to the elements and had *not* let the Indians eat his extra provisions, because—Whitney was particular about this—"recklessness of provisions was just as apt as not to end in our starvation, or, what concerned me more, failure of my trip." By Whitney's lights, you starved, quite literally, before you failed.

Well, Hubbard knew all that; he'd read the book. And he knew that with men like Robert Peary and Theodore Roosevelt writing for *Outing*, no staff writer was indispensable.

HUBBARD DASHED THROUGH the main entrance to Grand Central, his friend Dillon Wallace only a few paces behind. They were late—given the traffic and circumstances, there had been no helping it. Informed that the 7:30 from Montreal had indeed arrived, Hubbard walked several times up and down the platforms of arriving and departing trains, then canvassed the men's room, paced the sidewalk outside the Forty-second Street entrance, and surveyed the cab stands—searching for someone who looked Indian and swarthy, out of place in a city of millions. His name was George Elson; Hubbard had that much from the Hudson's Bay Company manager in Missanabie. But he had no idea what Elson looked like.

"We've missed him," said Wallace, who spoke with a moderation befitting his calling. Lawyers could pass along the worst possible news as if it were nothing more than another potato at the dinner table. "If Elson was on that train in the first place, he's surely left the station by now."

Hubbard continued looking this way and that, whirling like one of Edison's dynamos. How could Wallace just stand there?

Once or twice in a lifetime, a man puts everything on the line: his money, his job, his reputation. This was one of those times, and to let it skitter away, all for a missed train, would be . . . heaven to God, there was no word for it.

What would the half-breed do? Hubbard dreaded to think. Go out and get drunk, probably; it was impossible not to suspect the worst.

Hubbard knew the places in New York where a stranger might wander—the missions and the soup kitchens. Four years earlier, he had stepped off a train at Grand Central, five dollars in his pocket, a reputation in Detroit as an enterprising young newspaperman, and the intention of breaking into the upper ranks in New York. That first summer his last ten cents had gone for a few stale rolls and crullers before he sold a single story. Newspaper after newspaper turned him away; for several days he had staggered about the streets so unsteady from hunger that he hid from the police for fear of being hauled in as a drunkard.

So he knew the haunts to which Elson might eventually gravitate. The trouble was, there wasn't time to search them. The *Sylvia* would be sailing for Newfoundland on Saturday. If Hubbard missed his ship connections, the chances of penetrating far enough into Labrador to join the Indian caribou hunt would be ruined. He couldn't afford delay.

As the carts and trolleys continued their clamor Hubbard started downtown, Wallace in tow, for the offices of *Outing*. He set a furious pace, but his mind kept spinning out ahead of him.

Picking up a guide in Labrador seemed out of the question. There were no natives to be hired along the coast, he'd been told, and the inland Indians weren't coming out anymore—they starved too much.

Yet to carry out the expedition without a guide would be impossible. Hubbard's original idea had been relatively modest—a trek to visit the Cree Indians of northern Quebec. That was a trip that he and Wallace might have been able to undertake alone. But chance and opportunity had raised the stakes. On a snowshoe trek north of Montreal, Hubbard had run into William Cabot, himself an Indian buff and an engineer from Boston. Cabot was friendly, curious, ready with questions. Why settle for the Cree? he had asked. A bit farther north were the Naskapi, a really primitive tribe who still dressed in skins. No whites had visited their inland camps; at least no one who had written a decent account. Why not come in from the Atlantic side—from the Labrador coast at Northwest River? A lot of ground beyond remained to be mapped.

The more Hubbard looked into the idea, the more irresistible it became. It seemed as if he had stumbled, half a century after Livingstone, upon a new dark continent. Labrador was the largest unexplored wilderness remaining in North America, perhaps the world. It was a vast peninsula, comparable in size and climatic rigor only to the world's two other major peninsulas, Alaska and Arabia. A handpicked party could make its way cross-country by canoe, explore the barren-grounds, and cap the journey by reaching the Naskapis in time to join their search for the annual autumn caribou migration. To a writer of initiative, the project promised splendid adventure as well as the book of a lifetime.

There were risks. But the uncertainty was hardly greater than coming to New York and nearly starving in the streets. In any case, how much security did a job and forty dollars a week amount to? Three years before, Hubbard had enjoyed a steady position with the *Daily News;* one bout of typhoid and it was gone at a stroke. The future belonged in making a name, something nobody could take away.

One wintry night, on a snowshoe outing in the Shawangunk Mountains, Hubbard confided his ambitions to Dillon Wallace, an occasional hiking companion. The friendship that had grown up between them was, perhaps, a bit unexpected. Wallace was nearly forty, ten years older, and not at all impulsive, as Hubbard could be. But the two of them had fallen together during hard times—Hubbard convalescing from typhoid at the Staten Island infirmary while Wallace, in despair, watched his bride of only a year waste away from consumption. Her death had left him utterly at loose ends. Hubbard had reached out, insisting Wallace come along to the woods for weekend tramps and a dose of fresh air. Their walks together seemed to bring him a measure of peace. Although Wallace had never done any serious camping, on this particular wintry evening Hubbard's enthusiasm swept all before it. "Come to Labrador," he urged. "We'll do it together." And Wallace—sitting there before the fire, having washed down his sourdough and bacon with a cup of hot tea—Wallace said yes, he would come. They'd do it together.

The Flatiron Building was already in view. An odd, triangular structure looming over Madison Square, it was the dominant building of the neighborhood, yet also the most delicate. Hubbard passed by its lee, then pushed through the doors of his own offices and climbed the stairs, wondering why the Montreal Express couldn't have been a little late, or the morning traffic not so heavy.

He walked into the office and saw his colleague Meule busy as usual, Whitney's door closed, and—

A man sitting near the door with a blue railroader's cap in hand—calm and unruffled as if New York were some minor suburb of Missanabie . . .

"Here is Mr. Hubbard now," said Meule.

The man could barely climb to his feet, before Hubbard had bounded across the room, grinning a bit foolishly but feeling like someone who'd just been raised from the dead. George Elson it was, and Hubbard found himself pumping the man's hand and saying *my* how glad he was to see him! And what a fine trip they were going to have! A fine, *bully* trip—just you wait and see!

3

Forebodings

WHEN MINA HUBBARD saw the two men walking down the lane side by side, she knew there would be no turning back. The guide had actually come this time; they would sail aboard the *Sylvia* on Saturday, after all; her husband would cross Labrador as he had so long dreamed; and there was not a thing in the world she could do to stop him even if she wanted to, which surely she didn't. She tried not to think about it.

Laddie led the way up the walk, immaculate as always in his suit and starched collar and bounding up the steps to kiss her, while the other man followed behind. He wore a suit, too, but one that had seen plenty of outside work, leaving it rounded and rumpled with the creases of the weather.

He did not look particularly Indian. Tall and broad-shouldered, with a nicely trimmed mustache, his complexion was a bit darker than Laddie's, but that could have come from the sun. When she spoke to him, he took his cap off and his manner was open and friendly. There was a Scottish lilt to his voice, which made it sound almost musical. She showed him his sleeping quarters and where to put his duffel.

Their home, in the village of Congers, was an easy distance from New York. Both she and Laddie preferred to live in the country, having been brought up that way. For their last night at home, she prepared a farewell dinner, and Dillon Wallace came out to join them. With just the four of them, it made a cozy meal. Following grace, she brought in dish after dish of roast lamb, beef stew, hot rolls, rice pudding, sugar cookies, coffee. . . . Laddie talked as much as he ate, full of plans and last-minute details. Wallace sat at one end of the table, working away at his plate with methodic determination. He was heavier than her husband and balding. Normally a bit reserved, the prospect of the trip seemed to have cheered him a good deal. George Elson ate quickly and sat up straight, once his plate was clean, looking polite and a bit uncomfortable until Mina asked if he wouldn't have more lamb or stew or rolls, to which he quickly agreed and again cleaned his plate.

She couldn't help wondering how the men would get on together. Wallace would surely prove a help; Laddie said he had any amount of courage out in the woods. But he was so quiet at times; his wife's death had been hard. Consumption always was: that sad, resigned look Mina had seen in the eyes of so many of the patients she had nursed at Staten Island infirmary. And their loved ones powerless to act, knowing full well the slow death that was coming. Laddie had been a tonic for Wallace—their hikes, the occasional meal, even Thanksgiving dinner together. . . . The two of them would work out fine.

George Elson seemed pleasant—big-boned and strong. But it was hard to tell about guides until you were out in the woods with them. John, the fellow they hired the previous summer at Missanabie, had hardly launched their canoe before the rain began to fall and he began dragging his paddle. Laddie, of course, had come for trout and was not about to let a little rain stop him. But he was not going to yell either; that was not his way. He only paddled harder, until finally John said, "Better put on coat; you get wet"—hoping they would all go ashore to camp. "Oh, I *want* to get wet," said Laddie. "I've been in the city too long where I haven't had the chance." Impishly Mina turned to John, her face utterly solemn, and added, "It's such *soft* water too." That settled John; he got down to business. They covered sixty miles the next few days, most of it in the rain.

Then there was Tom—a white guide and even more secure in his knowledge. Laddie told him never mind the weather, he wanted at least one day of good brook trout. "You can't do it," said Tom. "Rain's ruined all the streams." Laddie harried him for three days until Tom said, "Well, there's a little spring lake back in the bush about ten miles, where the trout always bite. It's rough getting there. Madam can't go, of course. No white woman has ever seen this lake."

That was enough for "madam." She and Laddie spent hours wading up a tiny stream, fighting the underbrush, climbing ridges on their hands and knees until at last they reached a marvelous little lakelet, rocky peak to one side, sheer wall on the other. Laddie had his fishing and she had her own small triumph to savor.

This was one reason she loved him so. He was bold, but in a way that seemed to include her and sweep her up. After their engagement, he joked that he was going to "annex" a bit of Canada, for she had grown up in a farm village in Ontario before coming to New York. For her part, she was determined that the annexation would work both ways. She would go where he went and do what he did.

Of course, to cross all of Labrador was out of the question. Her husband's proposed route covered five hundred miles of harsh, unpredictable terrain. But if she could not join the expedition, she could at least journey to the edge of the interior. She could sail north, stand on Labrador's shores, and scent the sharpness of its evergreen forests, trying in a small way to understand the magnitude of the test that called him.

As for the days beyond—those she preferred not to dwell on.

The *Sylvia* sailed as planned on June third and, by evening, had passed the shelter of Long Island Sound. By Sunday the pleasant breeze had become a sharp headwind and the sky overcast and showery; on Monday a cold, slanting rain began in earnest. As the seas worsened, Mina's stomach began to flutter. Along with her husband and a good many other passengers, she descended below-decks to suffer in private. George, too, had become a bit ashen, though he remained always cheerful and uncomplaining. Of the four of them, Wallace alone seemed unaffected by the seas, taking meals with gusto and walking the deck.

Not until Tuesday did the weather lift, as the *Sylvia* steamed into Halifax harbor. Bundling up, Mina came on deck and Laddie escorted her to the bridge. In pale sunlight, the city spread out around the bay, while along the wharves hundreds of freighters, mailboats, and dories were unloading cargoes of all sizes. On the nearest pier, Mina noticed a robust man dressed in tweeds who seemed to be paying particular attention to the *Sylvia*. Laddie saw him, too, and stared. "By jove!" he said. "Can it be?"

"Cabot!" he shouted. "Ho! Cabot!" And gave a great wave.

The man waved back. William Cabot it was: the engineer from Boston who had run across Laddie snowshoeing in Quebec and convinced him to follow the Northwest River into Labrador. That was a year-and-a-half ago—and now here he was again, steamer trunk by his side and looking ready to travel. The gangplank down, Laddie made introductions all around. It seemed Mr. Cabot had his own canoe ready to load; he was planning to reconnoiter the Labrador coast in hopes of meeting any Naskapi who might come out to trade. "Why hang about the coast?" Laddie asked. "Come with us and see the interior for yourself!" Cabot bowed and promised to consider the offer. There would be plenty of time to talk plans in the days ahead, he said.

They spent the afternoon touring Halifax while the *Sylvia* loaded cargo, then were off again heading north and east for St. John's. Along the Nova Scotia coasts the land had been clothed in a marvelous spring green, but, on rounding the eastern tip of Newfoundland, the air became crisp and the water more pale. When the fog lifted, Mina spotted her first icebergs, sparkling blue and white in the distance.

In St. John's they hurried to the offices of the Reid-Newfoundland Steamship Company, whose vessel, the *Virginia Lake*, was scheduled to make the season's first run to Labrador. To Laddie's dismay, the steamer turned out to have left for parts north a week earlier. The ice had gone out ahead of schedule and so, it seemed, had the ship. The Reid-Newfoundland passenger agent, an unctuous man by the name of Morine, bowed, made elaborate explanations about the exigencies of the ice, and, in so many words, informed them that another week might elapse before the ship returned. As a token of his respect, however, he insisted on presenting them all with free passes for the *Virginia Lake*, and recommended they visit a fine spot for landing "mud" trout—whatever these were—some fifty miles down a narrow-gauge rail line operated by Reid-Newfoundland.

Laddie was exercised by the delay—every minute counted, given Labrador's short summer—but concluded there was nothing for it but to go fishing. That project proved not quite the effortless jaunt Mr. Morine had intimated. Reid-Newfoundland was having trouble with striking crewmen, who refused to take them the last ten miles, and then the "fine fishing hole" turned out to be located in some of the most desolate country imaginable—rocky, barren, and charred everywhere from recent forest fires. At least the outing offered Mina the chance to spend a few quiet hours with her husband. And, once back in St. John's, the conditions of the country seemed positively idyllic, for the Reid-Newfoundland steamer lay anchored in the harbor, presenting a truly imposing sight.

Mina had not been particularly fond of the *Sylvia*, with its cramped quarters and sickening roll. But the *Virginia Lake* was hardly larger than a harbor tug: a horrid old bucket with peeling paint and rusting metal. The deck and gangways, the hold, and even the cabins were covered with a film of oil. The slick was partly spilled kerosene, partly slopped fuel, but mostly the putrefying remains of baby seal from the spring kill. Theoretically, the ship was cleaned and refitted at the conclusion of each year's hunt, to serve as mail-boat and passenger ship to the northern coast. But the vessel could no more change its ways than a dolphin sprout wings. First and foremost, she was a sealer.

To Mina's inexpressible disappointment, it soon became clear why Mr. Morine had earlier indicated with a cheerful wave of the hand that there was no need to engage a stateroom in advance. After showing their passes, she and Laddie boarded to find themselves milling about with several dozen fishermen and their wives—all trying to squeeze into five staterooms, plus a small saloon reserved for the ladies. Under the pressure of such numbers, there was no hope of obtaining more than a berth apiece; certainly no way of managing private quarters.

She and Laddie were lucky. Poor George, being a half-breed, had ended up in steerage. And by the time Wallace came aboard, there was not a berth to be had. The Reid-Newfoundland steward, a minion well-schooled in Mr. Morine's ways, suggested that a man of Wallace's vigor might prefer sleeping on the floor in any event—a suggestion which sufficed to crack the surface of Wallace's usual demeanor. He drew himself to his full height, pulled in his stomach, and conducted the steward through a brisk cross-examination. Once determining exactly who was occupying which berths, he proceeded to invoke the law of eminent domain and moved his baggage into a certain cubicle while the steward, his ears flattened, removed his own duffel. Mina marveled. She had never been so proud to have Wallace as Leon's friend.

Dinner was served in a smoke-filled dining room crowded with passengers, mostly fishermen on their way to the cod banks, plus a few prospectors in search of gold, copper, and mica. The rolling of the ship took away most of Mina's appetite; nobody was particularly hungry except Wallace. Caplin was the meal's main course, with each plate populated by exactly three of the sardine-sized fish. Wallace, glowering, passed along some information he had picked up along the way, that caplin were used by the locals as bait for cod and as fertilizer for the garden patch; also, these same fish were harvested by the millions and sold in the villages for ten cents a barrel.

At the end of the meal, one of the usual Reid-Newfoundland minions made his way to the table, paper in hand.

Laddie was puzzled. "What's this?" he inquired.

The craven steward would not even meet her husband's gaze.

"Ah—your check, sir."

"My check!"

"Yess'r. That is . . ."

"You've seen our complimentary passes!"

The steward begged to inform Mr. Hubbard that for anyone using free passes, meals cost extra. And for three caplin (here the villain had some difficulty keeping his voice on perfect keel)—the charge would come to thirty-five cents. Two orders—seventy cents. Further interrogation revealed that the regular tickets *included* the price of meals, and that most certainly it would prove less expensive to buy a ticket rather than pay for the meals one by one.

Mina wanted to jump up and shake the man until he rattled; the whole lot of Reid-Newfoundland seemed worse than a pack of mongrels. But Laddie only thanked him for his explanation and replied that, after all, his party would prefer to purchase the regular tickets, meals included.

As the *Virginia Lake* traveled up Newfoundland's north coast it anchored each day at half a dozen tiny villages, putting ashore a longboat with mail and supplies. It was July already, yet the daytime temperature scarcely rose above freezing, with a sea rising and the breeze blowing strongly out of the northeast.

William Cabot seemed to be everywhere—mixing with the crew, watching the ship's log bobbing in the wake, taking crude observations from the deck, even climbing, bold as brass, up to the bridge and looking over Captain Parsons' shoulder at his maps and compass. Nor was Cabot's probing confined to matters nautical. Day after day, he talked with Laddie of the approaching expedition, questioning him about his canoeing plans, his hunting plans, his contingency plans—every aspect of the trip. He noted immediately that their canoes were identical—both canvas-covered Old Towns, eighteen feet long—and wondered why her husband, looking to carry three men and an entire season's outfit, had chosen the same canoe that Cabot had picked to nose about in for a few weeks alone. He inquired about the outfit and seemed astonished to find that it weighed five hundred pounds. Would that and three men besides even fit in an eighteen-foot canoe?

He asked about fishing gear. What size gill net was the expedition taking? Laddie explained that the netting could be selected only when it was known what size fish would be trying to swim through it. A. P. Low, the well-known geographer who had himself penetrated Labrador's interior, had written him personally, recommending that the net be obtained from the post at Northwest River, where the locals could suggest what to take. But Cabot wasn't to be stopped. Yes, yes, he agreed—sound advice. Had Laddie written ahead? Certainly, he didn't expect to find a net made up without placing an order, did he?

And then there was the matter of firearms. Cabot agreed that the expedition's rifles were good choices for going after caribou. But a shotgun, he suggested, would be better for bringing down geese, its pellets scattering over a wider arc. Laddie countered that shotgun ammunition was too heavy to lug around in the bush, but Cabot began talking of "small bores" and "reduced shot charges"—Mina could not follow all the details—and indeed, Laddie seemed a bit surprised by the suggestion himself.

Until now Mina's forebodings had been formless and ill-defined—frightening as a nightmare and equally insubstantial. But Cabot's queries—dark, dreary, detailed—drained her of courage and left her feeling bleak and defeated. His implied criticisms were like so many pricking daggers; they gave her no rest.

On the Fourth of July, as the *Virginia Lake* reached the northernmost tip of Newfoundland, the weather began to turn heavy. The northeast wind was climbing toward gale force. A rain had come in, but even in the downpour a fog persisted. Whether to chance crossing the strait was open to doubt. Mina stared out to sea, trying to find luminous spots in the fog, places where it looked like the sun was trying to break through. That would indicate an iceberg, Cabot had explained. In these seas, though, bergs were not as big a threat as growlers. Those were smaller chunks of ice, fragments that rode buried in the waves but remained large enough to sink a ship. Surely Captain Parsons would wait out the storm in port.

But then she heard the ship's whistle shriek and the engine throb. Storm or not, the *Virginia Lake* was sailing.

The vessel hardly reached the open water of the strait before waves began breaking over the foredeck. Steaming at a narrow angle to the wind, the *Virginia Lake* fell into a steep pitch that threatened to lift the rudder nearly out of the water. The whole ship began to creak and groan, her uneasy protests broken now and again by blasts of the horn as Parsons tried to locate icebergs by the return of an echo.

Mina went belowdecks immediately: so did all the passengers. She maintained no illusions about being able to ignore the ship's heaving and lurching. Almost at once she brought up the little food she'd eaten; not even tea would stay down. As the crossing progressed she became almost too weak to lift her head off the pillow in search of the bucket. The dank air of her room, acrid now with vomit, was suffocating. With every pitch, it seemed the boat was going to dive straight to the ocean bottom; with every roll, it seemed impossible that it would right itself. Was drowning so horrible a fate? Frightened at first that she was about to die, she soon became too sick to care. Long before the crossing was finished, she wished for death—anything to end the ordeal. Anything, too, to avoid the greater agony of the next stop, Battle Harbor. It was there she would leave the ship and her husband, to catch a steamer heading homeward.

Late in the afternoon the *Virginia Lake* reached the Labrador coast and the opening to Battle, but in the fury of the storm Parsons continued on to the safety and relative calm of Spear Harbor, a few miles up. The men opened the ports and the air cleared enough to become fit for breathing. The harbor waters lapped against the sides of the ship while the fog, thicker than ever, muffled the sounds of the crew setting anchor.

The fear in her grew. She wanted to be alone with Laddie, but on that ship it was almost impossible. Once, after nightfall, she managed a moment in the fog and the dark. He showered her with tender kisses while she hugged him with all the terror she felt inside.

"Will you miss me?" he asked, his voice so soft she could hardly hear him. "Will you miss me, sweetheart?"

She could only nod. The words wouldn't come.

With all her soul Mina hoped Captain Parsons would sail directly north without returning to Battle Harbor. That would mean a few more precious days together. But, at first light, the ship moved back down to Battle.

Standing on the forward deck with Laddie's arm around her, she caught her first glimpse of Labrador. The tiny cove, the merest notch on the rock coast, seemed not to have a green or living thing in sight—not a tree or shrub or blade of grass. Slick black rock jutted practically straight up from the sea and was broken only here and there by patches of snow that looked thrown down in a random, careless pattern. High and away, clinging to the face of the rock, was a little house, a shack really. There she would be confined until the next ship passed by to pick her up. The air was calm in the dawn haze, but rain was falling in a cold drizzle down her face and down Laddie's.

One of the roustabouts coughed. "The jolly boat, she's ready to be lowered, ma'am."

Mina could not maintain her composure, not even with all the strangers about. She threw her arms around Laddie and held him fiercely, crying in great, aching sobs. She cried for being left in such a dreary, lifeless place. How even more desolate Labrador must be another thousand miles to the north! She cried for her husband leaving her; the awful wrench of parting. And most of all, she cried because she knew she would never see him again. This was no foolish premonition; she felt it as an awful certainty.

Feeling small and frail in her heavy coats, Mina stepped into the launch. Pulleys creaking, the boat was dropped into the harbor and rowed to shore.

Turning in her seat, she watched Laddie standing at the rail, one arm raised in farewell. His features were already lost to her.

A whistle shrieked; black smoke blew. The *Virginia Lake* steamed away. Stepping out on black Labrador rock, Mina turned again and stared at the empty sea.

4

Good-bye and Godspeed

CABOT, STANDING BY the rail as the *Virginia Lake* made its way up the coast, watched whales spout to seaward and the terns wheel and dive for fish. Tickle-asses, the locals called them. He mulled the decision that had to be made—whether to throw in with Hubbard.

On that score he was undecided. Cabot was a cautious man, whose Boston engineering firm had not only constructed the City Hall of Cambridge but a section of the New York subway. Dynamiting through bedrock under Times Square had proved to be a tricky business, and Cabot had learned not to take chances. Yet, in his love for the outdoors, he had knocked around odd and sometimes dangerous corners of North America, from Montana and Utah to the wilds of Quebec. It had been he who pointed out to Hubbard the challenge Labrador posed, and he who suggested Hubbard forego a visit to the Cree in order to seek out the more remote Naskapi on the Labrador barrens.

Still, Hubbard puzzled him: it was hard to take the measure of the man. He was vigorous and energetic, certainly, and a natural-born angler. But something in his temperament made Cabot uneasy; a kind of "story-book" strain. In St. John's, they had spent an evening with Captain Bob Bartlett, the skipper of Robert Peary's ship during his attempt on the Pole. Hubbard had been like a boy out of school, aflame for every scrap of news about the famous man. When Cabot, after a time, remarked that the Pole held no attraction for him, Hubbard was taken aback. Of course Cabot was attracted!

Why else were they all up in the barren north? Peary was out to make his reputation and so were they.

"In the matter of northern exploits. I haven't the slightest interest in making a reputation," Cabot replied; and Hubbard had seemed quite put out. Cabot simply couldn't make him understand: He would rather meet one Naskapi in the flesh than stand on Peary's frigid, imaginary dot. The strange thing was, Hubbard seemed not only incapable of grasping such a proposition, but inclined to believe that Cabot was insincere in expressing it. It was troubling.

So was Hubbard's lack of experience. The man needed seasoning—a spin around the deck was all one needed to see that. Aft, their two canoes lay side by side: twin craft. But when the rain had started on the way north, Cabot immediately turned his boat over, to protect it from the elements. Hubbard's had gone neglected and now there was water in its bottom, the ribs and planks soaking up extra weight. That would not make portaging any easier.

If Hubbard's companions had themselves been old hands, the deficiencies of equipment might be remedied. In fact, the men were unknown quantities. Wallace seemed a good sort, but he had done little camping and had never traveled beyond the United States. Elson was a pleasant chap, ready enough and familiar with northern life, but he was young—perhaps in his midtwenties—and had worked mostly as a railroad cook in northern Ontario. He had never taken any long trips. As for Hubbard himself, his own "farthest north" was the Quebec snowshoe trip where Cabot had met him—only a week in the bush with a guide.

There was a bit of clatter in the gangway, and Cabot turned to see Hubbard coming his way, obviously agitated.

"This fixes me!" he called.

"What's that?"

"Parsons! He won't let me off at Rigolet! Can you imagine? He puts a longboat down to visit fishing huts every three or four miles, but when it comes to calling on the main Hudson's Bay post, he won't stop until he's been all the way north and started his trip back! If I want to go to Rigolet now, I have to get off at Indian Harbor and find someone to sail me the last fifty miles. I'm a week behind schedule as it is!"

Cabot began to speculate on possible alternatives, but before he could get half a word in, Hubbard was off. From time to time, he reappeared on deck, talking to one salt or another, but whenever he caught sight of Cabot, he seemed suddenly to veer away. It was as if, in his nervousness, he wished *not* to see him.

Cabot was perplexed. Had Hubbard changed his mind about wanting him along? Certainly the man was sensitive about "reputation." Perhaps he thought an older, more experienced hand would end up poaching on his territory. And there had been that business about Peary. Cabot couldn't fathom it. With dusk coming on, he gave up trying and went to bed.

The next morning, as the *Virginia Lake* dropped anchor at Indian Harbor, Cabot came on deck to find Hubbard with his outfit ready to go. He made no mention now of his earlier invitation; only said that he had decided to take his chances finding a ride to Rigolet with one of the locals. Wallace and most of the gear were ferried to shore in the ship's longboat; Hubbard and George paddled the canoe in. To a chorus of "Good-bye, b'ys, and good luck!" the crew waved them off.

Cabot waved his own farewell from the rail, relieved to have the decision made, yet a bit uneasy. It was he, after all, who had first encouraged Hubbard. Had that been rash? As he headed belowdecks to catch up on his diary he weighed the apprehensions that had come to vex him in the past days. Small things, really, when taken one by one. But in the aggregate? The men might face some difficult going. "Still it can be done," he wrote in his neat, level hand,

> though I am sure they have no sufficient foreknowledge of what is to come. I am afraid H. will get nervous and overdo and even barring accidents will fail to justify his hopes.
>
> They have two .45–70 rifles and two .22 × 10″ pistols. This battery is based on their visions of caribou and barrenground bear. George admitted readily that they should have a shotgun, but I think should have made himself felt earlier. Yesterday they were speculating as to having caribou to eat within the first few days, which is hardly to be expected as a rule. . . .
>
> I make record of these impressions because they (H & W) are in for hard work for a time and may not succeed. Being in some measure responsible for the trip, I wish to clear myself from connection with some of the important details mentioned.

H. knows my views; but I have told him that the trip can be made, without accidents, by means of his outfit at hand.

Now, at 11:00 A.M., we are off full speed after anchoring for a little while in their bewilderment as to our course and position.

THE WHARF AT Rigolet was a marvel of construction—a few planks held up by as crooked and spindly a thicket of saplings as Hubbard had ever laid eyes on—all driven seemingly haphazardly into the tidal mud. He didn't care a whit how rickety it was, so long as it held him. Four days to make fifty miles! And at that, bailing a leaky sailboat, navigating through fog and storms, camping on islands too barren even to have trees for tent poles . . . It was a relief merely to have arrived.

The entire population of Rigolet had turned out to welcome them, it seemed. The men stood tan-faced and solemn by the shore, pipes in hand, warily eyeing Hubbard's canoe. The women were gathered in twos and threes, wearing kerchiefs, simple shirtwaists and ankle-length skirts, some covered by aprons that in earlier years had seen duty as flour sacks. The children and dogs were like whirlpools at floodtide, swirling up and down the wharf, playing, wheeling, and fighting. Once ashore, Hubbard found himself surrounded by a group of huskies. The nearest growled before allowing himself to be petted and cuffed lightly behind the ears. "You see, Wallace, even the dogs are friendly!" he said.

Wallace seemed dubious. "They look to me only a little less than wolves in subjection."

On a rise stood the only two-story building in Rigolet and, beside it, the Hudson's Bay Company flag waving in the breeze. Hubbard looked about for someone in charge and soon spotted Mr. James Fraser, the Hudson's Bay factor, to whom he presented his letter of introduction. Fraser bowed and, with a thick Scottish burr, bid Hubbard and Wallace "mack themselves at hoom." His men would see to their canoe and to the accommodations of the half-breed.

Dinner was bully—salmon topped with a bread sauce. Fraser was a judicial sort of man who observed all the amenities: serving Mrs. Fraser first, then his guests, and finally the children, who sat off at a separate table. After tea the company adjourned to the parlor to talk with several of the locals who had come round. Hubbard started in immediately; he was eager to get information about the interior.

"I imagine there's fine country to be seen," he ventured.

"Yess'r."

"And you've seen a good bit, I suppose."

"Oh, yess'r."

He hesitated. The response was evidently friendly, but the "b'ys," as men called each other on the Labrador coast, seemed determined not to inflict two syllables upon the listener when one would serve.

"Quite a few caribou?" he continued hopefully.

"Yess'r. Lot of caribou."

"Do you see many of them about here?"

"Yess'r. Well, *no,* sir. That is—*some*times we sees 'en, in the winter mostly. Long about January, mostly, we sees 'en. *When* we sees 'en."

"Have any of you been past Grand Lake?"

Judging from the silence, nobody seemed to have been. Hubbard explained that he was hoping to visit the Naskapi Indians up on the George River, and that Mr. Low, the geologist, had suggested the best route would be to head upstream on the Northwest River. The men brightened.

"Ah, Mr. Low. I minds him—he was through here back a few years, wasn't he? Yess'r."

A few of the others nodded. "Low—that's it. Yes sir, Mr. Low. He was the Canadian that took an Indian for a wife."

"That's so. He went up to the big falls on Hamilton River. The Indians say there's three women that lives *under* that place, or near to it, so I'm told. Had you heard about that, sir?"

No, Hubbard hadn't heard. Hoping to make better progress, he brought out his copy of Low's map. The "b'ys" crowded round.

"This is Rigolet, with the Hudson's Bay post marked—"

"Ah, Rigolet! Yess'r . . ."

"—and Northwest River Post. Mr. Low suggested we leave from there and paddle down Grand Lake to the Northwest River."

"Ah! Grand Lake! 'Kipper Tom's for you."

"I beg pardon?" said Hubbard.

" 'Kipper Tom Blake. The Blakes trap down to Grand Lake. Talk to 'Kipper Tom—he's here for the summer fishin'."

Hubbard was intending to pursue this lead when the noise of

a most unholy row penetrated the parlor. It was the dogs, somewhere out in the night; but the yowling and snarling was so ferocious it seemed as if the entire canine population had answered the summons.

"Probably fightin' over a few cod heads," offered Mr. Fraser. "They're a fierce lot."

They had seemed friendly enough that afternoon, Hubbard observed.

"Yess'r," said one of the guests. "That is, some of 'en is, and some of 'en isn't. Some of 'en, ye'd best have a stone handy. We had a wonderful bad time the other day with Willie."

"Willie is one of your dogs?" asked Hubbard.

"No sir. Not a dog. He's a little Eskimo feller, not too many years old. Poor Willie was playin' about a hundred yards from the house, when about six of these dogs come round the corner and fastened right into 'en. Well, the boy's mother started peltin' rocks. All the proper dogs went away but not this one black one, he just stayed there and tore away at Willie."

Hubbard said nothing.

"The ma pelted that dog till he left off, then picked Willie up and had to carry 'en under one arm and throw rocks wit' the other hand to keep that old dog away, till she could get in the door and slam it. Willie had his head all tore up, you could pull his skin back and see his skull. Dr. Simpson wasn't around, so we sewed 'en up then and there, put bandages everywhere there was a bite. We had to do it whether we knowed how or not."

"That black 'un, I wouldn't be surprised if there's some wolf there," commented one of the other guests.

Outside, the howling of the dogs had stopped.

"Awoke from bad dream of trouble getting somewhere to realize that I was at a post," Hubbard wrote the following morning. "Mighty good awakening." After breakfast, he and Wallace went around to look up "Skipper" Tom Blake.

"Yess'r," said Blake. "Grand Lake. I knows it well. Trapped many years on 'en."

Hubbard showed him Low's map, which indicated Northwest River flowing into the west end of Grand Lake. The lake itself was quite long, stretching northwest for forty miles. Some miles above, the river split in two. One branch was labeled the Naskapi; the other the Northwest, which seemed to continue all the way to Lake

Michikamau. All these features were marked in dotted lines. Michikamau itself was huge—sixty miles across. To the north of it, somewhere along the George River, dwelt the Indians Hubbard hoped to find. Obviously, the first step would be to paddle to the end of Grand Lake, then up the Northwest River.

But Skipper Blake looked doubtful. He didn't know about the Northwest River, he said. Northwest River *Post,* yes; but the river—well, that was only the three miles of water running out of Grand Lake to the post.

"The Northwest River doesn't flow *into* Grand Lake as well?" asked Hubbard. That seemed hard to believe.

"Well, sir," replied Blake, "she don't that I knows of. The Naskapi River, now, that's the one who comes right into the far end of Grand Lake."

"Perhaps it's the Naskapi we're after," suggested Hubbard. "Does that flow out of Michikamau Lake?"

Blake couldn't say. His son Donald, though, trapped up the Naskapi. *Donald* could tell 'en all about it.

So Hubbard went round to see Donald that afternoon.

"Yess'r, you can paddle right up that river the first fifteen or twenty miles," Donald said. "I've sailed up it many a time. Fifteen miles up, the Red River comes in on the left—shallow, lots of boulders. After that, though, the Naskapi gets bad—tumbles right off the mountains."

Hubbard wondered if it went all the way to Michikamau. Donald said he'd heard so, yes; Indians said the Naskapi flowed out of Michikamau. He'd never been all the way, though.

Hubbard talked with a few other trappers but always received the same response. "Ah, Donald Blake—he's the one. Knows all about the Naskapi." So he found himself trudging back to Fraser's house in possession of little more than Donald's bare outline and the inevitable canine escort. With these companions, he now behaved more cautiously: the previous night's ruckus, it turned out, had resulted in one of the pack being surrounded, attacked, and eaten. In the morning, only a few pieces of fur remained as evidence of the deed.

On Sunday the fog was back, bringing with it the sudden arrival of Captain Gray and his *Pelican,* the Hudson's Bay Company ship that made its pilgrimage from England to Labrador once a year. The captain had sneaked the *Pelican* in unnoticed in the fog, then let loose with a blast of his whistle before anyone could hoist the flag. This he regarded as a tremendous joke. Gray was a jolly, cranky old fellow, cheerful in his pessimism. "You'll never get back," he told Hubbard genially. "But if you're at Ungava Bay when I get there, I'll pick you up."

It was frustrating. Everyone was friendly, but nobody seemed to think the interior of Labrador could be mastered. Simpson, the itinerant physician, was more diplomatic than Gray, but his conclusion was the same: "Don't leave your bones up there to whiten, boys, if you can possibly help it." Poor Wallace had to be bucked up a little, for he couldn't help feeling uneasy, his own camping experience being so limited. Hubbard, of course, had heard this kind of talk before; it only made the work seem bigger. "Prophecies that we can't do it don't worry me," he wrote in his diary. "Have heard them before. *Can* do it. WILL."

On Monday the *Julia Sheridan* finally arrived and took them down Groswater Bay for Northwest River. The bay was still salt water—actually only a continuation of the Atlantic. Within its shelter, though, the character of the country changed. Barren rock cliffs gave way to gentler hills. Whole forests of spruce mingled with others of white birch. The country seemed lush in comparison to Battle Harbor, where Mina had been rowed ashore.

At Northwest River Post, Hubbard finally found a Hudson's Bay man after his own heart, a lanky fellow named Thomas Mackenzie. Mackenzie was a bachelor, high-spirited and eager for adventure. Lonely, Hubbard thought, though pretending not to be. It took only a few minutes of listening to their plans before Mackenzie was won over completely. "If I wasn't tied down," he said, "I'd pack up this evening and be off with you in the morning."

There was one piece of bad news. The gill net Hubbard had been counting on was not available. Rigolet had run out of them, Northwest River had none, and at this late date, nobody had the time to fashion a new one. Mackenzie scrounged around and came up with an old net that had been lying in a corner. It was worn, but he got a couple men to patch it up as best they could. At dinner he talked expansively of northern life, and Hubbard savored the conversation. This would be his last meal for months under a civilized roof. "Oh yes," said Mackenzie grandly, "you boys will have a fine lot of adventures."

Wednesday morning, July 15, the sky was a brilliant blue and the air sharp with the aroma of spruce. For once there was no fog, no rain, no barren cliffs—a perfect day to set out into the unknown. By nine o'clock, the canoe was deep-laden with its outfit, prow resting on the shore of the strait leading to Grand Lake.

Hubbard brought out his Kodak and took several shots of the group standing by the water. Mackenzie was looking jaunty in tweed trousers and jacket, with a handsome, white turtleneck sweater and wool cap to match. George still wore his wool jacket and railroader's cap. Wallace stood strait as a ramrod, a bit of belly showing in profile, but determined to shed it when the work began.

"Now it's your turn, Hubbard!" he called, and took the camera as Hubbard walked to the water's edge.

Picture-taking completed, Hubbard crawled carefully over the gear to the bow seat. When he was settled, Wallace worked his way amidships, straddling one of the packs. Then George pushed off, hopping as he did into the stern seat. Hubbard dipped his paddle and the canoe, heavy with its load, glided up the strait toward Grand Lake.

"Good-bye and godspeed!" called Mackenzie. "I wish I were going with you!"

5

March to Your Front Like a Soldier

THE LOCALS HAD told Hubbard to expect a short stretch of fast water at the entrance to Grand Lake and said it would take some hard stroking to reach the big water. The entire stream was only a few hundred yards long—little longer than it was wide—but the current fairly ripped along. Hubbard hopped out of the canoe in the shallow water near shore and, wading with tracking line in hand, pulled the canoe upstream through the waves. With one final surge, the boat breasted the upstream lip of the drop and came to rest on the waters of Grand Lake.

It was quite a moment. He had crossed the threshold and was finally poised inside the last great North American wilderness. Even on Low's map, the most authoritative in existence, Grand Lake appeared only in hypothetical dots. On the way up the rapids, they had seen a trapper and his family standing in front of their cabin. Except for an occasional log hut along a winter trap line, that cabin was the last human dwelling this side of the Naskapi wigwams, hundreds of miles to the north.

The waters of Grand Lake stretched like an arrow piercing the interior. Hubbard fancied he could almost see the mountains and barren grounds far beyond. To either side, veiled in a thin blue haze, steep bluffs plunged into the lake. The streams rushing down the slopes caught the sun's light and reflected it back, silvery ribbons among the black spruce.

He marveled. Grand Lake looked nothing like the barren scene he had been anticipating. For all the world it looked like Lake George, nestled in the hills of the Adirondacks. The resemblance was uncanny. He thought of Mina: How many times had the two of them paddled those Adirondack waters, stopping on a granite outcrop for a picnic lunch? How many times had they hurried to the shelter of its evergreen forest to wait out a shower?

With only a light breeze they made good time along the north shore before stopping for a noon observation. The practice with the sextant now paid off. While George fixed lunch, Hubbard recorded their latitude—53° 35′. Strike a few dots from the map of North America.

During the afternoon, he set a diagonal course toward the south shore as they hurried to keep ahead of thickening clouds. There they camped for the night and, by five-thirty next morning, were off again, paddling in the lee of a massive bluff that rose a thousand feet into the air. As the canoe rounded the headland Hubbard could see for the first time the far end of the lake.

Along the left shore a line of evergreens advanced unbroken into a long, shallow bay. Down the right shore, a much deeper bay offered; Hubbard dubbed it the "northwest arm" of Grand Lake. But straight ahead, even on this overcast day, the light played on a gap in the trees.

Hubbard was both elated and relieved. Rivers entering and leaving large lakes could be devilish to spot from the seat of a canoe. From any distance, the shore tended to blend into a continuous line of green, giving the appearance of a dead end. Here, at least, Low had proven correct. The Northwest River obviously flowed into the gap at the end of the lake—not even a child could miss it.

Shortly after lunch they reached the river's mouth. It proved surprisingly narrow—about thirty yards—yet sufficiently deep to permit good paddling. For a mile or so, its channel swung in gentle curves between high sand banks, broadening here and there into pondlike expansions. Then abruptly the river changed. It widened to a hundred yards or more and became swift, shallow and strewn with boulders. Paddling against such a current was out of the question. Together the men headed to shore and cut two poles about ten feet long. To the butt ends George attached protective metal shoes.

With Hubbard standing in the bow of the canoe and George in the stern, each man angled his pole against the rocky bottom, then climbed hand over hand in order to creep the canoe a few feet upriver. Reaching the top of the poles, they lifted and swung them ahead and, in the brief moment that the canoe hung suspended in the current, quickly reset the poles farther upstream. With Wallace paddling amidships, they gained a few hundred yards this way, but the river soon overmatched them.

While Wallace and George worked the poles Hubbard took the bow painter and waded ahead to tow like a mule. Sloshing up a hill of rushing water, he groped for footing. But the riverbottom was boulders shore to shore, all irregularly sized and spaced, many slick with algae, and others ready to roll with the slightest pressure. Often Hubbard stumbled, only to have the boat bump and bobble downstream. Regaining his balance, he stepped into a hole hidden by the water's turbulence and floundered up to his armpits. To make matters worse, the current was numbing and, on this drizzly day, the air hardly warmer.

Yet the rain, the cold water, the rock-hopping, the rope-hauling—all this was as nothing compared to the real torture the river valley inflicted. From along the shore and out of the bushes, from the deep recesses of the moss came an army of winged pestilence—a legion of insects that were the veritable curse of Labrador.

Along the Atlantic coast there had been mosquitoes buzzing about the sand flats in sufficient numbers to prompt Hubbard to purchase cheesecloth at Rigolet for use as veiling. Now the bothersome insects of a week ago were revealed to be only the advance scouts for entire battalions awaiting them in the backcountry. These mosquitoes were deceptively delicate, dim-witted creatures who descended gracefully onto any bit of clothing or exposed flesh; they didn't seem particularly choosy. In reasonable numbers, they would have been little worse than an annoyance, easily dispersed by a wave of the hand. But their numbers were unreasonable beyond counting, even beyond imagination. Hubbard brushed one sleeve and, the instant he was done, columns of replacements took up their stations and started drilling anew, even through a full layer of clothing. He brushed the back of one hand, and the other, in the act of brushing, was assaulted by dozens, even hundreds of troops. Within minutes of arriving in the river valley, all three men were alive with a crawling, probing, mat of mindless tormentors.

Incredibly the mosquitoes were friendly by comparison with the black flies. When the humidity dropped enough to discourage the mosquitoes, the flies came out in clouds; they literally filled the air. With dense, black bodies the size of a tiny ant, the creatures buzzed in senseless, busy circles, propelled by short stubby wings. The flies dove madly for any seam in Hubbard's clothing. They flew and crawled into his pantlegs, shirtsleeves, collar, and, with special ferocity, into his ears and eyes. The hordes were so thick it was impossible not to inhale a few, whence they buzzed angrily inside his nose and bombarded his throat until he gagged or swallowed them.

While the mosquito delivered its sting and was gone before an itching welt appeared, the black fly had jaws for biting and left behind a bleeding scab that proved more than sufficient enticement for other compatriots. And not only black flies. The worst bite of all was delivered by what the natives called "bulldogs," a kind of giant, ferocious deerfly. Bulldogs were the size of a man's thumb joint—roughly ten or twenty times larger than the black flies, with jaws and apparently teeth to match. Their buzz was a horrible rasp; their specialty, a fast landing followed by an immediate bite. This wound was too painful to itch; rather it felt as if inflicted by a hot poker. The bulldogs appeared in no great numbers, but even with a dozen or two flying about, Hubbard became worn out listening for their approaching buzz, trying to anticipate the direction of the attack, and then—distracted by the bombardment of the black flies—would lose track of the big buzzards and fall victim to their butchery.

In midstream he and the others stopped, dug through their packs, and put on gloves and the cheesecloth nets. The veils kept out the flies tolerably well, but the weave proved too tight to see through. The net had to be lifted above the face and used instead as a makeshift hood over the ears and the back of the neck. That provided some defense against the mosquitoes, but the black flies simply crawled underneath, where they could not be easily swatted. Hubbard's wrists, exposed between glove and sleeve, were soon raw and bleeding.

Desperately he applied the insect repellent he had bought in New York. For a few moments it seemed to work, but the splash of water from the stream and his own perspiration washed the dope away almost as fast as it could be applied. There was nothing to do but suffer and look forward to the smudge of the evening fire.

The time for dinner and rest finally came. In the rain, it was less than a totally comfortable camp, but Hubbard's spirits lifted as soon as the falling temperature sent the bugs into hiding. "Looks like we've got our work cut out for us, boys," he said. "I shouldn't think we'll make more than ten miles a day, with the rapids and the river being so low."

Wallace was emphatic. "That river certainly is the limit! If the Indians have to travel on it much, I feel sorry for them."

George lit his pipe and said nothing.

"Blake told us we could paddle up the river eighteen or twenty miles," Wallace continued. "He said he had *sailed* his boat that far."

"Well, Blake was sorely mistaken about the distance, that's all." Hubbard thought the error was not that surprising, all things considered. The locals claimed Grand Lake was forty miles long, yet by his own calculations it reached barely thirty-two miles, end to end. Obviously, this had to be the place where Blake said the river tumbled off the mountain.

He pondered their progress. The sheer weight of their baggage was what made the situation so difficult. Loaded to the gunwales with equipment and provisions, the canoe seemed to snag every rock in the river. From the time they'd started upstream against the current, they'd made less than a mile an hour. He looked at the others. "What do you say to throwing away some stuff, boys? We'll never make any progress if we try to carry it all."

Wallace puffed contentedly on his pipe, but George shifted less easily.

"Let's stick to it a little longer," he suggested, effectively closing the conversation.

The rain continued all night. Hubbard awoke to a drumming downpour, the tent silk sagging practically into his face. He dreaded having to start out again, but the rain was not going to wash away his determination. He pulled himself out of his blankets quietly, so as not to wake the others, then fixed breakfast before calling them.

Despite the rain, they got off at six, after making a last-minute decision to abandon their extra change of clothes, heavy wool coats and a four-pound pail of lard. Out of respect for George's views, Hubbard desisted from throwing away any more food. They would lighten their outfit soon enough by eating through the provisions.

The second day on the river was worse than the first. The stream's gradient steepened, so that poling no longer sufficed. Wallace and George had to step out of the canoe and push and pull on the gunwales, while Hubbard hauled on the tracking line. Between river and rain, all three men were drenched. Then the river became even steeper. The only way they could make any headway was to lighten the boat by leaving half the outfit on the rocks, returning after taking the other half farther upstream—a strategy that committed them to negotiating each rapid three times.

Once or twice, despairing of their progress, Hubbard turned in to the riverbank to attempt a portage; but the shoreline was a tangle of alder branches and willows. After stumbling through this brush border, the men found the higher ground burned over from lightning strikes and crisscrossed with blackened, fallen trees. Far from being able to hike this country, they had to climb through it, an utter impossibility with heavy packs and a canoe. The horrible valley kept forcing them back to the water.

By the end of the day the men had advanced their position only two miles. The next day brought double that progress, but at even greater cost. The sun appeared and the temperature rose from the low forties to ninety in the shade. The air felt heavy and tropical. Yet the men could not remove their woolen clothes because of the insects.

How was it possible? In this heat, the flies seemed to increase in numbers. And were maddened to a biting frenzy. Under caked-on layers of fly dope, grease, perspiration, and blood, the men's faces became swollen and disfigured. Wallace's eyes were so puffed up, he could hardly see.

Respite came only with meals—four or five times a day. Hubbard arranged a schedule of breakfast at five, early lunch at ten, a noon snack, late lunch at three, supper at eight. And after the day's hard labor, evening camp seemed like paradise. All the delicious smells to whet the appetite and then enormous portions of everything. Hubbard's diary became a litany of foods. "Pancakes, bacon and melted sugar at three o'clock—bully. Dried apple sauce and hot bread, bacon, coffee with milk for supper at 8:30—bully. Apples and abundant sugar great comfort. Keep us feeling good and sweet and well-fed."

The dried apples came from his parents' farm in Michigan. It was so pleasant to think of mother and the apple tree; or wonder what Mina might be doing. "How the longing for home grips me," he wrote. "Wish I could see my girl for a while. . . ." Well, they must not get depressed—it was a good thing they *were* not. The boys were proving to be as hard workers as anyone could want. Accordingly, Hubbard announced that, the morrow being Sunday, they would take a day of rest.

When daylight came it was a blessing to be able to roll over in the blankets and idly watch the sun play across the peak of the tent. After a lazy morning, Hubbard and George explored upstream. Within a mile, they came to a rocky brook, which Hubbard judged to be the Red River mentioned by Donald Blake. A mile beyond, they could see two miles of open water on their own river. Best of all, they found hatchet marks and cuttings indicating an old Indian portage. There had been some talk in Northwest River about a Montagnais trail around the worst of the rapids, and this must be it. There could be no more welcome news, for surely, Hubbard argued, the Indians would never have fought such a rocky river unless there were lakes and open water ahead.

Monday, July 20, they set out to carry their gear to the open water ahead—their first long portage. The route led a mile and a half through an immense bog dotted partly with patches of muddy water but mostly with grassy hillocks the size of beehives, and composed of varying proportions of mud, water and vegetation—the exact relation of each element to the others never ascertainable until a moccasin had been committed to the question. Hubbard had hoped to master a pack of 135 pounds, but found he had to cut his load to 75. Even then, he needed George's help to lift the tumpline into place. Eyes up, head down: that was the working technique. The tumpline was a broad leather strap that wrapped around the forehead and attached to thongs that passed over each shoulder and secured the pack. The trick was to walk with a forward lean, tumpline tight, neck muscles bulging. With a heavy load, any sudden lift of the head would risk snapping the neck.

The weight was onerous beyond all expectation. A single trek through the swamp was hellish, every step kicking up a thicket of whirring mosquitoes. As it was, three round trips were necessary to bring up the full outfit of five hundred pounds. In the afternoon the trek led out of the swamp and up a steep hill. Climbing it was physical agony. Hubbard caught himself breathing in hard gasps; his legs turned to putty. The others seemed little better off.

Finally they reached the top of the ridge and for a mile followed a caribou trail to a camp overlooking the river. Hubbard was dead tired but kept on doggedly to the end. George worked like a hero. Wallace gave his best, but staggering along with the canoe on his shoulders, he suddenly collapsed about a hundred yards from camp. The others carried the canoe the remaining distance.

The work was nasty and hard but somehow cleansing. Each day was bringing them closer to Labrador's central plateau and Lake

Michikamau. The prospect buoyed Hubbard. He had never felt more confident about the ultimate success of his expedition. If he had any worry at all, it was a small one: Wallace seemed quiet and a bit off his feed.

Later, with the stars arrayed against a black sky, George and Wallace laid back and lit up their pipes. Hubbard did not smoke, but he led the evening entertainment with quotations from his favorite author, Rudyard Kipling, a poet with explorer's yearnings. Thinking especially of Wallace, who was most in need of training and experience, Hubbard put special feeling into one recitation:

When first under fire, if you're wishful to duck,
Don't look or take heed of the man that is struck;
Be thankful you're living and trust to your luck,
And march to your front like a soldier.

6

Thoroughly Lost

FROM THE VERY first, Dillon Wallace had expected the crossing of Labrador to be an arduous undertaking. The best evidence, it seemed to him, came by deduction: There was presumably good reason why the interior had gone unexplored these last four hundred years.

Yet he had, in a way, looked forward to the physical toil. He thought it might be just the strong medicine he needed. A shock to his system to jolt him out of his numb routine.

Wallace had never doubted his ability to manage the trip. He was no stranger to hardship. Taking over the farm when his mother had died and his father took to bed had been hard for a boy of fourteen. Losing the place to the bank three years later—that was even harder. But he had bounced back and made the long uphill climb toward respectability. Farmer, miller, telegrapher, secretary, private detective, legal clerk, and finally counselor-at-law.

Three years ago, it had all seemed worthwhile. Then his wife of one year—dear, sweet Jennie—died of tuberculosis, and he fell into the torpor he couldn't shake. A serious, even dour, mien proved no handicap in the law, but the pleasure had gone out of life. Without a wife and without a family, to what purpose were the long hours? What point was there in pursuing a career for its own sake? When Hubbard had come along with his snowshoes, optimism, and his plans to head out for a new world, Wallace might as well have been a marked man.

"Why don't you throw in with me?" Hubbard had asked.

"Why not?" he had answered.

Never—not once in his worst nightmare—had Wallace foreseen the agonies of this ordeal. The earliest warning had come too late, and it did not register in any case. Their first morning on the river, George came to him quietly to express surprise that Hubbard was intending to head out in the pouring rain. The Indians did not travel rough country in such weather, he said; certainly *he* had never before been expected to. Still full of vim, Wallace had only shrugged and remarked on the need for haste.

The vim was now spent, and Wallace was close to rope's end. One week into the bush, he was near physical collapse. The July sun was just one of the miseries he had not anticipated. Midday, the temperature was going up to ninety, even a hundred, degrees. The rapids kept forcing portages through wretched infested marshland and the flies were simply damnable! They were poisoning him—of that he was utterly convinced. Their venom made him feverish and nauseous; caused his eyes to swell and head to throb and muscles to ache. And then there was the torture of the portages. He was now falling regularly with his pack and doubted he would be able to walk even unburdened much farther. Exhausted, sick, he was hardly able to eat. How long could it be before he would have to call a halt? That question had no acceptable answer, for Dillon Wallace was fiercely determined that no breakdown on his part would be responsible for the failure of the expedition.

Relief came in a pitiable way, one that Wallace would never have wished. They all broke down together. By Wednesday noon all three men were too exhausted to eat, and so they just lay down and pulled the tent over them like a sheet, to ward off the flies. But Wallace was too far gone: not even this rest could quiet the rebellion of his body. He began to vomit.

"Wallace," called George—the habit of formal address having fallen away in the bush—"Wallace, you seasick?"

It was no consolation, but it was a fact that Hubbard was even worse off. Retching from overwork could not compare to the curse of diarrhea; and Hubbard had reluctantly taken to the bushes. How the flies must be reveling in the poor man's suffering.

Lightening the packs became a necessity; they were simply too weak to carry the full load. On the knoll where they had collapsed, they cached eighty rounds of .45–70 cartridges and three hundred rounds of .22's.

Hubbard's diarrhea grew steadily worse. The next day, July 23, he was forced to lie in the tent. Wallace poked his head in from time to time, to find Hubbard dosing himself with "Sun Cholera Mixture" and gazing at Low's map. He had been struck by a new idea—that the Indian route might leave the river and run through a chain of lakes directly to Michikamau. Determined to test his theory, he dispatched Wallace to investigate.

Carrying a sheath knife and a pistol on one hip, a tin cup and pouch of peameal on the other, Wallace struck for a high, barren hill two miles to the north. When he reached the top, there at his feet, like a silver setting in the dark forest, lay a beautiful shoe-shaped lake. Beyond, the spruce-covered country stretched to the horizon, an apparently limitless panorama.

His spirits lifted. A hard breeze scattered the flies, he was carrying no heavy pack, and he had been entrusted with a mission of his own. It was a challenge, exploring unknown country. His eye caught the glimmer of more water to the northeast, perhaps a larger lake, and he headed toward it. The route was more Labrador muck. Descending the ridge, he waded through a swamp to a second lake and then across several brooks.

After lunching on the peameal, he entered a swath of thick underbrush through which he could see no more than twenty yards. Pausing to take his bearings, he pulled out his compass, turned it over in his hand, and gave a scowl. He jiggled it upside down, tapped the case with his knuckle, then tried a sharp whack. None of these maneuvers had the desired effect; the needle was stuck and would not respond. It irked Wallace, not so much for causing any serious inconvenience—on a short hike he could hardly go very far astray—but because he and Hubbard had been having a running debate on the merits of each other's compass. This difficulty would put Hubbard one up.

Relying on his nose for direction, Wallace had passed two more lakes when a grouse fluttered up before him, making a small explosion with its wings. He brought it down with a single shot. *That* would provide a rejoinder to any remarks about the compass. Tying the bird to his belt, he turned back for camp. Instead of retracing his steps, he took a short-cut straight for his original shoe-shaped lake, tramping through more swamp until, just at dusk, he saw open water through the trees and hurried to a boulder at the lake's edge.

One look to right and left was enough. In no way was this lake shaped like a shoe. Nor did it resemble any of the other lakes he had seen that day. Somehow, in the monotonous, featureless terrain, he had gotten turned around and was thoroughly lost.

The old fatigue came back with a vengeance. Each foot weighed thirty pounds, his head hurt, and the mosquitoes were vicious. But a new fear gripped him as well. There were thousands of lakes in the vastness of Labrador, an infinity of swamps. They all looked alike, one leading to another, mile after mile. A wanderer who got turned around for a moment—confused—could spend eternity searching for a certain lake, a pond really, that looked like a shoe from a certain ridge.

He had to stay put for the night; he knew that much. Too tired to cook his grouse or even build a fire, Wallace settled himself on a flat rock, pillowed his head on a fallen spruce, drew a handkerchief over his face, and slept. At dawn he awoke feeling like the last person on earth. But he roused himself, heated a cup of porridge, and went to work on the compass. By rethreading the set screw with the point of his knife, he put the needle into working order. With that simple repair, all fright vanished. So long as he proceeded south, he would eventually come to their river, and that would lead him to camp.

He hiked for six hours through marshes that seemed wide as oceans and where the ground under his feet quaked up and down in waves. Toward noon he crested a hill and from its summit saw the river and, beside it, the ashes of one of their early fires. Eight more hours of fighting alders brought him into camp shortly after dark. George was off searching for him; the convalescent Hubbard looked drawn and worried.

Wallace hobbled into the light of the fire, his hat drooping below his ears. At his belt the grouse hung, a barely recognizable bundle of shredded feathers, skin, and sinew.

Relief flooded Hubbard's face, but his voice was wry.

"Look here, b'y!—you're limping!"

"Just blisters," Wallace replied. "Let me tell you, there are no trails in that direction."

"I had no notion you'd make such a thorough search of it."

Wallace made himself supper and gave an account of his wanderings. Then George returned and the story was repeated. As the details were wrung from him Wallace finally let it be known that the compass had rather failed to live up to expectations.

Hubbard lit up with a grin.

"Perhaps not to *your* expectations, Wallace. But I'm obliged to say your slender reed bore out *my* expectations quite predictably."

"That's all right," Wallace bantered. "Your turn will come, Hubbard. You haven't been lost yet because you haven't been out of sight of camp on your own. Anyway, I just stayed out for a quiet evening by myself."

The two men laughed and George joined in.

Progress upriver continued slow and difficult. The few adventures that punctuated the next several days were decidedly unwelcome. Fording the river a short distance above a falls, Wallace slipped in the current and was nearly swept over the drop with a pack entangled around his neck. Later that evening he and George found themselves portaging in the pitch dark, the rain pouring down. Exhausted, they had to abandon one of the packs in the middle of a swamp and hike two miles farther to where Hubbard was making camp. Wallace was convinced the pack had been lost forever; there could hardly be hope of finding it again in such trackless bogs. George astounded him in the morning by walking straight to it without benefit of blaze or compass.

By Tuesday, July 28, Hubbard was admitting to being "nearly blue" over their lack of progress. The river was growing distinctly smaller; indeed, to call it a river anymore was fantastically grandiose. The trip was becoming a monotony of one portage after another. The sensation grew on Wallace that the dreadful valley they were climbing stretched on forever, while the rest of the world—the one with trolleys and friends and farm fields—was but a figment of the imagination. Hubbard had the same odd feeling and the two of them mused over it, Wallace pulling on his pipe and Hubbard dipping his dessert of black chocolate into a mound of sugar.

The next morning their pace improved a bit; they were able to manage the next portage in just two trips. But the achievement prompted Hubbard to make a rude discovery. They were running low on bacon—also lard—and sugar too. Only seventy-five miles from Northwest River Post, with hundreds more before them, they had made a shocking dent in their rations. Hubbard issued a decree: There would be no more syrup for the pancakes. And another: They *must* get fish.

Equally alarming, the river and the alders were inflicting visible punishment on their clothing. Everything was brush-worn. Even the soles of their moccasins were wearing out. George had brought an extra pair for himself, but for Wallace and Hubbard, the matter was serious. Hubbard's feet were in especially bad shape. Two toenails had fallen off and a deep crack had appeared in one heel. He used electrician's tape to bind the wound, then wrapped his toes with cotton rags brought for cleaning the rifles.

Thursday, pushing through the woods on another portage, Wallace and George got mixed up and carried the canoe about three hours out of their way. Wallace cursed heartily and was placated only when he discovered that their stream divided in two and the country leveled out. Suddenly, it seemed, they had broken out of the river valley to emerge on higher ground. The Indian portage, the moss-covered barrens of the caribou, and the route to Michikamau could not be far away.

With the change in the country, the nature of their torment eased as well. Despite the strenuous labor, Wallace's nausea and Hubbard's diarrhea had passed. The whole party felt stronger. Wallace was pleased to find himself hardening to the life. He could carry a hundred pounds on the portages now without undue strain. The expedition's hardships were plain to see, plain as his worn trousers and Hubbard's Valley Forge footwear. All the same, they had advanced their position steadily. They had developed a rhythm of hard work during the day and unstinting comradeship during the evening. The river valley was behind, the plateau ahead. They had prospects. Wallace was astonished to discover that he had not been so full of energy and hope in years.

7

Goose Is Better Than Anything

GEORGE WAS DOING more scouting these days. Low's map wasn't much use. It didn't show any fork in the Northwest River—just one long dotted line. Mr. Hubbard had to decide for himself which way to go. What he did was climb a hill to look the country over while George went up the south fork to see if he could find anything.

Half a mile upstream, there was an ax blaze cut by a trapper. Fresh too—within the last year. Hubbard wanted to know how you could tell it was a trapline and not an Indian trail. Well, it was a winter blaze. Trappers would come through in the winter but Indians mostly only in the summer. Then Wallace wanted to know how he knew it was a winter blaze, so George showed how the blaze was high up on the tree; the fellus must have been standing on five feet of snow.

Besides the trapper's mark, there was some Indian sign farther up the creek. It was an old camp, with the wigwam poles already full of rot, but Mr. Hubbard looked hopeful. They still must be on the trail to Michikamau, he said. George thought it was pretty hard to say just from one wigwam, but he held his peace.

They started dragging up the south fork but it was raining hard, so they went into camp. The tent wasn't very dry either—been raining on and off quite a few days. Even the blankets were wet. Hubbard decided to stay put until the sun came out and they could dry things. Next day it was still raining. Mostly everybody just lay in, but George found he couldn't sleep the whole day and all night too. After a while, the ground began poking into his back and the muscles between his shoulders ached, and he got tired of being tired.

They talked some, crowded in where the tent didn't sag so much. Mr. Hubbard liked to talk the most. There must be lots of easy going ahead to make up for all the hard, he said. He spoke of Mrs. Hubbard—how by this time she would be at Wingham in Ontario staying with her sister, Mrs. Cruikshank. But mostly he talked about the grub running low. "We're going to have to tighten our belts some, boys."

So they cut down to two meals a day. Of course, that was no hardship, but all the same, it was a good deal less than the five meals they were used to. All it took was missing the first, and you got hungry enough.

Mr. Hubbard was a funny man. Sometimes it seemed he wanted to go one way, and sometimes just the other; but either way, it was never half a heart. First, he wanted to eat through their provisions to lighten up. So it was five meals a day and all the syrup they wanted on their cakes. Then the food seemed half gone, so he cut way back. With this rain, he had decided to wait for the sun and dry out—never mind if it kept raining three or four days. But coming up the river, when they still had plenty of grub and plenty of time, Hubbard wanted to travel, rain or no rain.

George had been so unhappy about that, he almost said something. But somehow he couldn't quite bring himself to. It wasn't as if Hubbard had stayed in the tent while George fixed breakfast—Hubbard let *George* sleep in and cooked the meal himself. In the rapids, Hubbard was always first to hop out and start pulling. He always did his share. And he treated George different than a lot of whites did. Some of the sports you'd hire out with—it was like you were their personal servant. And around the posts, of course, a half-breed always had to keep to his place. When Mr. Fraser put Hubbard up in Rigolet, he sent George off to stay with one of his servants. Matter of course. George didn't mind so much, any more than he minded sleeping in steerage on the *Virginia Lake*. But it had been nice, staying at Hubbard's home in Congers, that Mrs. Hubbard set a place right at table for him. Anyway, Hubbard seemed to like him. And he was usually so excited about what he was doing, you couldn't help wanting to try too. Even if he made you a bit uneasy sometimes.

The weather cleared in another day, so they dried their stuff and continued upstream. At the foot of a shallow rapids, Wallace was strapping his pack on to start the portage, when all of a sudden Hubbard looked sharp. "Drop!" he whispered.

He threw off his pack, hit the ground, and George did the same. Wallace was up the bank, but he lay down in the bushes.

They were on their stomachs and couldn't see much. Lying low. But, going down, George had got a look. Geese! Four of 'em, swimming right downstream.

Hubbard already had his rifle. George inched up, reached over the top of the canoe, and snaked Wallace's Winchester out of its case. His heart poundin' like a drum.

He thought to himself. Got to let 'em come easy, Georgie. Let 'em drift into view right around the bank. And hope Mr. Hubbard don't shoot too soon.

Quietly, he raised up onto one elbow, then the other. Took a bead on the silvery water beyond the marsh grass where they'd be sliding by, and held his breath.

Ah! There's the first one floatin' pretty—don't see nothin'. A little space behind the leader. Don't fire yet, Hubbard—not yet. Good. Let those others come along behind. One . . . two . . . three . . .

Bang! went one Winchester and then the other, both at the same time. The leader went down, one of the bullets going clean through the neck, the other in and out the body through both wings. The three other birds splashed, turned tail, and pumped their wings, rump feathers bobbing up and down. But they weren't about to take to the air—too soon after molting season! George took another bead, calm and easy, and squeezed again. Hubbard fired too, and two more went down. But one of them was only clipped, flopping along on one wing. George aimed and tried again, but—*click!* Nothing in the chamber!

In one big jump, he hopped over the canoe, grabbed a paddle, and splashed upstream. Hubbard swung his rifle that way too, looking to get number four. Tried twice and then he was empty too, up and rushing along the creek like a madman, scrambling through bushes and swamp to cut off a bend. Midstream, George slipped on a blamed rock, his paddle flailed, and then he was up again after the wounded bird—both of 'em flapping and splashing but George moving faster—until he reached out with his paddle and—*whack!*—put the bird out of his troubles.

Upstream, Hubbard burst out from cover like a flushed partridge, only now he was ahead of his mark. The bird saw him and turned tail, but George came splashing up from the other direction, and the bird was stumped. Hubbard finished him with two shots from his pistol.

Up the rise Wallace climbed to his feet and let out a cheer. Four geese to fill the hole in his stomach! He started skipping up and down. Hubbard and George stood there laughing—it sure was something to see Wallace jump! And they cheered too—Hubbard flung his hat into the air, Wallace threw his up, and George hallooed and sent his dirty old felt after.

With the water swirling pleasantly about his calves, George waded to fetch the other birds. When they were all rounded up, the boys hefted them. Fifty pounds of meat at least!

At lunchtime they had a second piece of luck. Stopping at another rapid, Hubbard got out his rod, cast a fly, and landed a half-pound trout. Then another and another. As fast as Wallace could split 'em and George could fry 'em, Hubbard pulled in fish. They kept eating until they couldn't force another bite down. And they were glad to have trout too—but it wasn't the same as meat. Somehow fish by itself wasn't ever filling: You could survive on it, but it didn't give you strength. Anybody who tried to work on fish alone was going to lose weight fast.

A mile or two upstream, the little branch creek branched again, and they went into an early camp. With goose, everybody wanted to stop and have a proper meal.

George built a big fire; then took one of the geese, all plucked and greasy, and hung it on a cord by the fire, with a pan underneath to catch the drippings. Now and then he gave the bird a twirl to keep it roasting evenly. Hubbard and Wallace just sat and watched the goose go round. Gave it a twirl themselves, sometimes. After a few hours, when the skin had turned brown and crisp, George stuck a splinter deep into the breast and white juice came out. Eagerly, he took the bird over to the mixing basin, got the joints separated, and put the bowl on the moss by the fire. He didn't bother setting out portions; everybody just got down to business. They ate and ate great chunks of that tender meat, much as they wanted, fast as they wanted, any way they wanted, nothing particular about it. "A good goose is better than caribou," George told them. "Goose is just about better than anything."

After a while the only thing left in the bowl was one morsel, plus the giblets. By the fire, Hubbard lay back on his boughs, reciting poetry from that Kipling he always knew so much of. Northern lights flickered across the sky, bright enough almost to make the moss glow. Watching them, Wallace had got himself comfortable with a log and didn't show any more signs of moving than the log did. George put the giblets on to stew for breakfast, took a look at Hubbard and Wallace, then eyed the last morsel.

"Maybe I'll just have that for a little snack before I go to sleep," he announced, to nobody in particular.

IN THE MORNING Wallace roused himself about six and prepared for another day of dragging and portaging. The fork of their little stream ended, after another mile or so, in a small lake with signs of an Indian camp at one end. Hubbard named the lake Mountaineer, after the Indians.

But Mountaineer Lake proved a disappointment. A thorough search revealed only one inlet, and that ended in a bog. The creek had petered out completely. This, then, was the ultimate source of their river—not the broad waters of Michikamau, but a nondescript, mosquito-infested, anonymous lake that stretched two miles from one swamp to another. It seemed they had picked the wrong branch: lost the Northwest somewhere downstream.

They poked around the far end of the lake and finally portaged into a larger body of water two miles distant. But search as they would, they could find no sign of either white or Indian travelers. So it was scout from the hills again. Hubbard and George fanned out in different directions, while Wallace set up camp.

With the tent in place, he proceeded to the lake's outlet with his fishing rod, where he set up shop on a rock in midstream, hoping for some luck in the gathering dusk. The days were shortening noticeably, and although George returned by eight, the sun was already down and its light fading. Appearing out of the bushes, he hailed Wallace, who was still casting in midstream.

"Come 'long to camp," George called.

"As soon as I land one or two more trout," Wallace shouted over the rush of the brook.

"You've got enough. Come back now."

Wallace bristled at being ordered about by a half-breed, but something in George's tone caught his attention. The man sounded breathless. Taking care not to hurry, Wallace waded back.

"I've been about lost," George said.

Wallace was astonished. George was the fellow who could walk two miles through a swamp to find a pack abandoned in the pitch dark. He loped around the country like he owned it.

"How did it happen, George?"

"I just got turned around. I didn't have any grub, and I didn't have a compass. And I was scared."

Wallace was fascinated, and a little unsettled, by this altogether unaccountable phenomenon. George getting lost—it certainly was odd.

"But you didn't have a canoe on your head," he persisted. "How'd you manage to get turned around?"

"I don't know. I just got lost. But I found myself pretty quick. I never got lost before."

By the time supper was ready, they needed the firelight to find their plates.

"What would you have done if you hadn't gotten your bearings?" Wallace asked.

George shrugged. "Gone to the highest hill I could see, and made a big smoke at the top, and waited for you fellus to find me."

There was no longer any hiding the anxiety that had crept into the conversation. Wallace surveyed the southern horizon, the direction in which Hubbard had set off. There was no smoke to be seen—but it was too dark anyway.

"Another man lost," he said.

Hubbard was gone for the night, at the very least. He had no food and no extra clothes. He hadn't even taken matches. Worst of all, he had no river to guide his return to camp. If he panicked and didn't think to retrace his own steps, the odds against his chancing on their camp, a pinpoint in this empty land, were intimidating. At intervals, Wallace took his rifle and fired a signal, but no answering volley came in reply.

8

Alone

To Hubbard, it had seemed such a simple matter. Upon leaving camp he had struck south for a set of high bluffs a mile or two distant. But in such monotonous country, features got easily mixed up. He had reached the bluffs—or some of them anyway—and on his return had intersected the stream that he knew flowed out of the lake by their camp. For some reason, however, the stream didn't lead back to his lake but into unfamiliar country. How could it be? At every bend in the brook, he fully expected to find his lake; yet, in the end, the stream had petered out in a swamp.

And then came the awful feeling of being absolutely and irrevocably alone; the desperate need to talk to somebody—anybody—for the comfort of another human voice. Sick at heart, he hurried back to the bluffs in order to regain his bearings.

But by then it was too dark to travel; he would have to find his way in the morning. Meantime, he would pay dearly for his indiscretion. The wet underbrush had left his clothes soaked, and the mosquitoes were out in droves. How could the little beasts operate in such cold weather?

Only one piece of information helped him through the night. From beyond the ridge, he heard a rumble, deep and unchanging. It could only be the bass of a major river—from the sound of it, larger than anything they had yet been on.

He dozed fitfully that night, lying on the tops of two dead spruce trees placed side by side. At first light he followed his bluffs eastward and then, sighting a different stream, followed it north. In an hour, he reached his lake and hurried to the familiar, welcome campsite. George was splitting wood for a fire and Wallace was just getting up.

"Hubbard!" he cried. "You had us worried. Did you have a miserable time of it?"

"I could certainly use a fire." Saying nothing of his misadventure, Hubbard retrieved his fishing rod and went to the lake in search of breakfast. Only at mealtime, when George told about getting "turned around," did he make his confession.

"Well, I was lost good and plenty. And scared some too."

A smile of supreme satisfaction crossed Wallace's face. "Lost, b'y, were you! Why, I'm surprised at an old hand like yourself. Been having trouble with your compass maybe?"

Hubbard was forced to endure more than a little of this good-natured chaff, for Wallace was determined to have his innings. But even the ribbing could not banish the evening's unpleasant memories. When it came time to search for the new river, Hubbard decided to send George to scout. Meanwhile, he and Wallace amassed a surplus of forty-five trout, which they smoked and dried to take along.

Sure enough, the river lay two miles to the south. Portaging to it on Friday, August 7, they beheld a glorious sight—water at least 150 yards wide. There were frequent rapids, but the upstream portages were short and the paddling good in between. When evening came, a full moon rose above the valley, turning the river a sparkling silver. Lying around the fire, Hubbard was again struck by a sense of isolation. This time, the feeling was grand and exciting.

Wallace noticed it too. "Let's organize a government!" he said. "There's nobody to stop us."

Hubbard smiled. "All right. What sort of government?"

"We'll make you head of the nation. Call you the Great Mogul—how's that? Of course, you'll be commander-in-chief of the army and navy and have unlimited power. We'll be your subjects."

Hubbard sat straight as a ramrod, then scowled. "I suspect you're angling for a political job. This is a serious matter, Wallace! However, it goes without saying that I stand ready, like our politicians at home, to serve the country when duty calls. As the Great Mogul of Labrador, I appoint you, Dillon Wallace, Chief Justice and also Secretary of State. George I shall appoint Admiral of the Navy."

Even George laughed at this. "Where's my ships?" he asked. "Admiral's got to have a navy."

"Ships!" exclaimed Hubbard. "Well, there's only one for the

present. But she's good and staunch—eighteen feet long, with a beam of thirty-three-and-a-half inches. As for artillery, she carries two quick-fire rifles."

High above, the moon cast a pale light near and far, across Hubbard's evergreen domain. He was content. What better fellows could you have along to share such adventures? Before retiring, he pulled out his journal and brought it up to date: "Fine evening. Fine river. Fine world. Life worth living."

The eastern breeze freshened during the night. By morning there came the familiar, unpleasant sound of rain. The wind drove it against the tent wall in sheets.

It was depressing to have to set out in such chill weather. Hubbard became soaked to the skin, a rivulet of water running down the inside of his sleeve with each stroke he took. He was determined to make progress, but there were limits to reasonable endurance. On Saturday, their first full day on the "Big River," as they dubbed it, he stopped at noon to prepare a sabbath camp. Monday, the rain was as bad as ever, and after three miserable miles, he called a halt. They went into camp on the strength of being on the right road, and needing fish.

Surprisingly, they did need fish—and rather desperately. At first, the four geese had seemed an enormous store of meat, but by the time they reached the Big River, the last of the geese was gone. There were the dried fish, of course, but it was amazing what a man could eat after a day's hard labor. Once cleaned and cooked, five fish apiece seemed barely enough for a meal. To satisfy the appetites of three men for three meals, they needed to pull in forty-five trout every day. Hubbard tried every angling trick he knew, but the raw east wind kept all but a few fish from biting. The boys were soon wolfing down trout, heads and all.

Without question, the rigors of the bush were taking their toll. One of Hubbard's trouser legs was ripped from the knee down, and he patched it with a piece of white duffel, proudly proclaiming the result "*distingué*"; but within a few days the trousers ripped again, and he had to cob them together with bits of twine. Disheveled hair, bushy mustaches, and stubbly beards gave them all the appearance of tramps. Hubbard joked about who would be thrown out of a restaurant the fastest.

Their inventory of remaining supplies was even more discouraging. They had started less than a month before with 30 pounds of sugar, and all but a handful was gone. The original 25 pounds of bacon was nearly spent. All 13 pounds of lard had been eaten. Nine pounds of peaflour—the same. Ten pounds of rice—all gone, except for a cup or two. And their mainstay, the original 120 pounds of flour, was reduced to 40. All that remained to tide them over was a sack of flour, a handful of bacon and sugar, dried apples, some tea, and 20 pounds of peameal—to be held back as emergency rations.

How Hubbard craved flour, or bread, or any baked dainty! But there was no avoiding a ration: one loaf to split among them each day. The "loaf" rose hardly at all and was only an inch thick, but he anticipated each day's portion as if it were a gourmet pastry. "I believe I'll never refuse bread again," he said, "so long as there's a bit on the table."

Finally, on Wednesday, August 12, the wind abated. Continuing upriver, they pulled hard against the current, portaged around four short cascades, and then were astonished to see open water. The boys gave a cheer, and leaned into their paddles. By mid-afternoon, they had covered eight easy miles. The river widened, and the country leveled out, opening up a broad panorama.

Sitting amidships, though, Hubbard's view was limited to the back of Wallace's shoulders. The first thing he saw was Wallace dropping his paddle for the rifle.

"Deer!"

Several hundred yards ahead, a caribou trotted into the water. It was a stag, with immense antlers sweeping back in a high, graceful arc.

Wallace raised the rifle and fired even before the canoe stopped moving. The report echoed across the river.

Nothing happened. The caribou tossed its head and looked at the men. It was in no hurry.

Hubbard slipped his own rifle from its case. Wallace was in the line of fire, but George gently turned the canoe. Hubbard felt strangely calm; he thought not of sport but only of grub, and how they needed it. The deer was two hundred yards away; at any distance over a hundred and fifty, the Winchester's trajectory would no longer be flat. He raised the rifle's sights to their limits, and even then aimed high.

"Good! You hit 'im!" cried George as the shot rang out.

The deer sank to its knees, stood again, and made a bolt for the bank. Hubbard and Wallace both fired as it struggled up, but their shots went low and the caribou disappeared over the rise.

Suddenly, the calmness was gone. The instant the canoe touched the bank, Hubbard splashed ashore. Charging through the underbrush, he burst over the rise to find the stag floundering helplessly on a bed of moss flecked with blood.

"All right, we've got 'im!" cried George.

Hubbard was aware of nothing but the caribou. Meat! Hundreds of pounds! The rifle felt weightless; floated to his shoulder.

"No, no!" cried George. "Don't shoot—you'll spoil him!"

But Hubbard had already fired. The bullet entered the deer's neck and passed down the length of its tongue.

George rushed in, caught the thrashing animal by the antlers, and held its head down. He motioned for Hubbard to draw his knife and cut the throat. They made a quick job of it.

Hubbard felt drained momentarily, then exultant. "Food again, boys—food again! We'll camp right here, dress the meat, and dry it. Venison for dinner, and plenty of it!"

They cut the prize into venison steaks, skewered them, and set a couple to roast. "Best day of the trip, bar none," Hubbard concluded. "This pays for all the hard work." It would take several days to dry their caribou, but there was good water ahead, clear skies, no wind, and—thank the Lord—plenty of meat in reserve. Best of all, they were on the right trail to Michikamau. They had to be.

Jerking the venison took a low, smoky fire, frequent turning on the drying rack, and several days of patient waiting. These were, far and away, the easiest times of the trip.

Why, then, Hubbard asked himself, did he feel so blue?

It had started as just plain fatigue, the morning after the hunt, when he and Wallace paddled upriver to scout. Wallace felt the lethargy too. "Maybe it's the meat diet," he speculated. "Being ravenous for the last week or so and then suddenly having all the caribou you can eat."

"Maybe."

For his part, Hubbard doubted that his exhaustion had any physical cause. It seemed more likely a product of the mind, a natural letdown after weeks of tension. To spend so much time in that valley, advancing two or three miles a day, had been awful. Even now, having found their big river and shot a caribou, the same worries haunted him. Exactly where were they? How long would their food last? Would his adventures satisfy Caspar Whitney and the readers of *Outing*?

The next day he dispatched Wallace and George to attempt a more thorough scouting trip. As the two men paddled briskly upriver Hubbard watched them go. At first he could hear the rhythmic splash of their paddles, but soon the sound faded and the boat grew smaller. Finally, there was only the double flash of blades in the sun: *dip-dip, dip-dip*. And then the boat disappeared around the bend.

Beyond this bend in the river was another. And another. Beyond these hills were more hills, all like the ones that preceded them. Once Wallace and George passed out of sight, it seemed they might be one mile away or a thousand.

A breeze blew gently through the evergreens. Not far from the fire, a Canada jay was singing. "Whiskey jack," George called the little bird. Hubbard watched it fly away.

There were chores to do. The drying stage was sagging under the weight of the meat and needed relashing. The deer hide was being tanned. Even so, it was a lazy schedule, with ample time for lying in the tent and dozing and thinking. Maybe the trouble was that he was thinking too much. But how could he keep from thinking? He tried to discipline himself, rationing the time he allotted for reveries about home and his darling girl just as he rationed their dwindling supply of flour. This trip was his big chance; he must not fail.

Dusk came and still no sign of the boys. The jagged ridge of hills was dark now, silhouetted against the reds and blues of the sky.

Out there, somewhere, the two of them would be settling down for the night. Without blankets they'd be chilly, but a fire would help. There wasn't anything nicer than a fire: You could sit by it and chat and joke. It kept you warm. A fire kept off the dark.

Morning dawned under low-hanging clouds. Hubbard pulled himself out of his blankets, but it took all his energy just to get the fire going. The slightest movement felt like heavy labor. At long last he cooked himself a "restorative stew" out of peameal, caribou meat, and a bit of bacon. When he saw a trout jump in the shallow water, he went out and landed it.

After a long while it was afternoon. Then late afternoon. A breeze blew gently through the evergreens.

Certainly both men couldn't have gotten themselves lost, could they? That was hard to imagine. An injury perhaps? A broken leg?

No. Hubbard dismissed such morbid thoughts easily enough. What he couldn't chase off was the longing he felt for the others. It was palpable, almost physical. He found himself imagining George's big friendly smile and dark eyes; Wallace's gruff, bearded face; the two men walking up the rise to camp. When the whiskey jack fluttered by again, he thought about how George would regale them with its Indian name or tell how big its eggs were. Then Wallace would want to hear how the bird tasted boiled and how roasted. "How about under glass and on toast?" he would ask. Strange—at home, he and Wallace were united by only the most casual of ties. They had two separate careers and went their own ways. It was their time in the woods that had pulled them together. And here was George Elson, a half-breed from Hudson's Bay and a complete stranger, working together with them, eating together, sleeping together, as if the three of them had been comrades for life.

He missed them.

Near dusk the canoe came around the bend; Wallace and George climbed out on the beach and walked into camp, looking like two lean and hungry wolves. They sat down at the fire and astonished Hubbard by the amount of venison they put out of sight.

Between platefuls of steak and cups of tea, they gave their report. There was a big mountain range ahead, running north and south. The river headed toward the mountains, but then split in two. They had followed one branch, but it ended in the mountains—just broke into a dozen rivulets. There had been no time to explore the other, but the mountains looked worrisome. Somehow they had to find a way by.

Hubbard said nothing. If the way to Michikamau was still so doubtful after a month of back-breaking labor, when would they get there? And when to the caribou grounds? And when home?

With the fire dying, George went to pull up the canoe. Wallace edged closer to the warmth of the coals. Their glow accentuated the hollow of his cheeks, lines drawn by hard work and short rations. Hubbard hesitated until George was out of earshot.

"It's bully good to see you again, Wallace," he said at last. "I took it hard when you didn't come back last night. I got thinking of my girl and home and good things to eat. I was dead lonesome."

He would not care to be left alone again.

9

Michikamau or Bust

THE RAIN WAS BACK again, unremitting.

From under the tarpaulin, the one dry spot within a hundred miles, Hubbard watched it pour down steady and cold. Camp this evening was organized vertically, like some sort of wilderness skyscraper. Bottom floor was the fire, with wood piled all around to dry out. Next came the boys, their heads in the smoke. The story above was the drying stage, with strips of overripe meat curling in the heat. And above it all, the canvas: straining on its ropes, its sag end forming a pocket of rainwater that grew and grew until, finally, Hubbard reached up and gave the bulge a poke, rolling the water over and out with a splash.

He was trying to take the latest setback manfully, but it was hard to keep off depression. Five days of searching had finally brought them to the source of the Big River. Far from leading to Michikamau, it evidently ended in a hundred nameless springs, one of which lay gurgling a few-dozen yards up the hill. Instead of cutting through the range of mountains, the river rose in them. Michikamau lay somewhere on the other side, and the Indians and caribou herd even farther away.

He shivered. What would Whitney say if Hubbard reappeared from the wilds having never reached the Indians? It was not something he cared to contemplate.

Failure displeased Whitney. He had no patience for it, no matter how justified by circumstances. More than once, he had told the story of a little "drastic medicine" he'd administered to an acquaintance of his—a good-natured fellow, really, but a tyro who was always putting his foot in it. Whitney had been hunting near a mining camp in Nevada, the tyro off somewhere on his own, and another companion stalking with Whitney. The two of them were skirting a thin growth of aspen, keeping just under cover, when—*bang!*—a rifle echoed and Whitney's partner swore and clapped his hand to his arm. Whitney whirled and spied the tyro, seventy yards away, standing in front of a tin-covered mining shaft and peering nearsightedly in Whitney's direction for another glimpse of his "deer." He appeared on the point of shooting again. Without a word, Whitney threw his rifle to his shoulder and opened fire—not *at* the tyro, of course, but around him; though (Whitney would add sarcastically) "I was not much awed by the possibility of a chance shot hitting him." After eight bullets spattered off the tin siding, and the tyro had collapsed in a trembling heap, Whitney called it quits. "The man *paid* for all the meat he ate after that," he said. "Never went hunting again."

No, Caspar Whitney was not tolerant of well-meaning bumblers. There must be no failure for Hubbard.

But he couldn't help wondering what the boys were thinking. Dear God, what if they wanted to turn back? He couldn't bear to hear that. They mustn't say it.

The rain hammered away at the tarpaulin.

"It's been hard luck, not being able to find a good river," he began at last. "It looks as though we might be in for a long portage . . . all the way to Michikamau."

The boys said nothing, only sipped their coffee. They had brewed the last of it that evening.

Hubbard persisted. "Do you remember the slogan of the old Pike's Peakers—'Pike's Peak or Bust'?"

"Yes," said Wallace glumly. "And very often they busted."

"Well, let's make it 'Michikamau or Bust!' What do you say?"

And to Hubbard's immense relief, Wallace thought, sipped, and smiled. "All right. Michikamau or Bust!"

The mountains took two days. They seemed formidable at first, but one little lake led to another, and, on August 23, Hubbard found himself breaking through a bouldery pass to a grand scene—as if the peaks had naturally parted to let him by. On either side, steep slopes of bare rock rose eight or nine hundred feet, but a narrow lake stretched westward to the plateau and the horizon. Could it be an extension of Michikamau's southeast bay? On the strength of their prospects, Wallace named it Lake Hope.

Two days of paddling, however, brought them only to a bog at Hope's end. Doggedly, Hubbard climbed a hill and spotted an even larger lake to the north. They carried to it and again headed west, looking for an outlet. Bay after bay, up and down the lake—nothing. After several days, and more than fifty miles of fruitless searching, Hubbard had to admit the game was up. This lake—Wallace called it Disappointment—had no outlet that they could discover. The Indian trail was finally, undeniably, and irretrievably lost.

The evening of August 27, Hubbard studied Low's map—measuring, calculating, staring endlessly at those damnable dotted lines, trying to make them coalesce. In a general way, he knew where Michikamau was. Low had charted most of its shores in firm, solid lines. But not the southeast corner—precisely the stretch of territory they were now approaching. That long bay was dotted. Hubbard's most recent observation put him at 53° 50′—far enough north, probably, to be parallel with the bay. But since he had been unable to compute longitude, he had no way of figuring how far to the west Michikamau remained.

Some things he did know. Their provisions were practically out—except for the peameal he'd been saving for emergency use. Yet, even if he decided to turn home, that supply would not carry them even halfway to Northwest River Post. One way or another, they were committed to living off the country.

And that meant caribou. Not fish, not fowl—caribou. One had only to look at the tally. The last few weeks they'd been pulling in sixty, sometimes eighty trout on good days, finding pike so big that Wallace was shooting them with his pistol, bringing in geese and grouse and rockers, getting all the berries they could eat. Why, they had even caught a baby loon once, with their bare hands. But the paddling, hauling, and straining made a man ravenous. Even under the best of conditions, the country yielded up the barest minimum.

Soon the geese would be taking to the air—and the party had no shotgun. The trout would be going deep—and Hubbard had already discarded the worn and useless gill net from Northwest River. Soon even the berries would be covered with snow.

Caribou. Caribou. Caribou. Where were they going to find

caribou? Ahead, along Michikamau's shores and the Naskapi hunting grounds? Or back in that first awful valley, where they had bagged a total of one grouse and a red squirrel? There really seemed to be only one answer.

"Saturday, August 29th. Temperature 6 A.M. 38°. Am writing a starter here, before beginning our march. . . . We must be moving with more ginger. It is a nasty feeling to see the days slipping by and note the sun's lower declination, and still not know our way." Hubbard collected his thoughts while the boys were eating breakfast. He'd had another bout with diarrhea and was sick of goose. He was sick, too, of how his body kept rebelling against his will. He intended to change that.

But after toiling all day, they achieved only the most discouraging results. It had become a matter of hopping tiny ponds and carrying the gear over one back-breaking hill after another.

". . . three miles. Not enough. Must get more snap into our game—too much scouting—not enough backache . . ."

One obstacle after another! How it galled him.

"Beautiful clear Sunday, but no Sunday rest for us. I jumped up early, called George, and built fire. Started at 5:54 A.M. . . ."

He worked and sweated and watched the landscape change before him. The wide plateau with its rolling hills was giving way to a succession of sharp ridges and a jumble of boulders, the debris left behind by the last glacier. The spruce forest fell away, replaced only by humble life forms—lichen and moss. The world turned from boreal to barren, from green to gray, with the azure ponds in the valleys providing the only visual relief.

It was a prize day, exactly the kind they needed. So when the old weariness hit shortly after lunch, Hubbard gritted his teeth and kept going. When the rumbling in his bowels struck again, he headed for the bushes and then, each time, returned to the trail, refusing to admit that his legs were becoming more and more rubbery. At day's end he was barely able to drag himself into camp. Saying nothing to the boys, he fixed a cup of tea as a tonic and, drinking it, was immediately overwhelmed by nausea. He turned again for the bushes but did not make it; his stomach came up before his legs could carry him. The vomiting stopped, it seemed, only when his body was too worn out to endure another spasm.

"That tea was powerful medicine," he said as soon as he could muster himself. "My cramps seem better."

"You sick?" the others asked. They were wide-eyed. Hubbard did not like that look.

"Indisposed, maybe," he said. "Just the diet. And the strain. Nothing a caribou won't cure."

To prove the point, he managed to hold down a light supper; then entered into the usual after-dinner round of menu-making. That was their great pleasure now.

Coffee, chocolate, pie, fried cakes and pudding—those were the selections for dessert. Hubbard ordered his pudding with a dollop of whipped cream.

"You *are* sick!" exclaimed Wallace. "Only a dollop! I want mine *buried* in whipped cream."

George chimed in, a serious look on his face. "Would'je believe it, fellus? I once threw away a whole batch of cookies."

"*No!*" Hubbard and Wallace cried as one.

"Fact," said George.

"For heaven's sake, how could you do such a thing?"

"Well, it was when I first went cookin' in a surveyor's camp. The cookies wasn't as good as I thought they ought to be, and I was so ashamed of 'em that I took the whole lot out and buried 'em.

"Supposin'," he continued in an awed whisper, "supposin' we had 'em now!"

"Why, what in the world would you do with them?" asked Hubbard slyly.

"Well, I guess we'd find a way to use 'em, all right."

NEXT MORNING Hubbard called a rest day. He was too sick to travel.

With nothing to do in camp, George went to the nearest mountain to scout the country. *Had* to do something; it was getting late. The geese had got their wings now; they were in the air and a much harder shot for a rifle. Oh, how he wanted a shotgun! Even Hubbard was sorry they hadn't brought one. It was already the end of August, and if they didn't get to Michikamau and the caribou grounds soon . . . well, George didn't want to think about it.

From the top of the mountain, he saw a long lake that looked like a river but wasn't. And beyond, far away where everything got shimmery, he saw *big* water that looked ten or twenty miles wide. That was more like it—they had to get past these little ponds and rough country. Portaging and hauling just took it out of you, especially on short rations. Look at Hubbard! He couldn't keep up like this. None of them could. They needed that big water for good traveling.

It took three days of hard going to reach the lake that looked like a river. It stretched five blessed miles without a portage. They tried some fishing there and landed about fourteen trout. George boiled up a few, then split them into three parts. He divided food carefully now, because the hunger in their sides had got a sharp point. Then he took two teaspoons of flour—same as Hubbard and Wallace—and stirred it into his share of the fish water. Using flour by the spoonful, they figured it'd stretch longer.

Later he climbed another mountain, came back, and told the boys their big water was one good day's march away—maybe three or four miles. But they hiked one day, then two and then three without ever reaching it.

George couldn't figure where that blamed lake had gone. It embarrassed him to be so far wrong. Hubbard said it must be the clear air that made the distance look so short. Wallace just shook his head and said it was like the wisp of hay you hung in front of the donkey's nose to make him go.

It was as hard country as George had seen. Raining every day; and when they weren't going nearly barefoot over the boulder patches, they were knee deep in mud. Hubbard's pack pitched him face down once, right into the muck. He pulled out in bad shape but kept on going.

Then the thermometer took a drop and it began to snow—big white flakes mixed with rain. The storm was coming out of the northwest, just where they were heading, so the only thing to do was lean into it and try not to think. That, and maybe talk to yourself; George tried that sometimes when the going was bad.

It was his turn to carry the canoe. He hoisted it to his knees, then swung it over his head so that the thwart lay on his shoulders. By now his shoulders were mostly bruises. And the canoe was so waterlogged, it weighed more than a hundred pounds.

Canoe keeps the rain out, he told himself. But he had to follow Hubbard and Wallace through thick brush and up some bluffs; things got gusty. Along the bluffs, the wind blew the boat around like a weathervane—blew *him* around with it and left his arms numb and tingling just trying to keep the canoe pointed straight. Don't let the bow rise too high, Georgie—don't let the wind under it. Once that wind takes a piece, canoe'll go like a sail and you'll tumble over the bluff. Forget about your arms. Just keep the bow down.

Except he had to see where the boys were. If he kept the bow down, all he could see was the ground ten feet in front of him. So now and then he tilted it ever so slightly—careful, careful—to find the boys.

Wallace was in sight. Pretty far ahead, though. Hubbard must've gone over the bluff.

Arms get to shaking—the blamed wind. Wind just keeps workin' the canoe. You got to keep goin', Georgie. Talk to yourself and tell yourself you have to keep at it. Hubbard keeps at it. If *he* can do it, you can too. Pull your arms up a bit—lift the canoe and take a look for Wallace.

Wallace is gone.

Heart beats a little faster. Tip her again, Georgie—watch it! Watch that wind!

Wallace is gone; nowhere to be seen. Hubbard is gone. There's nothing but snow swirling.

They'll be just over the bluff, won't they? That's where they were headed. But if you get there and they're not over the bluff, then what? You got one thing on your back, Georgie: a canoe. No grub. No blankets to sleep in the snow. No tent. No fishhooks and no matches to light a fire so the boys can find you. You got nothin' but a canoe, and you better not start foolin' around with *maybe* they went over the bluff.

With a lurch, he heaved the canoe from his shoulders, the wind catching it and bouncing it to the ground. He ran toward the edge of the bluffs.

"Hey, Wallace! *Wallace!*"

The snow seemed to eat his words.

Among the scrubby spruce he made out a shadow. When he got closer, he could see Wallace turn, hearing his call. A few more lopes and he caught up, all out of breath.

"You better wait for me," he said, taking the air in big gulps. "The canoe—I can't handle her the way she's blowin'. If I get separated, I might strike the lake one place and you might strike it someplace else. And *you* fellus got the grub."

Hubbard had already disappeared into the bush. Wallace hallooed, and a halloo came back. Pretty soon they could see Hubbard working his way back to meet them, blazing trees every few steps. George could tell by the look in his eyes he was glad to reach them. In this country and this weather, hallooing wasn't enough.

SUNDAY, SEPTEMBER 6th. Temperature 5 A.M. 38°. First snow came, mixed with nasty cold rain. . . . Crossed semi-barren ridges and plain and entered heavy spruce bush (small trees) alternating with swamps that make one wade and flounder. My trousers hanging in strips and tatters. My moccasins showing sock at most every angle . . .

It was ten days since they'd left Lake Disappointment. They had come nearly forty miles. But George's promised "big water" was still nowhere in sight. Hubbard brooded over their progress. Winter was already on its way, and what had the expedition accomplished? They hadn't reached the Naskapi. They hadn't reached the caribou grounds. They hadn't reached Michikamau. They had no idea whether their first river was actually the Northwest, or whether the second river was, or whether at Disappointment they'd simply missed the trail. So far, the expedition was a failure.

He confessed his fears to Wallace. What was there to write about? They hadn't *done* anything.

Wallace was true blue. "You've got plenty to write about," he said. "After all, we've come through country no white man has explored. We've had some great adventures—look at our caribou hunt. And plenty of close scrapes. It'll be a bang-up story."

Hubbard stared ahead. That wasn't much consolation. Not with Whitney waiting.

"Anyway," said Wallace, "we'll all reach the caribou ground and see the Indians yet. You can count on George and me to the last ditch; we'll stick by you all the way." And George nodded.

Hubbard was all smiles. *That* was the answer he'd been waiting for.

"All right. If you boys aren't sick of it, it's on to the caribou ground, late or no late. But I feel I've gotten you into a tight place."

"We came with our eyes open," said Wallace stoutly. "It's not your fault."

That night, Hubbard wrote in his diary: "Boys not scared. No talk of quitting. Don't just see where we are coming out."

September 8 brought them to a shoal bay where, at long last, George's "big water" spread for miles and miles before them. On the far side of the lake, perhaps twenty miles distant, stood one lone peak, gray and solemn in its isolation.

What lay beyond the mountain? Hubbard paddled all afternoon in a state of both anticipation and dread. Michikamau just *had* to be there. If it was, he and the others would be rewarded for all their struggle and hard work. But if they scaled the peak and once again saw nothing but hill stretching into the distance? His heart plumped down to his hipbones just to think of the possibility.

10

Limits

THEY REACHED THE far shore of the lake by ten o'clock the next morning. Leaving Wallace to harvest a bountiful crop of blueberries on a burned-over hillside, Hubbard and George headed for the mountain. Hubbard had his hands full trying to keep up. Even without a pack, his legs were leaden and the smallest steps deprived him of his wind.

As they approached the summit a flurry of brown and white caught his eyes. "Ptarmigan!" George whispered, and pulled his pistol. Sure enough, they had unwittingly flushed ten of the birds, who dashed madly ahead and then squatted in the arctic shrubs.

Hubbard was galvanized. He advanced with George, and both men fired as soon as they were in range. Hubbard's bullet found its mark. The other birds fled again, white wings beating against their mottled brown bodies. But none took to the air—just ran several feet and squatted in apparent terror in the next bush. Hubbard led the way, firing as fast as he could, dropping one bird after another. Within minutes he had bagged eight of them, George one, and only one had escaped. Nine birds for the larder!

"I knew we'd get 'em," said George happily. "They're tame as can be on a calm day. You just don't want wind, that's all."

A little farther on, their good luck continued when a rabbit hopped up ahead of them. Both pistols sounded and the rabbit went down. Hubbard figured they were ahead three meals.

The day was magnificent. Overhead, brilliant blue sky reached in every direction. Behind, the waters of their lake glinted silver in the sun, and to either side were many more lake expansions—hundreds dotting the countryside, so that in some places it was difficult to tell whether the landscape was really water filled with islands or land pockmarked with water. As they drew near the summit Hubbard kept his eye on the western horizon, where blue haze met the gray ridge of their peak. When the blue became deeper and deeper, he suddenly realized he was looking at water, not sky. He ran the last few feet and drank in the sight—no islands to the west, no hills rolling on and on, just crystalline water, stretching without ridges or boundaries or limits—water beckoning straight to the horizon.

He gave a cheer, and George grinned from ear to ear. This was Michikamau and no mistake about it! Hubbard stared, hardly daring to believe.

The air was so clean, it filled his lungs to bursting and made him light—almost giddy. What price could be set on it? To stand atop one lone peak, lord of all he surveyed, Grand Mogul of Labrador! Endless water, endless horizons, endless ambitions . . . Hubbard knew by the very air he breathed that the price was worth it. A few finite aches for a limitless sea of blue? It was a pittance! What human being with a restless soul would *not* pay it?

Together with George, he tried to spot a route from their own large lake into Michikamau. Both north and south, there seemed to be several winding connections through the many islands and twisting bays. But it was difficult to trace the exact course; they would have to find it from the water. Taking one last look at the lake of his dreams, Hubbard headed down the mountain.

WALLACE HAD PICKED three quarts of blueberries by the time he spied Hubbard bounding over the bushes yelling, "It's there! Big water, we saw it! Michikamau!" Wallace jumped for joy and then the two of them did a little dance, half jig, half bear-hug, while George stood to one side grinning with pleasure.

Then Hubbard directed Wallace's attention to the rabbit and the heap of ptarmigan at George's feet. Wallace was overcome. He counted the birds with nervous joy—nine of them! "You see," said Hubbard earnestly, "God always gives us food when we're in great need. He'll carry us through that way. We're in the wilderness, but he'll send us manna."

They built a fire by the shore. Wallace was ravenous. He'd eaten nothing but a few blueberries since their breakfast—what Hubbard called "porridge," though it was only three thin slices of bacon and three teaspoons of flour boiled in a big pot of water.

Now, each man roasted the black entrails of a bird on the end of a stick and ate them greedily. That was how the Indians did it when they were starving, George said.

At the evening fire, Wallace lingered with George to have a pipe, letting his imagination form pictures in the orange-and-black embers. George broke into his reverie.

"You hear the loons calling a few nights ago, Wallace?"

"Yes. It was different than I remember hearing earlier on the trip. Not their laughing cry, but the long, sad one."

George was silent for a moment. Then he said, "When the Indians hear the loon callin' like that, they think it's a sign. They think there's calamity on its way. That's what they say anyway."

Wallace said nothing; he didn't want to encourage such talk. All the same, he resolved to mention the conversation to Hubbard. George never seemed to worry when Hubbard was around—only when he was alone with Wallace.

The next day, September 10, the sky clouded up and with it any hope of quickly reaching Michikamau. The inlets and channels that Hubbard said could be seen so distinctly from the mountain now became a maze of spruce islands and shadowy bays. The search seemed depressingly similar to the one on Lake Disappointment, where so many promising leads had turned into dead ends. So Hubbard said they would try the southern end of the lake, where he had also seen water and channels. On the way, the wind picked up, whipping the waves and slopping an occasional crest over the gunwales. Sitting amidships, Wallace watched the waves dash against the canoe. It was unsettling: On a big lake like this they would have to be careful.

The last ptarmigan went for dinner that evening. After the meal, Wallace took his knife and worked another hole into his belt. He had lost two inches from his waist in the last week alone. Hubbard was in even worse shape; indeed, he had stopped bathing quite some time ago, confiding when George was out of earshot that he was too "ashamed of his bones" to go swimming. "The truth is," he told Wallace, "I'm a walking skeleton."

On Friday morning they ate one trout and a few ptarmigan entrails. George also stewed the last of the dried apples Hubbard's mother had given them. Then it was back to scouting.

But wherever they followed up a bay to the west, they found only dead ends. Whenever they climbed a hill, they could see only a band of green blocking their way. Chagrined, Hubbard vowed to give the other end of the lake one final try, and if a route couldn't be found, portage their way west. They *knew* Michikamau was there.

That evening they camped on a rough, rockbound island. It was a desolate spot, with only a few gnarled spruce and stunted fir trees. While Hubbard was chopping wood, Wallace helped George lift the canoe past the waves breaking against the bouldery shore.

"I used to be able to lift this canoe pretty easy," said George. "It's heavy now."

"Soaked up a lot of water," said Wallace.

"It's been soaked a good time before this. I'm weaker now, Wallace. I can feel it. I'm weaker in my arms when I paddle. I feel weak in my legs when I go to scout."

The two of them looked across the dark waters. Even in twilight, whitecaps were visible on the lake.

"I knew some Cree up on the Bay who was up against it once," George continued. "Came near starvin' to death. You get weaker and weaker, little by little. Doesn't happen all of a sudden. You feel hungry as the devil for a while. Then you don't feel so hungry, but still you're gettin' weaker. Pretty soon you don't feel like doin' anything. You just want to lay down and give it up and die."

"Well, at least we've got a few trout for supper," said Wallace. George was talking about starving Indians all too often these days—again, always when Hubbard was out of earshot. To be sure, George maintained his usual calm. Never once had he suggested turning back. Yet the worry behind the stories was evident. It seemed to Wallace as if two natures were at war within the half-breed. One, the Indian spirit, was haunted by superstitious fears. The other, the white element, rejected those fears and conquered them. Wallace admired George's ability to master his superstitions.

On the other hand, Wallace was worried himself. Except for the emergency reserve—twenty pounds of peameal, to be used only in case of a retreat—their provisions were virtually exhausted. The three of them were staking their chances entirely on living off the country until they reached the caribou grounds. Yet, so far, the fishing on these bigger waters had proved disappointing.

When he had a moment alone with Hubbard, he mentioned the Indian stories and George's fear of starvation. Hubbard seemed surprised. He hardly thought George could be worried. After all, the man worked unstintingly—was generally cheerful—seemed game enough about going on. He told Wallace not to read too much into an occasional story or two.

HUBBARD AWOKE Saturday to a loud flapping, the tent swaying wildly. One moment its walls would billow like a sail, the next they would collapse upon the men with a crack, as the wind gusted in some new direction. It seemed every moment as if the whole rig would be ripped from its stakes. Peering through the flaps, he was instantly greeted by a gust of rain and snow. The lake was almost unrecognizable, white foam everywhere, while the waves dashed against the island's rocky shore and sent spray high into the air.

One thing was certain: There would be no traveling. Bowing to the inevitable, he returned to his blankets, glad of the chance to sleep late. It was ten o'clock before he heard George rouse himself and disappear to cook a few trout for breakfast. Hubbard and Wallace were surprised to see him poke his head through the tent door only a few minutes later, a solemn look on his face.

"Well, that's too bad."

"What's too bad?" asked Hubbard anxiously.

"Somebody stole the trout we left under the canoe."

"Who?" they asked in unison.

George shrugged. "Otter or somebody. Maybe a marten." George habitually referred to animals as persons.

They all ran out to make sure the fish had not been left nearby, but a thorough search revealed nothing. Hubbard looked at the other two and they all laughed—what else was there to do?—and then settled down to a soup made of the usual tiny portions of bacon, flour, and rice. During the day, Hubbard ventured an occasional look outside, but what he saw only confirmed the noise of the flapping tent. They were windbound on the island.

Sunday morning it was blowing as bad as ever. By afternoon, however, the storm abated enough to let them escape. On the way to shore, they caught a *namaycush*—George's name for lake trout—and immediately put in to eat it, along with a cranberry stew made from berries gathered on a sandy knoll. The fish was good, but the sour berries made their gums hurt.

That evening Hubbard did not turn in early. Nights like this Wallace was so comfortable to be with: He sat solid as a log, gazing into the fire, listening to Hubbard's stories about his father's trek to California as a Forty-niner, or about maple-sugaring on the old Michigan farm. Every time the conversation hit a lull, Hubbard thought of the damp, dark tent, and started in on another story. Finally, though, bed could no longer be postponed.

The wind and sleet returned now and again during the night. And always, the ache in his belly was there. Hubbard would roll over, hug his blankets tighter, and try to sink back into the comfort of his dreams. At first light he jumped up nervously, but the balloon silk was flapping as hard as ever. So he slept almost until noon, when the gnawing in his stomach pulled him out. By the fire, he found George cooking the usual watery "porridge." The three of them sipped at it slowly.

The rest of the morning, Hubbard sat by the fire. George went out hunting but came back empty-handed. It was cranberry stew again for lunch.

The inevitable talk of food brought restaurants into the conversation. They were becoming an obsession. Hubbard brought out his diary and started a list of places to visit when they got home. The Chop House. The Marlborough. Cook and Foy. Parker's in Brooklyn. Fleischmann's Bakery in Lake George. Pearsall's Bakery near *Outing*. The Bowery mission, with beans and bread at two cents a plate.

The talk didn't help the ache, though. The ache was deep and wouldn't go away.

George was thoughtful. "There's a ridge up behind camp—good place for ptarmigan. Maybe I'll have a look up there." Wallace got up to join him, but Hubbard hung back. With the others gone, he could catch up on his journal. He threw another log on the fire.

But in the end, what was there to write? There wasn't anything he'd done so far today. He knew he should be out hunting—the discipline would be good for him. But the fire . . . you could sit and look at the fire forever. With some effort he turned his thoughts to the diary:

> I have learned a lesson in outfitting this trip. It is this—on a *Hard Trip* take only the essentials—leave the comforts out. When you are hungry enough you will not mind lack of sugar. . . . I'd take now: First—flour—a lot. 2d—peameal—a lot. A lot of oatmeal and rice. A few beans, maybe. Tea, sure. A good wad of bacon or fat pork—preferably the latter. Baking powder, some salt. Never mind sugar or coffee or choc-

> olate—or take a little to taper off with at the start. Just a little. Then use the whole lot conservatively. Boil bacon and rice and stir in flour. Same with oatmeal—use oatmeal, rice and flour with partridge, fish, etc. Go light on bread. Flour goes farther in soup.

It did, too. It was remarkable how much savor one teaspoon of flour gave the broth. As he thought about the soup his discipline weakened.

> But I'm not aching for more trips like this *just now*. Heretofore I have revelled in strenuous trips, trying to make them the real thing—*getting down to the essentials*. Now I've had a good taste of essentials, I want pleasant, easy trips. I'll take delight in the Congers woods, the Croton, the Hudson Highlands, the Ramapos, Lake George, etc., and with the outfit will go flour in plenty, sweet biscuits, bacon . . .

He couldn't help himself. No matter how he tried, he thought of food. He was obsessed by it. The pencil in his hand seemed to move of its own volition, on and on and on:

> . . . chocolate, milk, heap sugar, marmalade, lime tablets, canned roast beef, onions, potatoes, rice, oatmeal, raisins, figs, dried fruit, tomatoes, with chickens when we can get them along the way. Then good stew, soups, French toast, syrup, pancakes, omelettes, sweet biscuit and jam, with a broiled steak and a chicken roast when available, canned pork and beans and canned plum pudding must also go in the menu. Mina and I must study delightful camp dinners now and carry out the nice little woods dinners we started. I must study camp cooking, too. And what fine little dinners we can have.

George and Wallace came back with long faces. George had winged a ptarmigan, but it fluttered away before they could reach it. So it was watery porridge again for supper.

The talk about menus and restaurants had grown pretty threadbare. Silent, George lit his pipe while Hubbard watched uneasily. George knew how to be silent in many different ways; that was his eloquence.

What was he thinking? Hubbard desperately wanted to know.

Then again, maybe he didn't. George didn't want to turn back, did he? Surely he'd say so if he did. But according to Wallace, he'd been telling stories about starving Indians. That wasn't good.

There wasn't much to do other than call it a day. Hubbard wrote one final entry for September 14: "Later by campfire. Hard to keep off depression. Wind continues and all hungry." Then he followed the others to bed.

Wrapped in his blanket, he waited for the dreams to come. They wouldn't. The wind pulled at the canvas and set it flapping, keeping him awake with its noise, reminding him of the lake and the waves.

He listened. Wallace's breathing was full, regular. He was sound asleep. Hubbard couldn't hear George breathing.

George was awake. And silent.

Three slices of bacon. Three teaspoons of flour. Three teaspoons of rice. A pot full of boiling water. And the wind still driving across the lake, holding them windbound.

Hubbard brought out the food duffel. He made an inventory of their provisions. Two pounds of flour, eighteen pounds of pea-meal, less than a pint of rice, and half a pound of bacon. It was an easy task, but he spent a good deal of time on it. Just handling the food gave him pleasure.

George sat and watched. After a while, he cleared his throat.

"I knew some Cree on the Bay who was up against it once. Came near starvin' to death."

Hubbard looked away.

"You get weaker and weaker, little by little. Doesn't happen all of a sudden. You feel hungry as the devil. That's what they say. Then you don't feel so hungry, but still you're gettin' weaker. Pretty soon you don't feel like doin' anything."

They sat by the fire, staring at the logs. After a time, Hubbard rose and pushed the loose ends of the sticks into the blaze. He stood with his back to the flames, deep in thought. Then he turned toward the lake and walked through the brush to the water's edge. He faced the wind as it blew from the west, the sleet mixed with driving rain.

He wanted to be like Whitney. To think matters through and decide, in a hard-nosed way, what had to be done. And then go out and do it. Never mind the odds; no fussing over the risks—just *do* it. *Will* the solution into existence.

That philosophy had worked so far. It had brought him to the very edge of Michikamau . . . to the heart of an unknown country . . . to the brink of fulfilling his lifelong dream. He had every reason to press on. Everything depended upon the success of this expedition—his career, his self-esteem, his entire future. And now all they needed was one more caribou. A single caribou would carry them through to the Naskapi.

What were the odds of getting that deer? There was no telling, of course. You either got him or you didn't. When you were charting unknown territory, there was no banking on odds. If you did what Whitney did, you would hang the risk, put down your head, and keep on bulling.

Right?

But Whitney had been alone when he crossed the arctic—completely alone except for those Indians who couldn't speak English. And even if he had taken real companions, people he could talk to, he still would have been alone. That was Whitney's way—everything in the singular. But Hubbard's situation was different. He had Wallace and George. They were his friends. Their lives were in his hands.

He had tried to share the decision, but it hadn't worked. More than once, he had asked the boys whether they wanted to go on—asked them a lot of times. And each time they said yes. "Michikamau or Bust!" "Ho for Michikamau!" They meant it too; he knew that much. But he knew now that they hadn't meant it for themselves; they had meant it for him.

The waves rolled across the lake heedless of the man watching them. There was no limitless blue horizon where they broke along the far shore; no infinite vista like the one that had spread before him when he gazed out at Michikamau. There was only the black spruce forming a jagged boundary with the clouds. And behind him, two men feeding the embers of a fire.

There were limits. There were the people you loved.

Hubbard turned about briskly and, with quick, nervous steps, pushed through the brush to the fire where George and Wallace were sitting in silence. Suddenly, and without a word of introduction, he said:

"Boys, what do you say to turning back?"

11

Up Against It for Sure

FOR A LONG MOMENT, Wallace could not find his tongue. He sat dazed in front of the fire, trying to absorb Hubbard's words. Turn back? For months, he had reduced his life to one purpose: Get to Michikamau and the caribou grounds. His law practice seemed a part of a distant realm, vanished forever with the rest of the civilized world. Life had been distilled down to a compass bearing—north by west.

Hubbard glanced from Wallace to George and back, his eyes anxious as a boy's. Wallace still could not find his voice. Finally, George spoke up.

"I came to go with you fellus, and I want to do what you fellus do."

Hubbard's eyes held George's only an instant, then fixed upon Wallace.

Wallace swallowed. It wasn't just the change of direction; it was Hubbard asking. Asking Dillon Wallace, the novice of the trip. He'd never been asked to decide their course at any point along the way. Hubbard was the one who made the plans; he had a plan for every eventuality. Wallace accepted this as a matter of course—preferred it, even. He was content to push onward like a faithful packhorse, Michikamau being the wisp of hay that drove the donkey forward. Only once, when Hubbard took sick on the long portage, had Wallace considered stepping in to call a halt.

But really—how could he have done that? Hubbard would have been offended by even the suggestion of calling it quits. The poor fellow had staked his career on this expedition. No matter how sick he was, he had simply willed himself over the portage. Wallace understood that approach perfectly: It had taken him ten years of part-time jobs and night school to transform himself into a lawyer, years of plodding resolutely on. Now, here was Michikamau virtually over the next rise—and they were turning back?

"I don't see the point," he said finally. "We can't be far from the Indians now."

"Two weeks to the caribou grounds. Two weeks minimum."

"Well, but when we get to Michikamau we ought to see the smoke from their wigwams. And once we reach them, they'll surely help us."

"*If* we reach them," said Hubbard gloomily. "Look at these miserable gales."

"But your story. Without the caribou and the Indians . . ."

"I know," said Hubbard. "I've been thinking about that. But the migration must have begun already—perhaps it's even over. It would be too risky to push ahead."

"There are risks any way you look at it," said Wallace. "It's a long trek back to Northwest River. A lot of work on short rations."

Hubbard looked dreadful. "The Naskapi are most likely hunting along the George River," he said. "And we've got to find the headwaters. We don't have the food and don't have the time. We don't even know whether the river is canoeable."

Wallace found himself bending. Either way, they were trapped.

Maybe they should choose by instinct—trust sheer animal cunning. Wallace looked at George. "What do you think, George?"

George was prompt. "Oh, I'd like to turn back, and I think it's safest; but I'm goin' to stick to you fellus, and I'm goin' where you go."

"Well, then," said Hubbard, "what's the vote? Shall we turn back or go on?"

Wallace agonized. After all the miles, the hardships, the trials, it had come down to him.

"Turn back," he said at last.

"Very well," said Hubbard quietly. "Then that's settled."

George's face brightened immediately, and Wallace, to his surprise, found himself grinning. They were going home. No more wasting time scouting for some Indian trail—they'd be following their own path, as fast as paddles and legs could carry them; traveling light and living off the land.

Hubbard began pacing back and forth. Soon he was making

plans again, full of his old enthusiasm. "We'll have to catch some fish here on the lake and smoke them to tide us over the portage," he said. "If winter comes early, we'll build sleds, that's all. And caribou. What do you think of our chances for getting caribou, George?"

George shrugged. "We saw some comin' up, and there ought to be more now. I guess we'll find 'em."

Hubbard seemed immensely pleased. "I'll tell you boys, I'm dead glad we've decided to strike for the post. I lay awake most of last night thinking it over."

"I was awake too," George confessed. "My feet were mighty cold."

The conversation turned toward home. Hubbard couldn't resist planning their first vacation—to the lumber camp a few miles down the coast from Northwest River Post. There, he assured the others, they could count on some real treats: pork and beans, blackstrap molasses. . . .

"Will there be cake and pie?" George asked.

"Yes, in unlimited quantities," said Hubbard, "and doughnuts too."

"Gingerbread?"

"Yes, gingerbread is always on the table."

That night, Wallace drifted into a deep sleep. He dreamed he was going home; that he had arrived safely in Brooklyn to a grand welcome by his sisters. They had baked him a gingerbread. It was the size of an entire house. He was not at all troubled by the prospect of devouring it whole.

In the morning the waters on Windbound Lake, as Wallace called it, had calmed long enough to move camp to the lake's south shore, where they set about some serious fishing. Wallace went with George in the canoe to troll the open bays, while Hubbard headed for a nearby stream with his fly rod. At the end of the day, trollers and fly-rod specialist convened, each hoping for good news from the other. The final tally: two ten-inchers from the brook.

"Too raw and cold," was Hubbard's verdict.

Wallace was too disappointed to speak. Instead of building up a reserve, they were forced to dig deeper into their provision bag.

The next morning George shot a whiskey jack. It was about the size of a large robin. "They're pretty tough," he said, bringing his prize into camp. "This one'll take a long time to cook." The boys didn't mind; they ate the bird, bones and all, stewed in a pot of water.

That was breakfast. There was no lunch. Trolling along the lee shores of the islands, Hubbard finally hooked a huge namaycush, perhaps a fifteen pounder, and excitedly reeled it in. Reaching into the water just above its mouth, he gave the line a final pull. The namaycush arched into the air, flopped hard against the gunwale, and dived deep, back into the water. Wallace stared at the line in Hubbard's hand: a broken hook. Later they pulled in another big one, only to lose it in the confusion of trying to shoot it before lifting it out of the water. Near dusk, they finally landed two of their quarry, one weighing five pounds and the other two.

They hurried to camp and built a roaring fire. George cut the larger fish into three parts, the center section to eat immediately, the head and tail for the morrow. That gave them two snacks ahead and the second fish for the portage.

"I feel more satisfied every time I think of our decision to turn back," said Hubbard reclining by the fire. "I had a pretty hard night of it on Monday, though. I lay for the longest time thinking how I'd have to turn back without seeing the Indians."

George stirred. "I was awake too. I told you about havin' cold feet, and how they kept me awake." He finished abruptly, staring at the fire.

Wallace suspected more was coming. Soon George was out with it.

"Well, it was hearin' that wind out in the lake. The wind kept me awake more than the cold feet. I knew the wind was makin' the huntin' good down on the Bay. The game was comin' down there now, and I knew that the young fellus I used to hunt with had been wishin' for this very wind that was keepin' us here, and they were glad to see it and were out shootin' waveys, havin' a good time of it. And here we boys was, up against it for sure."

The rain was mixing with sleet; if anything, it was coming down harder than ever. When George retired to bed, Wallace and Hubbard stretched the tarpaulin between two trees that stood close to the fire. The canvas snapped at its ropes, but the shelter provided an eddy in the midst of the storm. Wallace watched as Hubbard fed the fire for a few minutes, then sank back next to him on their cushion of boughs.

"You don't mind sitting here for a while and chatting, do you, b'y?" he asked. "It's cold and shivery in the tent."

Wallace had noticed a change in Hubbard the past few days. Until lately, the work he had to do seemed almost wholly to occupy his thoughts. More and more, though, he craved companionship, and loved to sit and dwell on his home and wife. He spoke the word *b'y* now in the simple manner of the people on the coast. The old jocularity, the hint of mockery, was gone.

Wallace found that the custom came naturally to him as well.

"No, b'y," he answered. "Chat away. I would much rather be with you than in the tent."

Hubbard reminsced about his wedding. "Did I ever tell you the trouble I had?" he asked Wallace.

"No, b'y. You never took me into your confidence, you know."

"That was because we'd never camped together. If we'd camped together, I'd have told you all about it. Actually, Mina and I hadn't intended to get married so soon. But Whitney assigned me to a trip through the South. I knew it would keep me away until after our wedding date, and I didn't like that a bit. So I wired her and asked her to come on at once."

"Your telegram must have been a bit of a surprise."

"She was a brick, Wallace. Wired back that she was on her way. Then, the day of her arrival, I was so keyed up that by four in the morning I was at the station, waiting for the first train into Grand Central. I was taking no chance on missing her! So I sat there on the bench, thinking so hard about Mina and the wedding that the train pulled into the station, blew its whistle, and pulled right out again without me even noticing."

Wallace laughed. "And was the bride-elect kept waiting?"

"No, I hurried over to another line and took that one in. It all worked out right in the end."

Wallace rose to shake off some of the sleet that had iced up on the tarp. When he dropped back on the boughs, he saw that the drawn look had returned to Hubbard's face. He was staring wistfully into the darkness.

"What is it, b'y?" Wallace asked softly.

"That was a great trip, Wallace—our wedding trip. I would like nothing more than to repeat our honeymoon. Just to be with Mina and enjoy some southern cooking."

"Southern cooking?" Wallace ventured. In his straitened circumstances, he couldn't help concentrating more on the honey than the honeymoon.

Not until after midnight did the two men give up the talk of wild hog and hoecake and cornpone and honey. Even then Hubbard seemed loath to seek the tent; nights, he found it increasingly difficult to warm himself with his blanket. Wallace demonstrated an evening ritual he had developed, of toasting himself on all sides like a marshmallow, then pulling on a pair of socks that had been hanging before the fire, and making a dash for the tent. But even this prophylactic provided only temporary relief. After enduring another dismal and shivery night, he conferred with the others and, together, the three of them finally hit upon a plan. Spreading out their tarpaulin and one of their open bedrolls, they lay down side by side, pulling the remaining blankets snugly over them. The blankets were not wide; Wallace found himself huddled with the others shoulder to shoulder, hip to hip, and leg to leg. But their lank frames gave comfort too. For the first time in many nights, he slept warmly.

12

George's Secret

MONDAY, SEPTEMBER 21, the gale was still blowing and whitecaps were jumping on the lake. George looked over the distance they had to cross. Big swells kept breaking everywhere—the bay was shallow and studded with rocks. It was no weather for heading out in a canoe, but that didn't matter. They didn't have a choice anymore. Had to get off this lake. Had to get started for home.

Hubbard and Wallace knelt up front like always. They didn't have to do much thinking—just paddle. But George had to steer. He had to watch the wind and keep the canoe angled right with the waves. He had to think about the boulders too: Which ones were deep enough to slide over; which to slip around with a quick pry; which to stay clear of altogether. Going out in a wind like this was taking a long chance, but as far as George could see, they didn't have any choice.

It seemed to him, sometimes, he was the only one who could see this. It seemed that he held a kind of secret—unknown to the others and carried deep inside.

When he thought about the secret, it seemed a peculiar thing—something that should not be secret at all. It was something they should all know and talk about but didn't. Maybe because it had started out very small, deep inside where nobody else knew about it. Maybe the fellow thinking about it didn't even know himself at first.

George's secret had begun to grow long before they were windbound. It had begun before they went across the long portage for forty miles; back before they had spent so much time hunting the outlet of Disappointment Lake; before, even, they crossed the big mountain range. Back at Camp Caribou it had started, where they had eaten slice after slice of roast venison. Thick, juicy meat and all they wanted, bellies full, everyone content.

The morning George was packing up the dried meat, he noticed the four caribou hooves lying a ways from the fire. Now, a caribou hoof was just a lot of gristle and tendon. There was nothing to it. But George picked up one of the hooves, anyway, and put it in the bag with the other meat. Not all four, just one. Maybe the secret in his thoughts was so small, he didn't really feel it yet—just put the hoof in the bag and told himself, "We'll want this someday, maybe." Without thinking—or wanting to think—anything more.

But the secret was there: small, but riding inside, like the caribou hoof stuck in a corner of his pack.

And then they had paddled from one end of Disappointment to the other, bay after bay, looking for its outlet; and George got to feeling his secret spot. Toward the end of the search, when they passed their first campsite on the lake, he asked Hubbard to pull into shore. The campsite was where they'd thrown away the caribou hide. It hadn't dried well, was smelling something awful, and was crawling with maggots. But George hopped out and brought the hide down to the canoe.

Wallace had laughed. "Whatever in the world are you going to do with that?" he asked. And George saw that, inside, Wallace didn't have a secret spot yet. Neither did Hubbard. So George said, "We may want to eat this skin some day." Quiet, but he said it. And Wallace laughed again and Hubbard laughed too. Still, Hubbard saw George meant it, so he jumped out and helped wash the skin and put it back in the bag.

As the venison supply got lower the secret inside George grew. He could see something in the future, something coming, and it sure was something the other boys ought to be seeing. But somehow they didn't. Or acted like they didn't. And he liked Hubbard for helping wash the skin off, but it was the kindness he liked. Hubbard didn't really have the secret inside. Wallace didn't either, but he wasn't the leader of the trip, so George thought maybe he could talk a little to him. Maybe he could tell some stories about Indians starving down on the Bay.

Then Hubbard had decided to turn back, and a funny thing happened. Everybody felt good all of a sudden—wanted to talk. It seemed so easy, once the decision had been made. George could tell Hubbard how it hadn't really been his cold feet keeping him awake at night but thinking about the wind holding them down. Once they had shared secrets—once they told each other how they knew they were up against it—why, George figured there'd be no more silence between them. Everything would be easy.

But it wasn't, somehow. Because the wind kept blowing—pinning them down, first on the island, then along shore. The cold weather kept the fish from rising like they should have. And so the men didn't speak any more of how they were up against it, and the secret came back inside. They sat closer to one another around the fire and talked of food, or huddled in the blankets and spoke of days gone by. Each morning they would get up and see the wind blowing, and each evening they would see the store of grub grow smaller. And they all knew inside that if they didn't get started home soon—if they didn't act fast—well, they knew.

But they didn't say anything. They just let the wind blow them across the lake and the waves take them up and down. Steering the last twenty yards, George tried to keep the canoe lined up, but it got swung broadside by the swells crashing onto the bouldery flats. He scrambled out as the waves shoved 'em to shore—the others too—and staggered up to the bushes, dragging the canoe behind.

HUBBARD WANTED to take care—to plan methodically—their forty-mile portage back to Lake Disappointment. First he spread the gear out on a patch of open ground to let it dry. Then he shuffled from one pile to the next, looking things over. They had to lighten up.

The expedition outfit had lost its New York shine. The rifles were water-spotted and even showed a little rust. Hubbard's fishing rod was hopelessly broken and Wallace's much wound with linen thread. Off to one side lay a dirty canvas bag, tied with a string and hardly bigger than a man's head. It contained the last of their food—ten pounds of peameal. The fish from Windbound Lake were already gone.

Hubbard made some quick decisions about what could be thrown away. He discarded three pounds of tea, the pipes brought for trading with the Naskapi, the logarithm book. George tossed his old railroader's cap into the pile. What remained could be fit into three small packs. One piece of heavy equipment, though, couldn't be left behind. The canoe still weighed over a hundred pounds, too much for any of them to handle alone anymore. So they worked in relays—usually George and Wallace carrying the canoe while Hubbard brought up the packs.

The next few days one storm after another rolled in, pouring down rain and sleet and snow. The fish in the little ponds along the way refused to bite. Big game did not appear at all. Just once, Hubbard spotted a goose. Floundering through a swamp in mud over his knees, he got off a shot, but the bird flew away unharmed. Three times a day they drew on the bag of peameal: one sixth of a pound per man, hardly more than a mouthful apiece. Mercifully, Hubbard found his craving for food had become less intense; his very appetite was weakening.

By the third day he was unable to walk without staggering. He didn't know how much longer he'd be able to continue, and the others were in almost as nasty shape. Without fresh meat they were simply wasting away. Even Wallace was looking gaunt—thirteen inches off his belt so far. Every few days, he was busy with the awl, gouging a new hole.

That evening George poked at the fire. "Did you fellus hear those honkers go over while we were makin' camp?"

"Winging south," said Wallace.

"They was lookin' around," said George. "That's what I'd say from the sound of it. You remember that pond up ahead? I got a notion those geese stopped there for the night. If I could take your rifle, Hubbard, I'd have a go at 'em in the mornin'. Shouldn't be nothin' to bring one in."

At first Hubbard thought George must be joking. How could he possibly know where the birds would come down just by the sound of their honking? But his face wore a look of such confidence that Hubbard found himself handing over the rifle.

In the morning the balloon silk was drooping badly: a look outside told why. The ground was covered with wet snow, and more was falling fast. George paid no heed, just hurried off with his pack and the Winchester.

Hubbard and Wallace broke camp and trudged along in his tracks. Presently, they heard the gun in the distance. *Bang!* Then again. *Bang! Bang!*

"He's seen them," said Hubbard, hardly daring to hope.

"And shot one," said Wallace.

"Well—I'm not so sure. If they flew and he tried to wing them, the chances are against it."

They hurried along until they reached George's pack near the edge of the little lake. The bag's brown canvas was already white with snow. A few moments later George appeared out of the storm with the rifle in one hand, the other hand empty. His expression was glum.

"You can kick me," he said.

Hubbard's heart went cold.

George evidently read the look on his face and quickly added, "It's all right, fellus. I got two of 'em. I just meant, I wished I'd done a little better.

"I saw 'em out on the lake fifty yards from shore and bellied along through the brush, close as I dared. Then I fired and knocked one over. The others flew out about two hundred yards farther. I shot again and got another. Then the rest of the flock rose up, and I tried to wing one and missed. But there's two dead ones waiting for us."

Hubbard listened with awe and reverence.

"George," he said, "when we get home, I'm going to make you a present of two cookbooks and a big dinner."

After bringing up the canoe and retrieving the birds, they built a fire, dressed the geese, and set the giblets and entrails to boil. Then, as a snack, George cut three pieces of skin and fat from the necks. They put these morsels on the end of a stick and held them carefully over the blaze—just long enough to warm them without losing a single drop of oil from the melting fat.

Another gale howled all the next day and filled the air with flurries. Hubbard felt stronger as he pressed on, but still shaky. For supper they divided half a goose, then burned the bones and chewed them. After drying their clothes over the fire, they retired to the tent. Hubbard, last in, closed the flap and tied it.

The shared blankets were not wide enough to permit the men to sleep comfortably on their backs. Hubbard turned to his side and pressed against Wallace; then he felt George huddle spoon-fashion against his own back. At first the blankets were cold and clammy; it always took time for the wool to absorb their bodies' heat and feed it back. But Hubbard at once felt Wallace's warmth.

"B'y," he whispered, "I've been thinking about Thanksgiving. You must come to Congers for the holiday. Not just for dinner but the whole day."

"That sounds fine," said Wallace.

"Not just this year either. We should make Thanksgiving Day our reunion always. No matter what happens, we must make a special effort to spend the day together. We're brothers—comrades now, with all we've been through."

Hubbard could feel George's chest rising and falling steadily; he had fallen asleep. Wallace, though, was restless, stretching his legs, rocking on his hip.

"You're not sleepy, are you Hubbard?"

"No, b'y, not just yet."

"I was just thinking about the old farm. How I'd like to see it."

"Your farm?" asked Hubbard with some surprise. They had often talked of Hubbard's farm, but hardly at all of Wallace's boyhood home.

"I thought I'd never want to see the place again. Rocks and crabapples—that's about all it grew. But now I'd like to go back."

"A farm would be nice," said Hubbard sleepily. "I almost wish I had a farm to work now."

On Saturday they finally staggered to George's long "lake-that-looked-like a river." With the goose gone and the peameal down to a few handfuls, their only hope was to land enough trout here to carry them—how far? They had come six days' march from Windbound Lake and weren't even halfway across their long portage. On rubbery legs, Hubbard walked down to shore with rod in hand. He tried not to think about his chances. The air was cold—28 degrees that morning—and the water high after all the rain.

He planted his rag-bound feet on the frozen mud and whipped the rod. His arm was stiff, and the fly jerked awkwardly through the air. It plopped on the surface of the water and disappeared. A bite! He pulled in a half-pounder. Then another and another; big ones. By noontime, twenty fish! He ate a hurried lunch, then raced back to the lake and sailed the fly out in long, graceful arcs. Time after time a silver ripple flashed to meet the lure. By day's end he had 115 trout—one long line of shiny, dappled lakers stretching six feet or more on the mossy bank.

He had never expected such a miracle; he had expected—

well, something else. "It's God's way of taking care of us so long as we do our best," he said, and immediately began making calculations. One more day of good fishing would give them enough food to take them all the way to Disappointment. Another two days' paddle would bring them to the Big River and more good fishing. They were going to get through after all.

WALLACE ATE AS HE hadn't eaten in weeks and then felt completely washed out. They all did. The plan had been to continue on at least six miles the next day, but on Monday they went nowhere. It was from eating so much grub after the hard times, George said. The Indians felt the same way after they'd been starving.

All the same, they couldn't afford to stay in camp and eat up any more fish. On September 29 they launched the canoe from the mud beach with a wintry gale at their backs. An hour later the end of the lake appeared out of the snow: a steep bank topped by a fringe of spruce.

As Wallace helped George carry the packs up to a sheltered spot among the trees he noticed with concern that Hubbard had taken to the bushes again—his diarrhea was unrelenting. By the time he returned, Wallace had skidded down the bank to get the canoe. Hubbard marched to the stern.

"I'll take this end," he said.

Wallace hestitated. "Let's wait for George."

"No, b'y, I can handle it," he said.

The bank was steep, and, hauling foot by foot, the canoe kept getting caught in the brush. By the time Wallace reached the top, his canoe arm was numb and he was gasping for breath. He lay down his end of the canoe and turned to congratulate Hubbard. The words froze in his mouth.

Hubbard had sagged into a tree. His chest was heaving so hard that his breathing came with a rattle. For several minutes he stooped, doubled over at the waist, hands on his knees, elbows locked, his long hair falling over his face. When he finally spoke, his voice was faint and hollow, as if coming from an abyss.

"I'm dead tired and weak, b'y. I think I'll have to take a little rest."

Hastily, Wallace helped George build a roaring fire and tried to make Hubbard comfortable. Then they carried the canoe a mile and a half ahead. Upon their return, they found Hubbard huddled next to the blaze, just as they had left him. The leaping flame was the only splash of color in the whole scene, for the wet snow clung to every twig and tree, robing the woods in a spotless white. Even Hubbard was half-covered.

Wallace found Hubbard's condition alarming. He said little about it that evening, since George hadn't seemed to notice the extent of the breakdown, and Hubbard himself was so under the influence of his own indomitable spirit that he had not yet conceived the possible consequences. But Wallace saw it plain as day: The boy was close to total collapse.

True, he seemed cheered that evening—went back to speculating on their ability to catch up to their schedule. But, after a while, the conversation died out. Wallace watched Hubbard gaze at the fire's dancing flames.

"How much I'd like to see my girl now," he murmured. Not to Wallace, nor to George.

His face changed gradually to a peaceful smile. Wallace knew, somehow, that Hubbard was no longer seeing the fire before him but a blaze in the old hearth of his Congers sitting room. Mina was close to him, seated at his side. Together they were boiling tea, talking of a picnic they'd taken, or perhaps a snowshoe trip to nearby Haverstraw.

Wallace had no idea how he sensed these things. No matter; he knew what his friend was thinking, with a certitude born of so many days together. All the same, it surprised him, disturbed him profoundly, to see Hubbard smile, shift on the log, and extend his arm: reaching out dreamily to draw his girl closer to him.

September turned to October. To Wallace's relief, Hubbard rallied sufficiently to allow several miles' progress through some flat, swampy country and then over a series of boulder-strewn ridges. The weather, though, became only more fierce. The wind-driven sleet stung so badly that Wallace had to take refuge in the lee of thickets to recover his breath. As the gale continued rain would melt what snow had accumulated the previous day; then the flurries would begin again the next, only to turn back to rain. During these days, the evening fire remained its usual mainstay. Wallace thought they had talked food and restaurants to death, but one evening George fished around the pockets of his blue wool jacket and pulled out a large, battered card.

"What's that, George?"

George held the card out so Hubbard could see it.

"It looks like a railroad timetable. The New York Central?"

"That's one side," said George. "I'm reading the other. All about the buffet car."

It was a menu—an honest-to-God New York Central bill of fare!

Hubbard placed the first order. "Give me a glass of cream, some graham gems, marmalade, oatmeal and cream, a jelly omelette, a sirloin steak, lyonnaise potatoes, rolls, and a pot of chocolate. And you might also bring me a plate of griddle cakes and maple syrup."

"Can you have graham gems for breakfast?" asked George.

"You can eat *anything* for breakfast," Hubbard replied.

THE TEMPERATURE kept dropping. The morning of October 3, it fell to ten degrees. One of the ponds along their route was completely frozen over, and they had to walk around it.

Hubbard hiked along feeling weak and mean. Dirty; ribs sticking out; so unsteady, he was bumping into trees. He felt close to hopeless. At the same time he sensed that the worst thing would be for the others to lose courage. They must not be allowed to realize how desperate their situation was or they would surely lose heart.

So he talked: to distract the others and also, he realized, to distract himself. He told George that he would buy him a box of candy as a reward for several spruce grouse he had shot, and described the candies in loving detail. He told Wallace that they needed a vacation.

"I'm thinking of going to Bewdley, to see Mina's family," he said. "I'll take a box of Ridley's and some coffee to Mother Benson. Then from Bewdley, we'll go visit—"

He paused and fiddled a bit, as if he hadn't got the tumpline quite right. The truth was, he could not quite remember the name of Mina's sister.

He tried desperately to concentrate. He knew her quite well. Her husband's name was Cruikshank. But as for her first name, his mind was a complete muddle. Dear Lord, this was Mina's own sister.

He felt himself trembling; feared, suddenly, that he might go all to pieces. It was bad enough to see the body failing day by day. But with a little grit, he could hide that infirmity from the boys. It was simply a question of mind over matter. But now his mind was going. How could he hide that?

For several minutes he sat in the middle of the trail, his face buried in his hands as he strained for concentration. He had forgotten Wallace entirely.

He tried to remember her name. Mrs. Cruikshank. He would call her Mrs. Cruikshank.

The last portage to Disappointment was bad—through a swamp that was more lake than land. Wading through the ooze, Hubbard felt his lifeblood's warmth being drained through his feet. After the ordeal they stopped and had tea.

At least the long portage was over. They would make better progress on the lakes, then back through the mountains to the Big River and their good fishing spots. They would surely make better time now, wouldn't they? But oh, they had to get going and get out. He had to get the boys out soon or there would be trouble.

Crossing Disappointment the next day, the lake looked gray and roily. But they could not afford delay, or caution. As the canoe entered the widest reach of open water the skies darkened, the wind gathered, and the swell increased. The men had been trying to head straight for shore, running broadside to the waves, but now Hubbard felt George turn the boat to run with the wind. Otherwise, the waves would just scoop them up and roll them over in a trough.

The waves grew steeper, closer together, larger, all the while gaining speed as they swept across the lake. No matter how hard they paddled, the giant rollers overtook them from behind. As the canoe slid down the back of each swell the stern plunged into the trough. It was then that they had to paddle like men possessed, to give the canoe enough forward momentum so that the stern would rise on the upward slope of the next wave. But with the slopes steepening, the stern began to bury itself in the waves. The frigid water slithered over the gunwales a quart or two at a time.

There was an island ahead: rocky, with no shelter, but they had to try for it. They were shipping water too quickly. Any more and it would begin to slosh around and upset the balance. Then they'd be over and gone for good.

"Go for shore!" George yelled. "The island!"

Hubbard tried to quicken his pace but found it impossible. His arms had no strength left. When the keel crunched against the beach, it was all he could do to rouse stiff legs and stumble out as the boys hauled the canoe beyond reach of the waves. For the moment they were safe.

A close call—too close. They had to get home soon or they weren't going to get home at all.

13

Choose

WHEN THE SEAS subsided that afternoon, they launched the canoe. Every moment of good weather was precious.

Grand Lake lay yet a hundred miles away, but Wallace was traveling from point to point now, trying to think ahead only as far as the next leg of their trip. From Disappointment to Hope Lake; from Hope to the mountain pass; from the mountain pass to their "Big River." *Be thankful you're living and trust to your luck, / And march to your front like a soldier.*

Yet he could not go on thinking that way indefinitely. Once the Big River was reached, its waters would swiftly carry them to the place where they had first entered it. There they faced a choice that made Wallace uneasy.

In the past few days, Hubbard had made it clear he wanted to abandon both their canoe and the Big River, retracing the ground they had covered earlier in the summer. Carrying only light packs, he meant to hike down the first river valley to Grand Lake. There, one of the Blakes from Northwest River Post had a trapper's tilt where supplies might be found.

As much as Wallace tried to weigh this plan rationally, his response was instant and visceral. He dreaded returning to the river valley. The days of torment, the insects, the endless fighting through spruce thickets and impenetrable alderbushes—all rushed in on him like unreasoning nightmares. Never mind that the bugs would be gone, that the canoe wouldn't have to be carried. He never wanted to see the valley again.

He dreaded, too, what he could not bring himself to say openly: that Hubbard's weak condition would make it impossible to cover so many miles on foot. The long portage from Windbound Lake had already demonstrated how grueling the overland work was. On the other hand, if they stayed in the canoe on a river with good current, they would make better progress with much less labor. Why not follow the Big River out to its mouth?

"But where do we end up?" Hubbard asked. "Probably somewhere in Goose Bay on Hamilton Inlet. That's big water, and the weather's sure to turn worse. We could be pinned on shore miles from help."

George sided with Wallace. "When you're in the bush, stick to your canoe as long as you can," he said. "That's always a good plan."

Wallace could tell that Hubbard remained unconvinced, but nothing final was decided. Nor did Wallace press the issue; he hated to spoil their evening camps with debate. So they talked instead of home.

Nights, they lay huddled so close in their blankets, they had to sleep in unison. When one man's position became cramped, he would call "turn" as he rolled over, and the others would automatically shuffle and turn too. The custom became so natural, the three of them often turned without ever waking.

One evening Wallace called for an adjustment, except that instead of saying "turn," he called out "turn over." After the customary shifting, he heard Hubbard's voice, low and friendly in his ear.

"You know, b'y, that makes me think of the apple turnovers my mother used to bake for me. Heavens! I haven't thought of those in years." And for another hour the two men chatted quietly about spice rolls and other treats their mothers had baked them when they were young.

The portage through the mountain pass began with only a cup of watery peameal for sustenance. Then Wallace and George started up the rocky pitches, the canoe on their shoulders. It was pure torture. The rough ground made a steady pace impossible, so the canoe thwart jarred constantly against Wallace's shoulders, sending spikes of pain down his neck. Stumbling along on the return trip for the packs, he was on the verge of collapse, except that Hubbard was walking by his side, obviously in worse shape, obviously also as patient and determined as ever. "Speak stronger, b'y," he said. "Put more force in your voice. It's so faint George'll surely notice it, and it may scare him."

But there was no hiding their weakness. They desperately needed fish or grouse—food of any sort. At each rapids Wallace poled and paddled the canoe through the drops with George, while Hubbard walked ahead to fish the pools below. The only trout to be had were fingerlings—hardly any of them more than six inches long. Running the rapids, Wallace and George took greater and greater chances, dreading the prospect of carrying the boat along shore and knowing that speed was essential. "We may as well drown as starve," said George, "and it's a blame sight quicker."

One afternoon Hubbard offered to take the stern through a section of fastwater. Wallace obliged by giving him the paddle and then walked along shore watching the boat come down the course. His heart skipped a beat as the canoe struck a rock and one gunwale dipped dangerously. The canoe swung crazily, then bumped down the rest of the chute backward, George turning around in his seat to act as sternman for the remaining twenty yards. When they rejoined Wallace, Hubbard was subdued. "My fault," he said quietly. Wallace did the poling from that point on.

Once they encountered a four-foot falls, the first in several days to force a portage. After carrying the gear around, they returned for the canoe. All three stooped to lift it, but it seemed to be made of lead. Wallace's arms were shaking. With immense effort, he got his end of the boat chest-high, then strained with the others to swing it overhead. They gave a last, desperate lunge, but the effort was too much and the boat crashed to the ground.

They looked at each other. Up to that point, they had kept up the fiction that they were "not so weak." But concealment was no longer possible. No one spoke, but no one needed to. They knew they would be lucky to escape with their lives.

An hour before sunset they beached their canoe on the sandy spit that marked the spot of their most glorious feast, Camp Caribou. Without waiting to unpack, Wallace staggered up the hill with the others to search for the leavings. The head and antlers were there; also the stomach, though its contents had been partially washed away. George searched diligently for the hooves, but was vexed to discover only two. The third, which he had carried along with them, had long before gone into the soup to be boiled. But the fourth was nowhere to be seen.

"Somebody's taken it," he said. "Somebody's taken it sure—a marten or somebody."

They built a fire. George chopped up the hooves and bones

and put them in the kettle to boil. The resulting broth was greasy and rancid; "pretty high," he remarked. But Wallace eagerly took his cup of the mixture, downed it, then came back for more. They had three cupfuls each. The hooves had been covered with maggots, but no one cared. They only seemed like rice and made the broth richer.

Soup course finished, the men sat about the fire gnawing the larger bones. There was a good deal of gristle to work on, as well as some tough hide and bristly skin from the hooves. For a long time Wallace sat silently by the fire, paying heed only to the cracks and crannies of his own morsel. Finally Hubbard said, "I've often seen dogs eating bones and thought it was pretty hard lines for them. But it must be only fun."

They gathered up the other remnants. There was little left on the caribou head except the hide, but the antlers had been in velvet, and the velvet seemed fairly greasy. George promised to scrape it off and boil it for breakfast. He also eyed the *wenastica,* the half-digested contents of the caribou stomach. It looked pretty rotten, but he saved that, too, for another soup.

There wasn't much else to do, so they sat around the fire in silence. George seemed particularly blue; for the past few evenings he had sat mostly hunched over, eyes downcast. Now he appeared to be brooding over a problem of great moment. Abruptly, he got up and walked over to his camp bag. Wallace watched, curious.

George walked back to the fire and sat down again, setting his bag carefully between his knees. One hand went deep into its recesses, poking about.

He looked up and smiled, hand still buried in the bag.

"Well?" said Wallace.

"Sh-h-h," said George. Slowly the hand came up from the bag into the firelight. In its grasp was an unopened package of pure, cut-plug tobacco.

Wallace stared open-mouthed, first at the little treasure, then at George's glorious smile. For weeks now, they had been out of tobacco. In desperation, they had even taken to drying out tea leaves from the evening's kettle and smoking them. But real tobacco!

"I've been savin' it for the time when we needed it most," said George. "And I guess that time's come." He handed Wallace the package, and tenderly Wallace unwrapped it and filled his pipe. Then both men lit up with brands from the fire, pulling long and deep.

"George," said Wallace presently, "however in the world could you keep it so long?"

"Well," said George—*puff, puff*—"when we were gettin' so short of grub, I told myself the time's comin' when we'll need cheerin' up"—*puff, puff*—"and so I said to myself"—*puff*—"I'll just sneak this away until that time comes. We'll have a pipeful of this every night. One pipeful every night until it's gone."

"I'd try it too," said Hubbard wistfully, "but I know it would make me sick, so I'll drink a little tea."

He boiled some; then, after he finished his cup, got out the Bible. Together they read the first psalm and turned in for the night.

The river's current continued to pull them downstream, ever eastward. Wallace was grateful for the help, yet every mile they gained made him more uneasy. According to Hubbard's calculations, they would reach their take-out spot the next day. There they would have to decide on a course of action.

Despite the arguments for hiking overland, Wallace could not shake his dread of the idea. He had come to feel an almost irrational attachment for their weatherbeaten boat. "Stick with your canoe," George had said. "That's always a good plan." It seemed like an old friend who had endured the same hardships, the same toil, the same long days of suffering. To leave it behind would be like abandoning a faithful comrade. In any case, the pain of their short march through the mountains—everyone reeling, feet unsteady—made the situation evident. Even carrying light packs, a march into the valley would be folly.

Wallace broke his silence at the evening fire. Stick with the Big River, he urged again. But the three of them only covered the same ground as before. It was far better, argued Hubbard, to face the known perils of their old route than fly to others unexpected. What if the rapids got wilder and steeper? What if the wind pinned them down on Goose Bay?

Wallace couldn't help himself. "To go back into that valley means suicide," he said bitterly.

Hubbard was silent.

"We'll see how we feel about it tomorrow," he said finally. "I'll sleep on it."

Then his manner changed. He began to talk about how they would begin their lives anew once they were home and had regained their strength. And Wallace joined in eagerly. No more, they vowed, would the demands of their careers deprive them of the tender essentials. Home. Family. A sense of place and a sense of belonging. They would buy a farm together—Wallace could come and live with Hubbard and Mina, practicing law part-time. Hubbard could give up his staff positon at *Outing*, write only an article now and then. But the essentials had to come first. Despite their strong differences of opinion, both men went to bed comforted.

GEORGE LAY ON HIS side, as close to the others as he could get, absorbing the warmth of their bodies.

He was thinking about Wallace: what he had said. What surprised him was, Wallace knew the secret. Well, no—that wasn't it, because they all knew now. You could see that the other day when they tried to carry the canoe together and dropped it. Everybody looked at each other, but nobody said anything. Tonight Wallace said it right out, for everyone to hear.

"Leave the canoe, leave the river—that's suicide." If they went back down their old trail, they'd never get out alive.

And Hubbard was set on going. He said he'd sleep on it, but George knew better. Hubbard looked like he'd made up his mind.

Of course, nobody could make anybody do what they didn't want to. George had heard plenty of times about whites wanting to do one blamefool thing or another and the guides said no, straight out. Or just walked off and left. But George didn't like that. It wasn't keeping your word. Back on Windbound, he'd said, "I'm goin' to stick to you fellus, and go where you go." How far did that mean? Was it right to refuse to march all the way to your death?

By morning George's back had got to aching. It was lumbago; the muscles seemed to pinch up so bad, he could hardly pick up a kettle or swing a paddle. But there was nothing to do but keep going; paddle whether it hurt or not. They didn't get down the river as far as they thought that day. Come evening they were still three miles from where they had to choose.

The pain was pretty bad. Every time George bent to put wood on the fire, his back gave a twinge. When he walked, he had to walk crooked. Finally he told Hubbard what was worrying him. "I got a touch of lumbago," he said. "I don't know about travelin'. I hope I'll be better in the morning, but maybe not. If I don't feel any better, maybe you fellus better make your own way out. Leave me behind." He didn't really think they could do it by themselves, but they could try. "If I can't keep up, I'll delay you, and we're all pretty weak. Maybe if I get better, I could catch up."

Hubbard sat next to George and talked quietly. He said how sorry he was about George's back. He knew they were all not so strong now. They all must do the best they could. Maybe George would feel better in the morning. George came up to bed, said a prayer, and lay down to sleep.

Next morning, when he woke, the other boys were already up and had a fire going, They'd stole away quiet so he could rest a little longer. His back felt stiff but he hardly paid it a mind, because something important had happened during the night. He wanted to tell the others right off, but he didn't quite dare. He didn't know quite what they'd think. He decided to save it for after breakfast.

Wallace was boiling more of the caribou bones. There wasn't much to them. So George went and got the hide, the one he'd saved from the camp on Disappointment Lake. When the boys saw the skin, they laughed.

"You told us we'd want to eat that one day," Hubbard said. "And we didn't believe you."

They cut the skin up and boiled it with a bit of peameal. The broth tasted delicious. After breakfast Hubbard said, "Well, boys, today we have to choose."

Now was the time for George to speak up—to tell them what had happened the night before. But, somehow, he couldn't quite. So he held back while Hubbard and Wallace went over the same arguments about leaving the canoe behind. Nothing had changed. George took a breath and got up his courage.

"I had a dream last night, fellus. About our river."

"How did it go, George?" asked Hubbard.

"It was a strange dream," he said, and hesitated. White men didn't always think too much of dreams. "Well, I dreamed the Lord stood before me, beautiful and bright, and he had a mighty kind look on his face. He said to me, 'George, don't leave this river. Just stick to it and it will take you out to Grand Lake. You'll find Blake's cache there, with lots of grub, and then you'll be all right and safe. I can't spare you any more fish, George, and if you leave this river you won't get any more. Just stick to this river and I'll take you out safe.' "

He was uneasy, but the boys were listening. They didn't laugh. They wanted to hear him out.

"The Lord was all smilin' and bright, and he looked at me very pleasant. Then he went away, and I dreamt we went down the river and it came out in Grand Lake near where we left it comin' up, and we found Blake there, and he fed us and gave us all the grub we wanted, and we had a fine time.

"That was all there was to it."

He waited to see what they'd say—didn't know what they'd think of the Lord speaking to a half-breed. But Hubbard had always treated him fair. All those nights around the fire, they'd got to confiding to each other. George even told him once—a little bit—about the girl he'd fallen in love with and never married. Hubbard was as close a friend to him as any white man had ever been.

Hubbard thought about the dream. "It was unusual, all right," he said. "But George, we already know this river can't empty into Grand Lake."

And then he said: "Anyway, we talked about leaving the river last night, and you had it on your mind—that's what made you dream about it."

"Maybe so," said George. "But it was a mighty strange dream, and we'd better think about it before we leave the river. I think we should stick to the canoe; that's my vote. Wallace and I will shoot the rapids all right. They're sure to be not so bad as we've had, and I think they'll be a lot better. We can run 'em, can't we, Wallace?"

"There's got to be more water to cover the rocks farther down," said Wallace. "If George will take a chance in the bow, I'll go in the stern. We'll get the boat through."

But Hubbard only said, "I still think we should take the trail we know."

And then Wallace broke out with it again, what was in George's mind so strong.

"That means suicide. We'll leave our bones in that valley. We're too weak to finish that march."

But he didn't say anything more. And neither did Hubbard.

And neither did George.

Point to point; one bend to the next. Paddling downstream, that was all Wallace tried to think of. The canoe had gone less than a mile when something changed the current of his thoughts. It was George's hoarse whisper.

"Up ahead—little black duck!"

The duck was a hundred yards away, floating slowly downriver. As the canoe drifted silently to shore George took Hubbard's rifle and stole among the alders and willows, crawling on hands and knees through the marsh until he was opposite the bird. It seemed such a small target for a rifle. As George swung the weapon to his shoulder and took aim, Wallace watched with nervous concentration.

After an eternity George lowered his rifle, changed position slightly, then raised it again to his shoulder. He waited.

A breeze shivered the water, but the duck's wake still spread outward in a lazy V. Then the rifle cracked and the duck plopped over on its back.

No cheers echoed across the river; there was only grateful silence. Ragged, dripping wet with marsh water, George rose slowly and waded to his quarry, returning with it to the canoe.

"The Lord surely guided that bullet," he said reverently.

It was nearly noon when they reached their junction. George lit a fire and cooked the duck, which was small but wonderfully fat and greasy. It was the first decent morsel they had enjoyed in days.

Finally Wallace faced Hubbard. "Well, b'y, we can't postpone the decision any longer. It's up to you—which route do we take?"

Hubbard did not hesitate. "I firmly believe we should stick to our old trail."

Wallace nodded, said nothing. He felt numb. Hubbard was already at work again, trying to lighten their outfit. Wallace watched him put aside the artificial horizon, the sextant box, and one of the axes. Then the three of them dragged the canoe a ways from the water and turned it upside down.

Wallace lingered a moment. He felt an inexpressible sadness; did not want to leave that boat. Giving it a gentle pat, he nearly began to cry.

The others were waiting. He came up the bank and shouldered his pack. With George leading, they started over the hill and across a white, moss-covered field. For a while they could hear the deep rumble of the river, but soon the sound became weaker and then gave out altogether.

14

"I'm Busted"

FROM THE TIME they first turned back, Hubbard had been plotting his strategy for covering the ground between the Big River and Grand Lake. It was about forty-five miles in all: past two lakes to Goose Creek, where they had bagged their first geese; then down the creek to their original river. About twelve miles below the junction were a few pounds of wet flour they had abandoned in July. A dozen miles beyond that was a pound of powdered milk and, five miles farther, a pail of lard. From the lard, it was an easy hike to Grand Lake and the Blakes' cabin. If they could struggle from point to point, from one lifeline to the next, they had a chance of getting out alive.

The first part of the trek would be the hardest: twenty-two miles to the flour. But Hubbard was counting, desperately, on landing trout that evening at the first of the two lakes. The fish weren't rising on the river, he admitted, but the lake wouldn't be as cold. It *couldn't* be—it was a bigger body of water. But when he said this, the look on Wallace's face almost broke his heart.

"B'y, don't you think we'll get fish there?" he persisted. "Aren't you hopeful?"

"I hope," said Wallace, "but I fear too. Perhaps it's better not to let our hopes run too high; then if they fail us, the disappointment won't be so hard to bear."

"That's so. But it makes me feel good to look forward to the fishing there. We *will* get fish—just say we will, b'y; that would make me feel happy."

"We will," said Wallace. "We'll say we will." And somehow, it made the afternoon's hike easier to bear.

Hubbard was exhausted by the time he reached the lake, but

he got out Wallace's weatherbeaten rod. Back and forth the fly skimmed the surface, on waters that in August had been alive with trout. But every time Hubbard rested even an instant, the pond silvered over and was quiet, mirroring the gray sky. As he had known in his heart it would.

He had counted so much on those fish. Now there was only the flour to set his hopes on. That and the memories of home. He must use those to feed the will, when all other sustenance failed.

George ransacked their old campsite for scraps. He found a couple of goose heads and some bones, as well as an empty lard pail.

"I'll heat the pail," he said, "and maybe there'll be a little grease sticking to it." Then he set the caribou bones to boil yet another time, along with the rest of the deer's stomach and goose heads. When they finished the broth, Hubbard gazed into the fire. "Mina will be at dinner now. She'll have finished her meal just about this time. And there will be lots left over on the table. Oh, if she could only hand me a piece of bread!"

He dreamed of her that night—that they had met in New York for the first time in so many months. The dream was palpably real, and it made the pain of waking that much harder to bear.

Packing up, they set out north and east, skirting the lake where he had gotten lost, then heading toward Goose Creek. For footgear, Hubbard wrapped his feet in pieces of camp blanket, tied to the remains of his moccasin uppers with a bit of trolling line. The blanket soon became sodden and cold, wetted anew each time a foot sank into the ooze of a swamp.

At one point George ran off into the spruce, fired several times, and came back holding three grouse. Silently Hubbard shook George's hand and then fingered the birds lovingly, turning them over and over to make sure they were good and fat. He would have loved to stop right there and cook them, but George said no; they'd better be pressing on. And he knew George was right. He tried to concentrate, putting one foot in front of the other.

The pain of the march seemed unendurable. It was almost too much to look up, even, to see where George was going. Hubbard preferred to stare at the ground. He tried to think of the grouse and how it would taste for dinner. He tried to think of Mina, of the old farm, his parents, Kipling's poems—anything. He saw only the ground. His mind became a blank, despite all the efforts of the will. He began to dread looking up, because each time he did,

George and Wallace seemed to have gotten a little farther ahead. Ten yards, thirty, fifty . . .

At some point they must have stopped; rested. Then started again. George was closer now, and Wallace, somehow, had gotten behind Hubbard. Only just behind; Hubbard could hear footsteps close on his heels. It made it harder, because he couldn't slow down so much—if he did, the steps would run him over.

He was lightheaded. It was hard to keep one's balance with the pack on.

He heard water running, looked up to see Goose Creek two hundred yards away. They had camped at this spot in July, and the tent poles were still there, as well as the black char of the old fire. But he saw it all through a haze. Even his legs seemed distant and the ground in front of him sparkled.

He was on his knees. He wanted to get up, but it seemed easier to roll over and lie down. The steps behind him stopped and he looked up to see Wallace towering over.

"B'y, I've got to rest here," he explained. "Just a little while. You understand . . . My legs—have given out."

Wallace knelt by him. "That's all right—take a little rest. You'll be better soon. I'll rest with you; and then we'll leave your pack and you can walk to camp light. I'll come back for it in a moment."

By the time Hubbard walked up to camp, George had a fire going and a cup of hot tea ready. The boys looked worried.

They mustn't worry, he thought. They mustn't let their spirits go.

"It was a momentary slip," he said. "I'll be better tomorrow, after the grouse. I'm really quite happy now." And he was. The grouse tasted wonderfully good and greasy.

"I remember feeling like this when I first came to New York," he said. "I got caught in the rain—hadn't any carfare. I was soaking wet and good and hungry, and all I had in my pocket was a dime. I hadn't any friends in the city, and I didn't want to write home, because nobody in Michigan thought I'd make it in New York.

"I went to a bakery and spent my last dime on stale rolls and crullers. I took them and walked back to my room. Then I took off my wet clothes and got into bed to get dry and eat, not knowing where the next meal would come from. I was supremely happy. I sort of felt I was doing the best I could."

They were quiet for a while. George went to get the blankets ready. "Do you have your Testament, b'y?" Hubbard asked Wallace. "I was wondering if you could read me a little. If you're not too tired."

Hubbard asked for Matthew six, Christ's parable of the lilies. "Wherefore, if God so clothe the grass of the field . . . shall he not much more clothe you, O ye of little faith? For your heavenly Father knoweth that ye have need of all these things."

"How beautiful!" he said, when Wallace had finished. "It encourages me so much." He crawled into the tent to join George, but at the last moment turned to Wallace, still at the fire. "I'm so happy, b'y . . . so very, very happy. We're going home. . . ."

GEORGE AWOKE TO find the fire crackling and Wallace by it. Sliding out of his blankets, he left Hubbard sleeping.

Hubbard was in a bad way. They had to get him out.

For that matter, they were all in a bad way. George had gone off the other day to have a bowel movement and noticed there were blueberries in his stool, almost whole. It seemed his stomach didn't even have the strength to digest them. Standing there, he had been almost tempted to pick them out, wash them, and eat them again. And food seemed to do the least for Hubbard. His eyes were gaunt and his skin dirty and pale. He was just wasting away.

George cooked up one of the partridges for breakfast. It seemed to help some. Then he took the lead, hiking along Goose Creek back into the river valley. At each bend, he saw things he remembered from the way up—the country stayed in his mind clear as a photograph. But the season had changed. The moss was orange now, with the cold weather, and the creek had almost disappeared. There was hardly any water in it.

About noon they came to a spot where Hubbard had caught some trout. It seemed like a place they might rest. George was about to sit down when he caught movement out of the corner of his eye.

"Caribou!" he whispered, and they threw themselves face down in the moss.

George raised up for a look. The deer was coming toward them from a pond nearby. He had a rich coat, beautiful antlers, and plenty of meat on his haunches. The meat was the difference between life and death.

His scalp prickled. There was a clump of spruce between them and the deer, but the wind was blowing the wrong way. Any instant he was like to catch their scent. If he would just trot on past the spruce, into rifle range . . .

The boys were face down on the ground—they hadn't moved an inch.

Then the deer sniffed, pulled up sharp, and was off, and George was pulling himself out of the moss, too, and running after. It just about killed him to stand up so fast, and the world swayed around him.

Caribou had bolted left, so George went left, staggering through the trees, rifle catching on the branches, everything spinning except the hope of that caribou. He saw spots before his eyes.

He tried to think as he ran. A swamp he knew of: he remembered from walking the country in July. If the caribou comes to that swamp, he'll go round, he thought. He won't want to go through it. Go through—cut him off.

He stumbled and fell. Picked himself up and kept going, the branches grabbing at him. Oh, it was hard! He was dizzy and lightheaded and so very weak. Just to run nearly took the last breath from his lungs, but they were dead men if he didn't get that deer. He looked for the light of a clearing and saw it; ran, trying to keep his feet from giving way under him, trying to think how his shaking arms would hold the rifle steady and how his deer might bound just once into the space at the end of its sights.

He stumbled into the open, splashing across the swamp like some drunk. He ran till the world whirled from its swaying—and then suddenly everything in the clearing froze—still, silent, and sharp—except for a blur of antlers across the far end of the swamp, bounding away and into the trees. . . .

George took the air in gulps: ears ringing, heart beating, blood pounding. The world began to come to life again, except that now there was nothing at the end of the swamp.

He just stood and felt the breeze against his face. The clearing was quiet. It looked the way it had for years and years, still and empty.

More slowly now, he turned and made his way back to the woods, retracing his steps to the creek.

The boys were lying face down in the moss. They hadn't moved.

"Fellus," he said, "we missed 'im."

They got up slowly, the light gone from their eyes. George hated to see them so. Quickly he gathered branches and got a fire going. He boiled a pot of tea to cheer them up.

When the tea was ready he poured each a cup; then after they started to sip it, he asked them to pass their cups back. It was a little game he'd been playing the past few days: something to keep off thoughts of what lay ahead. "Pass your cups back," he said, "I forgot the sugar."

"Don't want any," said Hubbard, and managed a smile. "I don't like sugar."

George laughed. "Well, what about some bread? How about that? Or pie. You fellus want some pie?"

"Pie?" said Hubbard. "What is pie? What do you use it for? Do you eat it?" And George was glad to see them smile again. But it was hard to keep off thoughts.

They had the last partridge for lunch and then looked to lighten up again. The packs didn't have more than about ten pounds in 'em, but everybody was weak as babies. George threw out his extra clothes, even a new pair of long johns he'd been saving for the cold weather. He was going to put them on in place of the old, but he got too dizzy trying. He didn't even have the strength to take his clothes off. But at least his pack was lighter now, so he could carry Hubbard's rifle for him.

FOR THE PAST WEEK, Wallace had been tormented by Hubbard's condition. All of them, now, were little more than walking skeletons, skin sallow, eyes deep and gaunt, shirts patched, trousers tattered almost entirely below the knees. But Hubbard seemed almost a wraith, whose frail body might float away if the pack on his back didn't weigh him down. The day before, Wallace had quietly asked George to set a slower pace; then, to give Hubbard encouragement, had fallen to the rear. But with Hubbard directly in front, Wallace had only become more fearful, for he could watch his poor friend march. He was staggering along, hardly able to keep his balance, always on the verge of collapse. "We must get him out of here," Wallace thought to himself, over and over. "We must, we must!"

For nearly two weeks, the weather had favored them with

generally clear, crisp days. But on Saturday, October 17, a raw wind was blowing from the east, threatening rain. Cold and utterly miserable, they began their hike.

Wallace noticed that the bad weather seemed especially to affect Hubbard. "I'm cold and chilly, boys," he said. From time to time, George stopped and built a fire for tea and a rest.

Around noon they reached their first camp above the main river. George found an old flour bag with a few moldy lumps clinging inside. He scraped them into the pot to flavor the bone water. Then Hubbard called out. He'd made a wonderful find, a box nearly half full of pasty mustard. Each man took a mouthful of the precious substance; then George added the rest to the pot. He was about to throw the tin away when Hubbard asked for it. He took the box in his hands and examined it lovingly.

"This came from my home in Congers," he said, almost in a reverie. "Mina held this very box in her hands. She bought it at the little grocery store where I've been so often, and handed it to me before I left home. I wonder where my girl is now . . . I wonder when I'll see her again."

He bent his head and tears trickled down his cheeks. "She's been such a good wife to me."

Wallace turned away.

They followed their creek all afternoon, from clearing to clearing, from one resting point to the next. Each time they resumed their journey, they took fewer steps before Hubbard began tottering again. Wallace walked by his side now; Hubbard would set his face in a blank stare, focusing only a few feet in front of him, jaws clenched in frustration. At last they heard the sound of another river: the main branch they were seeking. Hubbard sank exhausted to the ground and Wallace collapsed next to him.

There were a few red berries nearby. George brought them and then went off to see if he could find more. Wallace felt he ought to go, too, but hadn't any energy left. He could only stare blankly at the ground around him. He watched George come back and kneel beside Hubbard.

"You don't want to lie on the moss," George said. "It's too wet. Why don't you rest on your knees? The camp we made near the fork of the river is just across the way. It's a little drier there. If I take your pack, do you think you could come over?"

Hubbard nodded. George took his pack. Then he helped Hubbard to his knees to keep off the moss.

"You fellus rest a bit. Then you can come up."

He left. Wallace watched Hubbard crouching on one knee in the clearing, staring at the ground. His face bore an expression of absolute despair.

At length Wallace stood and helped Hubbard up. The two of them forded the shallow stream, leaning on each other for balance, and came up the rise to camp.

There were a number of large boulders scattered among the evergreen. George pitched the tent facing one of them, a granite block with a flat face. Between the open tent door and the boulder, he built their fire, so the heat reflected from the rock would warm the tent. Then they arranged themselves in the doorway and had supper—more bone water and caribou hide. They chewed the hide, watching the fire with indifference.

"Well," said Hubbard at last, "I'm busted. I can't go any farther—that's plain."

Wallace couldn't find words to reassure his friend. He didn't trust himself to speak.

After a while George said, "Fellus, we got to talk. Not about restaurants this time. We got to talk about what's on our minds. We can't chop logs anymore. We can't run to chase caribou. We can't hardly walk. Our death is pretty near us now, it seems to me. If anybody else was in our place here, they would expect nothing but death."

He turned to Hubbard. "That flour is still ten miles away. I was thinking. Tomorrow, we could see how you are. If you couldn't get up the strength to go any farther, maybe Wallace and I could try for that flour. If we reached it, one of us could bring some back to you, and the other could go on to Grand Lake and Northwest River, as fast as he could, and bring back some of the fellus there to help out. I could try to do that, maybe."

Hubbard looked doubtful. "I don't know as there's any use, George. We're all pretty weak now—we know that. And if anyone sent a relief party, we'd be scattered and hard to find."

"Maybe," said George. "But maybe they aren't going to send anybody for a while. Maybe we'll be a long time waiting." He was silent, uncomfortable again.

"All right," said Hubbard at last. "Maybe you should try. I don't see how you're going to do it, but I've never come across a man as brave as you are. We'll just have to see what happens. What do you say, Wallace—are you game?"

Wallace had been thinking along the same lines. "I say it's well," he said. "We've got to do something."

"Then you both better start in the morning. When you get to the flour, Wallace can bring some back to me, and George can take some and keep going. But Wallace, if you don't find the bag—if some animal's taken it—you'd better go on with George. There's no use, then, your trying to get back here. I'll be quite comfortable until help comes."

Wallace felt awful. "I'll come back, flour or no flour," he said. Even the thought of Hubbard lying alone filled him with dread.

For a while Hubbard stared at the ground. He seemed troubled.

"What is it?" asked Wallace gently.

He shook his head. Wallace laid a hand on his arm.

"Oh, it's just that if I hadn't come on this trip, you'd be at home right now, having all you needed and going on with your lives." He shook his head. "I'm sorry, boys."

"We're here because we want to be here," said Wallace stoutly. "You know that."

"That's right," said George. "If we didn't want to come, we would have stayed home. So don't put the blame on yourself."

Hubbard's face cleared a little. "Well, we'll see what happens tomorrow. Maybe I'll feel better and can go on without a pack. But whatever comes, I feel happy and contented. I don't know why—I feel that our troubles are about ended."

He lay down in his blanket. They kept the tent door open for the warmth. Wallace sat quietly in the entryway as George got ready for bed.

After a little while Hubbard called softly to Wallace: "B'y, I'm so chilly; won't you make the fire a little bigger?"

Wallace threw on more wood, then sat down again in front of the blaze. "I'll keep this going all night," he said. "It's damp out, and cold."

"Oh, thank you, b'y, thank you." Hubbard's voice was hardly a whisper.

Soon he spoke again. "B'y, won't you read to us from your Testament? Perhaps we can each choose a chapter. It would comfort me so much to hear you read."

Wallace brought out his Testament. He picked the fourteenth chapter of John, and George asked for Christ's prayer in the seventeenth: "Father, the hour is come." Wallace leaned forward, so the light from the fire shone on the water-stained book. "Let your heart not be troubled," he began, "but believe in God, and believe also in me." He paused to glance at Hubbard. The boy had fallen asleep like a weary child.

Wallace kept reading. George stayed awake a little longer but was lost to sleep before the second passage was finished. Wallace read the last chapter anyway.

The wind blew restlessly up the river valley, from the east. It stirred the tops of the firs with a weary sighing. As the other two men slept peacefully behind him Wallace felt the darkness and the loneliness. He put on more wood and steeled himself for an all-night vigil. The dread in him kept growing. It was not so bad as long as you could talk with the others. It was not so bad if you could just keep plodding ahead—then even the pain came as a relief that kept the mind from morbid speculation. But alone, in front of the fire, Wallace felt a presentiment of something awful. He wanted badly to sleep; sleep was so comforting now. But he had told Hubbard he would keep the fire going, and he would. He had promised. What was there about Hubbard that made you promise?

He jumped suddenly. He had been dozing. Rain was falling against the tent roof, its random patter driving out all conscious thought.

Half-asleep, half-awake: gradually the real and the seeming blended. At the edges of the night, beyond the fire's glow, Wallace began to see black shapes that gathered and swayed. His limbs felt paralyzed, sunk in a sleepy torpor, yet he was terrorized by the horrid figures. They mocked him. They hinted at something dreadful. He jerked upright again, wide-awake, and heard only the sound of the rain and the sighing treetops. *Patter-patter, patter-patter.*

The noise of the rain was hypnotic. Why did he have to stay awake? Oh, that was it—for Hubbard. For Hubbard's sake. The black shapes beyond the fire began to grow again, taunting him, leering closer and closer. He heard himself yelling, *"No, no, no!"* and then sat bolt straight and stared wildly around him.

The rain had stopped momentarily. It was deadly silent. He listened in particular for one quiet sound and heard nothing. Urgently he turned about, crawled to the back of the tent and placed his head next to Hubbard's waxen face, listening desperately.

The breathing came to his ear; light, slow, calm.

Wallace crept back to his place by the fire. But he couldn't hear Hubbard's breathing, so he crawled back again, bent over, listened, reassured himself.

The rain began again and Wallace resumed his vigil, fighting the drowsiness and the confused sense of things evil and malicious, of starts and jerks, and the patter of rain as the night wore on.

After an eternity the black faded into drab. The trees in front of the tent, dripping with moisture, gradually took shape. But the east wind continued to sigh, bringing rain up the valley.

15

The Loons Had a Call Like This

NOISES. THEN AN eddy of cold air across his face. Then, through half-closed eyes, a shape at the door. Oh yes—Wallace. Still tending the fire.

Hubbard closed his eyes, sensed the cold again as George sat up beside him and tied blanket scraps to his feet, to walk down to the stream for water.

Daylight had come already. Should he try getting up? He felt quite warm enough where he was. When he raised his head to get a look out the door, pinpricks swirled before his eyes. He lay back dizzy but heard George say something to Wallace. Well, if the boys were up and about, he should be too.

He sat up and waited for the swirl to pass. Through the tent door the sky seemed gray, but he couldn't hear any rain against the canvas.

"How's the weather, b'y?" he asked.

Wallace grunted. "It makes me think of Longfellow. *The day is cold, and dark, and dreary . . .*"

Hubbard couldn't help smiling. "Yes," he replied, "but

Be still, sad heart, and cease repining,
Behind the clouds is the sun still shining."

Wallace looked up, astonished, and then his hollow face broke into a smile that pleased Hubbard beyond all reason.

"You're a wonder, Hubbard! You've a way of making our worst

troubles seem light. I've been sitting here imagining all sorts of things."

"There's no call to worry," said Hubbard. "We'll soon have grub now, and then we can rest and sleep—and get strong."

So saying, he actually felt stronger himself. He climbed out of his blankets and crawled on his knees to the tent door. Carefully he stood up. The pinpricks swirled again, and he waited until they were replaced by the overcast sky. He tried his legs, taking a few steps to the fire, and after that a few more to the big boulder. The wind, little more than a breeze really, set him to rattling. He turned, tottered back to the tent door, and sank down beside Wallace.

"I'm feeling stronger and better than I did last night," he said, "but I'm too weak to walk or stand up long."

Breakfast was bone soup and a bit of hide, boiled with a yeast cake. Hubbard sipped at the oily water and thought things through. He had to organize; get his plans laid out precisely and clearly. If he didn't plan well, even George and Wallace might not get out.

"I don't see any other way," he said. "We've got to split up."

Wallace agreed, although now he looked a bit reluctant. "I don't know if my strength will carry me to the flour," he said at last. "I feel weaker this morning. But if I get there, I'll get back somehow."

"Yes, we all must try," said Hubbard earnestly. "The odds are against us, I know, but there's nothing to do but keep on trying and do our best. We all must promise each other that."

George said, "If there's help at Blake's—or grub—I'll get it."

Wallace almost glowered at his friend; and this, more than anything, brought the tears to Hubbard's eyes. Dear, stubborn Wallace.

"I'll be back in three days," he said. "Flour or no flour."

"And I'll do my best to live as long as I can," said Hubbard quietly. "We'll all do our best. No one can ask more."

He sipped the last of his broth. After a time Wallace said, "You're going to need firewood." He went to fetch some.

"Good," said Hubbard. He needed a word with George alone. Rummaging around his duffel, he pulled out a small packet the size of his fist, unwrapped it, and pushed it toward George. It was about half a pound of peameal.

George looked at him, disbelieving. "I thought we'd eaten all that."

Hubbard shook his head. "I saved some. Not much, but you must take it with you."

"I can't do that. Why, I couldn't *ever* do that. You need it worse than we do."

Hubbard gripped George's arm. "Please—for my sake as much as yours. If neither of you get out, how will I?"

He pressed the packet into George's hands, afraid that Wallace might return and spoil everything.

"You *must*. For my sake."

"All right," said George reluctantly.

Hubbard was greatly relieved. He watched George stow the packet and then sank back against the log, no longer ashamed to rest while George refilled the kettle for him and set the remaining bones and hide within easy reach of the tent.

When Wallace returned with a pile of firewood, the three of them crawled inside and sat in a circle, the balloon silk sagging over their shoulders. Hubbard propped himself up as George and Wallace prepared traveling kits. They didn't take much: a compass, cup, small pot, a little tea, and matches. Their blankets, wet as they were, seemed too heavy; George suggested tearing them in half. Wallace hesitated, holding his in his lap for a time, and finally laying them aside. "They'd still be too much to carry," he said.

Hubbard understood the hesitation. Four months earlier he had presented those blankets to Wallace on the *Sylvia*, only a few days out of New York harbor. They had been a surprise from Wallace's sisters, a birthday gift entrusted to Hubbard for delivery at the appropriate hour. Wallace had been touched.

"If you don't want to tear your own blankets, cut mine in two," Hubbard offered. "They're a bit lighter anyway. I can use yours while you're away."

Wallace looked grateful. The wool was wet and somewhat rotten; it pulled apart easily. Next, Hubbard removed the pistol and knife from his belt and handed them to George, but George shook his head stubbornly.

Hubbard insisted. "I can use the rifle if I have anything to shoot."

George finally accepted the pistol and filled his pockets with cartridges, but he wouldn't take the knife.

Outfits assembled, the two men looked around the tent to make sure they hadn't missed anything.

"It might be well," said Wallace, "if each of us made a note of how we wished to dispose of our effects."

"Yes, that's a good idea," said Hubbard. "We should each make a will."

They took out their notebooks. George penciled a final entry and then asked Hubbard to write a letter for him to Mr. King at the Hudson's Bay Post at Missanabie. Wallace added one last note to his diary, wrote letters to his sisters and his friend at the law office, Alonzo McLaughlin. When they were finished, they placed the papers in their camp bags and put the bags at the rear of the tent. If worst came to worst, the tent was more likely to be found than their bodies.

Hubbard used the time to think a little. It was his last chance to put things right. When Wallace and George were done, they looked up expectantly.

"All right. Now, George—you know how you're set, do you?"

George nodded.

"If you get out to Blake's alive and somebody's there, send them with the grub. Don't come back yourself; stay there and rest up. You'll be too weak to go fast anyway. If you don't find anybody at Blake's, but you get out to Northwest River, then get Mackenzie. He'll find some men to send."

Hubbard paused. He wanted George to understand the situation, but there was no easy way to put it.

"If they get up here too late—well, don't worry. You did what you could. You've worked like a hero through all this. Mackenzie will help you. He'll see that you get all you need and he'll keep you over the winter. By the first boat next spring, you'll go to New York and see Mrs. Hubbard. Take my diary and give it to her. She'll know what to do with it. Don't give it to anyone else."

He looked away. "Tell her how things happened. Tell her that it wasn't so bad toward the end, and that I didn't suffer. Starvation isn't a bad way to die.

"I wish you could get out to Michigan to see my father and mother, or my sister, Daisy. I wish I could tell them how good you've been to me. But that's all right. You must go to Mrs. Hubbard, that's all. Do your duty and go to her, and she'll take care of you."

He turned to Wallace. "If you get out of this and I don't, you'll have to write the story. There's nobody else to do it."

Wallace faltered. "I wouldn't even know how to begin. I've never written anything like that. Besides—"

"Wallace—you're the only one I have. You *must* do it." He was pleading. "If not for me, for Mina. Publish the story for her."

"All right," said Wallace at last.

"You *will* write it, then. Do you promise me that?"

"Yes, b'y. I do."

"Oh, thank you. That puts me at ease. And now before you leave, won't you read to me again? I want to hear the fourteenth chapter of John and the thirteenth of First Corinthians. I fell asleep last night while you were reading, I was so tired. I'm sleepy now, but I'll keep awake this time."

Wallace took out his Testament and read, first from John and then from Corinthians:

"If I speak with the tongues of men and of angels, but have not love, I am become sounding brass, or a clanging cymbal. And if I have the gift of prophecy, and know all mysteries and all knowledge; and if I have all faith, so as to remove mountains, but have not love, I am nothing. . . . Love beareth all things, believeth all things, hopeth all things, endureth all things. . . ."

Hubbard let the words flow over him. Wallace was such a comfortable friend. He read as if they had always been together and always would be.

"For now we see in a mirror, darkly; but then face to face: now I know in part; but then shall I know fully, even as also I was fully known. But now abideth faith, hope, love, these three; and the greatest of these is love."

"Thank you, b'y," said Hubbard. "That's so comforting. I've faith that we'll all be saved. God will send us help."

"Yes," said Wallace, "we shall soon be safe home."

"We'll soon be safe home," repeated Hubbard. He felt supremely content, as if this were home and he need never leave.

Wallace continued to sit, now mute and still, as if stricken. He was facing the fire and Hubbard could see only his back: The same silhouette that had been there the night before, guarding the fire and keeping it fed. Several times Wallace rose and turned, picking up his kit bag as if to go. But each time the tears welled up, and he turned back to the fire. George sat alongside, his face haggard and drawn.

Hubbard just looked at them, content to gaze at their shapes.

The hunch of George's shoulders. The peculiar set of Wallace's rag-bound legs. Not wanting to think what the fire would be like once they had gone. Five minutes passed; then ten. The drizzle was turning into a steady rain. Finally George climbed to his feet.

"Well, Wallace, we'd better start now."

"Yes, we'd better."

Wallace seemed to take an eternity to stand. Then he turned and held out a thin, bony hand. Hubbard took it and clasped it tight, looking deep into Wallace's eyes.

"I'll be back," said Wallace. "Three days."

For one brief instant Hubbard saw those eyes glower with fierce belief. And then Wallace crawled close, threw his arms around him, and broke down. Weeping and sobbing, he kissed Hubbard's cheek with his poor, sunken, bearded lips—several times—and Hubbard kissed his.

George was crying too. He came over, stooped, and kissed him as Wallace had done. "The Lord help us, Hubbard. With his help, I'll save you if I can get out."

Hubbard hugged him to his chest. "If I were your father, George, you couldn't try harder to save me."

George slung his bag over his shoulder and Wallace picked his up. They started to go; then Wallace turned again, bent over, and pressed cheek to cheek. Finally he tore himself away. Hubbard watched the two of them go.

"Good-bye, boys, and God be with you!"

"Good-bye!"

"Good-bye!"

The footfalls of the two men swished softly in the moss. They soon faded away. The only sounds now were the sizzle of the fire and the patter of rain on silk. And, high above, the sighing of the trees.

Hubbard felt drained, yet strangely peaceful. He wanted to sleep. But he could not. He had work to do and needed strength to do it.

He added wood to the fire and, as soon as his heart stopped pounding in his chest like it was trying to get out, he poured himself a cup of tea, dark and strong. He also drank some more bone broth and chewed on the rawhide. The hide especially left him feeling full and warm.

Folding the tent flaps back to catch the reflected heat of the fire, he slid into his blankets and extracted his diary from the kit bag. With his knife he whittled a new point for his pencil.

> Sunday, October 18th, 1903
>
> Alone in camp, junction Nascaupee and some other stream—estimated (overestimated, I hope) distance above head of Grand Lake 33 miles.

There was so much to write. For the last two days he had failed to keep his journal. Now he had to catch up. He concentrated fiercely.

> On Thursday, as stated, I busted. Friday and Saturday it was the same. I saw it was probably hopeless for me to try to go farther with the boys, so we counselled last night and decided they should take merely half a blanket each, socks, etc., some tea, tea pail, cups and the pistols, and go on. They will try to reach the flour to-morrow. . . . I want to say here that they are two of the very best, bravest and grandest men I ever knew, and if I die it will not be because they did not put forth their best efforts.

Hubbard's eyes wandered from the paper and fastened on the fire outside. It was sputtering—already dying. The rain was coming in sheets.

> Last night I fell asleep while the boys were reading to me. This morning I was very, very sleepy. After the boys left—they left me tea, the caribou bones and another end of a flour sack found here, a rawhide caribou moccasin and some yeast cakes—I drank a cup of strong tea and some bone broth. I also ate some of the really delicious rawhide (boiled with bones) and it made me stronger—strong to write this. . . .
>
> I am not so greatly in doubt as to the outcome. I believe they will reach the flour and be strengthened, that Wallace will reach me, and that George will find Blake's cache and camp and send help. So I believe we will all get out. . . .
>
> I am not suffering. The acute pangs of hunger have given way to indifference. I'm sleepy. I think death from starvation

> is not so bad. But let no one suppose I expect it. I am prepared, that is all. I think the boys will be able, with the Lord's help, to save me.

Hubbard put away the diary and reached up to close the flaps. He noticed as he pinned the fastenings that his hands were shaking rather violently. It was curious. Shutting the tent was a simple chore, ordinarily.

He drew the blanket around, intending to take a nap, but a terrible foreboding came over him. He *could* sleep now, but he must not. Not yet.

He sat up in the weak light and fumbled through his bag for the diary. There! He reopened the journal and flipped to a blank page near the back. At the top was printed "Tuesday, December 1, 1903." He crossed the heading out with a thick black line.

> Sun Oct 18, 1903
> to my wife—Mrs. Mina B. Hubbard
>
> My sweet heart:
>
> Dearest, Dearest Girl:
>
> I want to write you a long, long letter, but first I must write a few short ones. I write them on these following pages. Deliver them, please, and write what words of comfort you can to the home folk. Your sweet heart—
>
> Leon.

He must hurry. He must write fast, but he had to be careful too. He had to keep his hand steady and legible. Mina had to be able to read what he wrote. But hurry.

The first letter was to Mr. King. He wrote just as George had asked. There was a bank account, he told Mr. King, and an insurance policy that should go to "said youngest brother Jim."

Hubbard looked over what he had written. He could not end the letter like that. He owed George something more. The strength he had taken from the rawhide seemed to be running out of him inexorably, like water draining from a leaky bucket; but he bent to the paper.

> George is a grand, heroic fellow and I thank you for sending him to me. If I escape, my life will be owing to him and my

white companion, Mr. Wallace. If I do not, they have still done their utmost.

The next letter, one to his mother, filled two pages. He asked after the farm and he said how sorry he was. He sent love to Daisy and to Father. He asked, after a fashion, that his family look after Mina. Not that his girl would need looking after. He told his mother that he would always, always be her loving son.

That brought him to Friday, December 11. He blacked out the date and beheld the open white space before him. That would belong to Mina. His long, long letter. He riffled the pages left in the book. There seemed to be plenty. But he had so much to say that he could hardly bear it. He wanted so badly to compose himself; to think carefully; to find tender words that would last a lifetime.

He rested a little—didn't know how long—then propped himself up.

"My dearest, dearest," he began.

No. More clearly this time.

"My dearest, dearest . . ."

His heart gave a leap. He could hear it pounding.

He stared awhile at the paper. He was not wrapping his fingers around the pencil properly. That was the problem.

With painstaking care, thinking all the while of Mina, he took his left hand and molded the fingers of the right.

"My dearest, dearest . . ."

Dear God. Each time was worse. The words were veering off the page in a wild scrawl. No one would be able to read them. Not even his sweetheart.

Dearest, dearest. Oh, one last time.

He had never felt so helpless. When he closed his eyes, he could see her face before him, sweet as ever, near as ever. Why couldn't he write her name? One last way to reach, with his own hands . . . to touch, to hold her.

He opened his eyes and looked around, frantically. The tent was a dim, bleak gray, without sun or shadow. The rain was pelting the silk furiously and hurt his ears with its hammering.

Wait! He heard something. He cocked his head and listened carefully. A long, low cry, coming from—from where? It came again, deep and mournful. The loons had a call like this, but the loons were gone now. Could it be the trees, creaking in the wind? No, it was a smaller sound, close to the ground. Close to *him*. There!

Again! More faint this time but even closer. It seemed to be coming from inside the tent!

He looked around and, seeing nothing except the three packs, a couple of kettles, and his own shape, he began to suspect. Then he heard it another time and, yes, was quite sure: the sound was coming from *inside him*. He had begun to moan. What did it mean—to be crying out so strangely? He wanted desperately to know, so he kept listening; determined to wait—to listen—to listen as long as necessary. . .

16

How Far to the Flour?

Several hundred yards downriver from the tent, Wallace struck a brook flowing into their river. Mechanically he splashed through in his blanket-boots and pushed on into the forest of stunted spruce. The water was icy but it seemed hardly to matter. His feet had been wet for days and the rain from the east quickly wet the rest of his clothes.

He walked unsteadily. Even the simplest obstacles presented a challenge. If his sleeve caught on a stray tree limb, he staggered and fell to his knees before regaining balance. If his foot dragged while stepping over a log, he plunged headfirst into the moss and had to wait several minutes before gaining enough strength to stand. George wasn't in much better shape, but he remembered the country better, so Wallace let him lead. About noon George threw down his pack.

"We'll have a spell here and a cup of tea to warm us up," he said.

Wallace collapsed without protest. Having been up most of the night, he was exhausted. He watched as George gathered firewood and pulled out his knife to whittle shavings. The rain had soaked all the natural tinder. When the fire finally caught, George put the water to boil, then pulled out a little cardboard packet. It was a half-pound portion of peameal.

It took a moment for Wallace to register. Then he remembered that Hubbard had emptied the last of their peameal into the bone broth several days earlier.

"George!" he cried indignantly. "Where did you get that peameal?"

"Hubbard gave it to me this mornin' while you were gettin' wood."

"How could you take it?"

"He made me take it. I didn't want to, but he said we'd need it. We ought to have it as much for his sake as for ours, he said, and I had to take it to make him feel right."

Wallace frowned. The argument made a certain amount of sense, but he felt bad enough already leaving Hubbard alone. Still, they couldn't take the peameal back. George boiled a third of it for lunch and they each drank a pint of the hot broth. It revived Wallace some, dispelling the sluggishness that crept into his limbs every time he sat down.

The rain fell in torrents that afternoon, dashing into Wallace's face as he walked down the valley, streaming down his back and legs in rivulets. Lacking any tent or tarp, the two of them at dusk sought out the most sheltered thicket they could find. It was not much. With no ax, and the woods so wet, the best they could do for a fire was to assemble a few half-rotten trees that had been lying on the ground. George got the logs burning, but the result was less a blaze than a smoldering, steaming smudge. The smoke hung everywhere.

The rain continued to come in sheets. After drinking more of the peameal broth, Wallace crouched as close as he could to the fire, with its smoke and hissing steam. He didn't even bother with the pretense of sleeping. George was lying curled up around half of the fire, his little blanket wrapped about his shoulders.

It was impossible to avoid the smoke. Wallace tried, but when he moved farther away he began to shiver uncontrollably. For a while he pulled his blanket completely over his head, but the smoke came in anyway, nearly suffocating him. His eyes stung and his lungs ached. There was nothing to do but dumbly endure.

Now and again he got up to throw wood on the fire. Around midnight the rain let up, then stopped altogether. For half an hour the evening was uneasily calm.

He could get no relief from the cold. If anything, the temperature seemed to be dropping, and soon a breeze stirred again. It had turned around and was now coming from the west. A few flurries drifted lightly down into the fire. The wind increased. There was no more of the mournful sighing, as on the previous night; the tone had become hollow and implacable. It began to snow in earnest—not the wet, squally snow they had encountered during their long portage, but in relentless, wind-driven gusts that obliterated the world around him, snuffing out the shapes of trees, bushes, everything but the orange embers of the fire. It snowed like Wallace had never seen it snow before.

By the time the sky turned gray, six inches lay on the ground. The wind died down and the clouds broke to reveal the sun, but Wallace saw the world imperfectly. A strange haze before his eyes stained everything a smoky, blurry blue. He stood up and went away from the fire; rubbed his eyes with a bit of snow, as if to wash away the soot; but the haze remained. George complained of it too.

They had the last of the peameal and started off, the countryside transformed into a world of white. Sometime before noon George crossed the tracks of a partridge and followed them into a clump of bushes. Wallace listened for the pistol shot, but when it came, it was followed by the flutter of wings as the bird flew away.

"Only scraped him—he nearly fell too," said George mournfully. "And I was so particular, aiming."

They continued downriver, shuffling along in the snow. George's tracks made it easier for Wallace to follow; he didn't have to look up so often. After a while George turned down the bank toward the river, and Wallace remembered that their flour had been left along the south shore, not the north.

"We'd better cross here," said George. "This is about as shallow as it gets."

Hardly pausing, Wallace followed obediently, wading into the river. Instantly the water sucked his breath from him, made his legs numb. He felt his way along the uncertain river bottom, trying desperately not to stumble. He kept his arms out for balance as the current swirled around his waist, then his chest, and nearly to his armpits. A few more steps and the worst was over. Wallace struggled to shore and up the snowy bank.

Almost immediately his clothes froze stiff, whitened with rime. George built a fire and they thawed out before it, had a quick cup of tea, and pushed on. But every time Wallace sat down, even for a moment, he felt he didn't want to get up.

GEORGE KNEW THEY had to get to the flour that night. The peameal was gone and they were both weak. They couldn't walk through drifts, nearly to their knees, without more food. The pace was getting Wallace too; George had to wait every so often, to let him catch up.

"How far yet to the flour?" Wallace would ask when he drew even.

And George would answer, "A few miles yet."

Wallace was very near his finish; George knew that. But he didn't dare ask him about it, afraid Wallace would be scared if he had to say so. George was afraid *he'd* be scared, too, if Wallace said he couldn't go any farther. They just had to keep going.

Come late afternoon Wallace was lagging way behind. George waited, watching him hobble along the broken trail until he finally caught up. He stood breathing hard, head down.

"How far yet to the flour?"

"About two miles."

Wallace thought some.

"You better go along. Don't wait for me anymore. If we don't get to that flour tonight, we may not live to see the morning."

"Yes," said George, "that's what I was going to say."

But he had only gotten forty yards when he crossed another partridge track. He followed it to a tree, drew his pistol, and fired. The bird fell to the snow. By the time Wallace came up, George had plucked both wings.

He cut one off and handed it to Wallace: "They say raw partridge is good when a fella's weak."

Wallace lit into the wing, bones and all. George ate the other almost as quick: It was still warm with the bird's lifeblood and wonderfully delicious. Another mile or so of walking and George crossed some caribou sign. A lot of tracks, going in all directions. The caribou were nowhere in sight, though, and neither was Wallace.

All those tracks might be confusing, George thought. Wallace might get there and not be able to tell the right path from all the others. So he waited again.

"How far to the flour?"

George pointed. "Do you see that second knoll?"

"Yes."

"Well, don't you remember it? No? Why, that's where we camped when we threw the flour away. We'd better eat a mouthful of this partridge. It'll freshen us up and help us on."

He gave Wallace the neck and ate the head himself.

"I just fancy I never ate anything so good in my life," said Wallace.

It was dusk when they reached the old camp. Snow had covered everything. "How'll we find the flour?" asked Wallace. But George went straight to a bush, ran his hand under the snow, and pulled out the bag. He had the place right in his mind's eye.

The flour, three or four pounds of it, was a solid lump of greenish-black mold.

"We'll boil the partridge in some of this," he said eagerly. "Have a real good stew."

The fire hadn't been burning long, though, when Wallace doubled up and put his hands to his eyes. They felt full of sharp splinters, he said—couldn't even open them. Well, it was the smoke blindness from the night before. Same kind of thing happened when you went snow-blind. George took Wallace's pipe and filled it with dried tea leaves and one last nugget of real tobacco; then lit it for him, since Wallace couldn't see to do it himself.

After dinner Wallace just pulled his blanket around him and fell asleep. He'd rested hardly at all the past three days. George sat up all night and kept the fire going. He thought of Hubbard a lot; wished Hubbard had been with them to enjoy the partridge. He worried about Wallace too. If they hadn't gotten that bird, they never would have made it to the flour; George was convinced of that. And now, Wallace had to turn around and go back. Could he do that and live? George wasn't sure.

He thought he'd better make Wallace some food, help him to keep going. He took some moldy flour and mixed a pasty dough, which he cooked thick and a trifle burned, the way the Indians baked *nekapooshet,* a dish George favored up on the Bay. Sometime after midnight he woke Wallace and gave him some to eat, then let him go back to sleep.

Wallace slept like the dead. Again at dawn George gave him a shake. "Time to be up, Wallace. We're goin' to have more snow to travel in."

The clouds were hanging low again and the first flurries had already started. Wallace tried out his eyes, found they could open, but everything still looked hazy.

George boiled some of the flour; in the light of day, he was surprised how black it was. He hadn't paid much attention the night before. After breakfast he put about two pounds in his pack and gave the rest to Wallace.

"How long can you keep alive on that?" he asked.

"Two days to reach Hubbard," said Wallace. "Then maybe the two of us might go three days more—in a pinch."

George looked Wallace hard in the eye. "Do you think you can live as long as that?"

"I'll try."

"Then in five days I'll get help to you, if there's any help to be had. Day after tomorrow I'll be at Grand Lake. Those fellus'll be strong and can reach camp in two days, so expect 'em."

Wallace nodded. "Five days."

"Well, we'd better go," said George. He didn't want to, really. When Wallace was gone, there'd be nobody left but himself.

Wallace seemed uneasy too. "Do you have your Testament with you?" he asked.

"It's the Book of Common Prayer. But it's got the Psalms in it."

He handed over the leather-covered book, but it was no use: Wallace's eyes were so bad, he couldn't even make out the print. "Maybe you can read one, George."

George took the book, flipped it open. "Ninety-first," he said. And read it as clear and strong as he could. By the time he finished, the snow was coming thick and fast. He looked at Wallace. "You'd better make a cape of your blanket. Let me fix it for you."

He draped the blanket around Wallace's shoulders, made two small holes with his knife, and tied the blanket together with trolling line. Then he did the same for himself.

"Stick with the river, Wallace," he said. "You can't get lost if you stick with the river. If Hubbard gets stronger after he has a bit of the flour, you may want to come on after me. But stay on the north side, and stay near to the river. If I get down safe, and I'm too weak to come back, I'll tell the fellus to stick to the north side, and they'll surely find you."

They shook hands.

"Good-bye, George," said Wallace. "Take care of yourself."

"God be with you, Wallace. Expect help in five days."

They were on a rise when they parted, Wallace heading upstream and George heading down. They could see each other a good ways. Every so often George would stop and call out good-bye, and Wallace would halloo back. Then they'd walk a little more, turn, and sing out again.

"Good-bye!"

"Good-bye!"

George turned one last time. Through snow, he could just make out Wallace climbing the far knoll. George stopped and waved and yelled.

"Good-bye!" And then: "Wallace! Stick with the river!"

But Wallace had disappeared into the snow.

17

Man Proposes

WITH GEORGE GONE Wallace began to walk in earnest, heading west into the storm. For a way he could follow the groove of their old trail, but it soon disappeared in the snow. The wind was terrific, heaving and gusting, and cold as the polar ice of its origins.

Wallace drew his blanket tight over his ears and trudged on. Over the barren knolls; back up the steep-walled valley; through the blackened forest.

This was the burnt-over country they had found so difficult to portage through in July. It seemed incredible now that they could have hated the hot summer sun. On the way up, the forest floor had been their nemesis, a delirium of fallen trees overgrown with scrub brush and seedling spruce. Now the small growth was covered by snow, creating a totally white world save for the black remains of the standing dead—mile after mile of scorched trees scabbed with char.

Wallace kicked his way along with the wind howling in his ears. Only once did another sound come to him: a snort from a quivery-lipped caribou that threw its rack back in astonishment at coming upon Wallace, then bounded off, hooves flying. The storm had so disoriented the animal that man and beast had almost collided.

Wallace was too stiff to draw his pistol in time. The best he could do was hurry on upstream, staggering along in an effort to get his river crossing over with before dark. Then he could dry his clothes by his night fire. But the going was slow. The snow was often to his knees and difficult to plow through. The wind regularly rocked him on his heels. Worst of all, the hot cinders came back to torment his eyes, obscuring his vision, and finally driving him to his knees with pain. For half an hour he had to sit in the snow with his eyes shut, waiting for his head to clear.

By the time he got to his feet the blizzard had obliterated his tracks. Half-blind in the featureless landscape, he looked up and down the valley. Or was it down and up? Blinking hard, he took out his compass and watched its needle swing. The dial was a hopeless blur; he could not tell "N" from "S." He could not even make out which end of the needle was the pointer. He wondered vaguely if he were becoming totally blind.

Darkness fell before he reached the fording place. Discouraged, he threw down the flour bag, gathered a supply of dead branches and started a fire. Melting snow in his cup, he added a few lumps of flour from the sack. The mixture looked blackish green and gave off putrid vapors, but he choked it down.

Polar winds blew all night and by morning the snow was up to his knees. Head down, mind blank, he wallowed ahead to the fording spot. The river here was forty or fifty yards wide. From each shore a jagged shelf of ice extended a few feet out over the water. Chunks of ice, miniature bergs, were floating down the broad open middle of the stream.

He stepped gingerly out onto the ice, testing his weight, bracing for the shock. Near the edge the crack came and he sank thigh-deep into the icy current. The cold caused him to gasp; his involuntary grunt mingled with the gurgle of the river as it tried to bowl him off his feet. His legs felt like two unconnected sticks, but he kept them moving. Leaning hard into the onrushing current, he sidestepped out to the middle, where the water rose to his chest and almost floated him away. A few more sidesteps, a near slip, and suddenly he found himself at the ice along the far shore. He raised one arm and let it fall like a deadweight. Crack! Something broke; he hoped it was only the ice. Both arms smashing, he chopped away at the shelf until it became thick enough to support him. Bellying up seal-fashion, he reemerged on dry land and fumbled for his matches.

Quite irrationally he had hoped to continue on without stopping for another fire, but the experience of reimmersion disabused him of any such notion. Without a fire he would soon become as immobile as a knight of old, encased in an armor of solid ice. With stiffening fingers he nursed the tiny phosphorous spark of his match into a leaping, crackling blaze fueled by the largest branches he could carry. While his clothes baked in the heat he brewed himself a cup of tea and drank it quickly, without relish. The delay was unavoidable, but it vexed him terribly. He was not far from the tent now, but he was already off the schedule he had sworn to keep. He had promised Hubbard to return in three days; this was the fourth.

Another delay, later that day, was even more galling. The smoke blindness attacked him again. He lost an hour and fretted the rest of the day. At nightfall he remained well short of his goal. Hubbard was still upriver.

The storm moderated the next day and snow fell only lightly. His jaw set, Wallace walked all day, not even stopping for a noon fire. He must find Hubbard. Night came and he kept going by moonlight until, around midnight, his weary legs could not be willed to take another step. He dozed in front of a miserable, smoldering fire, shuddering awake again and again with dreams too awful to recall.

By morning the blizzard had returned with gale force. Resuming his march, Wallace could see hardly twenty yards ahead. All the same, he sensed Hubbard's nearness. There was a small frozen brook; Wallace felt sure it was the one near camp. He would have to proceed carefully and do a thorough search.

The country here was no longer featureless, but full of features—all monotonously similar to one another, a jumble of knolls and swamps and balsam stands cluttered by innumerable randomly placed boulders. They had pitched the tent twenty or thirty yards from the river, so Wallace picked his way trying to judge his position by the sound of the rapids. Everything had been changed by the coming of winter. The river's rushing seemed muffled; trees and boulders were covered so that only their outlines remained visible. The contours of the land itself were being altered by drifting snow and the molding hand of the wind.

Wallace searched frantically for the tent and spotted it a thousand times. Scuttling from one white hummock to another, he found only crouching, silent rocks. Desperately he sniffed the wind like an animal. The cold air burned his nostrils, but he detected no telltale whiff of smoke. He shouted himself hoarse and heard no answer but the whistle of the wind. Almost delirious, he began an incantation: "I must find Hubbard," and repeated it over and over as he wandered up the valley. And then recited the chorus with each new step: "I must. I must. I must." But nothing worked. Hubbard was not to be found.

With daylight fading Wallace resigned himself to another open bivouac. More tired, cold, and disheartened than he had ever imagined a man could be, he cooked and devoured his gruel and tea. As night crowded in, his one constant companion, the wind, abandoned him. An unearthly stillness came upon the world. The unaccustomed quiet oppressed Wallace and tried to choke him. Hubbard's face came to fill the void, imparting an unspeakable dread. All night long the haggard features kept looming up—sunken, sallow cheeks, strangely peaceful smile, and those eyes, drawn back into the skull, but burning with longing and hope.

In the morning he drank the last of his tea, slung his bag of flour mold over his shoulder, and started again on his pilgrim's journey: zigzagging back and forth, straining to see beyond boulders for the peak of the tent, trying to remember what the clearing looked like and how it might appear now in the snow. Hoping to fit together the confused pieces of the landscape.

Periodically he came back to the river before searching again inland. The pieces he saw along shore now did not comfort him; in fact, they filled him with a new anxiety. He saw the river narrowing more than he remembered; he came upon a strange hillside with a chunk of unfamiliar ledge rock. And the trees squeezed in so closely. Had they really been so tight before? He stopped, staring for a long time up and down, down and up. Which was it? Had he missed the tent and gone too far? Missed Goose Creek and wandered up some other tributary where no white man had ever ventured, and no rescuer would ever look for him?

How many days had passed? He counted them, carefully. Seven from his parting from Hubbard; five days from George.

Five days. George had promised help in five days! But George might not have made it. He might be lying in some snowbank, exhausted, helpless, or even dead. Then again, maybe he had gotten to Grand Lake. Perhaps a rescue party had come up the river, looking for Wallace, looking for Hubbard. George would have told them where to find the tent. Maybe they'd found it already and were taking Hubbard out this very minute—and didn't know Wallace had gone on up the valley—too far. Every step he took was leading him away from Grand Lake, away from civilization, away from hope.

Wallace had no awareness of being afraid for his life. He was quite beyond fear. But a loathing came over him, born of a singular dread of being left alone in the awful valley. To struggle with the last bit of strength in his body, only to take himself beyond the reach of help, would be . . .

He did not complete the thought. He could not. He did not pause to consider his decision. He did not make a decision. He simply did what he had to do.

He felt himself racing madly. Not for home—that was too far. Not even for Grand Lake. But for some sign that he had *been* there before. He had to find something from a world he recognized.

He floundered though the snowbanks pumping his legs as fast as they would go. Sometimes he sank to his hips and had to pump his arms as well to extricate himself and keep moving. Soon his chest was pumping too, gulping the air with gasps and wheezes.

The country looked so strange. The snow-covered hills were now on his left, their shapes obscured by the storm. The river, on his right, had disappeared from sight under its own canopy of snow and ice. Where was Goose Creek? How could he have missed where the river forked? The alderbushes along shore tangled his feet and sent him sprawling. Look there! Was that a blaze on the far shore? One that George had cut?

Wallace stumbled to the river's edge, attention focused on the tree and its blaze. He walked out onto the ice, striking a diagonal across the river to get a closer look. Anyway, the walking was easier away from the alders and boulders of the shoreline. Dimly, he heard a cracking sound under his feet, but attached no significance to it. He kept angling out, eyes on the far shore. Then the ice cracked again and, too late, he knew.

The current hit him hard, but failed to knock him off his feet. He stood sucking the wind, with his feet dancing along on the streambed and the waves lapping at his chest.

A question came to him—so strongly that he spoke the words aloud—"What's the use?" Three soul-weary words. Why not settle into the water and take the long rest? It would be so pleasant and quick. It would be a relief to die.

He had almost let the river carry him off, when he thought of Hubbard alone in the tent. Hubbard had made them all promise to live as long as they could. And Wallace had promised, hadn't he? Well then, he couldn't let Hubbard down.

Drawing on his last reserve, he scratched at the ice and pulled himself from the river. Half-dazed, he crawled back to the north shore and gathered what little wood he could find lying under the snow. Then he broke a few fresh boughs for a mattress and collapsed on them, thoroughly spent. It was growing dark already and he didn't have enough wood to last the night, but he was too exhausted to move. It was then that he heard the woman's voice.

"Hadn't you better break a few more boughs? You'll rest better then."

The voice was clear and low and sweet. It was there by his side—real—or perhaps just over his shoulder: his dear wife Jennie, looking after him. To Wallace her voice didn't seem at all unnatural, or odd, or unexpected. It was just Jennie, taking care of him, watching over.

He rose and broke a few more boughs.

All night, as he lay by the fire, she tended him. When the embers burned low, her hand came to his shoulder. He felt immensely weary, sick of it all, but she was the one person he could not refuse. Whatever Jennie asked of him, he did it willingly.

In the morning she awakened him and he started again down the valley. No more zigzagging, he was going home. He tried to resume his search for Hubbard, but it wouldn't work. The old refrain wouldn't come. He could remember the words in a vague sort of way—"I must find Hubbard"—but they wouldn't come to his lips. Others came instead. They were more impersonal but comforting, in a strange sort of way. At times, they even made his soul laugh. He repeated them over and over, and the sing-song refrain carried him along: *Man proposes, God disposes. It is His will and best for all. Man proposes, God disposes. . . .*

There were plenty of hard places in the valley—places where the wind tried to blow his face off, places where his legs gave out, and he felt he could plod no farther. But Jennie always got to those places first and was there to whisper softly, "Do your best. Don't lose heart. All will be right in the end."

Time pulled apart. Events no longer happened in linked sequence, but simply burst haphazardly into his consciousness. Jennie spoke to him now and again, but once or twice it was his mother who appeared. Daylight came and went, but he no longer paid any attention. Only one element persisted to hold the world together, and that was snow. It was always snowing—sometimes in a blinding fury, sometimes in gentle flurries, sometimes with icy pellets, sometimes with powder flakes—but always snowing.

The stuff clogged in his moccasins, so he unwrapped the ragged leather strips from his feet and hung them from his belt.

That left two woolen socks on each foot, but the toes and heels soon wore through and exposed bare flesh to the snow.

Before long, both feet were complaining to him. They were like two little people, independent personages with their own domains. They talked to Wallace; said that they were cold and that it was his duty to take care of them. Wallace tried to pay attention, but they were so far off. He had enough to do to care for himself.

All the same, the moccasin shreds came in handy. The flour mold was making him so nauseous that he tried eating the old cowhide. He did this carefully, cutting out the brass eyelets and saving them for later, when he might get really hungry. With a little boiling, the leather swelled up and tasted delicious.

Rescuers seemed to pass nearby several times. He heard the men talking and joking. Each time, he shouted at the top of his lungs, "Over here! I'm over here!" But they never seemed able to find him and he would shake his head and say, "Man proposes, God disposes. . . ."

One evening he crossed the river. It was frozen solid now, murmuring only faintly under its winter blanket. On the south side of the valley he built a miserable little fire under an uprooted stump. It created very little heat, but it smoldered all night without having to be fed much new wood. He slumped in front of it and sat with his head in the smoke and his toes complaining vainly from their ice holes. He wanted to sleep and needed to, but Jennie wouldn't allow it. Whenever he started to doze, she touched her hand to his shoulder.

As the darkness began to lift he became aware that the sky no longer pressed down on him. It looked far away and was tinged with velvet. He was looking right through the clouds. No, there *were* no clouds. The sun was rising above the horizon. The storms had passed! The storms had passed!

In the rotten stump a few embers were still wafting a curl of smoke with each gust of wind. The air was biting cold.

He saw a dead tree a few yards away. It was a big spruce with long, low branches—just the kind he needed to stoke the fire. He pulled his frayed piece of blanket around his shoulders and tucked aching legs under him. Pushing with his arms, he raised himself to a standing position. It seemed for a moment as if he were floating, for he had no sensation of contact with the ground; he had no feeling whatsoever in his feet. Then he saw that the tree, his tower of firewood, was swaying dizzily; suddenly it toppled.

The snow felt cold on his face. He tried to get up again but couldn't. His legs refused his instructions. Finally, using the breast stroke, he maneuvered back to the smoldering stump and tried to think. His thoughts would only go in circles.

He caught himself dozing and, with a start, sat up straight. Through the veil of sleep he had become aware of an unusual sound. Was it a shout? It sounded like a man calling from a great distance, from the far end of a tunnel, from the bottom of a well. He staggered to his feet and, rocking back and forth on those unsteady, insensible beings, listened. There it was again! He felt *sure* it was a shout. Those men, maybe, who had been passing up and down the wrong side of the river looking for him. Up and down, down and up.

With every bit of energy left, he sent up an answering "Hello!" Then licked his cracked and blackened lips; moved his tongue carefully around the borders, to get it just right. Had he actually made any noise?

"Hello!"

All was silent.

Again and again, with mounting excitement. *"Hello! Hello! Hello!"*

18

You Can't Lose Me

As George set out downstream the morning of October 20, he paused on the knoll to wave and catch the faint sound of Wallace's last farewell. But the snow had swallowed it. In a snow like this, voices didn't go very far. Wallace waved, turned, and was gone.

Early in the trip the boys had talked about how alone they felt in the woods, like nobody else existed, and George didn't see it. He knew what they meant now, though. He wanted to hear Wallace's voice, anybody's voice.

"Well, Georgie."

He said the words aloud, to cheer himself up. To let himself know *somebody* was around.

Pushing over the rise, he was careful to keep the sound of the river to his left, even when he couldn't see it. Along the steadies the ice had just about shut the river up. But this stretch the water fell mostly in cascades and the ice hadn't got a good grip.

About noon he came on porcupine tracks. Fresh. He followed them into a clump of trees and, sure enough, there was a ball of quills, tucked in at the foot of a bent-over spruce. One shot with the .22 took him.

George built a fire and singed off the quills and hair. Talked to himself aloud, as if Wallace or somebody else was kneeling beside.

"There's them fellus up there without grub," he said. "Maybe I'd better turn about and take 'em this porcupine. But if I do, it won't last long, and then we'll be worse off than ever. This snow's gettin' deeper all the time, and if it gets so deep I can't walk without snowshoes, we'll all die for sure. No, I'd better go on with this porcupine to help me."

So he boiled a piece in his kettle and went on, always keeping the sound of the river to his left. The snow kept falling and swirling all through that day, all through the night, and on into the next morning. The drifts began to pile up, making the walking much harder, except on the ridges where the wind blew things clear. When he had to go down into the trees, it was bad business: The blankets on his feet were always slipping off and it was getting harder to retie the trolling line that held them. It seemed so thin and his fingers so thick.

Whenever he stopped to take a little rest or boil a kettle for lunch, things would come into his head. Notions about the boys who were waitin' on him and who wouldn't come out alive if he let them down. Or he would remember how Hubbard had said, "George, even if I were your father, you couldn't try any harder to save me." Such notions would come into his mind pricking him. Then he would jump up from sitting by the fire or whatever and push on again.

Nighttime wasn't quite so bad, because he would tell himself it was too dark to travel. No point travelin' in the dark. Then he would find a sheltered thicket and build a fire long-style, spread out five feet or so, so he could lie next to the blaze and keep warm from head to toe. Always he would talk to keep himself company. "This's been a tough day," he would say, "and I ain't where I ought to be. But I'll eat a good snack of porcupine with some of the flour, and in the mornin' I'll have another good snack, and that'll make me stronger so I can travel farther."

When he was done eating, he would put the rest of the porcupine in his sack, along with any leftover bones; then take out his prayerbook and read a chapter and, after that was done, lay the sack of food under his head for a pillow, so some animal couldn't get it. Feel around to make sure his pistol was handy. It wasn't but a little one—only .22 cal.

"If some wolves should come along tonight, they would see me pretty quick and make short work of me," he told himself. "But I guess I might just as well get killed by them as starve."

He looked around. Didn't see any wolves.

"Still, if they *do* come by, I'll make that first fellow jump a little with my pistol." He said it in a voice loud enough so the wolves would hear.

Then he went to sleep.

By the third afternoon the weather began to change. George could smell the difference right away, and it put fear in him. It was getting warmer. He could feel the moist air in his nose and the snow wasn't powdery anymore, but thicker, harder to push through. In the evergreens the drifts became heavy and wet. When George staggered, he caught hold of a tree and the snow would shake loose in great clumps, crashing down on him.

It grew warmer still and began to rain—worse than any snowstorm, because it wet him through as the snow had not. Every time he fell, it was into wet drifts that blotted up his warmth and stole it from him. Each stumble seemed his last, his legs so weary and heavy—and still they had to be lifted high: up and out of one snowbank, into the next.

Thoughts came into his head. "Maybe you better give up. Maybe you better just lie down." But he would not say these things aloud. If he didn't say them, maybe they weren't real.

Suddenly he came upon some tracks that caught his breath in his throat. *Human* tracks, fresh broken trail! He felt life tingling through him and began to run.

"Hey!" he called, and his voice faltered, weak. He had not tried to yell in a long time.

"Hey! . . . fellus!"

He staggered along in the tracks, stumbling, picking himself up with energy he didn't know he had. These were men's tracks, no doubt about it. Donald Blake, or some other trapper from down on Grand Lake. Had to be.

"Hey! . . . fellus!"

No, only just Blake. Blake, or some other. It was the tracks of only one.

"Hey!"

And then he stopped dead. *Why don't he have snowshoes?*

And then ran on a little; but the thought wouldn't go away. *Why don't Blake have snowshoes?*

He looked at the track. Where he'd come; where he'd gone. Always a steady bend to the right. He began to tremble.

They were his own tracks.

He leaned against a tree and felt the tears coming down his cheeks. He cried easily now. It was just—he wanted some rest from the weight he was carrying. Just a little rest. Let somebody else go for help.

But there wasn't anybody else. George Elson, that's who was left.

He tried to calm himself. He had to quiet down and do some thinking. "Listen for the river," he told himself. "You've got too far away."

There it was—faint in the distance. George left his circular trail and broke through new snow until the sound got stronger. Then he stopped. "Not so fast," he said to himself. "You're cold. You keep fallin' and your hands get cold. Before you go any farther, you got to fix that."

He took his knife and pulled at the sleeves of his undershirt, cutting the ends into tubes. Then he tied off the open end of each tube with a bit of string and slipped the tubes over his hands as mitts. He rested a minute or two more, until he could hear his heart slow down to what was natural. Then he stood up and spoke in a clear voice, so any marten or wolf might hear.

"Them fellus up there in the snow have got to be saved. I said to Hubbard, 'With God's help I'll save you,' and I'm goin' to. At least, I will if my legs hold out and there's anybody at Grand Lake." And then he continued down the river.

That night the Lord gave him four fat partridges, lined up nice and easy in a clump of spruce. Soon after, he came to the campsite where they'd left the coffee and the milk. Couldn't find the milk. The lid was off the coffee and the can was full of ice, so all its strength had gone. But the partridge freshened him up, and he made a fire and dried out some. After he read a psalm, he felt strong enough, even, to raise his voice for a hymn. If he was going to sing, he wanted to do it good and clear, like his father. He sang:

Lead kindly light, amid the encircling gloom,
Lead Thou me on.
The night is dark, and I am far from home;
Lead Thou me on.
Keep Thou my feet; I do not ask to see
The distant scene; one step enough for me.

By morning the weather had turned clear again—dry and cold, only not too cold. By next evening he reached the pail of lard. It was about three pounds in all. And the evening after that, he got four more partridges. Every night now, he would sing "Lead Kindly

Light," and each morning at daybreak he sang, *Come to me, Lord, when I first wake,/As the faint lights of morning break; / Bid purest thoughts within me rise,/Like crystal dew-drops to the skies.*

Every so often he counted the days, just to keep track. They'd left Hubbard on October 18. Nineteen, twenty—that was when Wallace turned back. Twenty-one, twenty-two, twenty-three—that was the rain. Twenty-four, twenty-five. This was twenty-five.

Six days ago was the last he'd heard Wallace's voice.

The Lord be praised, on the seventh he was out to Grand Lake by ten in the morning, and so glad to see it! Snow was all around the shore, but the lake was still open. A big lake like this wouldn't ice over for another month.

George was feeling light now and not minding the snow. The partridge had freshened him up some. He was just going along the south shore toward Blake's cabin, no ups and downs, no mountains, good walking. He'd gone about two miles when he heard a noise that bothered him. He pushed into a stand of evergreen and birch, then stopped and stared.

Before him lay another river—big, flowing into Grand Lake. It was right in the way of where he had to go, to Blake's tilt.

He shook his head. What was a river doing here?

He stepped back a few paces and looked some more. Tried to imagine it in summer, with leaves on the trees. They'd looked down this bay when they came by—and never seen any river. Must have been hidden by the trees.

It was bigger than the river he'd been hiking on, and running fast. Then he had a thought. "I bet this is the Big River we were on, and it come out to Grand Lake after all. Just like my dream."

He worked his way through the snowbanks, traveling upstream a ways, looking for a place to cross. But the bank only got steeper—twenty-five, thirty, feet high. When he dropped a log in, the current grabbed it and swept it away. Ice was floating down the river in big chunks. And when he got upstream enough, he saw something else. The part of the river he was following was only one branch. The whole thing came shooting out of the forest and split in two where it flowed into Grand Lake.

So what he'd seen first was an island, not the far side of the river. That was bad. If he crossed down there, he had two rivers to get by.

All afternoon he walked up and down trying to figure a way

to cross where the river hadn't split. But it wouldn't work. He gave up and came back to Grand Lake.

Near the lake was a rapid. George gave it a hard look. Maybe it wasn't so deep and he could wade it. Not all the way, but still—maybe he could walk out some and then just swim the rest.

He started out, but the water rose to his waist before he got more than thirty feet. Ice floes kept bumping him, throwing him off balance, and then his leg muscles cramped up. They began jerking so bad he couldn't help himself. He turned and staggered back to shore, fell to the ground, and held his legs. He'd got out just in time.

He rubbed his legs until the feeling began to come back. By then it was dusk, so he started a fire. He lay close and sang "Lead Kindly Light" before bed. But he couldn't forget the river. The noise of the ice rubbing the shore went on all night long.

Come daylight he had his breakfast—partridge. He thought maybe it would fix his legs up a bit. But when he tried to wade across again, the cramps came just the same. He could see there was no way to swim. He wouldn't last three minutes in that water.

Along the lake was a lot of driftwood. He thought he better try a raft. Hauling together the biggest logs he could find, he laid them side by side. Then he took his tumpline and cut it in two, using the pieces to tie the driftwood together at one end of the raft. He used his leather belt for another corner. For the last, he had nothing but a little piece of salmon twine. Had to make do.

He got a pole. He wanted it long, to feel the river bottom all the way across and make sure he knew where he was going. He couldn't afford any chances.

Finally he looked his raft over and then out at Grand Lake stretching as far as the eye could see. The wind was blowing toward the middle of the lake. If he didn't watch out, it would sweep him straight into heavy seas and open water. He looked again at his pole, to gauge how long it was.

He had to try it.

Once aboard, he could see by the way the raft sank down that it was too small. But he pulled his food bag close anyway and shoved into the current, using the pole to snub, the way he would in a canoe. It was more awkward than a canoe, though. The raft wasn't careful of where it was going and there wasn't someone like Wallace standing at the other end, ready to help in the tight spots. George could snub one end all right, but the current took the other and swung it farther out, into the deeper channel. So then he had to turn and put his pole on the other side to snub that. No use: the raft only spun again, out into faster water, downstream a little more, a little closer to the mouth of the river.

Chunks of ice floated downstream, jarring him. He had to fend them off with his pole, all the while trying to keep his balance; then punch his pole down quick again, to feel for the river bottom. He pushed deep as the pole would go—nearly leaned off the raft—and felt the bottom catch once, twice, as it went racing by. Then he couldn't feel bottom anymore and, looking up, had his breath taken away to see how fast the island was floating off behind him. He was going right out into Grand Lake.

The river's current was gone, but the wind had him—coming out of the west and blowing him straight into thirty miles of open water.

On his knees, George pulled his pole from the water and stuck it between his legs. It wasn't doing any good anymore. Waves began to roll over the raft, covering it as the crests went by, letting it breathe a bit in the troughs. But always working on it: straining the lashings first one way, then another.

The raft began to come apart. Piece by piece, the driftwood broke away. George crouched as the waves washed over, trying to hold the raft together. "Have I escaped starvin' only to drown?" he asked himself. It looked like it. "But if I drown," he said, "the boys will be up against it for sure, so I'd better not drown." Another wave washed over, and he tucked his food bag tight between his knees. "Hold on to that bag," he told himself. "It'd be just as bad to escape drownin' only to starve, as to escape starvin' only to drown."

The wind shifted slightly. George clung to the raft, hands numb, body numb. He looked at the water around him and the shore so far beyond reach. "Now if I jump," he said, "I'll drown; and if I don't, I'll drown anyway. So I guess I'll hang on a little longer."

For more than an hour he crouched over what was left of his raft, expecting the lashing to give, sure he was near his finish. The wind drove him to one side, a little ways out from the point of the island. It was a long point, and George could see by the set of the land that there would be shallows running out from shore. He took his pole and felt around, finding nothing at first and then just hardly touching bottom. He poled the raft closer to the island, and shoved along the sandbar until he made land. Staggering up the beach he threw the lake one last, stubborn look.

"You can't lose me," he said.

Wringing wet, he worked his way around the island to the far branch of the river. He knew he needed a fire and he sure wanted one, but he wasn't about to let himself rest. Not until he got across that second river and was safely off the island.

The raft was no good. Waterlogged, and too small anyway. He'd have to build a new one. Up and down the island he went, searching. No driftwood: The only thing around was a few rotten stumps. He began hauling them to a spot where the ice had frozen over a good bit. He lugged the stumps out onto the ice, eyeing it as he walked. The ice had to be thick but not too thick. It was the only thing he could try at this point; too weak to do anything else.

The rags he was wearing were beginning to freeze on him.

"You don't want to build a fire now," he said. "You're almost over. Just haul these stumps down and make your raft."

He pulled the twine and lashings off the old raft, talking all the while about what a fine new raft he was making, and how proud he was going to be of it. Then he got on the raft, as it sat on the ice, and tested it.

"You need a good pole," he told himself; "maybe a little longer than the one you had before." When he'd got it, he stood on the raft and began jabbing holes in the ice with the pole on the shore side; first one hole, then another, then another. The ice began to give along the shore side, and the raft floated free. Only, some of the ice stayed underneath the stumps and buoyed the raft better than the first. George stood up with his pole and oh! he was so proud of that raft, telling himself all the while how proud he was, and being so careful to touch bottom always, guiding it slowly across the river.

And when he touched shore finally, he hopped out light as could be and grabbed the food bag along with him and said, "*Now* I'll have a fire and dry out." He picked a fine campsite near a point, and the Lord liked it, for there were three partridges he shot for his dinner. Would have set right down to cook them, except . . .

Past the point was a deep bay. He got to thinking: What if another river came out of there? And he couldn't drive the thought from his head no matter how hard he tried; couldn't rest until he saw a little better if there *was* a river. So he put the partridges down and ran to the point.

He looked into the bay and saw no river. Good. But it was twilight; shadowy. He saw something else, maybe a hundred yards or so down the shore. Gray—like a boat. Or maybe just driftwood, caught funny in the day's last light. He went slowly toward it. If it was a boat and wasn't wrecked, he could sail it to the post.

Then something flew to him across the air that set his heart thumping wildly against his ribs. He wanted to yell, but his voice—his only voice these long and lonely days—failed him; and his knees went weak. From out of the forest came the sweet cry of a baby, calling strong and clear against the night, and all full of life.

19

Fair Starved

THE YOUNG GIRL was standing in front of the cabin, holding the baby—the blanket wrapped tight—when she noticed the brush shaking about, shaking every whichaway. Then a horrible thing burst from out of the dusky night, about the size of a wolf and coming fast. But walking on hind legs: Look there—it only got two legs! The girl screamed and flew into the cabin.

"Oh, Mrs. Blake! Mrs. Blake! 'Tis somethin' dreadful comin'! 'Tis sure a wild man!"

Harriet Blake came right over. She didn't hold much for wild men.

One look and the poor woman's heart jumped to her throat. '*Twas* a wild man—and the creature was there on her own stoop! Dripping wet, long black hair streaming in the wind, scraggly black beard twisted and kinked, thin chest heaving like it was trying to blow fire . . . why, it was the devil, no mistake. And where was her ax but all the way across the room!

"Lord ha' mercy!" she shrieked, throwing her arms up in surrender.

"Don't be alarmed ladies," said the wild man. "I couldn't hurt a rabbit. Ain't there any men here?"

It was a man! Near starved and the most raggedy thing she ever care to see—but a man.

Was it anybody she knowed? No; 'twasn't. But he didn't talk like an Indian out of the bush either.

Just to make sure, Harriet Blake kept talking. Devils couldn't get after you if you kept 'en talkin'. Yess'r, she told the stranger, the men be returnin' directly; they were right handy to the cabin, anywheres right near here. The men 'ud be her husband, Donald

Blake, and he's young brother, Bert. Well, folks called him Bert. Real name was Gilbert. Yes, sir. Gilbert Blake and Donald Blake.

She kept her eye on the stranger, and, by and by, he caught his breath enough to tell her how he'd come down the Naskapi River, been out of grub for a long time, and Hubbard and Wallace were still up in the bush in a bad way. . . .

"Oh, Mr. *Hubbard!*" she said. They all knew about Hubbard. Everybody was wantin' to know what had become of 'en. And this was George Elson, the guide who'd gone along!

"Dear lord, come in," she said. "You needs a mug up and a proper dinner."

GEORGE THOUGHT he had never been happier to see the inside of a house in his life. The cabin was log with a sod roof. Everything—even the floor—had been planed smooth and rubbed with oil so it looked bright and sparkly. Mrs. Blake kept telling him to sit and eat, but he couldn't hold still. He paced up and down, the ice on his rags melting to make tiny streams on the plank floor.

Pretty soon the food she was laying out smelled too good not to do something about it. There was a pot of grouse stew and hot tea with all the molasses he wanted. And biscuits—hot buttered! Those biscuits just looked at him from the plate, all tender and waiting. When they were gone, Mrs. Blake put more on and *they* looked at him too. He couldn't help himself; he ate and ate and couldn't stop. Finally he got up and went outside for a while, where he couldn't see the little biscuits. Otherwise he wouldn't stop.

Just after dark Donald and Bert arrived. George knew Donald at once: Skipper Tom's boy, who told them how he'd "sailed" up the Naskapi as far as the Red Wine. The other boy, Bert Blake, was only seventeen; shy and quiet with a round face that looked Eskimo.

Quickly George told how Hubbard had busted and how Wallace was going back with the flour, thirty miles up the Naskapi. As he talked Donald's eyes began to flash.

"Didn't you see Allen Goudie's tilt, sir?" he asked. "She's on the Naskapi, right handy to the bank and in fair sight from the river."

"If there's a cabin on the Naskapi," said George, "you can kick me."

Donald gave George a narrow look. "When did you come out to Grand Lake, sir?"

"Yesterday morning."

"And how did you get across the bay?"

"I didn't cross the bay," answered George. "I hiked the south shore around and rafted the big river with the island."

"How far'd you come from *your* river before you rafted?" asked Donald. " 'Bout three, four miles?"

"Yes."

"Why, you weren't on the Naskapi!" said Donald. "You weren't on no river a'tall! We calls that Susan Brook. The Susan's just a little creek, ain't she, Bert?"

Gilbert nodded. "Yes, and she don't *go* nowhere much either."

"Well, I'll be blamed," said George.

Then Donald explained how the Naskapi flowed into Grand Lake on the north, at the big bay five miles from the end. Hubbard must have missed it on the way in, he said. The river George rafted was called the Beaver, and it flowed the same direction as the Susan, only ten or fifteen miles farther south.

They must've been on the Beaver too, George said. Up in the bush. Only they didn't know where it came out. He was so sorry they hadn't stayed on their big river when they had the chance. It would have taken them right where they wanted to go.

George drew a map to show where Hubbard's tent was. Donald looked at it and said he and Bert would pick up a couple other trappers, Allen Goudie and Duncan McLean, across the bay. Then the four of them would go in for Hubbard and Wallace—George had better rest up until he got stronger.

After they left, George got to worrying. What if he hadn't got out in time to save the boys? It made his stomach knot right up. If they were dead, he'd be mighty sorry he didn't stay and die along with them. Word would spread like the wind: "Stay clear of George Elson. He's the one that took food from those fellus and left 'em to starve." Nobody'd believe he'd been trying to save them, that he was actually their friend. All the men at the H.B.C., everybody all over the north country would be saying he was just another half-breed who turned bad when he was up against it. That'd be the end of George Elson right there.

Before long the knot rose up to his chest and got tighter. The pain was terrible. It got so he couldn't think about his other troubles at all—just the gripping pain. Finally it came to him that it wasn't just worry; it was the biscuits. His stomach couldn't take so much food all of a sudden. The pain just kept getting worse and worse; so bad he thought he might explode. He tried lying down, tried walking around, tried the outside air. Nothing helped. It kept on all night and all the next day, but he wouldn't tell Mrs. Blake how her good cooking made him suffer so. All those biscuits. He just got quiet and very pale and went outside and walked up and down a lot. "Have I escaped drownin' and starvin' only to die of overfeedin'?" he asked himself. "What a mean trick."

BERT BLAKE WAS only seventeen, and this Hubbard business was the biggest thing he'd walked into. By Garge, it didn't take any convincing for *him* to come along. By noon the next day he and the other three men were hauling their boat out on the snowbanks by the Susan Brook's rapids. It was going to be hard going, all right. The snow was fresh, so they kept sinking deep and their racquets kept tangling in the bushes. All the same, they hurried along, running the best they could, hardly ever stopping to take a blow.

By nightfall they'd covered ten miles in dirty weather, and the snow was still coming down when they set out next morning. They kept to the north bank of the river, like Mr. Elson said, firing a shot now and again. No holler came back.

Next morning the weather turned. Good blue sky everywhere, with red streaks in the east where the sun was near up. Bert was rolling his blankets when Donald caught something on the wind. Donald had as good a nose as lots of dogs.

Donald sniffed, then covered his nose with his hand to warm it. The sharp air had frosted him. Bert checked the wind: coming *up* the valley, from where they had already been.

Allen Goudie walked over on his snowshoes, ready to go. Donald didn't say a word, just kept sniffing. Allen put his own nose to the wind.

"Smoke?" he asked.

Donald nodded. "Not ours either."

So they all started back downstream looking for a fire. They ran near to an hour, with no sign of anything. Bert begun to wonder. It was a long way to go on a sniff.

Then Donald's cry. "Tracks!"

Sure enough, leading across the ice was the tracks of a man

without snowshoes. They all stopped dead. Then, whooping and firing their rifles into the air, they crossed the river and ran up the bank. Climbing up, Bert heard a sound, low and wavery. "Halloo . . . Halloo . . ." Sounded like ghosts, almost—it put the shivers into him.

Top of the rise, there was a smudge burning in an old stump—that was where the smoke had been coming from.

But next to it . . . Was that thing really Wallace? He was up on his legs but teetering like he might fall any time. His clothes were only long johns and stockings, with his trousers torn to tatters below the knees, and a piece of blanket around his torn shirt and sweater. You could see just about right through to the skeleton, his skin lay so close to the bones. Wasn't any hair on his head, but a fringe hanging past his ears. His lips were split and bleeding.

He was looking right at 'en, but he didn't seem to see anything. Didn't seem to know who they were or *what* they were. He looked hard at Donald. Finally his eyes lit up a bit.

"Donald Blake," he says. Not the firmest but clear enough.

Donald stepped up and grabbed Wallace's hand like an old friend.

Wallace moved his lips a little. "Did George get out and send you?"

"Yess'r," said Donald, "it's he that sent us. He's safe at my house."

"Have you found Hubbard?"

"Not yet, sir. We smelled your smoke from about a mile-and-a-half above, an' came down to find you."

Donald nodded to the others and they set about building a fire, putting on a kettle, and making a bed of boughs. They hurried—it looked like Wallace might keel over and die if they didn't.

Wallace kept talking about Hubbard. "You must find him," he said. "Leave me a bit of food and go to him as fast as you can."

"The young b'ys can stay with you, sir," said Donald. "Allen and I will go on for Mr. Hubbard."

Allen handed Wallace a piece of bread—just a little crumb.

"You'd better eat only a small bit at first, sir," he said. "You're fair starved, and too much grub at the beginnin' might be the worse for you."

Even before the tea was boiling, Donald and Allen were strapping on their snowshoes. Then Allen says, "What if the other man be dead, sir?"

"Dead?" says Wallace. "He won't be dead. He'll be in the tent waiting for you."

"But if he be dead?" says Allen. "He may be, and we sure can't bring the body out now, sir."

Wallace said if he was dead, to wrap him in his blankets and put him on a stage where the animals couldn't get him. And to bring back everything inside the tent—especially the rifle and books and papers. He didn't like the idea of Hubbard being dead, though.

With the two men gone, Bert and Duncan served Wallace hot tea and gave him a smoke. When he tried to cut the tobacco plug with his sheath knife, Bert eased the blade out of his hands. "He's a big 'un, sir, to cut tobacca with. Let me."

All day long they watched over him. Built a windbreak, kept the fire going, buttered little bites of bread for him. That bread made him just about wild. He begged for more, even though it would only make him sick. When they weren't looking, he got into the packs and chewed up some raw salt pork. Bert called Duncan and together they led him away and sat him by the fire again.

He kept saying how Hubbard would be all right. Thin and starving and worn down, but all right.

Then the pork must've got to him, because he passed an awful night. He said his stomach felt like it was about to tie into knots and burst; his feet pained him too, because they'd finally begun to thaw out. Socks were so clotted with blood, he didn't dare pull 'en off, for fear of what'd come with 'en.

Next morning Donald and Allen came over the bank. Their packs were large as ever, and Donald was carrying a rifle.

Bert knew what that rifle meant. Wallace saw, and he knew too.

"Yesterday evenin' we found the tent, sir," said Donald. "He were fastened up tight with pins on the inside, an' hadn't been opened since the snow began. Says I to Allen, sir, 'The poor man's dead. 'Tis sure he's dead.' Allen, he opened the tent, for I had no heart to do it; and there he was, wrapped all up in the blankets as if sleepin'. But he were dead, sir, dead; and he were dead for a long time. So there weren't nothin' to do but to wrap him safe in the things that were there, an' bring back the papers an' other things."

Wallace was near killed when he heard that. He looked like he couldn't speak.

"There was deer tracks all 'round the tent," said Donald. "And we saw a place right handy where you'd had a fire by a brook, sir."

"Yes," said Wallace, "I built that fire. So that really was the brook near our tent."

" 'Twere the mercy of God you didn't know the poor man were there dead," said Allen. "You would ha' given up yourself, sir.

"Donald, he stayed outside the tent. He didn't care to get sick, sir, and the body was too much for me to lift all alone. I wrapped him good, though, and he'll be safe 'till we can come back to bury him proper."

Wallace hadn't said much, but all of a sudden he jumped like someone'd give him a hot coal. No, no, no—they weren't going to bury Hubbard up there. *He* was going to bring the body out. He'd do that, at least, for Hubbard.

Well, the boys didn't want to tell him, but it couldn't be done. 'Twas near a hundred miles to the post, and too rough country to be haulin' bodies around with winter comin' on. Donald and Allen tried to let him down easy. But Wallace said it most certainly could be done. Most certainly *would* be done!

"Well, sir, you'd have to wait till Grand Lake catches," said Donald. "Once that's froze, maybe you could bring a sled. But it'll be months before anybody can get up again."

Wallace said he'd wait months. He wanted Hubbard's body, no matter what. They'd come into the country together and, if *he* had anything to say about it, they'd be leavin' that way.

He didn't look so much like he was goin' to die anymore.

20

Bitterberries

WALLACE SAT QUIETLY in the boat as the boys rowed him across Grand Lake to Blake's cabin late the evening of November 2. Donald fired his rifle into the air as they approached, and presently Wallace could make out a lanky figure standing at water's edge, silhouetted by starlight and almost unrecognizable. His hair had been cut, his beard shaved off, and a new set of clothes had replaced the old rags. As Wallace stepped ashore on frostbitten legs George lent a helping hand and said, "Well, Wallace, Hubbard's gone."

"Yes," replied Wallace, "Hubbard's gone." And together they walked up to Blake's, where warmth and light awaited them.

Yet the memory of those gaunt, pleading eyes could not be so easily exorcised. For months Hubbard had been the center of Wallace's life. The two of them had paddled together, regaled each other with Kipling, shared their food, blankets, and closest confidences. Strangely, Hubbard had become even more dear once he had relinquished the goal of his trip. He was less fretful or driven by the need to make a reputation. Failure graced him, in a way; turning home had made him all the more generous and unselfish. What Wallace found hard to admit was that he, somehow, had survived, while Hubbard had not.

Allen Goudie loaned them his sailboat for the trip to the post. The snow had started in again, but what were a few squalls after the perils they'd been through? With Wallace at the tiller and George handling the sheet, they soon reached the ice-fringed harbor of Northwest River, where Tom Mackenzie, the Hudson's Bay man, was down by the shore sawing wood with his assistant, Mark Blake. Both men dropped their crosscut saw and stared. Then Mackenzie recognized George's emaciated features and turned wonderingly to gaze at Wallace, whose long, straggly hair had not yet been cut.

"Where's Hubbard?" he asked.

"Dead," said Wallace. "Dead of starvation eighty miles from here."

He told the story as Mackenzie walked him up to quarters; then told it again once he'd reached the kitchen. He couldn't seem to stop; it just poured out. Gently Mackenzie sat him down and listened, then set out a fine dinner. At the end of the evening he led Wallace upstairs to a small room where a stove was crackling and a big tub of water had been heated. Wallace eased himself in and the bath warmed him to the core, all save his feet, which were swollen twice their normal size and discolored a shiny mottled blue. The water made them prickle.

After five days of eating, he still weighed only 95 pounds, having begun the trip at 170. Mackenzie lavished him with hospitality, providing six meals a day. Even so Wallace snacked constantly. Slowly he put on weight.

A schooner arrived from Rigolet with news. The *Virginia Lake* had docked there and would be making one last trip to Newfoundland. If Wallace hastened on, he could be home in a matter of weeks; if not, he would be forced to winter over, trapped until the ice went out the following June. Mackenzie told him he should go: he needed medical attention. His feet, badly frostbitten, were turning gangrenous.

Yet Wallace declined the chance. Hubbard was still out there, lying in a tent. No one seemed, really, to understand. At home all the people would be waiting—by the pier, at the funeral, in the office—staring at Wallace just as Mackenzie had and asking, "Where's Hubbard?" And Hubbard would be lying in a snow-covered tent, deserted and uncared for. No, Wallace would winter over. If need be, he would drag Hubbard's body home himself, by dogsled all the way around the coast to Quebec.

This was a plan that even Thomas Mackenzie—romantic, high-spirited Mackenzie—judged near-suicidal. Labrador winters were brutal, he remonstrated; one blizzard after another, real blizzards, not just the storms they'd seen so far. The one man who sledded the length of the coast in winter was the mail courier, and he traveled light and managed the feat only once a year. To attempt to transport a body in that manner would be the height of folly. Wallace was unmoved.

The weather soon exceeded Mackenzie's predictions: It was

the coldest season in memory. The post's spirit thermometer had a scale calibrated to 64 degrees below zero, and night after night the spirit disappeared altogether. One week the temperature never rose higher than 40 below, even at midday.

Even more worrisome, the infection in Wallace's feet had begun to spread. In order to receive medical attention, he wrapped himself up and was hauled for six hours on a chilling, bone-wrenching sled journey across the bay to the lumber camp at Kenemish, where he immediately became feverish and took to bed. The only doctor on the coast was a medical student there, who lay abed himself, fatally stricken with tuberculosis. "There's only one way to save your life," he told Wallace, "and that's to amputate both legs. But I'm the only one here who knows how to do it, and I'm too weak to try. So we're both going to die."

Wallace, however, refused to die; inexplicably, his fever subsided and the swelling in his legs receded. Trying them in early February, he found that his knees buckled under his weight. It seemed he would have to learn to walk all over again. For weeks he plugged away at it, up and down his room. The lumberjacks—rough, good-natured men from Nova Scotia—stopped around from time to time to cheer him up, but he could not shake his thoughts of Hubbard, lying uncared for in the woods. Over New Year's he had urged George to lead a party up Susan Brook, but when George visited Kenemish in January, he reported only that a series of storms had made travel impossible. Wallace became so agitated, he tried to leave for Northwest River immediately. Only the lumbermen's firm pleas stopped him. By March he could be restrained no longer—weak legs or no, he would return to push matters forward.

BEING A HALF-BREED, George didn't stay at Mackenzie's house, but over to Mark Blake's. Blake was a breed, like most everybody at Northwest River. He made George at home, and it felt just wonderfully good to have all the food he wanted and not to have to worry what the next day would bring or whether there'd be a partridge waiting in a bush or how many miles the boys had to get to in order to stay alive.

Still, his mind wouldn't let him rest. He would wake up in the middle of the night, thinking about how they had missed the real Naskapi River. It would come into his head how they should have explored the northwest bay of Grand Lake. When he was up at Donald Blake's cabin, waiting for the boys to bring out Wallace, he couldn't help hiking over to the tilt where he'd been heading to get help, just to see what he would have found. He poked around the small cabin, examining the items one by one, trying to decide which ax he would have taken, which snowshoes, how much flour he might have carried back to Hubbard. All those things.

At Northwest River he talked with Robert Baikie, who trapped up the Beaver River—what *they* called their "big river." Baikie seemed to know right where they'd been. "If you had come over that rapid where you left the canoe," he told George, "you would go six miles and just come to another. Only about fifty yards you would carry your canoe, and from there smooth and deep water, no rapids, but swift current. Even if you didn't have the strength of paddling, the current would have brought you down, right to my house." Just as in George's dream.

Wallace wanted him to get a few trappers and go bring Hubbard's body back, but a lot of the trappers weren't interested in the idea of foolin' with someone dead. You had to watch out for "smokers," they said—ghosts you were likely to run into, especially at night. Finally Duncan McLean offered to come. Duncan was a good boy, ready to work and not particular when to start in the morning and when to quit at night. Skipper Tom Blake was the other man Wallace wanted along, but he was older and not so happy about it. He'd seen more hard winters and frosted toes and noses. Wallace wouldn't take no for an answer, so Skipper Tom finally agreed. They left in March.

It took two weeks to get up the Susan, because they couldn't bring dogs to haul the sledge beyond Grand Lake. Too rough country. Along the banks of the river the land looked different after so much snow, but George had a memory for places. He went straight to the spot and said, "We'll dig here." He and Skipper Tom and Duncan went down four feet before they found the tip of the tent, and another four before they got the spot cleared away. Hubbard was inside; no wolverines had found him.

After they got the body on the sledge, George decided to push on up Goose Creek. Wallace had asked him to bring back some of the gear they had dropped along the way. Tom Blake and Duncan were against it. How would he ever find things under eight feet of snow, with no signs to go on? But George wanted to try. They walked along a few miles until he stopped and said, "We'll dig here." Skipper Tom and Duncan looked at each other: The place didn't look any different than any other part of the woods. They dug in over their heads and, sure enough, the stuff was there.

George did this four times, in four different places. The last was a stump in the middle of a swamp, where he'd laid a tin of films in October. No trees to guide him—only a field of snow. George didn't know how he did it. He just *saw* the place by the set of the field. It was in his mind. They dug and the tin was there. Tom Blake said, "I been trappin' ever since I was a boy, and I think I knows somethin' about travelin' in the bush. But *this*—'tis wonderful! I never could ha' done it myself, an' no man on the Labrador could ha' done it. Not even Mountaineer Indians." So they came home safe and well, bringing Hubbard wrapped up on the sledge. At the post they packed him in salt and kept him in a shed nearby.

Mr. Wallace still couldn't rest. He'd been nervous about the body all winter and a little sharp with people. Even raised his voice to Tom Blake once, when he didn't want to travel. Now Wallace was worried about the canoe. He got it into his head that he should make a present of it to Mr. Mackenzie. He had asked George to bring it back along with the body and the other gear, but Duncan and Tom Blake would have none of it. In April Wallace asked again, but this time George spoke his mind. The whole business was a "piece of nonsense," he said. The canoe had probably been crushed by the ice anyway. It would be a trip for nothing.

"If you had dug the canoe out and put it on a stage the first trip in, you wouldn't have to go up again," Wallace told George.

"I *don't* have to go up again," he replied. "Hubbard hired me, not you or Mr. Mackenzie." It made him angry that Wallace should try to boss him around. Hubbard had never been so short. George didn't dare say so out loud, but he thought Wallace had no right to give away the canoe. Why did Wallace have any more right to it than George? Anyway, he had done what he was sure Hubbard would have wanted, and the other boys around Northwest River agreed.

WITH GEORGE remaining obstinate about the canoe, Wallace saw no point in waiting interminably around Northwest River for the ice to go out. On April 22 he directed that Hubbard be taken from his blankets, wrapped in skins, and laid in a pine coffin. Wallace bid good-bye to Mackenzie and his other friends at the post and, along with George and several dogsled drivers, began the trek south.

Day after day they followed the coastline, crossing from one neck of land to the next, over frozen bays and inlets. Each time they had to cut their way through the "ballicaters," enormous ridges of ice heaped up along shore. Once on land the men would join the dogs in hauling the sleds up the hills. Clambering back aboard, they would coast down the other side, with the dogs racing madly ahead to keep from being run over.

The weather was generally mild and the teams made forty to fifty miles a day. On May 9 Wallace reached Battle Harbor, where the ice-crusher *Aurora* had just anchored on its first trip of the season. With the help of the local physician, Hubbard's coffin was sealed with sheet lead and hoisted aboard. Wallace and George sailed to Newfoundland as guests of the captain and then transferred at St. John's to the *Sylvia,* the same ship that had brought them north a year earlier.

For Wallace it was a hard-won achievement. Through sheer strength of will, he had arranged the rescue of Hubbard's body from its grave on the Susan, though incapacitated himself. Battling gangrene, he had cheated death not once but twice, learned to walk anew, and traveled five hundred miles by dogsled and another thousand by ship. Hubbard was gone. There was no way around that. But at least he had been cared for in every way possible. There would be a decent burial; a memorial service, perhaps, and the long journey would be over. It would end decorously, quietly, and with a fitting sense of honor.

Wallace went home truly expecting that.

Arriving at the Brooklyn pier, he scanned the faces of the crowd from the ship's rail and found the ones he had so long ached to see. With George in tow, he hurried down the gangplank and rushed into the arms of his sisters, hugging first Annie and then Jessie, then both at once. They wept for him but kept saying how good he looked—so fit and trim, tan and perfectly robust. At length they gave him over to his friends—Marks, from the college; Roth, in from Cleveland; Goldberg, from the firm. To one side was O'Keefe, one of Hubbard's friends. Wallace shook his hand and gave him an awkward nod, suddenly uneasy about feeling so happy and well and alive.

But here was McLaughlin! It was Alonzo McLaughlin who had hired him after he earned his law degree at night school, who had been so understanding after his wife's death, and who had wished him well on his trip north. Wallace gripped his friend's hand and shook it heartily. At the same time, he felt a tug at his shoulder.

"Mr. Wallace! Mr. Wallace!"

He turned to see not one but a dozen strangers, all pressing forward, anxious for a word. The ranks of New York journalists, as he might have expected. His eyes swept the rest of the pier, anxiously searching for another familiar face.

McLaughlin understood. "She's in the city," he explained quietly, "but in seclusion. It's not been easy for her."

A reporter caught a few of the words. "Mrs. Hubbard won't be at the pier?"

McLaughlin shook his head. "Her husband's death came as a severe shock. She remains prostrated by grief."

The reporters turned to Wallace, pressing closer. Their questions came in a flurry. Had Hubbard achieved his objective? What *was* his objective? When did he die? How was the rescue effected? Where was the body now?

Wallace gave a full account of the expedition, as well as his own journey round the coast. But the longer he spoke, the more the reporters pursued him. He did his best to answer their questions plainly and directly, but there was no satisfying these inquisitors. At the urging of his friends, and with McLaughlin leading the way, Wallace began to make his way across the pier.

"What about your own plans?" asked one reporter.

Wallace found it difficult to be less than forthright, but as a lawyer, he sensed the need for caution on this particular inquiry.

"Hubbard's instructions to me were to carry on his work." He glanced once again around the pier; he had not seen Caspar Whitney or, for that matter, anyone else from the magazine. "I don't know what contract Hubbard had with *Outing,*" he continued, "but I am under no obligations myself. I have all of Mr. Hubbard's notes and his diary. I also have quite a few of my own notes, and independently of fulfilling Mr. Hubbard's mission, I shall write my own adventures for publication."

He was almost to the street when a final question drifted to him.

"What would you say was the final cause of Hubbard's death?"

"Hubbard died of hunger," replied Wallace briefly.

He took another few steps, then stopped. He became almost wistful.

"If we had gone into the interior with a fish net, or even an ordinary shotgun, I think we should not have had any trouble. We could have caught the fish that were not rising to the fly, and shot geese while they were on the wing. That's one thing, certainly."

He hesitated a moment, trying to find the proper words to explain, trying himself to understand what had gone so horribly wrong. Why *had* Hubbard died, while he and George survived?

"The cause of Hubbard's death was primarily starvation," he began again. "There was also his physical condition. He suffered during the trip from several illnesses, which left him at times weak and unable to travel. I also think that he may have started the trip a bit overtrained. Perhaps that had something to do with it."

"Overtrained?" asked the reporter.

Wallace had never considered the issue in quite this light, but now the memory of Hubbard's impetuous energy, the high state of his nerves, the hasty plunge into the awful valley—all these memories returned.

"Yes," he concluded, "Hubbard was overtrained for the work, I think. A bit overtrained, and the strain at first made him stale."

And then he felt the reassuring pressure of McLaughlin's arm in his, drawing him gently toward the carriage that stood ready to take him home.

THEY LAID HUBBARD to rest the next day. George came up with the others to be there. Up Hudson's River.

There wasn't any church service; just a few words said under the sky at Haverstraw, the village one down from Mr. Hubbard's. Haverstraw was right on the river but the cemetery was back about a mile, higher up the valley. It spread out in a big, open meadow, sloping upward until it reached a band of thick forest, full of trees of every sort. But the forest didn't run far, because just beyond, the hill turned steep and rocky. There was a high cliff with a dark, rough face reaching up several-hundred feet. High Tor, they called it. It would have been good for scouting.

Most of the white gravestones were set in the meadow near the road, but the horse drawing Hubbard's coffin climbed toward the high part of the field, up a gravel path past the lower headstones.

When George first looked back, climbing up, all he could see were trees and a few rooftops. But then there was a spot of blue down in the valley, and then more, and finally a whole band of river flowing south, well in view from where the horse stopped.

Wallace's friend, Mr. McLaughlin, led everybody around to their places; and then the minister, Reverend Howland, prayed with them. Just a few words to say good-bye.

Mr. Whitney was there, come out from New York. He was solemn-looking and standing straight, and had only a word to say here and there. Mr. O'Keefe came too, Hubbard's friend who had been to see them off in New York and taken George's picture, back in June (took it alone of George, nobody else standing with him).

Wallace was quiet, in a dark suit and good hat. He had cheered up some on the voyage home but was sad again. Thinking about how they'd parted from Hubbard in the rain; how they'd been the only ones really there at the end to say good-bye. George knew Wallace must be thinking that, saying one last good-bye.

And Mrs. Hubbard, trying to be brave. He knew how much she cared for her husband. George had seen at Battle Harbor how the two of them hated to part. And all through the trip Mr. Hubbard said such tender things about her; she was always on his mind. She stood now a little ways from the others in a black dress, black gloves, black hat, and a black veil over her face. The veil was so dark, you couldn't see more than the pale outlines of her face.

What would she do now that Hubbard was gone? Their little house in Congers had been sold—she couldn't stay there. Would she go back to her parents in Canada? Maybe find a new husband?

He wanted to tell her how it was at the end; Mr. Hubbard had asked him to do that. He wanted to tell her so many other things. How he and Hubbard had made plans to take her up to the Bay, show her some of the rivers around there, and go goose hunting. He wanted to tell her how they were always talking about that last fine dinner they had had together at the house in Congers; how she would teach them to bake this or that treat when they got back safe.

But how could he say that now? It all seemed so far away. All the quiet talks and conversations late at night by the fire—the little promises and sharing of secrets. George had been going to get a room in New York and learn pastry cooking. Wallace and Hubbard had decided to buy a farm in Orange County and settle down together. How could they talk about those things now—there in the bright sunlight? Wallace would write up the story the way he promised and then go back to his business at law. George would go back to Missanabie and Rupert's House and get himself a wife, he hoped. They wouldn't even see each other again—not without Hubbard to bring them around for a visit.

How could he tell Mrs. Hubbard what all those conversations meant—with her standing so silent and black, so sad behind her veil? *He* couldn't tell, and Wallace couldn't either. Wallace didn't find those things easy to talk about.

They came off the hill. George gave one last look for Hubbard's sake, the last he'd probably see of that resting place.

It was a bit like Labrador, after all. Not the forest and the trees. But the gravestones like small boulders, scattered here and there on a mossy highland meadow. And the rock summit you could climb, bare and treeless—that was like Labrador. Like the time he had climbed with Hubbard, searching for the waters of Michikamau. And found them, standing out blue as could be, as far as the eye could see, and seeming so close it would be hardly a walk down to the shore from the bare rock top.

You wouldn't think there was anything could survive up there. But there was, even in the high places. There were the ptarmigan fluttering from bush to bush, yielding themselves up when they were so badly needed. There were those low bushes with fruit the Indians called *uishitshimin*—bitterberries. And even among the highest rocks, there were mosses and lichens, just like the patches of green now up on High Tor. Tiny bits of green in every cranny and crack; even the hard places. All holding on however they could; all clinging fiercely to life, any little way.

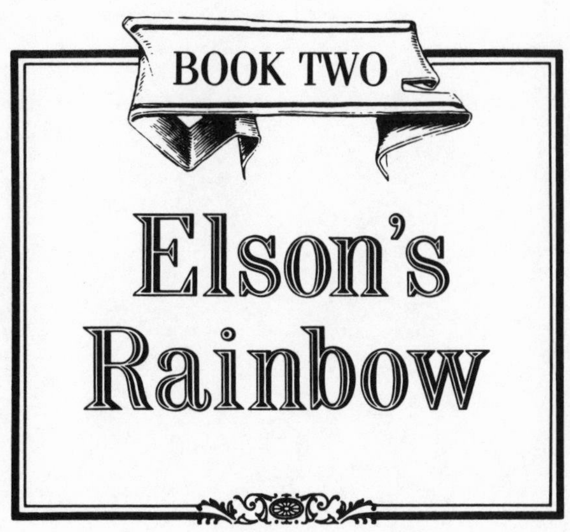

Elson's Rainbow

21

Trust Me

ON THE TRAIN. And this time no green anywhere. This time it was December, with the feel of winter in the air.

One station after another: each standing still, out the window, for half a minute, maybe two. Then the lurch of the train, the station slipping away, the wheels clicking on the rails. One station after another, each sliding slowly beyond reach. To George, it seemed like the iron rails were running him straight into a trap.

He stared out the window. This was the season, all right. Around Missanabie and Chapleau and Jackpine—all along the track—the traps were out. In Labrador, too, the "b'ys" would be off working their lines. You'd cover so many traps a day, and in one or two—well, maybe you'd find a fox. If he was still alive, you had to finish him quick, Indian style. In winter you could walk right over him in your snowshoes, pinning him down so he couldn't snap or claw. Then, with one hand, you grabbed behind the neck and pulled him up, hind end still pinned. With your other hand, you felt quick for his heart—pounding wild against his ribs—and caught it between thumb and fingers, pulling hard until the heartstrings snapped.

A yank, a quiver, and that was it—quick and merciful. And sure better than knocking his skull a couple times with an ax.

But George knew, now, what it was like to have to wait trapped like a fox. Listening for every twig snapping in the distance; waiting and not knowing who had put those steel jaws there or what was going to happen next. But knowing whatever it was, it smelled of fear and darkness.

George got his first dose of waiting at Grand Lake, just out of the bush. Three long days had passed before he heard what happened to the boys. Three days of not being able to sleep, wondering when the trouble would begin and somebody'd start to get after him because he survived and the white men hadn't. Oh, they'd get after him, all right! Half-breed and all. There'd be trouble. Three days he'd had to wait before he finally heard that Wallace had lived and everybody believed his story. Looking back now, those three days seemed like nothing.

The letter had come down the tracks to Missanabie like the trump of doom. Even before George opened it, he'd seen it was from her. But he hardly expected what was inside. The Lord himself wouldn't have. George had thought to find—well, he didn't know quite what. Maybe a bit of news and a note thanking him. At the funeral, there hadn't been time to say much. Before he left she'd asked if he wouldn't visit sometime when she was feeling a little better. And he'd said yes—anybody would. But he didn't really think she'd ever ask.

Well, she was asking.

She was doing more than asking; she was near about summoning him. There were things she wanted to find out, she said, about the trip; questions she hadn't got answered. The sentences read like lightning bolts.

She had reason to doubt now some of the things Wallace told her.

She wanted to know more of what happened to her husband in the last days.

She wanted to know what George had done after he left Mr. Hubbard.

She wanted to know what Wallace had done. Especially she wanted to know what Wallace had done.

What it amounted to was, she like as much accused them of leaving Mr. Hubbard out there to die. Just to think the thought made George's mouth go dry.

But why? Dear Lord Jesus—why?

Hadn't she read Mr. Hubbard's letter? And hadn't Mr. Hubbard said there weren't any finer men he could have with him? *Done their utmost*—that's what the letter to Mr. King said. She knew that!

But it was like none of it had ever been written. She wanted to see him, she said, at his earliest convenience. She had moved and was now living in Williamstown, Massachusetts. Mr. Wallace was staying in North Adams, nearby. If George would let her know the train he was on, she would make the necessary arrangements.

Out the window the stations slipped by one after another, somebody hopping on, somebody off. George wanted to hop off.

In Montreal he had to change trains. The way the schedules for Williamstown worked, you had to stay overnight. He put up at the St. James Hotel, two blocks from the station. At least he could get some rest before going down.

But when he tried to sleep, things kept coming into his head. What could Wallace have said that made her so angry? In the letter she seemed to be getting after Wallace worse than him. What would she want George to say? Would Wallace take kindly to him coming down without his say-so? The whole business made him uneasy.

Before leaving the next day, he got some hotel stationery. George didn't feel as close to Wallace as he had to Hubbard, but he didn't want to do him wrong either. He'd written once from Missanabie, but he thought maybe he'd better try again.

In haste, he scrawled

Montreal Dec 13th 1904

Dear Mr Wallace

just as told—I am on my way to Williamstown. I had promised Mrs. Hubbard before when she asked me if I could come and I gess I am am in a fix but—I hope I wont ofend you as I couldn't very well deny her as she might think at the same time we are guilty and you will hurt me. that—I will in telling her of our trip that Nothing may be blamed of us as I think we had done what Man could do and nothing more. I shall be very carefull and trust me. I am as always Yours

Truly

George Elson

And I hope to see you before my return as you will heare from me from Williamstown hoping to here from you Soon. Yours as always

Geo Elson

Then he was running to catch the train, dreading to think what waited in Williamstown, watching the stations slide by, each one an escape past taking.

This time, no green anywhere. This time, the feel of winter in the air.

22

The Purple Valley

WILLIAMSTOWN was the kind of place Laddie would have loved. Unlike Congers, it lay well beyond the metropolitan orb. Instead of trolleys and whistles, it belonged to farm wagons and lowing Holsteins. And the nearest trout stream, the Green, was only a short stroll away.

Upon taking up residence during the last slanting days of summer, Mina had been struck by the peculiar deep color of the landscape. The broad valley was almost purple. It came, perhaps, from a mingling of New England colors: the sun's bright yellow gentled by the mountain haze and then mixed with the lush green of the farmlands. Though remarkably rich and intense, the color was elusive as mist. Strolling into the hills, Mina found that the purple hue constantly receded; it seemed so very real, yet was impossible to reach.

In September, when the first frosts came and the leaves turned, she was surprised again. She had never seen such brilliant reds and oranges; had never lived in a place so bright and gay. In her present condition, it made her feel foreign and out of place—wretched and alone. Sometimes, walking in the evening, she would be treated to the most amazing sunsets, glorious displays of light that would sweep her up and lead her to forget; and she would think to herself that she must bring Laddie here to see the sky.

All her Williamstown friends, and even her pastor, Dr. Sawyer, the dearest friend anyone could have, told her she was making a fine recovery. She was strong, they said, and courageous. And they told her how proud they were for the way she had decided to enroll and finish high school, although Mina suspected from a few unguarded glances that some of the ladies thought returning to public school a rather strange whim for a woman thirty years old, not to mention a trained nurse.

With the passage of time, the day-to-day routine had become a little easier. The requirements of school distracted her. Casual acquaintances had ceased squeezing her hand in that cloying way of theirs, and the neighborhood children no longer scurried away when they saw her approaching in her plain black dress and bonnet, with the dark veil trailing clear to the bottom of her skirt—swirling, when there was a breeze, like a mist that refused to recede.

Despite an outward calm, though, it often seemed to Mina that her heart was heavier and her grief more difficult to bear than ever. Seventeen months had passed since she had hugged Laddie on the deck of the *Virginia Lake,* knowing in her heart that she would never see him again. Still, for half a year she had been able to hope . . . until that cold day when the telegram from Wallace arrived. When Laddie's body was finally returned, she had suffered a nervous and physical collapse. She was tormented, knowing that the sealed casket held only the mortal remains and not Laddie himself, knowing that her desire to open the box was foolish and irrational, wanting not to think about the wasted, decaying flesh inside, yet being unable to control her own imagination; then being horrified at what her imagination saw. . . . It still made her shudder.

The early weeks after he was laid to rest were an agony. But the present period, the time that was supposed to be one of re-awakening and beginning anew, was filled with the cruelest pain of all. No matter what people said or expected, she was not "re-covering" from Laddie's death. She would never recover and would never want to. Any little incident was enough to spark a cherished memory, and then she would imagine him smiling or sense the gentle touch of his hand, only to pounce upon the memory, savoring it again and again. She couldn't help herself. The melancholy seared her, yet it was also inexpressibly sweet. She wanted to linger with Laddie any way she could.

She thought often of his last day—October eighteenth. What had she been doing? Had she felt anything special? She had prayed for him, of course, and more than usual: It had been a Sunday. Again and again, she read the last entry from his diary. "My tent is pitched in open-tent style in front of a big rock. The rock reflects the fire, but now it is going out because of the rain. I think I shall let it go and close the tent. . . ." She tried to imagine what it had been like, wishing desperately to have been there, where she could have done something—at least nursed him properly, as she had nursed him once before when he was so close to death. "I am sleepy. I think death from starvation is not so bad. But let no one suppose that I expect it. I am prepared, that is all. I think the boys will be able with the Lord's help to save me."

But they hadn't. Wallace had never gotten back with the flour. Oh, how she wished she could have been there!

Thinking so, she would get down on her knees and pray. Dr. Sawyer encouraged her in her prayer, believing that it would give her strength. She had never dared tell him that as she fell to her knees she often found herself praying not to Jesus but directly to Laddie. Then the tears would come, and she would sob uncontrollably at the memory of his final, wrenching letter—the scrap of paper Wallace had given her out of the diary. All of Laddie's remaining strength had gone into trying to write that "long, long" letter to his sweetheart. And the effort had proved too much.

She would find herself at the writing table, pen in hand. She couldn't help it. She would just begin writing.

Dear Laddie . . .

She poured out her thoughts in these letters; what she was feeling, how she longed to see him. She told him what had happened since he had gone; what she was doing that day. The writing seemed to help—a little anyway. She would have days when she seemed to be doing quite well. And then, without warning, another sharp remembrance would send her into tears, and back she would go to her writing desk.

As for the future, she had stopped thinking about it. It seemed she didn't have one. Once she had been married to a loving husband, the two of them living a wonderful life together. Now she didn't even have a home, the Congers house having been sold to raise money for the expedition. So long as she was waiting for Laddie to return, she had been content to stay with her sister and parents near Toronto. But moving in with her family indefinitely was impossible: She was too stubbornly independent for that. Still, where else could she settle? Upon the encouragement of Dr. Sawyer and a few other friends, she had finally chosen Williamstown.

There she could also keep in contact with Wallace, who had family in North Adams, just five miles away. At first she had looked forward to their occasional meetings—had wanted to glean from him every possible detail about all that Laddie had done. But these conversations proved difficult. Wallace would try to be cheerful, not wanting to upset her; then, when he came to painful ground, would falter. The scenes he described seemed far away, as if across a broad dark lake. She found no solace in them.

All the same, the two of them managed to work out the business about a book. That last day in Labrador, Laddie had made Wallace promise to write the story of the expedition. He talked with her about the difficulties he anticipated. He was a lawyer, he said, not a writer. He didn't have Leon's talent with words or his literary grace.

She urged him on. It had been Laddie's wish, after all. And something needed to be done—of that she was fiercely convinced. The newspapers were ruining Laddie's reputation, pointing up his supposed "mistakes." *Forest and Stream* magazine had printed rubbish about the expedition plunging "fatuously into what they believed to be unexplored wilderness . . . insufficiently provisioned" and "unequipped with any knowledge of woodcraft which might sustain them." Dilettantes who had never even laid eyes on Labrador were writing letters to the press describing edible plants and abundant fish. One insufferable prig noted how "personally, I would rather be there now than to have the best room and board at the Waldorf-Astoria, though I dine there tonight."

Laddie deserved better; somehow Wallace just had to write a true account of what had happened—a story for all posterity. Finally they came up with a plan. Mina would use her savings to hire a professional journalist, a ghost, to help with the writing.

Wallace drew up a contract. She was to pay a fee of a thousand dollars—$250 immediately, and the balance upon completion of the manuscript. The contract specified that he was to do the best he could in telling the story; it made no actual mention of Frank Barkham Copley. Ghosts were, after all, meant to be invisible.

Soon after Thanksgiving, well ahead of schedule, Wallace arrived in Williamstown, with a thick bundle under one arm. Mina brimmed with anticipation. She could hardly wait for Wallace to depart so she might hurry to her reading chair, unwrap the packet, and begin reading:

THE LURE OF THE LABRADOR WILD
THE STORY OF THE EXPLORING EXPEDITION
CONDUCTED BY LEONIDAS HUBBARD, JR.

It seemed a good title. Carefully she lifted off the top sheet. A dedication page followed.

L.H.
Here, b'y, is the issue
of our plighted troth.
Why I am the scribe
and not you, God knows:
and you have His secret.
D.W.

The story began with the winter outing in the Shawangunk Mountains, where Laddie had proposed the idea of a Labrador expedition. Wallace seemed to succeed in catching his infectious enthusiasm. "Man, don't you realize it's about the only part of the continent that hasn't been explored? . . . Think of it, Wallace! A great unknown land right near home, as wild and primitive today as it has always been! I want to see it. . . ." If anything, she thought, the description went a bit overboard. In recounting the day Hubbard finally committed himself to the trip, Wallace noted, "I shall never forget the exuberance of his joy. You would have thought he was a boy about to be released from school." Well, Wallace was ten years older than Laddie. It was a point easily enough corrected.

The story proceeded pleasantly enough until the party was canoeing down Grand Lake. In describing their progress, Wallace admitted right out that they had been "mistaken" in missing the Naskapi River, instead going up Susan Brook.

> Perhaps it will be said we should have explored the bay. I know now myself that should have been done, but in justice to Hubbard it must be remembered that none of us then had any reason to suppose we should find a river at any place other than the extreme upper end of the lake. Time and again Hubbard had asked the few natives who had been there if the Nascaupee entered Grand Lake at its extreme upper end, and the answer invariably had been: "Yes, sir; he do."

Reading this, Mina felt uneasy. It was true that Wallace was defending her husband, but at the same time he was implying that Laddie was to blame for not scouting the bay. It was more the tone, really—to her, it read a bit as if Wallace knew better, even if her husband didn't. Even worse was Wallace's account of the conversation that took place around the campfire that evening on the Susan. Supposedly Wallace reminded Hubbard of Donald Blake's claim to having sailed his boat up the Naskapi eighteen or twenty miles. Wallace then continued, "I'd be willing to bet he never sailed it up this stream." But Hubbard, in Wallace's version, paid no heed to the remark, replying only, "Oh, he was mistaken in the distance. . . . What do you say, boys, to throwing away some of the outfit? We'll never make any progress if we attempt to carry it all." It was George, according to the narrative, who countered Hubbard's suggestion by saying, "Let's stick to it a little longer."

Mina frowned. That couldn't be right. Why, it sounded almost as if Laddie could have found the right river and had plenty of food if he had only followed Wallace and George's advice. Perhaps Wallace didn't mean to convey that impression, but that was how the passage struck her.

As she continued reading her anxiety mounted. Wallace kept saying how much he respected Laddie, but it still seemed to appear, somehow, that Laddie was continually bungling things. Wallace referred to Hubbard shooting their caribou a second time with "nervous impetuosity," over George's protest. When Laddie got lost in the bush, or had to stay in camp alone, Wallace had him confiding afterward that he'd been "scared" or "lonesome" or "homesick"; but when Wallace himself got lost, she found no such confession.

And then came the long portage. Wallace's description of it was awful. Laddie appeared "nervously active by habit," and therefore the search for an outlet to Lake Disappointment was "particularly trying on his nerves, and left him a prey to many fears." Again—Wallace seemed to be sympathetic, but the results were unfortunate:

> Hubbard was the leader of the expedition, and he felt himself responsible, not only for his own life, but to a large extent, for ours. It is little wonder, therefore, that he brooded over the possibilities of calamity; but with youth, ambition, and the ardent spirit that never will say die, he invariably fought off his fears, and bent himself more determinedly than ever to achieve the purpose for which he had set out. Frequently he confided his fears to me, but was careful to conceal all traces of them from George.

As the story of the portage continued it seemed to Mina that nearly every page divulged yet another glimpse of Laddie "homesick" or "worrying" or "anxious about the sufficiency of the material he had gathered for a story." And then Wallace would appear by his side, telling him not to fear. Really! Who was leading this expedition?

And then on Windbound Lake—oh, this was too much; it was shameful!—here was Wallace talking about a "great change" in Laddie:

> Heretofore the work he had to do had seemed almost wholly to occupy his thoughts. Now he craved companionship, and he loved to sit with me and dwell on his home and his wife, his mother and sister. . . . Undoubtedly the boy was beginning to suffer severely from homesickness—he was only a young fellow, you know, with a gentle, affectionate nature that gripped him tight to the persons and objects he loved. Our little confidential chats grew to be quite the order of things. . . .

By now Mina could hardly bear to read the descriptions of her husband growing weaker and weaker; failing, apparently, at a much faster rate than either George or Wallace. The manuscript described him looking so much like a skeleton that he was ashamed to bathe . . . staggering when he walked down the trail . . . "going all to pieces nervously" when his memory failed him. And then Wallace had the gall to conclude that "the most pitiable part was his fear that George and I should notice his weakness and lose courage." Courage! Who possessed the *real* courage of the trip? Who was left alone to face death calmly and bravely without flinching?

She finished the manuscript, white with anger. How could Wallace imagine that anything so distorted and unbalanced would serve as a memorial to her husband? Did he have the audacity to suppose she intended to pay him a thousand dollars for such a wretched account?

The manuscript totally unraveled her. A year ago she had felt far away from Labrador and from Laddie's adventures: His light had played off among the distant hills, and she had wanted desperately to be there. Now, the man who had the privilege of being with her husband in his last hours was making the expedition seem entirely unworthy. He was describing a world that could not have existed—*had* not existed, for anyone who knew Laddie as well as she did.

She began working the problem over, trying to fit the facts into a pattern corresponding to what she knew must be the truth of the case. First, she needed information. Straightaway she demanded that Wallace return her husband's papers. Wallace returned the diary but refused to part with Laddie's field book or photographs. What was he trying to hide?

Over and over, she read the diary. Yes, it was true some of the things Wallace said were there; but that was only natural. Laddie's longing for home and for his "dearest" were private matters. Unfortunately, Wallace didn't possess the refinement of character to omit such details from a public account. More important, there was nothing to suggest that Laddie had taken the wrong river at the outset. She had accepted what the newspapers and Wallace had said about the Susan; but really, how did she know whether Laddie had actually missed the Naskapi? Nothing in the diary said so.

Once this germ of a suspicion had been planted, she found it impossible to rid herself of it. She couldn't help thinking about Wallace in a new light. He was a rather vulgar sort; what had her husband seen in the man anyway? Leon had taken up with him in a moment of weakness, during the bout with typhoid; he had always been generous to a fault with his friends. It certainly seemed as if his confidence had been misplaced.

Her thoughts turned again to that fateful October eighteenth. Wallace and George had left Laddie, George to go for help at Blake's cache, Wallace to bring flour from a bag left along the trail. Mina had no reason to doubt that George had done his best. But what about Wallace and the flour? Wallace *claimed* to have made a heroic effort to find Laddie's tent, but then had become delirious, losing all track of time. Could she really believe that? Look how he had distorted the earlier parts of the story! Could she accept his word here, with no other evidence to back it up?

There was Wallace's earlier letter to his sisters, of course; that was another source of information. The letter was the first account of the tragedy to reach the outside world, and all the newspapers had published it. She found a copy. It was even more galling than she remembered—much worse than the manuscript. "We plunged madly into the interior of an unknown country," Wallace had written to his sisters; "into regions never before trod by white men, with almost no provisions. For our trip we should have had 550 pounds of flour—we had 120 pounds; we should have taken 200 pounds of bacon or pork—we had 25 pounds; and so on all down the line." To have such an allegation printed publicly was humiliating. No wonder the newspapers had been talking about "babes in the woods"!

She went on, reading carefully Wallace's description of his attempt to bring the flour to Laddie:

> The snowstorm never ceased night and day. . . . The next day I forded the river, breaking the thin ice on the edge until I reached ice thick enough to bear me. . . . The next day I was still far from camp when night came, and the third day I walked the greater part of the night. The river was now frozen. The snow had obliterated all landmarks, and after walking up and down several times where I thought the camp must be I was at length compelled to give up the search, and headed toward Grand Lake.

I was at length compelled to give up the search. . . . Mina pounced upon the words in anger and in triumph. There it was—much plainer than in the manuscript. Wallace hadn't become delirious—he'd simply given up and turned back, leaving Laddie for dead in the woods! All the talk about hearing voices and wandering aimlessly came later, and was probably exaggerated anyway. Wallace had convicted himself by his own evidence.

For Mina, that piece of knowledge—that certainty—made all of Wallace's other loyal declarations worthless. In her eyes the man had become totally unfit to uphold her husband's reputation. The book's dedication rang harshly in her ears now: "Here, b'y, is the issue of our plighted troth. . . ." Who was Wallace to be addressing her husband so intimately? She was the one who had "plighted troth" at the altar. She was the one who had remained faithful to the very end. And now his reputation, his honor, his achievement—all that remained for him in this world—were about to be destroyed by a hopelessly distorted account. It was almost too much to bear.

She had mourned her beloved for too long to expect balm or relief. She had pined and prayed, tried letter writing, tried seclusion, tried all the usual rituals. They had failed her.

But she would not fail Laddie. She would do whatever was necessary to redeem the honor of his name. With winter approaching, and the fields stiff with frost, she sat down at her writing table and addressed two letters. One was to George Elson; the other, to Dillon Wallace himself.

23

Hard Choice

After drawing up his contract with Mrs. Hubbard, Wallace had engaged Frank Copley and moved into his cousin's farm near North Adams. There, holing up with Hubbard's diary and field notes, plus his own journal, he and Copley went to work. To Wallace's relief the writing went more quickly and more easily than he could ever have imagined. He discovered that he had only to read over the water-stained entries of the diaries to trigger whole constellations of memories. Each day's events came back with a vivid clarity—all that had to be done was type them up, divide the whole into chapters, and add a few grace notes here and there. When he hit a rough spot, Copley smoothed it out.

When the climactic moment came and Copley rolled the last sheet from the typewriter, Wallace felt an immense sense of accomplishment. He had finished—and even ahead of schedule. But he also experienced a twinge of apprehension. Would people actually want to read the book? Would they like it? Would they be moved?

Mrs. Hubbard's response, once he had presented her the manuscript, was not long in coming: She sent a note asking to meet with him immediately. Any hope, however, that the swiftness of her reaction was an indication of enthusiasm disappeared at their interview. Wallace had only to see the paleness of her face and the reserve in her eyes to know that something was dreadfully amiss. His shock increased as she began to discuss the book.

There would have to be changes, she said. There were some . . . unfortunate statements. Grimly she began paging through the manuscript. Here, for instance. Mr. Hubbard was not shown in the proper light. The tone was wrong. And here: This passage was indelicately written. In any case, it was impossible for her to believe that events had occurred precisely the way they were described. Here. And here. The pages kept turning. She became more agitated and upset as she went along; her eyes started to flash.

Wallace was struck dumb—absolutely at a loss for words. More than anything else, it was the vehemence of her reaction that startled him. During the past months, he had immersed himself in his writing, reliving day-by-day the hardships of the trail. The task of finishing the book had come to fill his life, crowding nearly everything else out of his waking hours and even out of his dreams. Now here was Mrs. Hubbard: obviously distraught, obviously angry, telling him there would have to be revisions; stopping at nearly every page with something that seemed wrong to her.

Wallace tried to find his tongue. It wasn't so much what she was saying as how. She acted as if he had insulted Hubbard throughout the book. It was unbelievable. Why, the whole manuscript, from start to finish, was a tribute to Hubbard's memory. Hubbard was the hero of the thing. Wallace wanted to point out how unstinting his praise had been. There was the last chapter, where he described Hubbard's "noble character, his simple faith . . . his bravery, his indomitable will. . . ." All these qualities, Wallace had written, "shall not be forgotten; they shall remain a living example to all who love bravery and self-sacrifice." But that was only the end of the book—his devotion was clear throughout. How on earth could anybody think he was slighting his dearest friend? The book was dedicated to Hubbard!

As she continued to jump from page to page it occurred to him that the problem was not with the book after all. The problem was, Mina Hubbard could not believe that things had actually happened the way they had. She didn't like it when he described Hubbard as worried over whether he had a good story for Caspar Whitney. She didn't think it right to admit that Hubbard was homesick. How could Wallace possibly write that Hubbard's memory had been failing?

But . . .

But all these things had happened. You couldn't change what *happened*. Nobody could do that.

If anything, he felt he had been rather diplomatic about some of Hubbard's weaknesses. The nervousness, for example. Hubbard's high-strung nature, combined with the strain of all the early delays, had made him more fidgety and anxious than Wallace had cared to reveal in his account. As for the homesickness—that was simply the plain truth. Hubbard himself had admitted as much more than once in his diary. Furthermore, Wallace had not said a word about a deficiency that, in retrospect, had become clear to him. That was Hubbard's lack of experience. In the manuscript he was introduced as an outdoorsman who had made "several long trips into the wild," including visits to the "Hudson Bay region" and the "winter hunting ground of the Mountaineer Indians." In point of fact, this so-called "Hudson Bay region" was merely the Missanabie railroad station and its environs—the fifty or sixty miles where Hubbard had paddled with Mina on his vacation, a location hundreds of miles to the south of Hudson Bay. As for the winter hunting trip, that had been hardly more than a weekend hike.

Wallace tried tactfully to explain a few of these circumstances to Mrs. Hubbard. Any explanation seemed only to make her fiercer and paler and more upset. She could hardly entertain thoughts of further progress on the project, she said—not unless the necessary changes were made.

For his part, Wallace didn't see how he could change circumstances. He couldn't change what actually happened. He understood how stricken she must feel about the loss of her husband, and how difficult these past months had been, but . . .

It seemed the interview was at an end. Perplexed and feeling totally at sea, Wallace gathered up his papers, bowed stiffly, and took his leave.

GEORGE STEPPED off the Williamstown train, feeling like a fox ready to have his heart pulled. Nothing to do but wait for the blow.

When he first caught sight of her, he was near to trembling. She still had on her widow's black, with the veil hanging behind now, instead of over her face. Her face looked pale. But she didn't glare or mention any of the things she'd put in the letter.

She introduced him to Reverend Sawyer, who was the minister of her church. The Reverend was the one who saw to George's sleeping arrangements. He visited with Mrs. Hubbard and George a lot of the time; seemed interested in George and easy to get along with.

Finally the time came George was expecting.

She asked him to tell the story, and he told it, start to finish. The early part, down Grand Lake and up the Susan, seemed easiest to talk about. The work had been hard then, but there had been good times too, around the evening fires or catching the geese and caribou. Once George began talking, it seemed impossible to stop—he had to keep on, telling about each pond and lake they traveled on the long portage, how they crossed the mountains and ran the rapids of the Beaver River. He remembered these events like they'd happened the day before. When he came to the part where Hubbard busted, he couldn't help himself; he began to cry. But he kept on to the end.

She asked questions. And to these George listened anxiously, trying to hear the tone in her voice; where there was blame in it, and where reproach. He wanted to see what had pricked her so.

There did not seem to be blame. She did really trust him and believed what he had to say. When she asked if Mr. Hubbard had really missed the Naskapi River, he told her straight out how Duncan McLean and Allen Goudie showed him the mouth of the real Naskapi later. Hubbard had missed it. They all had.

And she accepted that.

But when it came to Wallace, that was a different story. Wallace was where the wind was blowing. You'd only have to mention his name to see her face grow dark.

She wanted to know what Wallace had actually done when he left George to go back with the flour to Hubbard. Wallace claimed, she said, that he had traveled up Susan Brook well past Mr. Hubbard's camp before turning back. He claimed he'd spent a great deal of time looking for the tent.

George was uncomfortable. He'd been hiking toward Grand Lake when all that happened. He'd only heard what Allen Goudie and Duncan McLean said—which was that they'd followed Wallace's tracks up the brook, and the tracks stopped by that brook a hundred yards from the tent. It looked like Wallace had never got beyond. Well, Mrs. Hubbard picked right up on that. She said it proved what she thought all along—that Wallace's book was full of wild stories and exaggerations. His book made it sound like Mr. Hubbard had made one mistake after another. It made Wallace out to be the real leader, with Mr. Hubbard depending on him to get through.

George hardly knew what to say. He hadn't seen what Wallace wrote. It seemed hard to believe Wallace could make things up like that.

On the other hand, the two of them hadn't gotten on so well that winter at Northwest River. Wallace had tried to order George into the bush a second time to haul Hubbard's canoe back—trying to boss him around when it had been Hubbard's expedition, not Wallace's. Mr. Hubbard had always treated George like a partner—let him make a lot of the decisions and gone by his plans generally. Wallace didn't seem to do that. He treated George more like a servant.

The more Mrs. Hubbard talked about the awful things Wallace had written, the more disturbed George got. Maybe Wallace *had* tried to grab the credit in this book.

Mrs. Hubbard spoke so quiet and earnest. Her husband was gone, she said. Nothing could bring him back, and they all prayed and believed he was in a better world than he had ever known before. But she did want his memory to be preserved. He was a man who should be remembered for many years after. That was why she wanted to tell his story in the proper way—not the way Wallace had done it. And why she was counting on George to help.

The back of George's neck began to prickle. Help?

She wanted to publish Mr. Hubbard's diary, she said. But the diary couldn't tell the end of the story. Only George could say what had happened afterward. Would he write down his own memories for her? He could do it day by day, like a journal. And then she would publish his story along with Mr. Hubbard's.

George hardly knew what to say. Coming down on the train, he had tried to imagine every possible fate that lay awaiting him in Williamstown. Never in his wildest dreams had he imagined being asked to help write a book. How could he refuse?

Yet it came into his mind—what would Wallace think? All things put together, Wallace probably wouldn't think too much of it. In fact, he probably wouldn't like it at all—seeing the way Mrs. Hubbard was feeling toward him. But George would only write the truth. He made that plain to her. He would not make up any stories about Wallace. And she said, of course; she wanted him only to say what really happened. How could that hurt Wallace? George had to believe—how could the truth hurt Wallace?

A real book—and his own words in it! When George thought it over, he really had no choice. Hubbard was the man he owed his loyalty to. He had never met a man like Hubbard. If she wanted him to write what happened in their last days together, he would do it.

When he got back to Missanabie, the snow was piling up. Christmas came and went and the snow kept falling, but that didn't stop the Canadian Pacific. Engines with plows came barreling down the tracks, pushing the drifts to either side so the trains could go through. It brought not only passengers but mail. And Mrs. Hubbard's letters were about as regular as the mail.

George had never had so many letters from the outside. Each one gave him a twinge, just to look at it. After that first one, he never knew what to expect.

Sometimes there was news about the book. She had written the story of Mr. Hubbard's boyhood, she said; told how he went to the university, got his job with *Outing*, and so on. She planned to use that as an introduction to the diary. But then, in early February, he got another letter. This time, she said she was convinced that the only way her husband's name could be fully associated with Labrador was if his work was completed. She had considered seriously and decided the proper way to accomplish that was to organize an expedition of her own to Labrador.

George set back on both heels. Her own expedition?

That was what she was saying. In June, she intended to catch the first steamer to Northwest River. With a fully-equipped wilderness party, she was proposing to explore the Naskapi River all the way to Lake Michikamau. After she got to Michikamau, she intended to search for the headwaters of the George and visit the Indians. After she saw the Indians, she wanted to see the herds of caribou migrate across the country; and after she saw the caribou, she wanted to paddle north on the George River all the way to the Hudson's Bay post at Ungava. Also, she wanted to map all the country along the way. Well, what she wanted to do was everything that Mr. Hubbard had tried to do but hadn't.

George kept reading.

She knew she couldn't do this trip by herself, she said. She had to have a guide—somebody who could recruit other trustworthy men; somebody who could put together an outfit and know what to do in the bush. That was George, she said. He was the only man qualified to guide her expedition. And she knew he was the only one who would truly appreciate how her success would be a lasting tribute to Mr. Hubbard's memory.

George just shook his head. Labrador was no place for a woman like Mrs. Hubbard. She was full enough of spirit, but she was so delicate—just a wisp of a lady, and pale. Hadn't she listened to him in Williamstown when he told her how hard the country was? Dear Lord—hard! Mr. Hubbard had starved to death trying to do those things!

Besides, what would people think? What would they think of a man—a man like himself—going off into the wilderness with a white woman? That kind of thing, mixing like that—it just wasn't done. What did Mrs. Hubbard mean, anyway, saying he was the only person fit to accompany her? He wasn't fit at all!

And then—more trouble—more puzzles. Toward the end of the letter, she asked him in the strongest of terms not to speak a word of her project to anybody. Not yet. Because no matter what happened, she wanted not a hint of her plans to reach Wallace.

George spent days mulling that one over. He couldn't go, of course. He couldn't even begin to imagine Mrs. Hubbard wading those icy streams, fighting the black flies, gnawing on caribou hooves. And it sure would cause some awful talk, George Elson going into the bush with a white woman, a young attractive white woman. What if she got hurt along the trail and couldn't walk, or fell into the rapids and drowned? Or what if the same thing happened to her as happened with Hubbard? If George came out without a woman, he'd never be given a chance to explain—just skinned alive. He'd have to be crazy to hire out to Mrs. Hubbard.

All the same, he put off writing back. For one thing, he couldn't say outright that he wouldn't guide her because she was white; he just couldn't do that. And the devil was, he couldn't say that he didn't think he could get her through all the way to Ungava, because he thought he could. He knew Labrador now and wouldn't repeat the mistakes they made first time around. But most of all, he didn't write because he got a feeling, reading her letter, that this trip meant an awful lot to her. He knew how much she cared for Mr. Hubbard and wanted to do what was right by him. And George didn't want to let her down.

He was still worrying this point and that when another letter came down the tracks—this one postmarked New York and the name of the sender typed in big letters. Dillon Wallace.

It was getting so George didn't want to *open* letters. But he could guess pretty well what was inside—some of the developments Mrs. Hubbard had been hinting at. Sure enough—Wallace wrote to say he was heading north again, hoping to finish off what Hubbard had started. He was recruiting a few younger men to help with the hard work, he said. But he wanted George to guide—was counting on him—and hoped to have a reply at his earliest convenience.

So now there were two trips and two letters to write. And one hard choice.

On the face of it, he ought to go with Wallace—it was more regular. Certainly that was what Mr. King would advise. But George already had a taste of how Wallace might boss him around on his own expedition. On Mrs. Hubbard's trip, George would be the real leader. She trusted him to put the expedition together—get his own men, organize everything. If they were going up the Naskapi River and down the George, he'd want Job Chapies to come along. They'd been friends since boyhood days, and there wasn't anybody more trustworthy in the rapids. If George went with Wallace, though, who knew what men would go along? George surely wouldn't have any say.

Every way he thought it over, Mrs. Hubbard was the one he wanted to go with—if he dared. But she'd told him not to breathe a word of anything to Wallace. How could he get around that? George had to write something . . . couldn't just leave Wallace hanging. If he wrote and told what was really happening—that he was going with Mrs. Hubbard—Wallace wouldn't be any too happy. And *she* wouldn't be any too happy.

He thought a long time. Then wrote her saying he'd come. Thought a while more and wrote Wallace. He couldn't come, he told Wallace. He was getting married in the spring. With his new wife, he couldn't manage any trips away from Missanabie. He hoped Wallace would find somebody else to guide, and have a good trip.

George didn't like that, but what else could he do?

Then toward the end of April, something came down the tracks that stopped George worse than any letter and made him feel all over again like his heart was about to be pulled. What came down the tracks was Dillon Wallace. Himself.

George could hardly speak. He tried to be cheerful and act like nothing had happened, but it was pretty hard. Wallace looked uneasy too, though trying not to show it.

It was getting to be that time of the year, Wallace said. He was about ready to leave for Labrador.

Yes, George agreed. He'd been figurin' Wallace would be off pretty soon.

It was too bad George couldn't come along, said Wallace. He surely would be missed, not only by Wallace but all George's friends on the Labrador. Who was the lucky bride?

George studied the ends of his bootlaces like they were the only items of interest from there all the way to Chapleau. They were dangerous things to trip on, bootlaces.

He coughed. Well, the truth of the matter was . . .

The truth of the matter was, he wasn't getting married after all, he said. That is—well—that was it.

Wallace brightened. There was still an extra place, he said. George could still come.

No, said George. Thinking it over, he guessed he couldn't.

Wallace didn't seem to know what to say. He wondered if the pay wasn't as good as George might have hoped.

No, wasn't the pay . . .

Maybe someone else had hired him for the summer?

Well . . .

No, he just didn't think he could go, that was all. He was sorry about it, but he didn't think he could go.

He wanted to disappear into a swamp, that was what. He wanted to walk right to the end of the mudflats on Hudson's Bay and let the tide come in. But he'd promised her he wouldn't tell.

Wallace left looking pretty disappointed, like he'd been counting right from the start on having George along.

But it was over anyway, once and for all. George had made his choice. There was no going back.

24

Headed North

THE TRIP BACK to New York—alone—gave Wallace ample time to ponder, time he desperately needed. With the expedition scheduled to depart May 30, in less than a month, he still had no guide; and even worse, no lead to a replacement. Mr. King at Missanabie had been unable to help. And so, despite every exertion to the contrary, Wallace found himself in almost precisely the predicament Hubbard had faced two years earlier, scrambling about at the last minute to pull things together.

It was remarkable, the similarity of their situations. Wallace's initial hurdle had been the one that had first bedeviled Hubbard: how to finance his ambitions. After the failure of the first expedition, Caspar Whitney of *Outing* had quickly backed away, claiming he had been "frankly not in sympathy" with Hubbard's plan, "because I considered it not worth the time and money." But when Wallace's *Lure of the Labrador Wild* appeared in February 1905, the book proved remarkably popular, receiving favorable reviews and going into a new printing almost immediately. Whitney quickly agreed to sponsor the new expedition and publish Wallace's account of it.

Wallace had other financial schemes too. In 1903 he had met several prospectors on the *Virginia Lake,* all heading to the Labrador coast in search of gold. Why not keep an eye open for valuable ore while traveling inland? He might just hit upon another Klondike. Even if he didn't strike it rich, a scientific survey would add to the value of his trip. Wallace placed newspaper advertisements for young volunteers with training in geology or related natural sciences. A college student would be just the thing: someone willing to come along for the sake of adventure rather than cold, hard cash.

The strategy worked. By March he had signed on a Columbia

student, a strapping fellow by the name of George Richards. Richards looked young; at times his rounded features and full lips gave his face an almost babyish cast. But he had a big, strong frame, a confident manner, and his undergraduate studies gave him passing familiarity with geology.

Wallace was also approached by a twenty-one-year-old forestry student named Clifford Easton. Easton had studied at the Biltmore School in North Carolina and the previous summer had completed a seven-hundred-mile canoe trip in Canada. He was a spare, thin-framed lad, but he possessed an earnest enthusiasm. Wallace took him on.

Still, there was no venturing north without an Indian guide or camp servant of some sort. Returning to New York, Wallace canvassed his sporting acquaintances and came up with the name of Peter Stevens, a full-blood Ojibway guide. Hailing from Grand Marais, Minnesota, Stevens hunted along the old fur-trading routes of the voyageurs and came highly recommended. The Montreal Express brought him to Grand Central late in May. He proved to be a swarthy young man who spoke only halting English, of slighter frame than Elson and not nearly so ready to look a white man in the eye. Yet he seemed healthy and willing.

As for Wallace's own spirits, he was determined to put the unpleasantness of Mina Hubbard behind him. At least he would be shut of the matter once the *S.S. Rosalind* sailed from Brooklyn for Halifax and St. John's. To the outside world, of course, he maintained a confident demeanor. "Poor Hubbard's fate doesn't scare me," he told reporters. "It only teaches me a valuable lesson. In the first place, I shall take care to make the expedition much better provided than was Hubbard's. Then, too, I have learned a great deal about the country." Referring to George Richards, he couldn't help making a little joke. "He's a young man," said Wallace, "and young blood, of course is preferable on an expedition of this kind." He paused. "I am myself over forty. . . . I suppose I am too old to make this attempt. But I assure you—a younger man will find it a hard job to keep pace with me."

BY THE END OF MAY, Mina had moved headquarters to her parents' home in Bewdley, Ontario. Over the spring she had marshaled the support of several important allies—a publisher named Phillips, who persuaded her to combine Laddie's diary and George's tale of 1903

with a narrative of her own crossing of Labrador; Herbert Bridgman, himself a well-known newspaper publisher, who obtained for Mina the backing of the Peary Arctic Club; and William Cabot, Hubbard's friend from Boston. All those months, however, she remained in deep mourning, insisting on her privacy—and convinced that the success of her expedition depended upon stealth.

By meeting George in Bewdley, she could be sure that no premature word of her plans reached her rival. George arrived on schedule with a small mountain of gear and two companions, both from the Hudson Bay region. Job Chapies was a full-blood Cree who spoke hardly any English but who had such a fine, broad smile that it seemed vocabulary enough. Joe Iserhoff was half-Cree, half-Russian, with a lean face and quiet manner. Despite his ancestry, he spoke in a pleasant, low, Scottish accent.

As for the outfit, Mina gave clear instructions. The only way, she believed, to prove Wallace wrong about her husband would be to duplicate the original expedition in every way. By surviving with the same kind of food and equipment, she would prove her point.

Certain differences, of course, could not be avoided. For one thing, George intended to hire Duncan McLean once they got to Northwest River. Duncan would raise the party to five and allow for two canoes. Accordingly, Mina agreed to increase the rations: 392 pounds of flour, for example, up from 120 pounds; 200 pounds of bacon instead of 25; also a new entry, 20 cans standard emergency rations. To carry the extra men and gear, she further acceded to George's suggestion that the canoes be nineteen footers instead of the original eighteen. George also packed two gill nets, taking care this time to bring them from home. But she drew the line when it came to the matter of a shotgun. Wallace had practically blamed Laddie's death on his failure to carry one. The 1905 Hubbard expedition would bring two rifles and five pistols. That was all.

By the first of June she was growing impatient. Wallace's itinerary was well known. He was to have left New York on May 30 for Halifax, Nova Scotia, and then Newfoundland, there to pick up the *Virginia Lake* for its usual run north. Mina, meanwhile, had made arrangements to sail directly from Halifax to Labrador, on the lumber ship *Harlow*. By avoiding the stopover in Newfoundland, she hoped to beat Wallace to the Labrador coast. At long last word came of a break in the winter ice; on June 5, Mina and her party left Bewdley, anxious to be headed north.

25

Bricks Without Straw

SAILING NORTH on the *Rosalind*, Clifford Easton found out what he already knew—that Mr. Wallace walked about ten feet tall in these parts. Everywhere they went, he turned heads. Was this *the* Dillon Wallace, people wanted to know, the explorer and noted author? After Robert Peary, he was about the biggest man in the North.

On their first stopover, Mr. Wallace was guest of honor at the Halifax Club and later was interviewed by the local newspaper. It was a fine session. He praised Labrador for having a great future, then talked about his own feeling of confidence heading into that fateful land again. He introduced his companions, and the way he did it ("George M. Richards, the geologist from Columbia University; C. H. Easton from the Biltmore School of Forestry"), you'd never guess they were just a couple of college kids. When somebody asked the whereabouts of his former guide, George Elson, he didn't drop a beat—just talked about Pete Stevens like he was a cross between Geronimo and Daniel Boone.

The fifth recruit for the trip also joined the party in Halifax, a chap by the name of Leigh Stanton. Stanton was closer to Wallace's age—somewhere in his late thirties maybe. He'd been working at the lumber mill in Kenemish the winter Wallace was sick there, and the two of them had gotten to be pals. Stanton wasn't exactly a woodsman, but he'd knocked around a lot and been off to the Boer War with the First Canadian. Folks around Halifax knew him from his railroad career on the Canadian Pacific, mainly working the dining car between Truro and Brownville, Maine.

Stanton brought more than his baggage—he had news. He'd been hanging around the wharf, and the word there was that Mrs. Hubbard was due in town in another week, planning to take a trip of her own to Labrador! *That* was good for a few hairs out of Mr. Wallace's mustache. The other firecracker in the string was that George Elson was coming along too, as part of her crew.

Easton was burning to find out more. There was bad blood between Mrs. Hubbard and Mr. Wallace—he knew that much. But Wallace was a quiet man, slow to anger, and he didn't air grievances publicly. Easton had to respect him for that.

What they had to find out now was how to get to Labrador by the quickest route. Mr. Wallace talked with the lumber operator, Mr. Gillis, who said that the *Harlow* was going direct to Labrador but not for another ten days. So Wallace stuck with his original plan of going on to St. John's and connecting with the *Virginia Lake*. Anyway, who wanted to hang around Halifax? The coffee was terrible everywhere, the Halifax Club excepted.

The sail to St. John's took two days. There, they checked into the Balmoral Hotel and settled down to wait. It turned out the *Virginia Lake* wasn't due to leave for another ten days either, so things came out pretty much a draw in the matter of boats.

With plenty of time on his hands, Easton chummed around with Richards. They were the youngest on the expedition and it was only natural. Richards seemed a pretty burly fellow, never at a loss for an opinion and always confident of the lay of the land. Easton, on the other hand, worried about his thin, bony frame, and whether he would be able to keep up when it came to hauling loads along the trail. The two of them took long walks in the countryside around St. John's and up to Signal Hill, which overlooked the harbor. Out in the bay lay a massive iceberg that immediately seized Easton's imagination. It was a genuine piece of the Arctic, shimmering like a diamond! Day after day he climbed the hill to admire it. Finally, yielding to temptation, he borrowed a skiff from one of the salts and talked Richards into serving as first mate.

Rowing out to sea turned out to be tricky. The tide was running in, and, even though the harbor had only a chop, it was filled with swirling currents. More than once a rip grabbed the skiff and spun it around. But the two of them kept the oars flying and eventually made progress.

Up close, the berg loomed like a mountain. Easton sized it up, undaunted. After all, what did you do with a mountain?

Climb it!

Judging by the look on his face, Richards would have rather rowed to Ireland. But having gotten this far, Easton wasn't about to give up. The front wall of the iceberg was practically sheer, so the two of them maneuvered around to the back, out of view from shore. There they found a broad shelf above the reach of the waves and, rising beyond, a fissured slope that offered a route to the top. Easton hopped out of the skiff and started up. Richards stayed in the boat; his confidence seemed to have deserted him.

Underfoot, the berg didn't appear quite so grand—more a dirty gray than blue and silver. With every kick the surface crumbled into a mixture of crystalline ice loosely bound by granular snow. A few traverses across the open slope, a shimmy up an ice chute, then a boost over a little headwall, and Easton was at the summit.

"What's it like?" called Richards.

Easton waved his hat grandly, king of the mountain, surveying the harbor and shore. He knew that Stanton and Wallace were out walking the countryside somewhere. Could they possibly see him?

The salt air was in his nostrils and the breeze ruffled his hair. The only sounds were the sloshing of the waves against the berg and a little grinding noise, no doubt from the ice. And perhaps the barest, barest tremor.

Time to get down, Easton thought to himself.

Then the ice under his feet gave a lurch and the sea below made a horrible sucking sound.

Easton flailed, then began to slip and slide. The berg was apparently too rotten to hold together in the shearing of the cross-currents. Small cracks opened, then yawned into crevasses. Before he could scramble to the water's edge a chunk of the pinnacle broke off entirely, toppling toward the skiff. Easton had a glimpse of Richards' white upturned face and a wave lifting the boat as the ice crashed into the sea; then he was tumbled head over heels as giant slabs, some as big as houses, plummeted into the water with him.

The shock of the frigid currents made him gasp, while the momentum of his fall carried him deep underwater. Seawater filled his nose and sinuses; he gagged, only to inhale more water. He tried to kick to the surface, but the salt burned his eyes and he became so disoriented that, for all he knew, he was swimming straight for the bottom.

Ears ringing, lungs about to burst, he felt his face brush against something fiercely cold. In that moment he knew he was going to drown. He must have come up under the berg.

Water washed over him again—then the searing cold slapped a second time. He blinked open his eyes.

The cold was the wind wicking the water off his face. He gulped a huge breath, then gulped again, only to swallow the top of a wave.

Sputtering, chattering, he looked for the skiff. But on either side rose steep white walls, ice cliffs swaying in the lop. If the wind drove the fragments together, he would be crushed.

The numbing cold drained his strength. Even treading water became an effort. Desperately he paddled to a small icepan riding in the troughs. By throwing his arms around it, he was able to keep his head above water without having to swim, but the ice sucked away his warmth. His arms felt heavy and dense; he lost all feeling in them.

From out of the blue-and-white mountains, he heard a voice. "Easton!"

Easton managed a hoarse reply and turned numbly, trying to locate the source. The skiff hadn't capsized after all! He saw it making its way between thick chunks of ice, Richards' broad shoulders powering the boat like a two-cylinder.

"Grab the rope!" called Richards.

Easton couldn't move a finger.

Richards drew closer, leaned over the gunwale, and dragged Easton aboard by the scruff of his collar. Then he rowed away from the cliffs as fast as oars could carry him. Easton lay in the bottom of the boat, gasping; it was all he could do to breathe. Once on dry land he began to recover a bit, but he still felt pretty green around the gills. What on earth was he going to tell Mr. Wallace?

He decided to take his medicine like a man. When they got back, he reported what happened straight out; admitted that climbing the iceberg was a piece of hairbrained lunacy; that the dunking he'd taken was nothing compared to how badly he felt risking Richards' life and putting the entire expedition in jeopardy.

To his amazement Mr. Wallace never so much as uttered a cross word. He thought about it some, looked at the two of them, and said the whole business was probably a good lesson. He supposed they would keep clear of icebergs henceforth.

Easton supposed so too. As for Richards—Richards didn't even want to see ice in his tea.

ARRIVING IN Halifax on June 10, Mina found Mr. Gillis, owner of the *Harlow*, awaiting her. Also Mr. Merlin was holding in storage a few provisions that William Cabot had been kind enough to forward. The very sight of the little city with its citadel on the hill brought back sharp memories of her previous visit, Laddie on her arm. But still, all seemed to be going according to plan. The last thing she expected was to be approached by a perfect stranger.

The fellow seemed to know exactly who she was. Perhaps one of the *Harlow*'s crew had pointed her out to him. Perhaps he recognized her by her mourning attire. He turned out to be a Mr. Lumm, a reporter for the Halifax *Herald*, who had interviewed Wallace coming through the previous week.

Mr. Lumm had nothing but praise for Wallace. That alone should have put her on guard. But he seemed a pleasant fellow at first and kept up a steady stream of patter. He commented on her baggage. It seemed a remarkable collection, he said. Did those canoes belong to her?

Mina did not want to be rude. After all, Laddie had made journalism his career. She found herself admitting what could no longer be hidden in any case: that she was, as a matter of fact, on her way to Labrador.

Mr. Lumm did not seem particularly surprised. He said that he had guessed as much. Was she, he wondered, planning to venture into the interior of that fateful land?

She gave him a sharp look. She did not care to be drawn into particulars. All the same, she had to give some kind of answer.

"I will be taking up where my husband left off," she said.

"One final question," he said. "Just where will you be joining Mr. Wallace?"

This was too much. The man was hopelessly forward, and she bid him a firm "Good day."

That evening the *Herald* carried a short dispatch noting her arrival in Halifax and stating the general purpose of her expedition. It was almost laughable to see how the reporter had garbled the facts. According to his account, her party included "five Americans, besides Indians and other guides." The man was obviously determined to link her with Wallace.

The next day Lumm was back again—this time bristling with questions. He wanted to know about any ill-feeling between her and Wallace. What was her opinion, he asked, of Wallace's book? He wanted to know if Wallace was aware of her expedition and asked skeptical questions about George Elson.

Mina was taken aback. She could not imagine how this man knew so much about her own inner feelings, but she was determined to maintain a correct bearing. It might be Wallace's style to run on in public about shotguns and Leon being "overtrained," but she was not about to imitate him. Confident that not even the *Herald* could make bricks without straw, she refused all comment except to repeat the bare facts: She was enroute to Labrador to complete her husband's unfinished work.

The headline on June 13 stunned her:

HUBBARD EXPEDITION IS RIVAL
OF DILLON WALLACE

Mina read the article with dismay. The source of this gossip turned out to be Wallace's sister, who had accompanied her brother as far as St. John's and now was passing through Halifax on her way home. Annie Wallace professed to be shocked that Mrs. Hubbard was undertaking her own expedition, scandalized that George Elson was accompanying the party, and distressed that her brother was in ignorance of Mrs. Hubbard's plans. Mina's cheeks burned as she read the story. George Elson had every right to guide for anyone he wanted to! He understood what it meant to be faithful to Laddie.

Things went from bad to worse. Two days later, the *Herald* ran another headline: MRS. HUBBARD DOUBTS WALLACE'S STORY OF TRIP. Outrageous! How could this be? She had herself declined any more interviews. Was Mr. Lumm now resorting to mind reading?

Of all people, the source turned out to be Edgar Briggs, Wallace's editor, who called the "unfortunate misunderstanding" between Hubbard's partner and his widow "a dispute that has been waged for months." Seeing the dateline, Mina's heart sank. New York. This was a wire story. Obviously Briggs had been approached in New York about her statements in Halifax, and now the stories were bouncing back and forth. No doubt the loose talk was carried in the New York papers and, from there, was being dispatched across the country. It was vulgar beyond belief.

There was no way to undo the unwanted notoriety; simple physical escape offered the only relief. On June 16 Mina supervised the loading of her gear aboard the *Harlow*. That afternoon, she sailed with her party of "assorted Indians" from Pickford and Black's

Wharf, thankful to be at last beyond reach of newspapers, controversy, and Dillon Wallace.

BY TEMPERAMENT and training, Wallace was not an individual given to high feeling. He was a patient man; forebearing to a fault. But there was a limit to persecution—and Mina Hubbard had crossed the line.

P. T. McGrath, editor of the St. John's *Herald,* was in Wallace's rooms with the news. The story was one garbled paragraph, featured prominently in the morning's public dispatch. But one paragraph was enough.

Mind you, McGrath was saying, she never directly states what she obviously has in mind. "Responsible for her husband's death" is the way she puts it.

Wallace was furious. What more did a man have than his own good name? The woman was shameless. Wasn't it enough to turn George against him? What a miserable dog *that* fellow had turned out to be, with his lies and treachery. But Wallace was not deceived. Mrs. Hubbard was the demented spirit behind it all. And she had timed her attack so that he would have no chance to reply for months.

Her claims, he told McGrath, were totally preposterous. Hubbard's diary was a matter of public record. McGrath could read it, the wire services could read it, anyone could read it. He and Hubbard had been dearest, closest friends. As for the circumstances of Hubbard's death, Wallace courted the fullest investigation.

Politely but firmly he showed McGrath the door. He did not trust himself to remain circumspect under such aggravating conditions. Alone again, he sat down at his writing table and gave full vent to his wrath, in letters to McLaughlin and Whitney.

He would do more than *court* an investigation, he told them. It was his intention to have Mina Hubbard arrested upon her return for criminal slander. Let a jury decide which of them was telling the truth.

Unfortunately, events overtook any further drafting of plans. As if to confound Wallace once again, the ragged and rusting *Virginia Lake* sailed promptly the following morning at ten. Wallace and the others had to rise early and scramble to get their gear aboard. Then, true to Reid-Newfoundland form, the little ship just as promptly veered off schedule—making an unscheduled stop at the hamlet of Brigus, where a crowd of over a hundred fishermen and their wives clambered aboard, attracted by a discount rate on the tickets. The *Virginia Lake* left the harbor loaded to the rails and soon headed north into the grip of the Labrador current. Easton and Richards amused themselves by counting icebergs, though now always at a safe distance. Once across the Strait of Belle Isle, Labrador greeted them with snowstorms, a gale, and pack ice that Captain Parsons had to ram through.

Wallace found the landscape drearily familiar; his only concern was hurry, hurry, hurry. But the *Virginia Lake* did not know the meaning of hurry. The ship stopped at even more ports of call than usual, met more ice and wind than expected, and was slowed by one vexatious delay after another. Six full days passed before they neared Rigolet.

On the way up two years earlier, Hubbard had been keyed up by nervous agitation—worrying about the weather, worrying about the ice, worrying about passage to Northwest River. Wallace was tormented by all these matters now and one other besides. Where was the *Harlow*? She had been scheduled to leave Halifax on the sixteenth, the day after the *Virginia Lake* left St. John's. But having no intervening ports of call, the lumber ship was expected to arrive at Rigolet on the twentieth.

This was already the twenty-first. Wallace had been keeping a lookout for days, but had seen no sign of her. By now he was convinced that the *Virginia Lake* had been passed. It was galling. Instead of Mina Hubbard being on his trail, he was in all likelihood on hers.

Giving up hope of making Rigolet before morning, Wallace retired to his stateroom. He was dozing when he heard a voice and a knock at his door. One A.M. It was Captain Parsons, come to say they had made Rigolet after all. Wallace hurried into his clothes and came up on deck. A slight haze hung over the water but no fog. He could barely make out the Hudson's Bay Company's "Big House" outlined against the dark hills.

Parsons pointed across the water to a twinkle of lights whose reflections were mirrored in the water. It was another steamer, anchored still and silent in the night.

26

Christ Shall Give the Light

George stood at the *Harlow*'s rail and watched the evening go its way, slow and easy. Finally it was dark.

Rigolet hadn't changed much. Same old flag wavin' in the breeze; same old dogs into everything. Mr. Fraser was still the H.B.C. man but even quieter than before. The fellus said he lost his boy, Stuart, and took it hard.

Exactly when George noticed the lights way down the narrows, he couldn't say. It was misty, and the yellow pinpricks looked like they might have shone from a hut or two on the far shore. But gradually they moved closer, and he could guess well enough who they belonged to. He waited until it drew into the harbor, just to be certain.

Should he wake Mrs. Hubbard and tell her? He wasn't sure. She might think it strange, him knocking on her door after she'd gone to bed. And she had a lot on her mind already. Only a day out of Halifax, Joe Iserhoff had taken sick. He'd been running a fever for days, and about coughing his heart out. If Joe had consumption, they were in for a bad time. They couldn't head into the woods with him being that low, but they couldn't just drop him off in Northwest River either, like a bad potato.

Joe being sick made the other piece of news all the worse. Mr. Fraser said the Hudson's Bay steamer was making rounds early this year. The *Pelican* came over from England, bringing supplies for the settlements around the top of Labrador and into Ungava Bay. It was the only ship that visited George River Post, where Mrs. Hubbard was planning to come out. It was due there early,

Mr. Fraser said—probably sometime the last week in August. So they had barely two months to cross all of Labrador and meet that ship. If they missed it, they'd be stuck on Ungava Bay a whole year. Mrs. Hubbard didn't like that idea at all.

Still, she'd been pleased to get to Rigolet so quickly and George didn't have to ask why. They'd beat Wallace. Everybody seemed to think that the *Virginia Lake* wouldn't dock until tomorrow; and by then the *Harlow* would be gone. It was scheduled to sail at daybreak, about two hours from now.

But here were running lights pulling into the harbor, and George knew the *Virginia Lake* when he saw it. Could be, two hours wasn't going to be lead enough.

AT THE FIRST RAP, Mina jumped. Cautiously she sat up.

"Mrs. Hubbard, it's George." The voice floated muffled from the other side of the door.

"Yes?" she called anxiously.

"I thought maybe you should know. The *Virginia Lake* is here."

She hesitated. "Can you find out the news?"

"I'll go now," he replied.

She lay back and tried to think. There was no point in rising; nothing she could do.

The day before, coming up the channel to Rigolet, the suspense had been almost unbearable. Where was Wallace? Had the *Virginia Lake* beaten her to Rigolet? She had scanned the cove from end to end, her pulse racing, until she was absolutely certain there was no other steamer at anchor. Even then the uneasiness wouldn't go away. What if he had jumped on some other fishing boat? What if he was sitting in Mr. Fraser's office when she went up to the post? What if she ran into him walking around the huts? But there was no sign of him anywhere and the Frasers had received no word.

If he really had arrived on the *Virginia Lake* now, she would just have to avoid him at all cost, that was all.

But had he arrived? The more she thought about it, the more unlikely it seemed. Dozens of boats traveled up and down the coast, transporting fishermen from Newfoundland to Labrador. Wallace might be on any of them. At first she could hardly wait for George to return. But the rippling of the harbor waters lulled her under the weight of her blankets. She became drowsy and let her thoughts drift.

Another rap and she was out of bed instantly, searching for her robe. Wrapping it about her, she cracked open the door to find George looking solemn.

"He's here. Him and the others and all their gear. He's at the Big House now, looking to buy tickets."

She managed to nod—wanted to say something—but felt lightheaded. George looked away mostly, her being in her robe; then turned to leave. She shut the door.

A strange thing happened. She began trembling—just standing there in bare feet, trembling like a leaf. At first she thought it was the chill, but she lay on the bed with blankets over her and still trembled. She hardly knew what she was doing. Her cheeks flushed hot and cold, and she was thinking all kinds of things, all stirred up. She wanted to walk on deck, but she wanted to stay in bed. She never wanted to see Wallace again, but she wanted to shame him directly, to his face. Whatever she wanted to do, she trembled to think of it. The shaking wouldn't stop.

She thought of Mr. Gillis, the *Harlow*'s owner, and had an idea. Mr. Gillis would never let Wallace on board. It was his ship; he could do as he pleased. In Halifax he had said, "Mrs. Hubbard, all I am thinking about is to help you all I can in your plans." Now he could, by simply forbidding Wallace's presence.

Her thoughts seemed to tumble one over the other. Mr. Fraser had been so quiet and undemonstrative. Had he known Wallace was coming all along? Had he meant to slight her, not escorting her to the wharf this afternoon? No—more likely he was only sad about his little boy, Stuart. Mr. Fraser had loved Stuart. There was so much sadness in the world . . . so much death . . . .

Yet she couldn't help thinking that no one had been so beautiful as her Laddie, none so loved as he. Not even little Stuart.

The chills and trembly mixed-up thoughts went on for fifteen minutes, half an hour, an hour.

Then there were boots tramping about on deck, seemingly inches above her head; boots on deck and the sounds of loading.

It came as no surprise to Wallace that every berth on the *Harlow* was taken. These ships were all the same—never enough space. After getting the gear deposited on the foredeck, he settled down with his companions on the duffels to watch the tars prepare the ship for departure. He pondered whether or not to take a stroll.

Unfortunately, the *Harlow* looked to have only so many places a person might walk without chancing to meet another doing the same. For the time being he decided to stay put.

A little before six, he caught the echo of footsteps coming up the stairs. He had become increasingly alert to sounds from below. An instant later a familiar figure rounded the corner and strode along the deck: It was George. He didn't notice Wallace at first, for his eyes were fixed on the wharf—searching. When he finally spotted all the gear laid out and the five men sprawled across it, he stopped dead and stared; first at Wallace, then at the others, and then back again at Wallace. He seemed almost stunned to see them on deck, big as life.

Wallace got to his feet, a little less uneasy given George's confusion.

"Hello, George," he said. "How are you?"

"Oh. Hullo, Wallace."

Wallace offered his hand. George took it, sheepishly.

"I guess you'll be traveling with Mrs. Hubbard."

"I guess so," said George. He looked as if he wanted only to be somewhere infinitely far away.

Wallace offered a few pleasantries, being careful not to betray any irritation over the way he had been treated. George fidgeted all the while, and then beat a hasty retreat below decks.

ANOTHER KNOCK, another hurried conference. Mina agonized over what to do. She could avoid Wallace by staying below, but generally she believed it better to meet trouble than to hide from it. With the boat underway, she was determined to take in the prospect of Groswater Bay. George alerted her to where Wallace's gear was piled; she would simply stay on the opposite side of the deck. If Wallace chose to wander aimlessly, that was his business.

At ship's rail she and George watched the country pass before them. He liked to tell stories about the seals in the water or the birds overhead. Sometimes he'd go off to have a diplomatic "look around," with Job and Joe as reinforcements; then return to relate the news, his companions standing obediently to one side like a mute Greek chorus. Wallace didn't look well, George said. Not sick or anything but not quite well.

Mina wanted to know about the other members of the crew.

George said he recognized a fellow named Stanton, but Stanton had only been around the lumber camp at Kenemish. Never traveled in the bush. There was an Indian who seemed friendly enough, but he wasn't Cree. George had talked with him some and so had Job. He didn't seem to know too much.

Mina looked anxiously at Job, who nodded agreement.

And then there were a couple of college students. That was all. One of them seemed pretty white and thin.

Mina couldn't help glancing at Joe Iserhoff, who looked rather anemic himself. He claimed to be better, but it was hard to tell. She would just have to trust to him pulling up in time.

She couldn't stay at the rail all day. There was the noon meal to eat, and she returned now and then to her stateroom. Perhaps it was inevitable that she should encounter Wallace at some point. When she finally did come upon him, it happened too suddenly to turn and flee. To her surprise, she discovered she didn't want to. The trembling of the previous evening had vanished. She felt only anger and a determination not to yield one iota.

Their eyes met and she refused to look away. She kept walking, her gait steady and her stare burning with a hot resentment that bored through Wallace and beyond him to the Labrador barrens where Laddie had been left to die.

He said nothing, only passed in silence.

At Kenemish the usual swirl of people appeared at the sound of the *Harlow*'s whistle. As Mina watched the crowd on shore she felt as if she were coming out of a dream. After weeks of traveling, it was finally time to act, though she was unsure of just what to do. The ship had hardly dropped anchor before Wallace hurried into a longboat and went ashore. George, thank heavens, jumped in too. Mina watched from the deck as he hastened toward one of the huts on shore. He was hoping to find Duncan McLean and recruit him for her party. Meanwhile, Wallace was talking to some local with a skiff. The rest of his party began transferring their gear to the man's boat.

She fumed. Wallace was scurrying about while she stood by helplessly. Once the skiff was loaded, he would row the last dozen miles to Northwest River and have a clear head start.

She spotted George making his way back to the wharf with that easy lope of his, but there seemed to be no longboat at hand. He waited calmly. Mina wanted to reach directly across the water and shake him by the shoulders—make it clear that at all costs they mustn't let Wallace seize the advantage. But when George finally returned, she couldn't bring herself to say out loud what she was feeling inside. George sensed these things, didn't he? Surely he understood the need for hurry?

"Duncan's not here," said George. "Still out trappin', I guess. Or maybe he's over to Northwest River."

She tried to control herself. "I suppose we can't very well leave tonight with Joe sick."

George was studying Wallace and his skiff.

"Northwest River's only about three hours' paddle," he said. "I was thinkin'. Maybe Job and me might go ahead. We could get a little business done while Joe is gettin' better."

"Go, then," said Mina. And it seemed that before she could turn around, George and Job had lowered one of the canoes and jumped aboard, paddles in hand. As they slipped across the bay Mina watched from the deck, bursting with pride. George knew, all right. He knew just what had to be done and who was going to do it. "I could have just taken off [my] hat and shouted and jumped round," she wrote that night.

THE TWO OF THEM beat Wallace to Northwest River Post, all right—dark had about fallen when he and Job pulled in. But Wallace still had a few surprises for them, as George found out soon enough.

He knew Wallace would be staying at the Hudson's Bay Company post, just as before. Mackenzie wasn't there now; he'd been replaced by a new fella, name of Stuart Cotter. George headed for the French post on the other side of the narrows. The Hudson's Bay post on one side of the river and the French post on the other were rivals for trade—each keeping a sharp eye on the other, though still on speaking terms. Monsieur Duclos gave George a fine welcome, but Mrs. Hubbard was the person he was really looking for. He was fixing a special room for her, he said. Along about one in the morning, Wallace and his crew pulled in on the other side of the river. They sent up a big halloo and got Mr. Cotter out of bed.

Next morning was the first jump Wallace got on George, when Duncan McLean came walking, bright and early, into Mr. Cotter's kitchen. He'd come straight from the bush. Before he heard George was across the way and looking to hire somebody, Wallace signed him up. Even so, Duncan agreed to guide only as far as Seal Lake. That was as far up as he trapped and as far as he was going. With

Hubbard, July 15, 1903, Northwest River Post

George Elson, in Newfoundland on the trip north

Dillon Wallace, Northwest River Post

LEFT: William Cabot in 1903 at Davis Inlet, wearing a Naskapi caribou-skin coat. BELOW: Thomas Mackenzie, Hudson's Bay Company agent at Northwest River Post. BOTTOM: The day of departure, July 15, on the beach at Northwest River. Mackenzie stands at left, Wallace far right, and Elson next to him. As always, children, dogs, and old salts are in abundance.

ABOVE: Wallace and George haul against the current, not far above Grand Lake.
BELOW: The river's rocky course. Wallace *(left)* and Elson both wear mosquito netting under their hats. Wallace carries a cup at his belt, as well as a pistol.

Lake Hope in 1903 *(left)* and in 1980, as the authors photographed it. The water level has dropped slightly and the middle evergreen of three in the mid-distance has passed its neighbor by a few inches over the course of eighty years.

Wallace portages from Goose Creek toward Mountaineer Lake, tumpline across his forehead, a goose hanging from either side.

LEFT: Hubbard, already ragged at Disappointment Lake on the way toward Michikamau. ABOVE: Wallace on September 21, as the retreat from Windbound Lake began, the folds of his cinched-in trousers barely visible at the waist. BELOW: Poling down the Big River in the retreat toward Grand Lake. In mild rapids, George stood in the bow while Wallace sat in the stern. (By this point, Hubbard had become too weak to steer accurately.)

Hubbard on October 17, the day before the parting.

Hubbard's last entry: October 18, 1903. The final sentences read, "I think death from starvation is not so bad. But let no one suppose I expect it. I am prepared, that is all. I think the boys will be able with the Lord's help, to save me."

June—Cash	Rec'd	Paid	July—Cash	Rec'd	Paid

bone broth. I also ate some of the really
delicious rawhide (boiled with bones) and
it made me stronger — strong to write this.
The boys have only tea & ½ pound of
pea meal (Erbswurst). Our parting was
most affecting. I did not feel so bad.
George said, "The Lord help us, Hubbard; with
his help I'll save you if I can get out."
Then he cried. So did Wallace. Wallace
stooped and kissed my cheek with his
poor, sunken, bearded lips — several
times — & I kissed his. George did the same,
& I kissed his cheek. Then they went away —
God bless & help them.

I am not so greatly in doubt as to
the outcome. I believe they will reach the
flour, & be strengthened — that W. will
reach me. That George will find Blake's
cache & camp & send help. So I
believe we will all get out. My
tent is pitched in open tent style
in front of a big rock. The rock reflects
the fire but now it is going out because
of the rain. I think I shall let it

go & close the tent, till rain is over,
thus keeping out wind & saving wood
tonight or tomorrow perhaps the
weather will improve so I can
build a fire, eat the rest of my
moccasins & have some more bone
broth. Then I can boil my belt and
oil tanned moccasins & a pair of cow
hide mittens. They ought to help some.
I am not suffering. The acute pangs
of hunger have given way to indifference. I'm sleepy. I think death
from starvation is not so bad. But
let no one suppose I expect it.
I am prepared — that is all — I
think the boys will be able with the
Lord's help, to save me.

Wallace's rescuers *(from left):* Gilbert Blake, Duncan McLean, Allen Goudie, and Donald Blake. "Bert" Blake, only seventeen at the time, joined Mina Hubbard's expedition in 1905; Duncan joined Wallace's.

Hubbard fishing. *Outing* published this photograph, not from the expedition, after it learned of Hubbard's fate.

Mina Hubbard, in a portrait drawn by J. Sydall; BELOW, LEFT AND RIGHT: George Elson and Dillon Wallace in 1904.

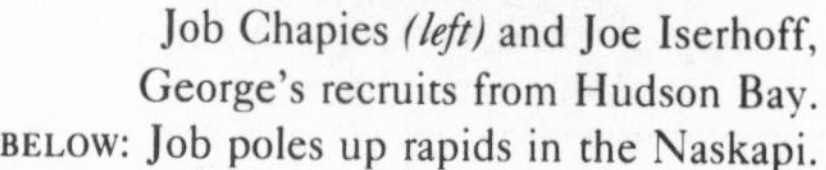

Job Chapies *(left)* and Joe Iserhoff,
George's recruits from Hudson Bay.
BELOW: Job poles up rapids in the Naskapi.

ABOVE: Gilbert Blake. Mina called him Gil; everyone else called him Bert. LEFT: Mina in hiking attire—"short" skirt, rifle in hand, moleskin pouch on her belt. BELOW: George swats a fly while resting along the trail.

RIGHT: Wallace, at the shores of Lake Michikamau. BELOW: Peter Stevens, Clifford Easton, and George Richards aboard the steamship to Labrador.

ABOVE: Duncan McLean enjoys a pipe; Leigh Stanton gives Pete Stevens a haircut. BELOW: Easton and Richards fight an upstream current along the Montagnais route to Seal Lake.

ABOVE: Mina in camp at Lake Michikamau; with the Naskapi women along Indian House Lake. BELOW: The arrival at George River Post on Ungava Bay. John Ford greets Mina.

ABOVE: Writing letters home before Wallace's party divides at Lake Michikamau.
BELOW: Wallace and Easton before the departure; a Montagnais boy along the upper stretches of the George River. Easton stands in the background.

ABOVE: George Elson several decades later, probably in Moosonee, Ontario; Mina Hubbard in England, the day of her marriage to Harold Ellis in 1908. BELOW: Dillon Wallace in 1913, with the inscription he carved at Hubbard's last camp; and his son Dillon Wallace III, who returned to find the marker in 1973. *(Photo courtesy of Rudy Mauro.)* Wallace refurbished the inscription, which had become nearly invisible, and in 1976 placed a permanent bronze plaque at the site.

Duncan hired away, George had to scramble. He looked up Bert Blake, the boy who'd gone up the Susan with Duncan and the others to rescue Wallace. Of all the Blakes, Bert was the runt of the litter, only nineteen. But he'd trapped up the Naskapi too, and he jumped at the chance to go with George—not only to Seal Lake but all the way to Ungava.

George also talked to some Montagnais who were camped nearby. They told him the Naskapi was full of bad rapids and that it would take three months to get to Michikamau. The best route, they said, was to leave the river opposite where the Red Wine came in and go by the old portage trail. John Ahsini promised to draw George a map—do it later that day. But Wallace went round to the Indians afterward too, and they gave him the map John had just done. That was the second time George got beat.

Saturday night he went to Kenemish for Mrs. Hubbard. She was packed and ready to go. Joe was feeling stronger too, which was a relief. Coming back, they hadn't even pulled into the French post before Monsieur Duclos was down on shore—bowing and paying Mrs. Hubbard the greatest of courtesies. He led her up to the room he'd fixed, and afterward set a fine dinner in her honor—the last goose from the fall season.

Meanwhile, George had to get the outfit settled. His friends at Northwest River sewed flour sacks and duffel socks, and even made a pair of sealskin boots for Mrs. Hubbard. All the while Wallace kept to his side of the river, never showing his face; but the two college fellus came over and poked around, trying to look like they didn't care a bit what Mrs. Hubbard was up to.

Monday afternoon the boys disappeared back across the river, and after supper Wallace got his two canoes launched for Grand Lake. George didn't see them go, but Cotter skinned over from the Hudson's Bay post the minute Wallace was gone. He didn't want to miss out on anything. George worked on into the night; it wasn't till next morning, June 27, that he was finally ready to load the boats.

Mrs. Hubbard stepped out of the post ready to go, and the sight of her about stopped him in his tracks. He tried not to stare. For a year now he'd not seen her dressed in anything but mourning—not in Williamstown, in Halifax, nor on the *Harlow*. But the black crepe, with the veil behind, was gone now. She was wearing a short sweater with a skirt that fell about her ankles and swung when she walked and then took a couple of extra swings when she stopped walking. Her moccasins were so freshly oiled, they looked alive. Cinched to her waistbelt was a revolver and a hunting knife; also a moleskin pouch that hung by a strap from her shoulder, for little things she wanted to keep handy. On her head was a soft felt hat with a brim that bent in the breeze. She looked like a woman made over—and she was smiling too.

He was trying to remember what he'd been going to do, when she spoke up and said she needed to cross the river and get a couple last things from Mr. Cotter's. George called Bert to come help paddle, but Mrs. Hubbard came up and touched his arm.

"I'll take the bow," she said.

George just looked at her.

She laughed and hopped into the canoe. When he saw she meant it, he handed her a paddle. "I guess maybe I'd better bring a couple more," he said. They paddled across and got what she needed.

By 3:15 the last packing was finished. Bert climbed into the bow of one canoe, with Joe in the stern. Mrs. Hubbard went in the other, with George and Job. She sat in the middle. Then George pushed off, hopping into the stern.

Monsieur Duclos was on hand to say good-bye, and Stuart Cotter too. Mr. Cotter had been awfully curious about their plans—like all the white men who wanted to know what George was up to. But at least he'd been friendly about asking. He hadn't had any little "talks" like Mr. Gillis, to try and scare them into bringing Mrs. Hubbard out safe. On the way up from Halifax, Mr. Gillis had put the fear of God into George, and even worse into Job and Joe.

Cotter looked them all over and finally said, "You'll be all right, Mrs. Hubbard. At first, I didn't think you could do it, but I've changed my mind. You *can* do it, and without any trouble too."

Christ shall give the light, thought George, and pointed the bow of the canoe toward Grand Lake.

27

Trail or River?

FOR WALLACE, entering Grand Lake was a tonic: back into uninhabited lands and away from the quarrels, the jockeying for position, and Mina Hubbard's stony stare. The morning had begun overcast, but almost immediately the lake turned blue under a clearing sky, and the sun sent shimmers across the water the way it had two years before.

Monday evening Wallace had wanted only to get out of Northwest River, no matter how late the hour or how brief the march. The moment Duncan presented himself (a day late, indolently cheerful, with no inclination to leave for anywhere, at any time, in any particular haste) Wallace got his men into the boats and paddling. In an hour he had reached the foot of Grand Lake and Tom Blake's cabin—the same Blake who had helped retrieve Hubbard's body from the Susan. Tom was delighted to see Wallace and pleased to put his party up for the night. Mrs. Blake furnished a big breakfast the next morning and made them a present of some buns, several loaves of bread, and a handful of eggs. " 'Twill be a long time before you has eggs again," she said.

Duncan, predictably, was nowhere to be seen. He hadn't left Northwest River with the others, promising to come later in the evening. After breakfast Wallace eyed the channel as he loaded gear, half fearing that Mina Hubbard's canoes might appear rather than Duncan's rowboat and sail. But at ten Duncan arrived, and, within half an hour, Wallace was pointed west down Grand Lake, blessing the sun, the breeze, and the azure skies. Nothing seemed to have changed.

Yet nothing was quite the same. In 1903 Wallace had been the novice, content to paddle obediently along. This year he had to make the decisions. Should he hurry down the lake and open a quick lead over Mrs. Hubbard? Or study the lake point by point as he went? He determined not to be stampeded by a woman. He was engaged in serious exploration, not popular entertainment for the penny newspapers. He would explore carefully, just as Hubbard had set out to do, and he would still get to Ungava before her.

He followed the northern shore of the lake at first, then cut a diagonal to the south shore, where the college boys, Richards and Easton, could climb a high bluff for a view of the country. Richards put his geological training to work, collecting samples of what he called "compact amphibolite" and "pegmatite dikes." In the afternoon the party cut back to the north shore, arriving just in time to make camp at the mouth of a stream called Watty's Brook.

All in all, a fine day. Twenty miles to the good, and Wallace had taken his first latitude reading. Best of all, Stanton had bagged a couple of porcupines. Already they were living off the land.

"Porcupine is a northern delicacy," Wallace assured Richards and Easton. "It tastes a bit like lamb, only more succulent."

Young Easton was dubious. Skinned of quills, the beasts looked rather more like large rats.

"Give it a try, boys," urged Wallace, and attacked his own plate with a bit of vigorous knife work. He popped a fair-sized chunk into his mouth and chewed. After a time his jaw tired. His expression became impassive. He took a sip of water, then chewed again. He tried to swallow, nearly choked, and went back to chewing. Finally he gave it up.

He tried another piece. They all did. The meat was impregnable. It had a gummy texture that mastication only rendered more elastic.

"Must be the oldest porcupine in Labrador," said Wallace glumly.

Pete came to the rescue. "This porcupine, he must boil long," he declared. "I boil him again tonight and boil him again tomorrow morning. Then he very good for breakfast. Porcupine fine. Old one must cook long."

So the evening meal became coffee and some of Mrs. Blake's bread. As the men finished, the aurora lit up the sky. Wallace sat a long time, sipping his coffee. Through the gathering darkness, he could barely make out the lake's opposite shore, where two years ago a small cove had served as his first Labrador camp. The fire had been leaping high then (George liked his fires big), a tarp lean-to had been rigged under the pines, and Hubbard had returned from the nearby stream, empty-handed but terrifically charged up. Wallace still felt the intoxication.

But tonight the mist was rising. Though the cove was only four miles across the water, Wallace could see little more than a vague silhouette, deeply shrouded in shadow. He finished his coffee and turned in.

AMONG THE PINES of the cove, just up from the beach, the fire was jumping—the way George liked it. Mrs. Hubbard seemed to like it too. Even though it was after midnight, she was still writing her journal by the light of the blaze.

She was pleased with how far they had come. Twenty-two miles, she figured, using her instruments.

Which sounded right to George. After leaving Northwest River, they'd paddled almost eight hours, right up to eleven o'clock. He wanted to get as far as he could down the lake before a wind stirred up; otherwise they could get stuck good. So they'd paddled straight through the afternoon and along into the dusk, using the weather while they had it.

After he cleaned the dishes, George got out his own journal and did some writing himself. It was different for him than her, though. When Mrs. Hubbard wrote, her pencil just flew across the page. He had to go slow, thinking about what to say. And he kept having to cross words out, till he got them spelled right.

They turned in about one o'clock. Mrs. Hubbard slept in her tent, but the fellus just laid their bedrolls out under the trees. Two hours later, as soon as the sun came up, George was calling "All aboard." He stretched it out just like the conductors did—"Allll a-*boord*!" The boys laughed, and it became a regular joke.

The calm held and by 8:00 A.M. they were rounding Berry Head. Another couple hours and they had reached the mouth of the Naskapi. George didn't have any trouble finding it now; he knew right where to go. Once they got inside the valley where the wind couldn't hurt them, they pulled into shore, fixed some lunch, and settled down for a good nap. That was the difference between whites traveling and Indians. Whites traveled by the clock, every day the same. Indians went by the country, sleep when they could.

It wasn't easy for Mrs. Hubbard, traveling like an Indian. The boys just laid down under the willows and fell asleep, till George stirred and called "All aboard." But Mrs. Hubbard didn't look as if she'd slept a wink. She didn't say a word about being tired, though; just climbed into the middle of the canoe like it was home to her.

The river was big and deep and the current something brisk, so they followed close to shore, cutting the slack water on the inside of the curves, going upstream. Casting his eye along a low ridge, George was the first to see the brush moving.

"Who's that?" he asked.

It was a bear. A big black one shuffling after berries.

A bear was about the last thing they needed just then. They had all the food they could carry, and they surely hadn't any use for his pelt, ragged from the winter season. But Job couldn't resist sending a couple rifle shots after him for fun, not expecting a hit or anything. The bear didn't seem to like it and clambered to the top of the ridge, where he went back to browsing like he owned the hill.

Seeing that bear amble, his shape so clean and dark against the sky, was just too much for temptation. George knew very well what Job was thinking, and he knew what was on his own mind too.

Without a word he dug his paddle in deeper, and Job, feeling the surge, dug his in too. Quick, sharp strokes. The canoe shot straight for paradise. The moment the keel touched shore, Job was up the hill with his rifle. George would have gone too, except he had to tend to Mrs. Hubbard. No telling what she might do if he left her alone in a spot like this.

She did about the last thing George would've guessed. She got a fierce look on her face and started up the bank. Right after the bear! George scrambled after, trying not to seem too surprised.

The hillside was steep and brushy—trees blown down everywhere. Mrs. Hubbard kept tripping on the deadfalls and getting her skirts caught on the branches. George would dart near, kind of, but then hop back, not sure what to do. The thing was, suppose her skirt snagged? He couldn't just grab ahold and pull—it might rip. If she stumbled, he sure couldn't just reach out and catch her. A lady like Mrs. Hubbard had too many soft places he hadn't any business touching. It put him in a regular sweat.

Halfway up, they heard a shot and a whoop from Job. The bullet winged the bear and knocked him so hard, he rolled like a ball off the ridge and down the bank. He got back on all fours, though, and charged upriver.

George popped off a pistol shot: sort of a final salute. There was no way they were going to bring him down in country rough as this. He turned to head back.

Bang! Bang! Bang! Bang! Four shots practically in his ear! And Mrs. Hubbard standing there with her pistol smoking!

"Did I miss?" she asked. She was some sight—shaking all over, cheeks red, eyes blazing.

George had to smile. The bear was almost a mile away and she expected to drop him with her .22. But he didn't laugh. He couldn't do that.

"Maybe I can give you a shooting lesson a little later," he said.

They didn't see any more bears that afternoon, but they did get a porcupine. He wouldn't be too good to eat, George warned. Wrong time of year for porcupines. Sure enough, they cooked it and she didn't like it.

There was animal sign everywhere. On the river, the next day, they flushed a rabbit. And then a muskrat lying upstream in the willows. The poor rat made the mistake of paddling into the current before he figured where he wanted to go. George and Job just smiled and loaded their pistols and waited for the river to sweep him to his Maker.

Mrs. Hubbard saw him pawing away full speed, like he *wanted* to go straight toward the pistols. The current was so smooth, she forgot all about it. Her eyes opened right up.

"Why, what's the matter with him? Is he hurt?" she asked.

The rat almost got away, the boys laughed so hard. The rest of that day, if anybody got tired or bored, all he had to do was roll his eyes and ask, "Why, what's the matter with him? Is he hurt?" And they would all laugh and feel fresh.

The joking stopped, though, when they came around a bend and saw the mouth of the Red Wine. The old Indian portage trail was supposed to be across from it. Finally they'd find out what they'd all been wondering: whether Wallace was ahead or behind. First thing on shore, George walked up and down looking for sign—footprints in the mud, broken twigs, scuff marks in the moss.

Nothing.

He came up to Mrs. Hubbard, smiling. And she figured it out

and smiled back. Somewhere on Grand Lake, they must've passed Wallace. For good, they all hoped.

The boys fanned out to scout the Indian trail. George finally traced it through underbrush that looked ten, maybe fifteen, years old. It was faint, all right, but there, climbing straight out of the valley like the Indians said.

He had to make a decision. Either take the trail or stick with the river. The Indians always took the trail, hopping from one pond to the next all the way to Seal Lake. But the breeds from Northwest River—Donald Blake and the others—always stayed with the river. That was in winter, of course. The river was mostly frozen then, and they hiked it on snowshoes to get their traplines. This time of year the rapids would be open and George taking canoes. Nobody'd ever tried that before; nobody'd ever tried to bring canoes up the Naskapi.

George spoke for a bit with Job in Cree, and then with Joe and Bert. Finally he went over to where Mrs. Hubbard was standing. He switched to English.

"Hard to know what to do," he said. He had to tell her that.

Mrs. Hubbard looked at him, not saying a word. But she knew this was their big decision.

He laid it out the best he could. He told her how Bert had been up the river in winter and how he said it was hard going. Maybe harder than the Indian trail.

Mrs. Hubbard looked at Bert. He was hardly more than a boy.

"But the Indian trail is awfully cold," said George. "We could use up a lot of time scouting."

He thought about how they needed to hurry, and of Wallace. But he didn't say so. He just told her a little about old trails. Maybe this one would get better as it went along. But maybe it'd just peter out in a thicket. Maybe once you got off it, it would take a lot of climbing and looking around to get back on again. He didn't say he wanted to stick with the river. He just told her how old trails like that could behave, and let the idea kind of hang there.

Mrs. Hubbard looked out at the river. It was flowing by so quiet and gentle.

After a while, she spoke. She said it had been her husband's wish to reach the interior by way of the Naskapi. That was her wish as well, so long as George thought the route was possible.

George gave the sign to the others and, straightaway, they slid the canoes back into the water. They had a lead on Wallace, but how big, George didn't know. There was no sense waiting for the man to paddle around the bend.

WEDNESDAY, JUNE 28, Wallace awoke to the aroma of boiling porcupine. It was Pete's reputation on the line now, and he had arisen ahead of the others to push the kettle to a full roll.

Wallace walked down to the beach and stretched. To wash his face, he had to break through a fringe of ice that had formed during the night. Then he scanned the lake, an unbroken sheet of silver-blue. No sign of the other party: he couldn't help but feel relieved. With breakfast almost ready, his crew would be off by 8:30—a late start but reasonable enough.

The porcupine carcass looked softer and grayer. It smelled delicious. Pete pulled apart the ribs, and the meat just seemed to fall off the bones. But the men's assaults upon the redoubtable creature were firmly repulsed. The extra boiling had wetted the gristle and made it soggy, but left it stringy as ever.

"The rubber trust ought to hunt porcupines," suggested Easton. "They're a lot tougher than rubber and just as pliable."

"I don't know why," said Pete sadly. "I boil him long time."

They continued their course up the lake, reaching the mouth of the Naskapi in time for lunch. In the afternoon they turned their bows upriver. Wallace's thrill at entering unknown waters was all too quickly spent. Though smooth, the current was remarkably swift. Not only did Duncan trail as before; he zigzagged from one side of the river to the other. Worse, Wallace's own canoe was encountering difficulty. Richards suddenly seemed incapable of paddling a straight line. Wallace fumed and redoubled his own efforts, but the canoe kept veering off, first in one direction and then another. Easton and the others, scraping along near shore, were actually making faster time than his own canoe in the main channel. After three aggravating hours, he called a halt and put into shore, having made only three miles upriver.

The next day Richards did better. Wallace also had to admit that the current wasn't quite so stiff close to shore: they made a dozen miles for the day's effort. The sun was low in the sky when the ruddy waters of the Red Wine came into view, flowing in from the left. And on the right was a knoll topped by the weathered poles of an old Montagnais camp. This was where the Indian portage started, according to Ahsini's map.

Getting out to investigate, Wallace discovered skid marks on the bank and, nearby, some trampled bushes. Then he spotted the moccasin prints. At first, he thought they must be those of a trapper. But Duncan insisted there were no trappers hereabouts this time of year.

"None that I knows of, sir. And I knows 'en all."

Wallace experienced a sinking feeling. Could it possibly be? But how? All the way down Grand Lake, he had seen not a flash of a paddle, nor even smoke from another campfire. There could hardly be any doubt, however. Some of the tracks were hobnail, like the boots worn by two of the men in Mrs. Hubbard's party. The more Wallace's crew searched for the old Indian trail, the more signs of George and Mina they found. Yet the tracks stopped only a short way up the hill. Evidently George had been looking for the trailhead himself—no doubt had raced here to get the jump on Wallace—and then failed to find it. That was Wallace's only consolation.

The trail *was* hard to spot. It hadn't been traveled in years—light years, Easton remarked. Indeed, at first they lost it themselves in the underbrush. Never was it wider than a rabbit run. But Pete was an absolute bloodhound. Just when Wallace might have been inclined to give up the search, the guide gave a shout from deep in the bushes. "He here—I find him!" Ever higher he climbed, up, up, following the trace to the top of the ridge.

Still, the best course of action was not entirely clear. The Indians at Northwest River had touted this trail as a good portage, but even they admitted it would be hard going. This was rough country to hike: Wallace had been over enough of it in 1903 to know that. Duncan, for one, had no enthusiasm for the route. "All I knows about it is what they tells me," he told Wallace. "I always follows the river. That's what I say, sir, if you asks me."

But Wallace didn't want to hear it—not with Mina Hubbard farther upstream. No doubt the Indian trail would be tough. But why was he here? Certainly not to avoid hardship. Did he really want to shut himself up in the river valley? Wouldn't it be better to get an overview of the country—a view Mina Hubbard would never see?

He made his choice. Tomorrow it would be the Indian route. Out of the river valley and up the trail.

28

Climbing Hills of Water

THURSDAY NOON, only a few hours after passing the Montagnais portage trail, Mina and her party reached the beginning of the rapids. For the first time she could see why the Indians chose to leave the river. It was still broad—nearly half a mile wide in some spots—but everywhere the water rushed madly over boulder bars and shallows. Huge masses of ice were piled here and there, left behind from spring break-up and looking like dingy steamboats run aground on the bars.

The men beached the canoes below the rapids on a point, and Mina walked to the end of it. The sight was unnerving. Somehow she had always conceived of rapids as fast current on a gurgling stream, like the quick water of Laddie's trout brooks. This was a broad chaotic swath of white, not a smooth stretch of green anywhere. She knew all too well that even a sharp stick could poke a hole in the canvas skin of a canoe. A heavily laden boat running onto a single rock could be ripped open, end to end. If the men ever lost control in water like this, the canvas would simply be torn to shreds.

Upstream, the base of a mountain squeezed the river into a steeper, even wilder, course. The water appeared to shoot out in a foaming, impassable torrent. Mina began to wonder if the Indian route would not have been more prudent after all and glanced at the men to see if they shared her apprehension. But George was cheerfully fixing lunch with Joe and Gilbert, while Job was nowhere to be seen.

Soon enough Job appeared from the woods hauling four stout

poles, each about nine feet tall. After lunch he made himself comfortable among the boulders at water's edge and pulled out his crooked knife. Taking the first of the poles, he began skinning it top to bottom. Something came alive when he held that knife—something in his eyes.

When the poles were skinned and each fitted with an iron shoe, George said, "All ready, Mrs. Hubbard. We'll get in above the point."

The canoe was rocking uneasily in the wash of the current. Mina settled herself amidships as carefully as possible, trying to hide her nervousness. Then the men got in—only now they didn't kneel, they stood! Poles in hand, George and Job pried the canoe into the current, and then upstream, with strong, sharp strokes. Time after time, the hull slid so near a boulder, Mina could have reached out and touched it. The splash of the waves spilled practically into her lap. Why the canoe wasn't pitched straight to the bottom of the river she couldn't imagine. But the instant the poles reached the end of their stroke the men flicked them out of the water and set them anew. Push, dip, set; push, dip, set—miraculously, the canoes made headway.

Eventually the water became too rough and they pulled ashore to portage. While the men made up packs Mina climbed over ice heaps and walked along the river. Here and there a few flowers were beginning to bloom, and she spied two tiny violets. At the deepest part of the bay, she turned to look for the men and could scarcely believe her eyes. Job had reloaded two heavy packs and was now proceeding alone, straight up the rapids. Not just against a rushing current, but through a boulder field of foaming chutes and waves. Mina could hardly breathe. She never dreamed any number of men could pole a canoe where this one was being taken singlehandedly.

She discovered she was not the only one to stop and look. George and Joe had never seen anyone try waters this rough, and they watched with professional interest. As for young Gilbert—Gilbert's eyes nearly stuck out of his head. He'd been with trappers some but never seen the likes of this.

Out on the river Job just smiled and smiled, eyes shining like coals, pole dipping this way and that. The wilder the rapid, the more he seemed to enjoy it. As Mina watched him set his course, she began to sense the craft in his work—the way he used the river's currents to his own advantage.

All that day and most of the next, Job climbed hills of water, first in one canoe and then the other, while the men ferried the remaining loads along the bank. When Mina wasn't watching Job, she walked along, studying the rapids. The water moved with such irresistible power, never stopping, swirling in lissome forms around every obstacle. She felt she could gaze at it for hours.

At one point she hopped out onto a boulder to have a closer look. The torrent there was particularly enticing, foaming in a surging pattern caught by the sun. As she watched, the men came winding along the riverbank with their loads, heads bent over, necks straining against the tumplines. George happened to glance up and, catching sight of her, stopped dead. He dropped his pack and came running, full of consternation.

"Mrs. Hubbard, you mustn't do that!"

"Do what?" she asked.

"Stand on that rock. You'll get dizzy and fall in."

She laughed. George looked so serious he was comical. Clearly he wanted her down, but there was nothing he could do to force her. He could hardly jump onto the boulder with her; it was too small.

"But I don't get dizzy," she argued.

"Maybe you think you don't," said George, "but you will."

"I've been standing here a long time, and nothing's happened."

George was unmoved. "It's all right when you're looking at the rapid. Nobody has any trouble with that. It's when you turn that you fall. It's very dangerous. If you're going to do that, we will just turn around and go back to Northwest River."

Mina flushed. She didn't care for George being so severe, but she was trapped. She couldn't go on without him.

"Well—all right," she said finally, and jumped back toward shore.

Above the boulder, the river became so wild that even Job hesitated to try his luck, and they turned to the bush. The gear had to be hauled up an eighty-foot bank littered with fallen trees. Mercifully, only a few flies and mosquitoes had yet taken the wing, but the hot sun made the underbrush steamy. It took four trips apiece for the men to get the gear to the top, each pack weighing more than a hundred pounds. At the end of the effort, Joe nearly collapsed on the ground, trembling like a leaf. Gilbert was hot and tired, and even George looked a bit shaky. Mina, amazed at their labor, sat by quietly.

"In a week George and I will be hardened up," said Joe. "Then there won't be any trembling."

"Always hard," said Job, though he seemed least affected.

With progress slow but steady, the daily labor fell into a natural rhythm. Late afternoon George would select a campsite along the ridge or in a moss-covered dell. As the men set up camp they chatted to one another in Cree. George and Job Chapies seemed particularly close; Mina watched them as they put up her tent. Job's face was sometimes thoughtful, sometimes full of fun like a boy's, always lighted up with affection when he talked to George. *Georgie,* he called him.

The tent up, Gilbert would proudly produce one of Mina's few luxuries, an air mattress. From camping with Laddie, she knew that she slept only fitfully without one and, when overtired, lost her confidence and was afraid to try anything. Unfortunately, the tube to her air pump had been mislaid their second night on the river. She had been on the verge of sending someone downriver to look for it when George had the idea of turning Gilbert into an air-pump, a chore he accepted cheerfully.

Mornings she awoke by four-thirty to the sound of rapids in the distance, birds calling, and the soft voices of the men. They often sang a song in Cree as they went about their work. If anyone slept too late, George would pipe up with one of his "All aboards!" The men loved the little joke, except for Gilbert.

"No trains in Labrador," said Gilbert.

"No," agreed George. "You ever see a train, Gilbert?"

"No."

"Would you like to?"

Gilbert looked dubious. "Yes. But I wouldn't like to go on one."

Mina laughed. "Would you rather walk, Gilbert?"

"Yess'r," said Gilbert, "I'd rather walk."

Saturday afternoon Mina kept an eye out for a Sunday rest camp. The first possibility, a small rapid with a pretty gravel bar, was rejected by George almost immediately. "Oh, no," he said. "There'd be no Sunday rest for me. I'd have to be watching you all the time for fear you'd be falling into that rapid." But a mile or so upstream they came to an even prettier point. There were no noisy cascades here, only the river slipping quietly by. On the far shore, gravel flats covered with spring green were cut by little waterways, still as glass, reflecting the sunset.

George pulled the canoes out of harm's way and then returned to the river. He stood quite still for a time, arms folded, looking upstream. Mina walked over and stood by his side.

"What are you thinking, George?"

"I was just thinking how proud I am of this river," he said.

Sunday she savored the luxury of waking late and then lying still, listening. No voices. The men weren't up yet.

Quietly she ran to the river for some water, brought it back to her tent and bathed. Then she went to her duffel, got out fresh clothes, and put on a shirtwaist brought especially for Sundays.

The men rose about nine; she could hear them splashing down by the river. They came back shaved and wearing Sunday best, Joe and Gilbert looking especially elegant in white moleskin trousers.

It was a lazy day. She took a nap; then did her laundry and walked up the river a little. Near a secluded cove she came upon Gilbert cutting Joe's hair. Later the men sat by the river, reading their Bibles and singing hymns. They sang softly in unison, almost as if afraid of disturbing the stillness of the woods. Job took a canoe and explored upstream, returning about nine. The others were sitting by the fire when he floated by, paddle dangling lazily. "Good-bye, good-bye," he called with a broad grin; then took a stroke and swung the boat to shore. There were plenty of rapids ahead, he said—white as far as he could see.

And then on Monday the unexpected happened, casting the entire expedition into jeopardy. The men were engaged in the usual poling and hauling, around a boulder near shore where the current swept by. George and young Gilbert had attached a tracking line to the first boat and were taking the line upstream, while Job and Joe Iserhoff stood in the canoe, pushing off from the boulder with poles.

Mina had seen Job accomplish so many miracles that she started up the riverbank with some of her gear. As she reached the top she turned in time to see the canoe waver slightly and then roll. One of Joe's hands flew up for balance, and Job leaned hard on his pole, but the canoe suddenly turned bottom up, pitching both men into the foaming rapids.

The shock left Mina paralyzed, unable to speak. Almost immediately Joe came to the surface sputtering. He flailed, caught the tracking line and held it. Struggling, he worked his way up the line and staggered ashore. Job bobbed up, groped for the line but missed it, then grabbed desperately for Joe's leg. He had it an instant, but the current peeled him off and swept him away. As his face floated by Mina could see fear; he was unable to swim. An eddy slowed him, but then he was sucked under by a crosscurrent and disappeared. He washed into the shallows a bit downstream and tried to stand, but the current again knocked him off his feet, carrying him belly up toward the main channel. He couldn't seem to right himself.

During these agonizing moments, George and Gilbert had remained motionless; suddenly Mina realized that they couldn't move because the lines they held were straining to contain the drag of the submerged canoe. If they let go, the boat would spin away to destruction. Joe was staring blankly near shore, still dazed by his own thrashing. Mina found her voice just as George did, and both yelled, "Run, Joe!"

Joe splashed downstream into the river. He stretched out his hand and Job lunged for it, holding on for dear life until Joe pulled him up so he could stand. Then the two of them stumbled to shore, Job only half on his feet. "Where's Mrs. Hubbard?" he gasped. "Is she all right?" Assured that she was, he collapsed to the ground, apparently unable to get up.

George and Gilbert hauled the canoe into shallow water and righted it. To their surprise, much of the gear was still inside, the current having somehow wedged it in place. This piece of news revived Job somewhat, whose prostration seemed to owe at least as much to the fear that his capsize had doomed the expedition.

It was difficult to assess their losses at first, for they had no exact notion of what had been in the canoe. There was a paddle gone, Job said; also his pole and extra pole shods, the crooked knife and a frying pan. A bit more rummaging revealed that the stove was lost, as well as a tarpaulin and two tumplines. George and Gilbert hiked downstream to see if they could spot the gear, with no luck. When they came back to build a drying fire, they made the most unwelcome discovery of all. All three axes were gone.

Mina's first reaction to the capsize had been relief—simple gratitude that Joe and Job were still alive. But as the losses mounted she began to fear for her expedition. The frying pan and stove were hardly indispensable, but what about the axes? And traveling by river, pole shods were a necessity. If the present ones wore out, how would they manage?

She thought about turning back, and the possibility made her sick. Turning back would leave Wallace alone in the field, free to reap all the glory. She would have to paddle lamely into Northwest River and answer question after question about her defeat. In Halifax the reporters would be hanging about like vultures, wanting to know why she had conceded the race and whether she now considered her expedition foolhardy.

She wanted to ask George how serious the situation was, but she couldn't quite summon the courage. What if he told her they had to turn back? If he did, she supposed she couldn't really refuse. On the other hand, if she didn't ask, he wouldn't have to commit himself one way or the other. She decided that silence was best.

She watched as the men ate lunch. Job was pale, not very hungry; Gilbert and Joe were quiet. After a while George began to upbraid himself for stowing all the axes in one canoe. Gilbert pointed out that there were several trappers' tilts along the river—they might find an ax or frying pan there. To Mina's relief, George nodded, and neither he nor the others talked of turning back. If anything, they seemed anxious to go at the work harder than ever.

After lunch George improvised new tumplines and soon they were on the march again. By midafternoon Job had relaxed enough to relate in Cree a fish-eye version of his underwater exploits, which reduced George and Joe to fits of laughter. Mina couldn't help smiling, even though she didn't understand a word. The relief she felt allowed her to put aside the somewhat unsettling discovery she had made at lunch.

Whether she wished to admit it or not, George was the one who made the final decisions. Whether they should push on, what routes they ought to take, where to camp each night. Even though the men all acknowledged her as leader, her expedition depended on a sort of unwritten compact. And her partner was the man who had once accepted Laddie's life as his own responsibility, and who now—again unsure of where the trail might lead—had accepted her life too.

29

The Way She Was

In the days after the capsize, hauling loads along the portages, George had lots of time to think. Had to think about something, take his mind off the flies. They were beginning to get along now like they meant business.

He thought about her. Was she really angry with him because of the bears?

She was sitting about a mile ahead on the trail, on a pile of gear, waiting for him and the boys to bring the rest of the stuff up. The trail he was on—the one she was on too—ran right along the ridge, which was nice for walking. The trouble was, bears liked ridges too, and this was still the season when mothers worried about their cubs. George couldn't help thinking what might happen if a bear came along while Mrs. Hubbard was alone.

Well—she didn't like him fussing that way. She'd glared at him, taken her rifle out and propped it next to her, so it was ready if she needed it. She'd be fine, she said. Hadn't she chased that bear the very first day on the river? And fired as many shots as George had?

Well, she had. More than him.

And hadn't they practiced shooting together just the other evening? Hadn't he said she was doing very well?

Well, he had.

But to see her sitting there by the gear, it sure didn't look like she was worried about bears. It looked like she was almost *hoping* one would come along. She made him nervous.

Sometimes he would tell her to do something, and she'd do it. Other times he'd tell her to do something, and she wouldn't.

She'd just laugh at him like she was thinking—all right, George Elson, see what I do if a bear comes along.

But she was laughing, so she couldn't really be angry about the bears, could she? You didn't laugh when you were angry at someone. He could pretty well tell, now, when she was angry.

Like—the other morning it had been kind of showery when he opened his eyes. So he just rolled over and let it rain. The boys had been working hard; they needed the rest. Then along about seven he heard Mrs. Hubbard's voice calling, "All aboard! All aboard!" To get them up. She seemed like she was joking, the way George did with the boys, but it was different. She did it because she thought they were late and wanted them going, rain or no rain.

George thought about that. She was joking but she wasn't. Now, how could that be? When you made a joke, you wanted people to laugh. And if you wanted somebody to laugh, could you be angry with them? Hard to figure how that could be, but the thing of it was, Mrs. Hubbard's moods changed so fast. She never behaved quite the way George was used to having a woman behave.

That night around the campfire, she was quiet. At first he thought she was angry with him, but it wasn't that. She just didn't seem to care. She had been the same way the night before.

George got her making bannock, a simple bread you made with flour and water. He showed her how to knead the dough; tried to draw her out. Then she asked him, Why not add some shortening to make the dough more tender?

"No, no," he laughed, "with bannocks, you want 'em tough. Then you can throw 'em around, or sit on 'em, or jump on 'em, and they're just as good after as they were before." He showed her how to heat a flat rock by the fire, then move the rock away and cook the bannock on top. She tried it herself.

"You're getting on fine," he told her. "There's been some pretty rough places on the river where we've had to go. I know lots of fellus who would've jumped right out of the canoe if we'd taken 'em where we took you."

She smiled. "Really?"

"That's right. Lots of fellus."

It was true too. And after that, maybe she wasn't quite so sad.

The next morning was slow going and she didn't say much. But come afternoon she cheered up, and he felt better. They saw a fish eagle circling above, worried about her nest in a tree. Mrs.

Hubbard wanted to climb the tree and get a picture, but she couldn't—the nest was up sixty feet. She said she wished she was a man and could. Well, if she was a man, of course, she wouldn't've wanted to. After a while she got the boys to try and teach her some Cree. They'd say a word or two, and she'd say it back, only she said it so funny, they all just laughed and laughed. She didn't mind either.

It started to rain hard toward evening, so they stopped to set up camp. "Come over here and sit on the gear," he told her. She laughed at him ordering her around, but she did it. He propped the tarpaulin over her, with her rifle on one side and her fishing rod on the other, so she'd have a shelter from the rain. Then he got a good fire going. "This rain's going to stay around," he said. And it did, all next day.

There was nothing to do but stay in camp. When the rain let up a bit in the afternoon, she came out and watched him mend one of her moccasins. Mice had nibbled the end off the toe. After he finished, he worked on the moleskin pouch she kept her cartridges in. He was going to sew it to her belt, so she'd have it handy if she wanted bullets in a hurry. She watched him work, a big smile on her face. She seemed so pleased to have him doing it for her. Then he handed it back, all done, but she wouldn't take it. She only laughed.

"What's the matter?" he said.

"Look at the sheath and holster."

Well, he'd sewed the pouch on backward. If she wore her belt right, the holster and the sheath would be on wrong. He had to start all over again.

"That's good," she said. "You'll have something to keep you out of mischief."

So there she'd stumped him again. He couldn't understand her at all. She'd ride through some wild rapids and not turn a hair, then get all worried and want to send someone back a whole day's march for an air mattress pump. She'd walk along boulders by the shore and be angry with him for telling her not to. *Was* she angry, really? Sometimes he thought she did it just to get *him* angry. She'd joke and be more familiar with him than any white woman he'd known. But other times she'd joke and wouldn't seem to mean it—or at least, mean something different than he first thought. He'd work a long time sewing her pouch, and then she'd tease him for getting it backward.

Well, he ought to let her sew the pouch herself! He could go to his tent and write his diary or sing with the boys or do something nice. But he didn't. He stayed around and showed her how to make a rabbit snare. He couldn't figure it out. Somehow, he kind of liked the way she was.

On a wet day, build a big fire.

The blaze at their rainy camp brought the memory back. In her diary, July 7, she wrote, "Had a fine fire and I thought of Laddie's proverb, 'On a wet day build a big fire.' Sometimes it seems as if he must be standing just near and that if I turn I must see him. Strange part of all this experience is, it seems so perfectly natural." One moment the men would be sitting by the fire, George pulling out a snare. Then the rain would hiss in the flames and Laddie would be behind her.

She knew his diary nearly by heart. She knew each night where he had been, and that made some of her own days difficult to bear. Three days ago, July fourth, was his last night with her, still aboard the *Virginia Lake*. Today, he was still on the coast, just getting off at Indian Harbor. He had more than a week before he even reached Northwest River.

And then George would knead the bannock and say something funny and—here they all were. 1905 again.

They were making wonderful progress. Out nearly two weeks, and this their first rainy camp. George kept saying the weather was so good, it hardly seemed like Labrador. There had been no hardships, no suffering. She tried, at least, to feel a sense of keenness and wonder at opening new lands. She could not. The river was beautiful, certainly—far more magnificent than she ever imagined. It was just that, now and again, her memories and feelings would take and spin her, leaving her unsure of her bearings. Why was she out here—really?

On Saturday the sun returned and they continued on. The underbrush was quite thick, making difficult going. At one point a brook came tearing madly across their path. The men tied one of the tracking lines to a stump while Job waded across to hold it, so she and the others had a rail to help them cross. Toward evening they reached a barren meadow, boulders strewn everywhere and covered with an evil-looking black moss. George suggested setting up camp, but it was Saturday and Mina shuddered to think of spending Sunday in such a spot.

"Couldn't we reach the head of the rapids before dark?"

George looked restless. "The other provisions are still a ways back."

"Well," she said, "we haven't gone very fast today. I'll bet you could reach the rapids if you wanted to."

He shot her a queer look and then said, "All right, let's go." Before she knew it, he had his pack and tumpline in place and was starting down the trail.

She followed hastily, snatching up her rifle. Almost immediately she fell behind. It was amazing how agile he was, even with a hundred pounds on his back. Over logs, around boulders, brushing scrub spruce aside almost casually. And he never looked back, which was surprising. Usually George was most solicitous when the path was difficult.

Then she realized, of course, that he wanted her to fall behind. With a grimace, she redoubled her efforts, trying to make her legs imitate that loping step of his. But no matter how she tried, she couldn't dodge bushes as quickly as he. It was infuriating.

Finally he turned and waited for her to catch up.

"Let me carry your rifle for you," he said.

"Thank you, no."

So he was off, she following determinedly behind, half at a walk, half at a trot.

When they finally reached the river, she was immensely glad of the effort. A pretty brook tumbled down the far bank, and where she stood a gently wooded terrace provided ample space for tents. She turned to George. "Now, won't this make a nice Sunday camp?"

"Oh, yes," said George. But she couldn't quite tell if he was still angry with her.

"When you get to walking fast," she said, "you go so quickly. It really is impossible to keep up."

"Well," he said, "I guess you do pretty good." He pondered a moment. "You know, you do walk faster than Wallace."

And she laughed at that, quite pleased.

On Sunday the men slept late, had a leisurely breakfast, and then fetched the rest of the gear while Mina did laundry. When George returned to camp he dropped his pack, walked over to where she was sitting and handed her a tiny bouquet. The flowers were a delicate pink.

"George! They're beautiful."

"I found 'em by the trail," he said, and went to see about the rest of the gear.

Job, for his part, did some scouting and discovered a tributary flowing in from the west. This was the route the trappers used, Gilbert said, to avoid fifteen miles of bad waterfalls on the Naskapi. The trail returned to the river at Seal Lake, the halfway point to Michikamau.

The men were up bright and early Monday, ready to go. The country was more open now, and George was delighted at their progress. "It's just fun with this kind of portaging," he said. Turning up the brook, the slope was steeper, but the country remained open. Soon they came to a tiny cabin with a door so small one had to stoop to enter. It was one of Duncan McLean's winter tilts, from which Job emerged triumphantly with an ax. Gathering wood for evening fires would no longer be quite so time-consuming.

All week they followed the brook as it wended its way higher into the hills. The gain in elevation was striking. They were now level with peaks that, twenty miles back, had seemed distant and imposing. For the first time Mina began to feel like an explorer. The higher elevation affected the vegetation too: the forest was open and the hilltops barren. She was delighted at one rest to have Gilbert present her with a dandelion he'd found sheltered along the bank of a pond.

In fact, all the men were working out beautifully. "They are gentle, considerate and polite always," she wrote one night, "not only of me either but of each other as well, and have such good times together. . . . How easy I feel in the midst of them all. I could not feel more so if they were my brothers. And no one except Laddie was ever more thoughtful and kind to me than they have been."

At one evening camp she began to clean her revolver, having taken "target practice" at an owl earlier in the day. She enjoyed such sessions with George, so long as the target was at a distance she deemed eminently safe for it. But in truth, she was not enthusiastic about shooting *any* living creature; she had gone after their bear earlier in the trip only in order to enter into the proper spirit of the chase. Now, as she was putting some grease into the revolver barrel, she noticed George watching, a broad grin on his face.

"Don't put too much grease in," he warned. "If you do, why, the bullet will just slip and—"

"Might kill something," she finished for him.

Oh, he just tilted his head back and laughed like a baby! She enjoyed it immensely.

He went back to making bannock, smiling to himself. Pretty soon he said, "When you were shooting at that bear—you know, back down the river?"

"Yes?"

"Where did you aim?"

"Oh, any place. Just at the bear."

He and the other men laughed so hard at this remarkable revelation, their dinner preparations came entirely to a halt for several minutes.

Another evening they camped in a marvelous spot where the brook cascaded over a series of ledges into mirror pools. The men pitched Mina's tent near the water's edge above a little fall, right next to an otter landing. George came over to admire the view. He was in a good mood.

"You'll have to keep your boots on tonight," he said.

"I will?"

"Oh yes. You're right by the otter landing. You never know about otters—one might come along and get hold of your toes and drag you into the brook."

Mina gave him a look. "Would an otter really harm me?"

"Well, it might be a bear instead of an otter," he replied, evading her question. "They're all great fellus for tin or any kind of metal. If it's a bear, he'll just get hold of that screw on your mattress and take it right off." His eyes danced with amusement. "You'd better put a bullet inside the mattress, and then when he takes off the screw—why, your weight on the bed will blow the bullet straight into his mouth. He'll think a fly flew down his throat, and cough. Then you'll have time to run."

She laughed and George stood there beaming at his success, trying not to smile too much.

By Sunday they had left behind their brook and were camped between two of the highest hills in the area. Beyond was a new stream, this one descending into Seal Lake. Hoping to trace its course, they climbed one of the hills after supper, arriving at the summit about sunset. The country spread empty before them, caught in the oranges of the dying day. George pointed north. "There's Seal Lake," he said. From their perspective it looked hardly a lake at all—more like a river winding among the hills. Then he turned to the southwest where a ridge of mountains lay on the horizon.

"Those are the hills we had to cross two years ago, from Beaver Brook into Hope Lake. I can almost see where we went through."

She gazed at the mountains a moment, then turned to look the way they had come. Their brook, a black ribbon among the spruce, ran toward the valley to join the Naskapi River, which in turn twisted its way toward Grand Lake—far beyond view.

July sixteenth. Laddie was there.

The thought came crowding in that he really was out there and had started down Grand Lake only yesterday. It made her sick with longing. As she came off the mountain all she could think was *If only he were here.* "I have to keep reminding myself that the hills he is climbing now must be so much grander and more beautiful in view, and escape an ever-recurring feeling that it is wicked for me to be here when he is not and, oh, how desperately hungry and desolate and sad. . . . I never dreamed it would be so splendid, and the grander and more beautiful it grows, the more I hunger for the one who made all things much more beautiful by the spirit which he breathed into them."

With dawn their new brook pulled them quickly along, around one bend and another. It felt marvelous to be riding with the current instead of against it. Two quick portages, two brisk runs in bubbling fastwater, and they were looking straight eastward into Seal Lake.

The morning shimmered in light: pale blue sky, golden sun across the country, translucent air—and silence. No sound of rapids, no rushing cataracts, only gentle waters lapping at the lake's shore.

The men scanned the horizon anxiously. So did Mina. Ever since committing herself to the river, she had no way of knowing which route Wallace would take. If he too had chosen the river, then she was clearly ahead—there had been no sign of him anywhere. On the other hand, if he had taken the Indian portage, he would return to the Naskapi here, somewhere along Seal Lake.

Its waters were long and narrow, twisting in a slow curve. Gilbert led the way, having visited the area with his brother, Donald. As the men rounded each new point they watched the view open up, listening for the dip of other paddles or the sound of a human voice.

30

Sweat, Groan, and Strain

ALTHOUGH CLIFFORD Easton was still a few weeks shy of twenty-two, he figured he'd been a member of the human race long enough to know what real work was, and what real heat was, and what it meant to sweat, groan, and strain. Beginning the first of July, he found out he hadn't even got an elementary education.

Nine o'clock they started up the trail with the packs, and there was only one direction to go: up. Fifteen hundred pounds of gear and a thousand vertical feet to haul, right straight out of the river valley. After an hour of bulling against the tumpline, his temples throbbed and his neck cords stood out taut enough to snap. He'd stop to rest for a moment and steamy heat would close around him, a suffocating heat, with not even the hint of a breeze, and the flies would swarm past his neckerchief, biting everywhere, scrambling under his net and jabbing at his face; more flies buzzing in his ears, crawling up his nose, all of them in a frenzy. In the cool of the river valley there'd been hardly any.

The men pushed beyond the tree line to the ridge's summit in the broiling sun—still no wind and the flies fiercer than ever. Every nerve was calling quits, but Easton wasn't about to give in, for he could see Richards through the sting of perspiration and the haze of his mosquito net—Richards hauling his pack along. Richards had taken a hundred pounds, even though Mr. Wallace said to go easy till they got used to the work. Easton took eighty-five, ashamed to try less, convinced he couldn't bear more. In addition to the torture of packing, he felt utterly fagged out from the laxative he was taking—some patent medicine out of the first-aid kit. The tablets were potent enough, but they went directly to his head and limbs—never, it seemed, to the seat of the problem.

They had lunch at the top of the hill, hoping in vain for a breeze. Richards consulted a thermometer that had been placed under a low bush.

"Eighty-seven in the shade, but no shade," he remarked sourly. "I swear it's a hundred and fifty in the sun."

There wasn't much else to say, and nobody wanted to. Not with another pile of gear waiting below. Somehow Easton got his legs going again and headed down the tangled slope, plugging away all afternoon until his last pack was in camp and he had collapsed on top of it, oblivious of the flies. The other men weren't any better off. The strain from the heat made both the Indian guide, Pete, and Duncan McLean bleed from the nose. For a long time nobody had even seen Stanton, Wallace's lumberjack pal, but finally he staggered in, face nearly purple, veins standing out, legs trembling, eyes so glassy it seemed he would have a seizure right there on the trail. He dumped his pack and just gave out—didn't want to talk, didn't want dinner, didn't want a tent, didn't want boughs for his bed—just lay down on the rocks and went to sleep. You'd have thought he was dead.

That was the big hill, and the big hill was the worst, but there was plenty more to come. The Indian portage trail—what was supposed to be the portage trail—led up over the ridge and along a series of ponds. After a while the trail was supposed to hit the Crooked River, which after another while was supposed to lead to a big lake called Nipishish. John Ahsini, the little Montagnais Indian who'd drawn the map, hadn't been much help. The circles he scratched for ponds looked all the same, except the big one for Nipishish. The lines between the circles were supposed to be *miam potagan*—"good portaging"—but as far as Easton could see, it was mostly a case of find your own way.

Thank heavens for sleep. Sleep had the ability to make a new man. Stanton looked like a corpse that night on the hill, but sure enough, next morning he was up early as anybody, amusing himself by clambering around the rocks, catching large black ants and eating them. Stanton could be a bit of an odd duck at times.

The Indian, Pete Stevens, was another case. He didn't speak much English, and when he did, it was mostly the cigar-store variety. But mention anything about hunting, and he was ready to talk turkey in any tongue. One morning, about five—not the morning Stanton was after the ants—he poked his head through the tent door, all out of breath and excited.

"Caribou! Rifle quick!"

Winchester in hand, he was out the door and gone. Pretty soon they heard from down the trail: *bang—bang—bang*—seven times. Then silence.

Ten minutes later he walked into camp, face long as a fiddle and looking in the mood for humble pie. Didn't say a word—only leaned the rifle against the tree and went to cooking. Mr. Wallace saw what was up and said, "Well, Pete, how many caribou did you kill?"

"No caribou. Miss him," says Pete.

"But I heard seven shots. How did you miss so many times?"

"Miss him," says Pete. "I see caribou over there, close to water, run fast, try get lee side so he don't smell me. He hold his head up like this. He sniff, then he start. He go through trees very quick. See him, me, just little when he runs through trees. Shoot seven times. Hit him once, not much. He runs off. No good follow. Not hurt much, maybe goes very far."

Well, Richards couldn't resist.

"You had caribou fever, Pete," he says. "Caribou fever, sure thing!"

Pete was indignant. "No caribou fever, me! Back in Minnesota, kill plenty moose, kill red deer; never have moose fever, never have deer fever." He looked at Wallace imploringly.

"You want caribou, Mr. Wallace? Plenty sign. I get caribou any day you want him. Tell me when you want him, I kill him."

But Wallace wasn't in the mood for hunting—no chasing around except for the Indian trail. That was hard enough to find.

Maybe twelve years ago those scratches on the map had been *miam potagan*, but not now. For nearly two weeks the men worked one pond after another, inching toward Nipishish. For all their efforts, they gained maybe twenty, twenty-five miles. Two or three miles a day. It was about as bad as Hubbard on the Susan. They had the consolation of Pete actually bringing down a caribou, but the caribou took time to skin and smoke. And even with the extra meat, Mr. Wallace made a solemn announcement that flour was going to have to be rationed if they all didn't cut back some on the bread. That sobered everybody up.

Miam potagan: the trail would lead out of a pond clear as could be, then disappear dead in the middle of a thicket. Or it would be clear enough coming into a lake, but the lake would have two or three arms to choose from for the trail out. Like as not, they wouldn't find signs on any, so Mr. Wallace would have to go to the nearest high hill, or send somebody to look. Usually somebody like Pete or Richards.

Wallace didn't send Easton so much. That stung a bit, but Easton couldn't really resent it, because he respected Wallace, and—well, Richards was pulling more and was a huskier fellow, and it made sense. He deserved it and Easton didn't. But that didn't make Easton any less determined to do better. He'd joined the expedition because it offered him the chance to prove himself—not only to the folks at home but to himself. Easton knew he was a bit impulsive; still had a little too much of the boy in him. The iceberg incident—that had been bad judgment. But he meant to show Mr. Wallace that he could pull his own weight.

On July 12 they finally struck the Crooked River—at least what Ahsini's map said was the Crooked. From there it was only a hop, skip, and jump to Nipishish. But they had to track through several rapids, wading up to their waists in icy water, which meant slow going. Then next day, just when things were beginning to look better, the river split into two branches and the trail didn't go up either. Climbing a hill, Easton and Pete could see that one branch was the better route, so they came down, roused Stanton from his torpor, and began poling up it. Mr. Wallace was still off exploring the other branch. It wasn't till seven that he came hauling along and caught up, not too happy they hadn't waited. With no sign of the trail, they should have retraced their steps, he said. Well, maybe so, but you could see Nipishish from the hill, and both branches of the Crooked led there. Looking for the trail every step of the way ate up time something awful.

The weather had been mostly hot and sunny, but now it turned gray. When Easton heard rain on the tent next morning, he figured he was in for a wet day's work, but Wallace said no, might as well stay in camp and wait for things to clear. He got their stove going and everyone sat around and loafed. In the afternoon Easton and Richards got out a few crayons and drew pictures on the outside of the tent—scenes from the expedition. After dinner Pete brought out his harmonica and surprised everybody. It turned out he knew lots of tunes. Then Stanton chimed in with "Auld Lang Syne" and "The Holy City." Nobody could beat Stanton's tenor: He sounded like some opera virtuoso. He also did "My Good-for-Nothing Brother

Bob," a song about a fellow supposed to be the greatest liar of all time. The verses went on and on, all funny. Then Mr. Wallace pulled out a vest-pocket copy of *Hiawatha* and let Stanton recite from it. Pete perked right up: He knew his Indian legends, all right.

"Hiawatha, he the same as Christ," he explained. "He do anything he want to."

Next day it was still raining, and Wallace made no move to go. Nor the third day. Easton was getting restless. The rain wasn't coming down all that hard; they ought to be traveling. A stove was a fine thing on a damp day, but it wasn't getting anybody across Labrador. "I do not intend to criticize Mr. Wallace," he wrote that evening in his journal, "but I firmly believe that taking into account the indefinite ending of our trip and the difficulty experienced so far . . . we should push on, rain or shine." It was difficult enough finding the portage along these small lakes, let alone the bigger ones they'd encounter later.

Even Mr. Wallace got cabin fever. He went out to fish with Pete and as he was hopping out onto a rock, in the lower swirl of the rapid, suddenly slipped into the river head over ears. Pete laughed his head off until Wallace came crawling out like a drowned rat and told him to tuck it in.

Next morning was cloudy, but Wallace had reached the end of his patience with the weather, so they were off again. Easton could have sworn Nipishish was only around the bend; he and Pete had seen it from that hill. But every crook in the Crooked brought only more bends and rougher rapids. More rain too. After three days of icy wading and wet brush, they still hadn't reached big water.

Nothing seemed to go right. One day Pete had to hike back to find a couple of cups and a tracking line they'd left at their last camp. Another, Richards mislaid his rifle along the trail and spent the afternoon looking for it. That night the rain turned to sleet, so Wallace went into an early camp. At least Pete came back with good news: He'd hiked over the last portage and saw Nipishish. Wallace felt a lot easier.

"Once we hit Nipishish, the lakes get bigger," he said. "We'll have more water and fewer and easier portages. We can travel faster."

"Maybe better, I don't know," said Pete. "Always hard find trail out of big lakes. May leave plenty places. Take more time hunt trail maybe now. Indian maps no good. Maybe easier when we find him."

As for Easton, he was still worried. They had covered a pitiful three-quarters of a mile that day. If he were running the trip, he would make use of every moment, wet or dry, to keep plugging. It was July 20. They had been out twenty-four days and hadn't done more than sixty miles—including thirty easy ones on Grand Lake. There were 440 more to cover, and a third of their flour was gone. The caribou meat had helped some, but they hadn't smoked it long enough, and with all the rain it had gone moldy and had to be thrown away. Easton couldn't help thinking of the 1903 trip, and the last entries in Hubbard's diary. But Hubbard himself had written "it is a man's game," and the game had to be played out.

The rain howled for two more days, but the sun reappeared about noon of the third. Wallace decided to dispense with Duncan McLean's services and send him back early, with letters for the home folks—he'd been looking pretty wet and quiet the past couple of weeks. After Duncan left, they pushed on until July 24—finally—they struck Nipishish. After so many days it seemed almost a mirage, especially with the sun and good weather. But the arms of the lake spread out exactly the way Ahsini had drawn them, and the trail led out right where he said. In the distance Easton could see high hills—the ones overlooking Seal Lake. The lake itself couldn't be more than twenty miles away.

Funny how a little sun and good paddling lifted a man's spirits. Easton still suffered from a touch of constipation, but he was beginning to think Pete's advice on that point had been the best. "No tablets, you. Eat balsam gum. Like Indians. Little balsam gum fix right up." Easton had tried it only once, but the results had been awe-inspiring.

WALLACE WAS BEGINNING to regret a certain inevitable arithmetic that had crept into his routine, something that hadn't plagued him on the trip with Hubbard. Each day had its balance sheet now, pluses or minuses to be totted up: number of miles gained, where they should be if on schedule, how to make up lost time if they weren't. In 1903 Hubbard had spent hours fiddling with these probabilities while Wallace sat contentedly by the fire, resting up so he could plug dutifully ahead the next day.

There were human factors in the balance scales too. Did each man pull his share? Was morale good? If not, what could he do to boost it? If high, what should be done to keep the men from becoming careless or overconfident? He'd already spoken about flour rations. Pete loved to melt a hunk of pork grease and fry the bread dough pulled out thin, a delicious concoction that tasted like doughnuts. Richards, who had never sampled it before, asked Pete what he called it and Pete said he didn't know.

"Well, I call it darn good," said Richards.

"That's what we call him, then," retorted Pete, and so they did. "Darn goods." Richards couldn't get enough of them, not to mention Easton and Stanton. The flour sack got lighter and lighter. Wallace took Pete aside and asked him to bake less bread.

Pete thought a bit. "Bread very good for Indian," he said. "Not good when white man eat so much. Good way fix him. Use not so much baking powder, me. Make him heavy."

But Wallace said no, bake it as usual, but not so much. He'd speak to the men about it. Just the possibility of going on rations made them turn solemn. But words of caution proved inadequate. Only five days past Lake Nipishish, Wallace rummaged through the provision sacks with increasing consternation and found that only two bags of flour remained out of the original six. Bread was cut to one loaf a day per person, to be eaten at each man's pleasure. Easton made another inventory a few days later and discovered a third bag, but Wallace let the ration stand. One couldn't be too careful.

On the other hand, if he were too strict, morale would sink and that wasn't good either. Their continual slow progress made for a fair amount of frustration. Lose the trail, search the lake, climb a hill, find the trail, paddle the next stream, lose the trail again. Tracking up a swift brook one day, the whole business had gotten his goat. The other boat was in the lead as usual, having breezed right up the rapids. But when Wallace tried to follow, his bow got stuck. He pushed and shoved to free it, got angry when it didn't budge, shoved again, and suddenly found himself up to his waist in icy water, holding on for dear life as the current swirled around him.

"Why in hell did you bring us up here?" he shouted to the lead boat, and they mumbled something inaudible.

Usually he'd been pretty good about his temper. Their caribou hunts had certainly taxed his patience. "Free-for-alls" was perhaps a more accurate term. Two days in a row they'd gone after deer and come back empty-handed. First time it had been a buck, a doe, and a fawn swimming toward shore. Both boats took up the chase in wild enthusiasm and got within seventy yards just as all quarry reached shore. Easton swung Wallace's end of the boat into position, while Wallace stood and fired twice, but his arm was shaking from having paddled so hard and the shot went short. Pete fired, missing the shoulder of the buck by a foot, then missed again as the deer took to the woods. Next day there was another buck and another wild chase. In Pete's boat, Easton had the rifle and should have been the one to fire, but instead of swinging the canoe into position, Pete grabbed a shotgun and pulled both barrels. Way out of shotgun range. Easton couldn't shoot without plugging Stanton, so he stood and fired over his head, missing the deer entirely due to the swaying boat. Stanton's gun was propped steady on his knee; he fired twice, missed. It was like a Coney Island shooting gallery.

Wallace said nothing. He didn't want the men discouraged. July 28 was Easton's birthday, and, in his honor, Wallace named their latest unknown lake after him, as well as ordering extra rations of bread all around. Stanton made up a prune pudding. Fortunately, Pete had also managed to bring down three geese with the shotgun, so two of those went into the pot. Easton seemed quite pleased at having his own lake, not to mention the chance for a feed.

"Smells just like home," he said, waiting for the goose to brown.

"I haven't been filled up for a week," Richards chimed in, "but I sure am going to be tonight."

Encouragement here, caution there. Always having to balance up. Wallace's impression of his recruits kept changing. There was Stanton: hail fellow well met and a fine companion. Wallace had been eternally grateful to him the winter they'd spent together at the lumber camp, when Stanton had helped him regain the use of his legs. His songs around the campfire were a morale booster and his occasional antics amused the boys. But it had become increasingly clear that he wasn't quite the workhorse the others were. Stanton was usually last with his loads along the portage trail, and he preferred cooking up a meal by the fire to going out scouting. Pete, on the other hand, was turning out to be a real peach of a guide, despite his rabid enthusiasm for the chase. Wallace had been disappointed upon first meeting him in Grand Central—he seemed timid and not at all sure of himself. In answer to inquiries on whether he could perform this skill or that, he had only lowered his head and answered with an aggravating "I don't know," leaving Wallace to fret about what kind of scout he had ended up with. In the woods, though, Pete had proved himself tenfold—his ability to nose out the trail was remarkable.

Still—there was the Indian side. A fox barked one day and Pete informed them earnestly that it was a sure herald of death for one of them. Richards and Easton scoffed, of course, and Wallace didn't take it seriously, but it was hard not to be reminded of George's starvation stories. Was Pete hinting at something? No, probably not; after enduring more chaffing, he revised his opinion and said the fox's bark came from off to one side, so it meant only a death in someone's family.

Then there were Richards and Easton. The youth of the trip, the packhorses. Even there, Wallace's opinions were changing. Richards was the bigger of the two, and cockier. Wallace had always assumed he'd be the one to help pull the trip along. Richards was doing well enough, certainly, although sometimes he seemed just a bit too cocky. He wasn't one to hold back a complaint. As for putting away "darn goods," he was the worst offender. And when Wallace reduced the bread ration to a loaf per man, Richards had taken to hoarding chunks to eat between meals. Wallace got hungry seeing him munch away; the habit rankled.

Easton, on the other hand, had started out seeming the weak link of the trip. He was lanky; one might almost think frail. Pound for pound, he was no match for Richards. But he never quit work ahead of anyone else, was always up early, always eager to push on. The last few days, in fact, Wallace had to take him aside and tell him to let up a bit. He seemed a bit under the weather. It was the laxative tablets, Easton said. He'd taken an extra strong dose, and now ruefully opined that nothing short of dynamite would cure the ailment. Then he went back to work, seeming to go at it as hard as ever.

The last day of July came and went, with Seal Lake seemingly no nearer. The flies were hellish. Bulldogs had joined the battle, leaving bloody welts on everyone. Wallace's face was swollen and disfigured; Easton's forehead, neck, ears, and chest were raw and covered with dark clots from the bites. Meanwhile, the evening army of mosquitoes left the wall of the tent black with their numbers. Morale was at its lowest, for not only were the insects fierce, the course led across a sand desert that seemed more like the Sahara than Labrador—no moss, not a drop of water anywhere, and only a few stunted bushes.

With immense relief, Wallace reached a large stream flowing in the direction of Seal Lake. At last they were over the watershed. Before he knew it, the current sped them along seven miles. The following day the canoes picked up more speed and even ran a few riffles. Wallace and Richards were the only ones on the trip with any experience in rapids, so their boat went first. Pete and Easton followed, nervous about the challenge and exhilarated by their success. They had a few wild rides and narrow scrapes, but came through unscathed.

The morning of August 4 everyone climbed a nearby ridge and looked westward. The river snaked around a few sand hills and then emptied into fine open water that stretched for miles. There was no doubt about its identity. The men gave a rousing cheer, and Wallace joined in.

"Seal Lake at last! That's what all the work's for. Now it's 'Ho for Michikamau,' boys!" Hubbard's rallying cry echoed strong as ever.

It was a simple matter to run the last rapids, and by noon they were on Seal's peaceful waters. Wallace could hardly believe it. He had been disappointed so many times that he climbed another hill to make sure the lake matched Duncan's detailed description. Then they all paddled to a spot called the Narrows, where one of Duncan's winter tilts was set. The men walked up and surveyed the cozy cabin, logs chinked with moss, and a weathered toboggan lying outside the door. One of the men lifted the toboggan and looked it over, then motioned for Wallace.

On one of the smooth runners was a message, scrawled in pencil. Wallace moved closer, squinted, read:

Arrived here all well and safe Hurrah for Michikamau 1905
George Elson

31

"You Have Just About Had Us Crazy"

George was in a good mood, and so were the boys—had every right to be, this only the third week of July and Seal Lake behind them. When Mrs. Hubbard did some housecleaning and threw away the cards her fishing leaders were wrapped around, George scooped 'em up. He laid the cards on a box by the fire.

"Time to get your tickets punched," he called to the boys. "Where do you want your ticket to?"

"Michikamau," said Job.

George made a show of stamping a card and handed it over. "That'll be fifteen dollars."

Job went through his pockets. Finally he pulled out a piece of gun rag and plunked it down. That got him by.

They'd paddled nineteen miles down Seal Lake, with no sign anywhere of Wallace. Then, after a rain day, gone another nineteen farther up the Naskapi. The only problem was the weather. The storms seemed to be getting down to business and not at all particular when to start or stop. Considering Labrador, it was a providence the sun had stayed as long as it had.

The morning of the twentieth the rain was so bad he called to Mrs. Hubbard to see if she wanted breakfast in her tent. She said yes. But her voice floated out so low, George dragged some big logs onto the fire and strung up the tarp, then went over again and stood by her door. The rain was running off his brim like a regular river.

"Maybe, after all, you had better come out by the fire," he said. "It will be warmer for you."

She got dressed and come out. Under the tarp, George served fried goose liver and bannock. She really liked the liver—called it a luxury. After breakfast the other fellus drifted off with things to do. That left George and Mrs. Hubbard to talk, the rain still beating against the tarp and the fire sparking like it does when the wood is wet. George put another log on. He wanted the fire to roar.

Mrs. Hubbard sat with her hands wrapped around a hot cup of coffee. Awhile back she'd lost the glove for her right hand, and it was swollen some from the bites. The left was soft and fine, though, with a little line of blue where the veins ran.

Somehow, George got to talking about Rupert's House, where he'd grown up. Mrs. Hubbard liked to hear about those things, just as Hubbard had. She seemed interested. Of course, George had lots of stories—about hunting or the pranks he played with Job when young, one thing or another. But this morning he got to talking about how he'd taught himself to write. He hadn't told this story to hardly anyone: Whites didn't care particularly, and Indians sure weren't interested. But somehow he thought she would be. As a boy, what he did was gather up little pieces of paper and stitch them together like a book. Then he marked down what he'd done every day. He never heard of a diary then or knew that anybody ever wrote such things. But he kept putting his little books together and writing stories in them. Then one day his father learned about it and gave him some real notebooks.

Well, this story lighted Mrs. Hubbard up like he'd never seen before. Something came into her face. All of a sudden she wanted to know everything about those books. Where were they now?

As far as George knew, they were still in the trunk back in Rupert's House. The trunk belonged to Jim, his brother.

It was marvelous what he'd done, she said—and without anybody's help. Was he sure the books were safe? He oughtn't to let anything happen to them.

The more Mrs. Hubbard asked, the more George got to worrying. Maybe they'd been thrown out by now; it had been a long time. He told her he'd happened to write Jim about the trunk before he left for Labrador. He guessed he'd know if the stuff was safe when he got back.

Mrs. Hubbard had a "capital idea"—her words. What George should do was take his stories and use them to write a book for boys. *She* was writing a book. Why couldn't he?

He had to smile. Why, he couldn't even spell right. *Porcupine* came out different every time he tried it. But she pointed out that he'd already written the story of Mr. Hubbard's last days for her. All he needed was an editor to polish things up. And then she said *she'd* help him, and he didn't have anything to say to that; it was something he never dreamed of. But she said it right out—she would delight in it. Dr. Sawyer would help too.

That was when he knew she wasn't just talking. Dr. Sawyer was an important man. As a minister, he'd published lots of things himself. George had got to know him while visiting in Williamstown; had even written a letter to him this summer from Northwest River, before they went into the bush.

She talked of these ideas a good while more, and then went back to her tent for a nap. But George stayed by the fire, feeding it and watching it burn.

By Sunday, the twenty-third, Mina had done enough "resting" to make any sane person tired. Being cooped up in a damp tent for more than a day seemed to her almost like prison, especially when the men went off on one of their scouting trips. Fortunately, George agreed they might travel on the Sabbath, to make up for lost time. He was just coming down to the canoes with the last gear when he stopped, eyes fixed on the lake expansion upstream. His genial smile had disappeared.

"What's that?" he asked in a husky voice. "A duck?"

Gilbert spun around and stared. "Not a duck—a deer!"

In the distance Mina could see what seemed only a dark speck moving across the river. Before she could say a word, George threw the last of the gear in the canoe and steadied the boat for her. As she stepped quickly to her place he drew his knife, cut the mooring rope, and pushed off in one motion. Job was paddling like a man possessed, before the keel had even cleared the shallows.

Caribou! This was one of the things she had come to see. Yet she trembled, for she really did not want the deer killed. Earlier in the trip the men had been in the habit of asking if she wanted to shoot game, but by now they knew she preferred not to see any living thing killed unless necessary. In any case they were entirely oblivious of her, their eyes riveted on their quarry, arms working so hard the canoe seemed to lift nearly out of the water.

They said nothing; only paddled sharp strokes, each surge

making the tendons in their necks stand out like ropes. Mina could feel the canoe's thrust, see the men strain with each pull and the water rush by the hull. Job barked a few words of Cree and George replied in kind. She could not fathom the content—only that the talk was of killing.

The deer seemed no longer a speck, but he was still some four hundred yards away. To her relief, he had nearly gained the shore, where he could easily scramble out of harm's way before the canoe pulled within rifle range.

Job called out, low, and both men laid down their paddles as the canoe swung round. George raised his rifle and aimed—a desperate shot, Mina thought. Still, she held her breath; he had astounded her before.

The rifle cracked and she relaxed. The bullet had splashed harmlessly in front of the deer.

George remained motionless a moment, then smiled and laid his rifle down. She looked at him, puzzled, then back to the deer. It was hesitating now and, frightened by the splash, began to turn away from shore back toward the middle of the river. Mina was nearly sick with dismay. George had tricked her! She wanted to call out and warn the creature away. It had been so close to safety.

The men were paddling again, sweat staining their shirts, the beat of their paddles spreading a wake like a steamer's. Finally the boat was close enough so that the men could almost touch the deer with their paddles. As if in a dream, Mina found her camera and tried not to shake as she snapped a picture. Then she pulled her hat over her eyes.

George fired with his pistol.

She looked up. The animal was still swimming as strongly as before. Could George have missed? Then the deer gave a shudder and she saw blood filling the water. The deer's eye swooped wildly—bulging, beseeching.

"George, use your rifle! For goodness' sake!"

George picked up the Winchester and shot a second time. This time the sound of thrashing ceased. She opened her eyes. The men were joyous, shouting in Cree, working to tow the deer to shore. She felt bleak and exhausted. When the canoes pulled up on a nearby sandbank, she walked a good distance down the beach. She did not want to look at the men or, for that matter, have them look at her.

MOSTLY GEORGE wrote in his journal after supper, once the evening chores were done. But sometimes he'd get a chance in the middle of the day. And with rainy camps, there was time to write just about whenever.

Diaries were funny things. You wrote 'em to yourself, not intending anybody to see them. Those little books he'd made as a boy—now why had he done that? If they were things only *he* was going to read—why, he knew those things before he put them down. Why trouble to write them, if they weren't for anybody else? Of course, Mr. Hubbard wrote a diary so he wouldn't forget things later. But he was meaning to write a book. Mrs. Hubbard too. But, when George was a boy, that wasn't so. He sure didn't know Mrs. Hubbard was going to take an interest years later. He hadn't even known other people kept diaries. Why did he do it?

Even now—the journal for this trip. Being only for himself, it really didn't matter how he spelled or what he said. Still, when he got down to writing it, he found he was particular. Some things seemed to fit on the page easier than others. The miles you'd come, what the boys shot, whether it was raining—that was easy. Whereas you'd go to put down other things and they didn't seem to belong. What he put, sometimes, was "See page 155" and then turned to the back and wrote it there. Other times, things didn't even want to go in the back. He would get out a second book. In his first journal he would write, "See other book."

And all this to himself. What did it matter where it went?

Now, Mrs. Hubbard. When she was getting along well, that was easy to write about. "Mrs. Hubbard making good shooting at an little owl." "Mrs. Hubbard doing very well indeed in her travelling through such a rough country." You just put it down easy, right next to "Joe killed two spruce partardjes, country very very rough and ragged." But the times when she seemed to keep to herself—that was harder to write about. "Just near the river and some nice sandy banks where I ~~*killed*~~ shot the caribou, Mrs. Hubbard after was shading tears. I suppose it just remined her of the one Mr. Hubbard had killed on our trip which we had out here in Labrador. I felt very sorry for her."

The hardest times were when she seemed angry or disappointed with him. Any time the rain stopped them, or they had slow going on the portages, she began to fret. And for a while after he shot the caribou she fretted even worse, because the boys got sick from eating too much deer meat. Two whole days they had to rest up, and these were sunny ones, good for traveling. She got quieter and quieter all the time, and finally came to him at night, her eyes anxious and full of distress. She told him she had given up hope of making it to Ungava in time to catch the steamer. There were nearly four hundred miles yet to go, she said. "I'm trying to do my best, but it seems such a poor best to me."

She had better not feel that way, he told her—straight out. Then he said, "We fellus haven't hurried ourselves any. We've taken it easy." Because, of course, they were afraid she couldn't stand the hard traveling. If she wanted, he said, they were willing to go a good deal faster.

Her eyes seemed almost to reproach him for going slow. As if she would fail now and it was his fault. It made him tremble to think about it. In his journal he wrote, "Well I hope we will be able to take Mrs. Hubbard through to Ungava. . . . Hope we will not be too late for her." But when he tried to say what he felt about their conversation, the closest he could come was "Sorry and tremble about—" and couldn't go further. Just wrote "so and so," and put a period.

Next morning he was up before three. They would blame well make up for lost time, especially with the hard country ahead. Upstream the mountains closed in like a canyon and the river got steep, with lots of waterfalls. Job found they could portage to the south of the river by hopping from one lake to another. He and the boys took the first load of gear along before breakfast, so she could sleep.

She was up by the time they got back, and she nearly scared them to death.

She came out of her tent wearing—well—a *bag* over her head. With holes in it. She looked like some kind of Indian conjuror. It was one of the grub sacks, except she had cut eye and ear holes, and one for her nose, and sewed them all over with mosquito veiling three or four layers thick. The holes were so dark you couldn't even see her eyes.

"Do you think it will work?" she asked. "Against the flies?"

"You'll have to take it off when you get to the Naskapis," he said. "They will just shoot you."

And they would too—he was dead serious. The way she looked,

she would scare the livers out of anybody, especially Indians that didn't know her. He tried not to smile but couldn't help himself. How could you talk serious to a bag?

"I won't care next time a bear comes along if you have that on," he said. "I'll just know you are safe. A bear would never touch you. You really don't know how you look."

But she said she didn't care and wore it anyway. Like he knew she would.

The next two days the boys moved right along, hauling up the hills and pushing through the marshes. Country very ragged. Mrs. Hubbard loved the high hills; in fact, she kept wanting to climb 'em, to see what the country was like. George said no at first. After all, hadn't she just told him she wanted to go fast? But she gave him such a look that his knees buckled, and said she meant to go whether he came or not. So he went, of course—what else could he do? Afterward he was glad, for he could see it meant a lot to her:

> This mountain so very high and see all around and how pretty. . . . Mrs. Hubbard was so much delighted on this mountain and of all the other scenary around she enjoyed it very much and could of taken some nice pictures if she had brought along her cameras with her. She felt so sorry she did not bring them along as she left them at the canoe.

Which was when he made his terrible mistake—standing right there on top of the mountain. Dear Lord, how could he have been so foolish?

"Why shouldn't I come up here after dinner with my Kodaks, and take pictures while you're making the portage? The walking isn't rough. I couldn't lose my way if I tried."

Mina was prepared for a refusal, as usual. Instead, George surveyed the surroundings carefully and walked down the other side of the hill a short distance, to try the angle of the slope.

"Well," he said after a long pause, "I guess you might try it. You could come back this afternoon and keep an eye on the lake. You'll be able to see us coming along in the canoes, and can come down the far side. We'll meet you there."

After lunch she armed herself with notebooks, two Kodaks, a

revolver and cartridges, bowie knife, barometer, and compass. She felt ready for anything. "You'd better take your rubber shirt too," said George. "It's going to rain this afternoon."

She looked at the sky. Only a few silvery clouds floated over the hills. Anyway, she was carrying enough of a load as it was. "No, I don't think I shall," she said. And to her satisfaction, George said nothing.

The afternoon was glorious. It seemed wonderful, going off without a guard, free to spend an hour or two alone on the hill. From the summit she took her pictures, jotted in her notes, and, after the allotted time had passed, began looking toward the lake for the men. They had not yet appeared, but Mina decided to head down.

Descending, she looked toward the clearing where she was to meet the men. To her surprise she saw a large brown object lying on the ground. A bear! She gulped; then stood quite still watching it. She hardly knew what to do. Her eyes could play tricks on her, she knew that. Several times already on the trip she had spotted bears, only to have them dwindle upon closer examination into ducks, old stumps, and other such objects. Now she racked her brain. The bear had not moved at all. Was it probable that he would lounge about on the moss and rocks for so long? Finally she concluded that the quickest way to settle the issue was to go and see. She had her revolver, and this time would aim at the chest—not "any place, just at the bear." Hurrying along, she tried to keep the object in sight but could not. When she reached the valley floor, it was nowhere to be seen.

There was no sign of the men either. To make matters worse, a thunderhead had appeared, making its way swiftly up the valley. She saw a sheet of rain sweeping over the lake; soon it reached her and swirled about. The downpour seemed to stir up the mosquitoes and flies, who buzzed at her madly.

Where were the men? She decided she could hardly be expected to remain rooted to one spot while being both drenched and devoured. Impulsively she set out for the ridge on the far side of the lake. It was no more distant than the hill she had already climbed, and it promised a view of the river.

She splashed across the lake's outlet, feeling vaguely like a girl running away from home. The men had warned her never to stray, but she was not going far and they were the ones who had failed to keep their rendezvous. Besides, any time she showed the least independence—wanting to explore along the river or climb a mountain or even look at a waterfall—George would warn her about bears or dizziness or some other peril. It was irksome to be so well taken care of.

From atop one end of the ridge, she got a marvelous view of the river, with its turbulent falls. Back on the lake, however, there was still no sign of the men. So she followed her ridge along the arch of its smooth spine, the ground dropping away abruptly on either side. Twenty minutes' march brought her to the farthest precipice, where she could see the bay to which the men were to carry their gear. Sure enough, there were the two canoes far below, turned upside down to keep the outfit dry. But her relief turned quickly to annoyance. The men were resting comfortably under some trees, drinking tea by a fire. While she was getting soaked, they were enjoying themselves regally.

Then she remembered. George and the rubber shirt.

So she was being given a lesson on the advisability of taking good advice. She flushed—then had an idea and smiled. They would see who was good at giving lessons.

She drew her revolver and fired two shots—just to put them on their mark. Then she trotted back along the ridge looking for a place to climb down—not to the lake but to the ridge beyond, an even higher one where the view would be spectacular.

Soon enough, two shots came in reply. The men had just realized where she was. She fired an answering round and disappeared over the far side of the ridge. The going was quite steep and she laughed to think how terrified George would be if he could see her. She slid down a wide crevass, careening along and grabbing bushes as they flew by. In the valley she encountered a bog, which she tried to cross, but the mud got too deep and she had to go around. Never mind—the freedom was delicious! Climbing the big ridge, she heard two more shots, this time from the end of the lake where she had agreed to meet them. The men were moving quickly now.

Up she climbed, faster than ever. She was determined to get as far as she could before being rounded up and returned to camp. Reaching the crest of the ridge, she walked along for more than half an hour, until she scaled its highest point. There she rested. The rain had passed and a fine breeze put the flies to rout.

The breeze also carried the faint noise of shouting and an occasional rifle shot. Presently she spied a small speck moving along the first ridge. She watched with satisfaction as it disappeared. Then shots again—a long series of them in quick succession. Mina surveyed the scene and laughed. Who was lord of the wilderness now?

For what seemed a very long time, she saw no one. She felt giddy, knowing she would soon be caught but not knowing by whom or from which direction her captor might appear. Finally a figure popped into view, far down on her own ridge. He was waving his arms wildly and seemed to be shouting or wailing. Then a second figure appeared, also running toward her.

Suddenly she became frightened. The two men seemed utterly frantic. Had something dreadful happened? Someone hurt or drowned? She started toward them.

It was George and Job. Perspiration soaked them and they were shaking all over. Their faces were pale, filled with a mixture of indignation, anxiety, anger, and relief. George ran up, gasping for air; then slowed to a walk; then stood for a moment, catching his breath. Reproachfully he folded his arms across his chest. Mina smiled, but he did not smile back. His chest was still heaving from the exertion.

"Well," he said between gulps, "I guess you very near done it this time."

"Very near done what?"

"You have just about had us crazy."

"Had you crazy! What about?"

"Why, we thought you were lost."

Mina laughed. "Didn't you see me on the ridge when I fired those shots?"

"Yes, we did. And when we got up to the end of the lake, we thought you would come back down. I went up the ridge to meet you and when I saw you weren't there, I was sure you went down to the rapids. Then I ran down there, and when I didn't find you I thought you either fell in or got lost."

"But I promised not to go to the rapids."

"Yes, but you promised you wouldn't go off alone too."

"Well," she said, "when I got to the end of the lake and saw you weren't coming, and the rain was coming on, I thought I might as well be doing something while the storm was wetting me and the flies were eating me."

"Yes, that is just what we said. 'Who would ever think of her going up there in that storm?' "

She laughed again, but George remained solemn.

"Job, he come running too, and he was sure you were lost. When we couldn't see you on the ridge or find you at the rapid, we began to walk faster and faster, and then to run like crazy people. Job could hardly speak, and neither could I, and out of breath and half-crying all the time. Oh, we can never trust you to go away alone again!"

"Very well," she said. "I'll make a bargain with you. If someone will go with me without fuss whenever I want to climb a mountain, or do anything else I think necessary for my work, I promise not to go away alone again."

And he agreed to that immediately.

But as they walked the ridge back to camp he kept going over and over the afternoon's events. How he had watched her climb along on the first mountain; how the next thing he knew two shots came from the *other* side of the lake. That puzzled them immensely. Joe was the one to catch sight of her at last, but even so they couldn't imagine who it was. Then Joe said, "Why, it's a woman!"

"The men got on me too," George continued. "They said they never saw a woman act anything like the way you do. They've been on lots of trips before—where there were women too—but never where the women didn't do what they were told."

She laughed heartily at this, but George only scowled. "Yes—you don't care a bit, do you?" he said, which only made her laugh more. And this time he laughed too, a little.

"Oh," he said, "I thought I was never going to see you again. I'm never going to forget it. I was thinking how you would feel when you knew you were lost. It's an awful thing to be lost. If I hadn't ever been lost myself, I wouldn't know what it means. And what would we do if you got lost or fell in that rapid? Just think what *could* we do? Why, I could never go back again. How could any of us go back without you?"

She reddened. This aspect of the situation had not occurred to her.

"We couldn't, that's all. We'd have to go live with the Eskimo or hide out. But even then, they'd hunt us down." And she saw that he meant it. Their wild looks and pale faces no longer seemed so comical.

George walked silently, eyeing her. "And to see you too, the way you look. Just as if you would never scare anybody."

Before he was done, Mina felt almost ashamed to show her

face in camp. She had never intended to frighten them so. When she arrived near dusk, Gil and Joe were putting up her tent. They smiled, but were pale and quiet. Their hands trembled as they worked.

She had packed no medicine for a quaking heart, except possibly the brandy at the bottom of her pack reserved for special meals. The men really looked as if they needed a bracer. After debating with herself, she dug down and brought the bottle out.

In the tent—lit only by the glow of four pipes—George took another pull and felt his throat warm. Then sent the bottle around again.

She said take only a little. Well—this was a little bottle to begin with. When they finished all but a few swallows, they laid on their blankets and talked a while more, with their big heads.

Joe couldn't get over it—how she'd got all the way to that ridge. Thought it was somebody else, till he saw those skirts billowing. Job never run so hard in his life, not even after deer.

George stared at the top of the tent. You could almost see the northern lights through the silk. He kept thinking how she looked climbing that mountain in the sunshine. She was running around up there like a Labrador fly, so busy—like a little girl building things. And she was so quick getting to the other side. Who would think to see her, with those little steps she took?

He ought to be mighty angry. But to have caught up to her finally, the way he did, and see how she looked: walking toward him so easy and smiling at him like she would never scare anybody—

He rolled on his side and pulled out his diary. Then lit a candle. The brandy felt good.

He wrote:

> Mrs. Hubbard is really so good and a really kind hearted woman she is. She is more than good to me. My sister could not be any kinder to me as she is. How glad and proud my sisters would be if they knew how kind and what a good friend I have.

He frowned at that. Words took off so in their own direction.

> Still I don't only want to say she is only a friend to me but that she is my sister. God will help her and bring her again to her good friends home to where she came from. She is so bright and smart and I am glad that she does trust me.

He thought a good while more. Somehow, the pencil didn't quite want to leave his hand.

He wrote: *See other book*.

32

The Verge of Success

By Monday, July 31, Mina was relieved to be back on the river again, heading upstream. The sun was out, and with it came a humid heat. Perspiration dripped from the men's faces as they carried gear and canoes up the slopes of several gorges and around waterfalls. The heat brought the bulldogs out too—buzzing, biting viciously, leaving welts and blood. The mosquitoes were never bad when the bulldogs were out, the men said; bulldogs ate mosquitoes.

Occasionally a breeze scattered the brutes and raised her spirits. The river's upward course was dramatic: huge reddish rocks thrusting at all angles, their tops seared by a fiery vermilion lichen, while fields of pale moss formed a backdrop. The river flowed broad and black into the drops and was dashed into a luminescent white spray. The vivid hues stirred Mina deeply.

For weeks it had been a matter of climbing hill after hill as the river wound its way higher, and now, finally, they came out upon a shimmering tableland where the river expanded into one long lake after another, mirrorlike under the noonday sun. Gone were the bright colors of the jagged gorges, leaving only the grays and greens of low ridges that pinched the river into an occasional cascade between lakes. Everything seemed to hug the horizontal—shrubs and berry bushes, the dwarf spruce, even the haze that burnished the landscape.

On August 1 they came to a solitary hill that George announced they would climb. He had the feeling Michikamau might lie just beyond.

The slope was wooded, almost to the top, and the walking

rough. Every conceivable bush seemed to snag Mina's sweater, every deadfall to catch at her skirt. George walked a few steps ahead, waiting every so often for her to catch up, but she paid him no heed, alone with her thoughts.

The heat was terrible. She felt she should almost strangle from it. In desperation she considered the possibility of turning back and letting the men do the scouting. Yes, she *would* turn back: never mind what they thought. But she caught herself. She knew that, in a strange way, she was afraid of getting to the top—not afraid that she wouldn't see Michikamau but that she would. The peculiar turn of her feelings frightened her. She was on the verge of success; yet with every step she took, she dreaded more what lay ahead.

Several nights earlier she'd had a dream of climbing hills of water—water cascading everywhere in a crystal rush. She climbed higher and higher and was reveling in the water, the climb, the achievement. And then at almost the last step, the difficulties and trials became too much. What the trials were she couldn't say—just, she wasn't able to go any farther and was defeated. Or rather, woke up.

The dream had been puzzling. Was she anxious that, after all the favorable progress, she might fail at the last moment? Or was it rather the prospect of success that disturbed her—the thought that once she finished climbing her hills of water, there would be nothing left in life for her?

Surely she did want to succeed. Yet there was no denying the strange feeling that it would be wicked to do what Laddie had not done or go where he had not been. It was as if a voice inside were whispering that it would be more beautiful, in the end, to fail. That she should somehow experience Laddie's disappointments and privations and join him alone, the two of them together, sharing the same fate.

At the summit she was afraid to look around at first; then wanted to look and get it over with. Through the summery haze, she saw the Naskapi winding all the way back to the portage where she had run away. Ahead, along the tableland, the river expansions snaked toward another lake that stretched northwest into a vast, blue expanse forty or fifty miles long. It could only be Michikamau.

George nodded his confirmation and then walked ahead another forty yards. She followed. He was looking not so much at Michikamau as the land to the south. Almost in a whisper he said, "I know the hill there. That's where the two of us stood."

It was surprisingly close; perhaps six or seven miles away. Mina followed the sweep of his arm as it passed over the plateau to a dip in the hills.

"That's where we came on our long portage."

And then below, nearly at their feet:

"Windbound Lake. We paddled up the bay there looking for a way through. We never did find it."

His gaze returned to the hill, searching with eyes that could lay bare a tin of films under eight feet of snow. He seemed almost in a dream.

"See the second knob there? Comin' off the top of the mountain? That's where Mr. Hubbard and me shot our rabbit."

His finger moved a fraction. "Just to the left, there's a shadow a little darker than the rest of the hill. Those are bushes. That's where our ptarmigan were hiding—nine of 'em. The tenth got away."

Mina watched in spite of her dread, straining to see the features through the haze. She didn't trust herself to speak. What she wanted so badly was to see two men running after ptarmigan, only seven miles away. But this was the first of August. They were too early by a month and nine days. Somehow it felt almost wicked to be there so soon.

GEORGE DIDN'T feel like staying, so they come off the hill pretty quick. It made him shivery to see that land, and to remember how wet they'd been, how hungry, and how cold.

In the canoes they started working their way toward the big lake. About six they come around a bend and looked straight into the sun. It was low on the water, everything dazzling, and sure enough, there was Michikamau—just like he'd told her. Gilbert said, "Rice pudding for dessert, Mrs. Hubbard?" and she laughed in that nice way of hers. Way back, she'd promised to give them all rice pudding when they got to Michikamau, to celebrate. She said, "Yes, Gil, rice pudding for dessert."

The pudding caused a bit of a problem. The one time she'd made it before, she fixed brandy sauce to go along, the brandy being from the medicine bag. Usually she carried it with her own stuff, but since the night she ran away, George had kept it in his dunnage. She called for it now and he got it out. Looking at it, it seemed like he and Job and the others had drunk a little more than he remembered. What was left you could count in swallows. Three swallows, maybe, so long as you weren't that thirsty.

She looked at him and didn't say anything—but oh, he knew what she was thinking. About how bad Indians and breeds were with their liquor. It made his cheeks burn. He wanted to say something to make her understand—remind her how there'd been some gone from the bottle to start, and with four of them dividing what was left, one bottle didn't go so very far. Especially after she'd had 'em all nearly crazy that evening.

But it seemed those things were too hard to get around his tongue. It just wouldn't come out. It would sound like George Elson making excuses. And she just looked so sad and reproachful but didn't say anything, so that in the end all he could do was study those three ounces in the bottle like he was looking 'em over very, very careful, and say:

"Guess we won't have any for our pudding. Better keep that for medicine."

She didn't say any different either.

That was the first bad thing that come of seeing Michikamau. Then the next morning it turned out the blamed sun had been playing tricks, because when they got to paddling they found they weren't in Michikamau after all, only in a lake with another thin strip of land blocking the way. He and Job picked up the faintest pull of the current, coming from a direction they didn't suspect, so they started paddling that way. But Mrs. Hubbard was suspicious of him now, not trusting him, and when he and Job talked in Cree, she stopped him and wanted to know why they were headed this way. Wasn't Michikamau straight ahead?

So he explained, and she thought it was a pretty good joke and gave him a time of it. Every time the current took a new turn and they came to another riffle, she would say, "You said we were in Michikamau! I thought we were done with these rapids!" The other boys joshed him too, because Bert and Joe had already taken off their shoes and were going barefoot—they figured no more hauling.

That afternoon they had to climb another hill, and this time the boys nearly ran to the top. George trailed behind Mrs. Hubbard, and, before the two of them even got all the way up, he could see Job standing on a boulder, hopping around and waving his hat and then the others waving hats too and giving three cheers—*hep-hep-oh-ray!* This time the channel was clear, and no mistake. By six o'clock, they paddled through the last bends of the river, and what a pretty sight! Water from one edge of the sky to the other. Just a few chunks of ice here and there to sparkle in the sun. It felt almost like being home on Hudson's Bay and it made him think of scripture. *Your joy no man taketh from you.*

Next morning the lake was flat as a flapjack. Not a bit of wind, and paddling up the eastern shore was nothing—a regular boatman's holiday. When a lake as big as that got quiet, there wasn't anything like it anywhere. The air still, the water still—nothing breathing. They went along seeing how quiet they could be; didn't even want to hear water dripping off the paddles. Then a couple of loons called from so far away even Job couldn't spot 'em. But their voices floated along like they were right next to the canoe, echoing one way, then back, calling each other for miles and miles across that lake. The fellus just set their paddles on the gunwales and listened. Those loons had a call so sad it would fly through the air straight to your heart.

A smart headwind come up next morning. Later it switched around, so they strung up tarpaulins for sails. That was nice enough, but George never liked the smell of south winds. You couldn't trust 'em. The boats reached the end of the lake without any problem, but then they had to cross three miles of open water to the bay they wanted. He and Job had a few words in Cree. The wind was rising and so were the waves. They decided to chance a crossing. Three miles wasn't much.

Heading across, George could see the waves beginning to work on Joe and Gilbert's canoe, swinging it first up on a crest and then down in a trough—so deep only their heads showed—then up again. George's canoe was doing the same and he began to worry. Storms on a lake like this could blow up in minutes. The waves would get steeper, the canoe would begin to roll and plunge—and next thing you knew, the boat would start filling up. If they went over, he didn't think much of Mrs. Hubbard's chances in her long skirts. He begun to kick himself for getting into such chancy seas.

Every time the canoe pounded through a wave, he wondered if they'd taken any water over the gunwales. It was likely to come in amidships, just behind him. Mrs. Hubbard was sitting only a couple feet behind, but he daren't turn around all the way to see what was on her face. All he could do was follow his paddle stroke with his eyes, till he got to the end of it, and then glance out of the corner before bringing the paddle back to the front again. Then he could just see her.

She was sitting silent as a bird, with one hand in her lap—the left one with the glove on. Her bare right hand rested along the edge of the gunwale, where the water was lapping close when the boat went through the crests. The water slithered over once or twice and ran across the tips of her fingers, but she never moved a bit.

He and Job didn't say a word—only put their heads down and paddled with all their might. Just as the wind started to really blow, they cut through the breakers at the far point. The boat bounced some coming into the beach and shipped a good one. George clambered out and held the canoe off the rocks. Then Mrs. Hubbard stepped out, calm as if she'd been for a Sunday carriage ride. *The dear Lord Jesus,* he thought.

Once on dry ground, she brought out Mr. Low's map. Up ahead was a smaller lake called Michikamats that drained into Michikamau. Then, somewhere above that, the ponds were supposed to start draining north, into the George River. That was what they had to find.

At the moment, though, George didn't care a bit. They'd got off Michikamau by the skin of their teeth and this being Saturday, the sabbath was coming. To fix matters even better, the Lord sent along a family of ptarmigans, which they shot, all but the father. So they wouldn't have to kill any birds on Sunday. With fresh food in hand, they paddled across to an island and set up camp.

George didn't come up for air the next morning until after nine, when he heard a *rat-a-tat-tat* on the mixing pan. It was Joe's call to breakfast. Sitting around the fire, the fellus were pretty pleased. Here it was only August 6, and they'd passed Michikamau. Why, with Hubbard, George hadn't even got onto the Beaver River by the sixth. He couldn't help thinking about what Wallace and his crowd might be up to. There hadn't been a trace of them anywhere.

"How far behind do you think he is?" asked Joe.

"I don't know," said George grinning. "But with this wind, he won't make much progress on Michikamau."

"I bet it's blowin' pretty hard on Seal Lake too, don't you?" said Bert. And then he laughed like a kid. He thought Wallace might be all the way back there.

"How good does Mr. Wallace follow trails?" asked Job.

"Sometimes he follows 'em and sometimes he don't," said

George. The other fellus had already heard about the times on the first trip when Wallace got turned around and carried his stuff to the wrong end of the portage. Also how he'd spent a night out alone.

"Maybe he'll get lost again," said Job.

"Stanton will get lost," said Bert. Bert knew Stanton from lumbering days over to Kenemish.

Mrs. Hubbard sat next to the fire, with a mug of tea, listening with a big smile on her face. "What's the matter, Gilbert? Isn't Stanton good at following trails?"

"No sir! If Stanton falls off the seat in his own canoe, he'll get lost."

That afternoon she asked George to give her another of his Cree lessons.

The Cree lessons had impressed him—that she'd even ask. Most of the sports who came fishing to Missanabie—the ones out of the city—didn't have any use for talking Indian. Even Mr. Hubbard never asked about it. But Mrs. Hubbard was different. She was always wanting to know what this word or that meant, and she loved to surprise them.

Every night when they'd light up their pipes, George would say to the boys, "*Nekupetan anganescen.*" It meant, "Now we'll have a good smoke." One day Job carved her a nice pipe out of a root, just for fun. When he gave it to her, she took it solemnly and pretended to take a pull. Then she said, "*Nekupetan anganescen,*" only it came out so funny they all just laughed till they held their sides. She knew it too—she was just having fun.

This being a rest day, she wanted a Cree lesson. She came over by the log, sat down next to him, and took out her diary so it'd be handy to write down the words. He taught her *ahtsigahsipuk*, which was a vine the Indians dried and mixed with their tobacco, but she twisted the sounds so much that George started laughing again. Each time she tried it, it seemed funnier, until he laughed so hard he fell backward off the log and poked himself on a little stump and jumped up right quick. She stopped laughing, afraid he'd hurt himself.

"Are you all right?" she asked. And when she saw he was, she said it faster, and he was off again. It was a while before he managed to sit up and say, "*Uipelashiu.*"

"What's that?" she said.

"It means good, good." But he couldn't stop laughing.

In the afternoon he walked with her down to the shore. The wind was coming fierce from the south, and they watched a couple gulls try to make headway against it. No matter how hard they tried, the gulls had to turn back. So *she* tried to lean into the wind, to see if it wouldn't hold her up, maybe, and it pretty near did. She wanted him to take a picture of her in the storm, so he took it of her standing next to the campfire, the wind blowing through her hair, with Joe lying by the fire, smoking his pipe. And then she went back to the shore alone.

George sat down and watched Job make fried cakes. He was going to give them to her for a special treat that night. That would be nice. What a fine lady and a fine Sunday! What better Sunday could there be?

BY THE SHORE's edge Mina looked across to the point where George had shot the family of ptarmigan. The men were a jolly crew, but for the moment she felt drawn to the wind and the solitude, the waves breaking against the beach.

She thought about those ptarmigan: a mother and three little ones. The father had barely escaped—flown in fright and then, after the men had gone, fluttered back, looking for his family. It was one of the succession of wilderness tragedies that occurred day in, day out. Yet such was her state of mind that she could not help wondering whether, even now, the mate were still huddled somewhere alone, wishing he had stayed behind to share the fate of his family.

33

Regular Conspirators

ON AUGUST 4 Wallace paddled out of Seal Lake with fine prospects. Mrs. Hubbard could not be far ahead and the Naskapi was smooth as a ribbon. The strength of the river's current, though, was deceptive. Before long they were hardly making any headway against it. Worse, Wallace and Richards found themselves unable to keep up with the other canoe.

By the eighth a cold headwind was blowing half a gale, so he polled the men. What did they think about calling an early camp? There were axes to be sharpened, rifles to be cleaned. . . .

After the tents were pitched, Wallace was surprised to find that Easton, instead of getting to work on the chores, hung back a bit. Except for his earnest expression he seemed almost comical, lanky legs barely covered by patched-over pants and his felt hat warped by the rain. He asked if he might have "a word" with Wallace, and, from the way he said it, it was clear he meant alone.

The problem was the bread rations, Easton began. Pete was a fine baker, but with everyone's share down to one loaf a day, the loaves were coming out—well, a little larger than before. Nobody was complaining, of course—that was only natural. Easton liked the bread as much as anyone. But for the good of the party, Mr. Wallace ought—they *all* ought to keep a stricter watch on the provisions. Flour squandered now might be needed badly later.

Wallace was somewhat taken aback. The last thing he expected was anyone to be asking for less grub. He promised to keep a closer eye on the ration.

But it seemed Easton wasn't finished. The wind was blowing

bad today, he continued. It made sense to camp. But in the future—in Easton's opinion anyway—they would do well to get earlier starts. Better to be hiking by six or seven and then camp a bit early. It would give the men something to shoot for when the regimen got tough—a pleasant hour or two at the end of the day. But, rain or shine, they should press on. Steady progress was imperative.

He seemed to hesitate before continuing.

They had all seen the signs of the other party. . . . The tracks along the portage this morning; the campsite Saturday with the muskrat remains. Elson must be pretty hard up if he'd taken to serving muskrat. Still, Pete figured the tracks were at least ten days old. That meant a good lead for Mrs. Hubbard.

Now, there was no sense to paying too much attention to what she did. But their own expedition had to succeed. It was imperative. They had to reach Michikamau and catch the caribou migration and find the Indians. It was either that or go back looking like a pack of fools.

Wallace nodded. Perhaps he should have been offended by Easton's remarks. But he felt strangely heartened by the show of spirit. As leader, it was terribly difficult to make one decision after another, never quite sure how much the others were behind him. He had come to appreciate much more keenly the nervous strain in Hubbard's optimism: his relief that there wasn't "a quitter in the bunch." In the bush you were entirely dependent on your comrades, not only for surviving but for your ultimate success and reputation.

This time around, there were five people in the expedition instead of three, and, for indefinable reasons, the group seemed less close-knit. There were no open antagonisms—just not quite the warmth Wallace had shared with Hubbard and George during the worst of their privations. What was different? Was it simply a matter of personal character? The size of the party? Such things were hard to estimate.

But in Easton he had a man willing to stick as close to him as he had stuck to Hubbard. It was a piece of knowledge to weigh carefully, for the Indian maps indicated another difficult choice ahead—whether to continue up the Naskapi toward Lake Michikamau, or take another long portage to avoid the next series of waterfalls and canyons. The Indians had urged the portage. They admonished Wallace that any white men venturing into the rapids would never come out alive.

On the other hand, if the Ahsini brothers' second detour proved anything like the first, the expedition's pace would again slow to a crawl. The chances of getting to Ungava in time to catch the *Pelican* would be slim. And if they missed the steamer, the only way home would be a return along the coast by dogsled. Teams being as scarce as they were, he could hardly hope to hire enough dogs to take five men around.

The conclusion seemed clear. If Wallace couldn't be sure of getting out before freeze-up, he would have to send some of the men back to Northwest River early. He would have to split the expedition.

But who should return and who continue on? Richards was the only member of the party other than Wallace who had experience running rapids, and there would be rapids aplenty on the George River. But Richards was also the youngest and, in any case, was due out in October to continue his studies. He was also a bit too ready to complain, Wallace felt, and too easily discouraged. Richards should return, then, though he certainly could not be put in charge of the retreating party. Stanton should return as well: a wonderful chef when it came to stews and roly-polies, but he tired easily, was no trailfinder, and lacked a certain initiative. Wallace did not quite trust him to lead the return party. To be completely safe, Pete would have to be sent too. With him for a guide, the trio would be safe.

Easton seemed the best man to go forward. He certainly was determined. The two of them traveling alone in the lighter canoe could move quickly, get the job done. The big risk would be traveling without a guide. But if the party split at Michikamau, the only scouting that remained was to find the headwaters of the George. From there it would be a matter of following the river down to Ungava Bay. Sending Pete back also meant that Wallace would have the distinction of completing his trip without being guided every step of the way by an Indian, a feat Mrs. Hubbard could hardly claim, given her retinue of half-breeds.

Sometime soon Wallace would have to tell the men. It worried him, for he was not at all sure how they would react to being sent home. No wonder Hubbard had fretted so much about whether George and Wallace had wanted to turn back. Wallace decided he would have to approach the subject diplomatically.

For four more days the party fought the river's current, making slow progress upstream. The Naskapi narrowed in places to less than 120 yards and rushed along so swiftly that even three men paddling full tilt could hardly make headway. For a time they tracked the canoes from shore, pulling them against the current with long painters. Meanwhile Wallace searched anxiously for signs of the Indian trail. When a few rotten teepee poles were spotted near a small tributary on the north shore, he sent a party out to scout. Before they left, however, he called Easton aside.

"I was thinking about what you said the other day," he began.

Easton nodded.

"So far, I think we've kept close enough to schedule. But any delays now would bode ill. If we have them, and the gamble comes down to the wire, I was thinking you and I might take the eighteen-foot canoe, plus a little grub, and push ahead at top speed."

Easton's eyes widened slightly, and Wallace hurried on.

"It means taking some risks, I know."

"We would go ahead?" asked Easton. "The two of us?"

"That's right."

He swallowed. "All right, sir."

THERE WERE NO likely looking lakes. Just ridges and ridges, plus a few ponds too small even to bother floating a canoe in. If this was a portage trail, Clifford Easton was Baron Munchausen of Bavaria.

Easton and Richards had followed Pete at a fast pace for several miles up a steep brook, then up an eight-hundred-foot mountain to spy out John Ahsini's portage route. Seeing no sign of it, they trotted down the hill toward one of the little ponds, where Pete picked up the faintest, faintest markings of a trail—hardly even a caribou run. How he sniffed these things out was beyond Easton. The trail went up and over several steep ridges, always climbing, becoming a little plainer as it went. Eleven miles from camp, they finally reached a lake about a mile long. The surrounding countryside was barren, burned over, charred stumps everywhere, moss blackened, the boulders bleak. . . . Absolutely desolate.

They loped up another hill to see what lay beyond. More of the same.

It would be a brute of a march. Eleven miles to the first lake, three trips each. With all the back-and-forth, that meant fifty-five miles of walking, and even then no big water in sight. Still, they didn't dare continue up the river. Everybody figured the Indians must have had good reason to keep out of those canyons. Everybody except Richards. He was so blue about the prospect of the long carry, he left the others on the return trip and cut over toward the river to see what that route promised.

Back at camp the smell of venison hash was in the air. Easton savored the aroma hungrily: The day's hike had covered about thirty miles and he was exhausted. Wallace and Stanton kept the grub warm, waiting for Richards to turn up with his scouting report, but as dusk fell, there was still no sign of him. Worse, it started to rain—first a drizzle and then in sheets. They bolted down their hash and quickly retreated to the darkness of the tent. Still no Richards. After a time Wallace lifted a flap and peered into the storm. "He'll never get in tonight," he said.

"No, and he'll have a hard time of it out there too," put in Stanton.

Pete rummaged around and brought out a candle, then sharpened one end of a stick, split the other end down the middle, and wedged the candle between. With a light in place everybody cheered up, and the tent glowed like a Chinese lantern, so Richards had something to aim for. The rain was tatting on the canvas like a drummer. After what seemed ages the flap swung open and Richards crawled in and threw himself down. It looked as though he'd been swimming. Stanton handed him a plate of hash and he set to work.

"What do you think of the river?" asked Wallace.

"The river! That's the only thing within twenty miles I *didn't* see. I've been looking for it for four hours, but it kept changing course and I never found it till I struck camp just now."

So much for the scouting report.

Even without having seen what was ahead, Richards held out for the river, but the vote was four to one against. Everybody else figured the Indians would choose the easiest route, and the Indians took the portage. Then Easton made his own suggestion: They ought to cache some grub. If they had to come back this way, he argued, they could use it for their retreat. Meanwhile, the portaging would go a lot faster. They could take their load over in two trips instead of three. The vote was unanimous, in favor. Easton was pretty pleased.

For their cache they dug a hole in a sandbank, lined the bottom with rocks, and lowered a bag of flour and a few cans of pemmican emergency rations. Easton felt as if they were burying their best friend.

Then it was back to the usual. Haul, haul, and more haul.

The flies were hellish as ever—worse, even. Wallace's bites made his face puff up like a fat old woodchuck's. Easton had a lump on his forehead the size of a robin's egg, and his cheeks were like a squirrel's in nut season. Even so, he was not complaining, for his constipation had at last deserted him.

Then they had two setbacks that nearly fixed them all. Coming along the trail Sunday, Wallace started to unload his rifle and—*boom!*—the darn thing went off, sending a bullet whistling about three inches off the end of Richards' nose. Richards nearly jumped out of his pants. After a bit everybody calmed down—there was nobody hurt. Monday, though, Easton was chopping and the ax slipped, glancing off the log and striking him in the shin. Blood gushed out—a two-inch gash clean to the bone. That looked like the trip right there. But Stanton the handyman rushed in with electrician's tape and pulled the wound together. The bleeding stopped and there was hardly any pain.

After a few days on the portage, Easton began to wonder whether Richards hadn't been right about the river. Every day they hauled gear until they dropped. The country was a wasteland: huge boulders to get around, bleached dead trees, and only a pond or two to ease the pain. They'd collapse at the end of one day, start tired the next, and it would be that much easier to stumble going through the muck of a swamp or over moss slick with the rain. When everybody sat down for a rest, Richards would pull out a chunk of bread he'd saved from the morning's rations and start munching the tidbit, until Mr. Wallace finally jumped on him for eating in front of everybody. Easton was with Wallace on that one.

Pete had begun to worry more. At the start of the trip Easton had thought the Indian a bit of a character, with his tales of Hiawatha's mighty powers and superstitions about barking foxes. The two of them had been scouting on a high hill one afternoon when Easton rolled a boulder off the top; as it crashed into the valley, Pete turned white at the gills. Bouncing boulders was a bad sign, he said. But as the days went by Easton couldn't help growing to like his canoeing partner. After the accident with the ax, Pete had become downright solicitous, wanting Easton to rest up for a couple of days. He even offered to carry extra loads for him.

He talked a lot, too, when they were alone. There wasn't enough bread in the ration, he told Easton. Indians needed more bread than white men—their bodies didn't work so well without it. He was getting weaker. Of course there was nothing to the idea, but Pete believed it.

Heading west and north from the Naskapi, it took five days to get to the first water of decent size, a lake about six miles long. August was already half-gone. On the lake they found a few wigwam poles, but they were so rotten they crumbled at the touch. After a day and a half searching, Pete located one ancient blaze on the far shore, and a wisp of a trail that led dead into the worst swamp ever. Easton was up to his knees in bogs and the gash on his shin kept pulling apart. To top it off, the next lake they came to was as bare of signs as the hair on Mr. Wallace's head. Not even Pete could raise a scent.

It had been rainy and cold along the portage, but now the clouds disappeared and the mercury dropped. Easton had been sleeping badly, so that night he sewed his blankets in the shape of a sleeping bag, thinking to keep off the chill. Instead he dreamed of ice, home, and zero weather. About 4:00 A.M. he could stand it no longer and got out of bed. Wallace was awake, too, and came out to build a fire, the two of them pulling their blankets over Stanton, who was sleeping away in fine style, lumberman that he was, his teeth chattering audibly.

Easton wrote a little in his diary and talked plans with Wallace. The two of them were getting to be regular conspirators. Wallace said he was convinced now beyond all doubt that the party must separate—there was no way five men could make it to Ungava on their dwindling rations. But he wasn't sure yet when to make the separation or how to divide the party. For his own part, Easton backed Wallace a hundred percent. "No matter what we have to go through I shall stick with him through thick and thin without a murmur," he wrote after their talk. "Think there will be grumbling and hard feelings if Mr. Wallace should send some of the men back; do not know what arrangements he has made with them, but he is sure to give everyone a fair deal."

After breakfast Mr. Wallace made for a nearby mountain, taking Pete along. Late in the afternoon he was back, not looking happy. The hill gave them the first good view they'd had for a week, and it showed clearly that they'd missed the Indian portage several days back, along one of the small ponds they'd crossed. The real trail cut farther south, across a number of large lakes. The signs they thought they'd been following weren't from summer portaging, only winter trapping camps. To Easton, the mistake looked as though it had cost at least a week's delay, and it was already August 20. But there was nothing for it but to keep pushing west toward Michikamau.

That night, after supper, Wallace summoned everyone for a powwow. "Now boys," he said, "we need to talk. Up to this point, we've had no hardships to meet. We've had hard work and it's been trying at times, but there's been nothing to endure that might not be met with on any trip in the bush. If we go on, we *shall* have hardships; pretty bad ones maybe. The sleet and snow aren't far off, which means cold days and colder nights, and the portages won't be any easier. Our flour and pork are getting low, the lentils and corn meal are nearly gone; we're on short rations already, with hungry days to come if we don't strike game. And you know how uncertain that is."

Easton knew what was coming. He eyed the others, trying to gauge how they were taking it. He couldn't be sure.

"I can't say what's before us," Wallace continued, "and I'm not going to drag you into trouble. I've thought about it some and decided to take one man with me to Ungava in the small canoe, and let the rest retrace our route to Northwest River, carrying what grub they need to take them out."

He paused and looked around. "Well, that's the way things stand. Who wants to go home?"

It stopped them right in their tracks. Nobody said anything for a minute, and then Richards spoke, almost angry. "Do you think there's a quitter here?"

Wallace apologized; he hadn't meant it to come out that way. There would be absolutely no stigma attached to being in the return party, he said; it was merely what the situation required, if success were to be had. He looked around the fire. Richards announced stoutly that he would continue on. Stanton asked to go on too. So did Pete. Easton was in, of course. Nobody was ready to admit yet that they'd seen the elephant.

"Well, we'll wait on the decision for now," said Wallace at last. "At least until we get to Michikamau."

Easton had a feeling, though, Wallace had made up his mind.

34

Long Chances

FOOD. MORE AND more these days, when the grub was dished out, the men got right to business. Easton for some reason ate more slowly than his companions. Without fail, the others wolfed down their portions, wiped up every drop of grease with a bread crust, and licked their plates for good measure. Then they sat and watched him, like a pack of ravenous huskies.

Everybody was hungry now. Not that they didn't have food; just never quite enough. There was that empty ache that wouldn't go away, whether pushing along the portage or crawling into blankets at night or even just finishing supper. Never quite full. Mornings were a torment. Mr. Wallace would come out and rub his hands in front of the fire and describe in meticulous detail the culinary delights he had dreamed of the night before, while Easton, listening politely, suffered the torments of the damned.

The country didn't yield much either. A number of years earlier forest fires had swept through, not only charring the landscape but flushing the game clear out of the territory. It seemed even the fish had been scorched from the ponds—the gill net was bringing up nothing. If it hadn't been for the owls, they would have been in real trouble. All of a sudden owls were appearing from out of nowhere. As soon as camp was set up, one would land on a blackened stump or a nearby tree and sit there twittering wisely, as if he wanted to find out what everybody was up to. He found out all right.

Pete was getting pretty flighty. Every time he and Easton went off to scout, they'd hardly get beyond earshot of camp before he began worrying. "Before trip, Mr. Wallace promise me, take plenty grub out in woods. Get low on grub, turn back. Now—out of pork. Flour almost gone. Maybe we turn back when we get off this portage—you think?" Pete was certainly right about the grub. Of the six bags of flour they'd brought, four were gone, one had been cached by the river, and they were quickly working their way through the remaining fifty pounds. Pete estimated that only about two week's rations remained, aside from the emergency pemmican.

As for Richards—Richards was getting cold feet or Easton didn't know ice. The meals never filled him up and he said so. When Easton countered that their allotment didn't seem so bad, he replied, "I'm a huskier fellow than you—I need a bigger ration." One night, after they'd advanced only a mile and a quarter, he came over gloomily and displayed the latest entry in his diary: "If we get out of this country alive, it will be by the grace of God."

Times like that Mr. Wallace was a real comfort. It got so he and Easton would hang around the fire every night after the others went to bed. With the aurora flashing up and down the heavens, it was exciting to sit there, smoking pipes and mulling things over. "I think Richards is having a change of heart about wanting to press on," Wallace commented that evening. "He spoke to me today about all of us having to turn back if the grub gets low." Stanton, though, was still talking enthusiastically about the trip to Ungava—he was going to be disappointed when he found out he was going back. Wallace was hoping to "ease the sore" a bit by giving him a commission to visit the big falls on the Grand River on his behalf. He could go with the trappers when they left on their winter runs.

As for pressing on to Ungava, Easton and Wallace both agreed that grub was the main problem to be faced. Wallace was determined to give the others enough supplies to reach the food cache on the Naskapi. That left mostly the pemmican emergency rations for the two of them. Easton had been skeptical of the stuff to begin with: an Indian-style concoction of dried ground beef, sugar, raisins, and currants, all suspended in tallow fat. But Wallace had opened a few tins for everyone to try; they each had a ration, and it seemed palatable enough. With any luck, he and Wallace could get down the George River on that.

Still, Easton couldn't help thinking of Hubbard and his long portage toward Michikamau: plodding from pond to pond, not knowing exactly where they were, and all the while watching their supplies dwindle. The same thing seemed to be happening all over again. Mr. Wallace didn't say anything, but he'd been awfully quiet, the last few days, trying to come to a decision.

"Long chances," he said. "Even with the pemmican, that's what we'd be taking. It won't leave much margin if we have trouble finding the headwaters of the George."

Easton didn't care. "Any kind of chances are better than failing," he said.

Wallace didn't say anything to that, only pulled at his pipe.

From the ponds they were struggling through, a lone peak could be seen through the haze of the westward horizon. Easton figured it had to be pretty near Lake Michikamau. On the twenty-eighth of August they finally struck open water and were boiling their kettle on the shores of a lake that stretched as far as the eye could see.

"I call this lake Kasheshebogamog," said Pete.

"What's that mean?"

"Lake of Many Paths."

And there were too. Almost everywhere they looked, fir-topped islands divided the waters; long bays stretched this way and that. Luckily, there was the mountain to aim for.

All that day and the next they ticked off mile after mile, until finally the last bay came into view and the mountain loomed ahead. Easton thought for sure they were back on the Naskapi's upper lake expansions, with Michikamau a short stretch of river away. But the bay just got shallower and shallower, danker and drabber. Almost before they knew it, they were staring at a marsh, with the merest trickle of a creek running out the end. No Naskapi. No Michikamau. Just another swamp. It was one of the bitterest disappointments of Easton's life.

It was difficult not to get pretty angry about their predicament. That night, Easton gave vent to his feelings—but only in his journal.

> This delay may mean our lives, but this is a country of disappointments and I tried hard not to show mine for Wallace's sake. . . . Wallace said to me today that he is tired of the grumbling and so am I, we are hungry as the others but it does no good to growl about it. . . . Richards sits beside me while I write, biting his nails while his face is as long as a fiddle. He nearly drives me mad—now is the time to be a man. . . . Shall be glad when we are rid of him, and Wallace and I face what is before us alone.

It started to rain, but Easton only tucked his journal closer into his lap and continued writing.

> Am very doubtful after today's work whether I come out of this alive; we may not be able to find the George or doing so will doubtless be short of grub. But if I do not, they cannot write on my tombstone, "He was a quitter."

WALLACE AWOKE the next morning to heavy rain and a stiff knee. Still lame from a spill he had taken a few days earlier, he resolved to send Easton and Pete up the mountain.

Pete was looking glum. Wallace tried to cheer him with the hope of seeing Michikamau, but the effort seemed vain. He thought a moment, and then went to his pack and brought out a corncob pipe. "Why don't you take this along?" he suggested. Pete brightened up some. "All right," he said. "I smoke him when I see Michikamau—when I climb hill, if Michikamau there. Sit down, me, look at big water, feel good then. Smoke pipe, and call him Corncob Hill."

Wallace laughed. "Good. I hope the hill gets its name."

It was a long day: so many hours and nothing to do but brood. Richards and Stanton went off to scout for several hours, leaving Wallace alone with his thoughts. If the news came back that neither Michikamau nor the river had been sighted, then the game was up. He would go back a failure. Whitney would have no story worth printing, the New York papers would be clamoring to know why he had turned back once again, and, to top it off, Mina Hubbard was apparently well on her way to the George. If Wallace failed this time, there would be no third chance.

But missing Michikamau was not his real worry. From the look of the country he thought it quite likely the big lake lay just beyond the horizon. What worried him was that he had seen this all before—had *lived* it. Hubbard had climbed a mountain and seen Michikamau too. He had come back full of hope and determination. And then for ten days the winds had pinned them remorselessly on a lake much like this, until Hubbard had finally walked back to their campfire, weary from staring at the waves, an almost pleading look in his eyes. "What do you say, boys, to turning back?"

Wallace's instinct then had been to say no. He had wanted to push on, march to his front like a soldier. But even now the look in Hubbard's eyes still seared him. Here were five people's lives. For three of them, Wallace was voting as Hubbard had. But for two, he was marching on. Was he being foolhardy? More to the point, was he being fair to young Easton?

In their talks by the fire he had tried to state the case as plainly as he could. So far, they had come 250 miles in a little over two months; Ungava Bay lay another 400 beyond, across territory farther north and more barren, and in weather totally unpredictable as the autumn season advanced. Yet the more Wallace pointed out such risks, the more Easton seemed determined to brave them. In fact, whenever Wallace had doubts of his own, Easton seemed eager to cheer him up, to press on harder than before. It was an open question as to which man was bucking the other up.

What had Hubbard seen as he stood on the shores of Windbound? Was it something, perhaps, that Wallace should be seeing too? Or had it been merely a failure of nerve? The frustrating thing was, no matter what news Pete and Easton brought, Wallace wouldn't have the answer. There was no knowing for sure unless he kept going.

Dusk came around eight, and, in the fading light, Wallace saw the silhouette of a canoe making its way up the creek. Easton and Pete beached the boat and came running up to camp.

"We see him! We see him!" Pete called. "We see Michikamau!" He could hardly contain himself. They had crossed several lakes and swamps to get to the foot of the mountain, then began climbing.

"When we most up, I stop and look at Easton. My heart beat fast. I most afraid to look. Maybe Michikamau not there. Maybe I see only hills. Then I feel bad. Make me feel bad come back and tell you Michikamau not there. Then I think—if Michikamau there you feel very good. I must know quick. I run—run fast. Hill very steep. I do not care. I must know soon as I can. I shut my eyes just once, afraid to look. Then I open them. Very close I see much water—big. So big I see no land when I look one way; just water. Very wide, too—I know I see Michikamau. My heart beat easy and I feel very glad. I almost cry. I remember corncob pipe you give me and what I tell you. I take pipe out my pocket; fill him and light him. Then I sit on rock and smoke. All the time I look at Michikamau. I feel good and I say, 'This we call Corncob Hill.' "

Wallace was deeply moved. More, he felt his decision was no longer quite so difficult to make. He stayed up late that night with Easton and settled matters.

At breakfast he asked the men to get their pipes. Then, with the whole party sitting at solemn attention, he went over the points he had rehearsed with Easton. How he had promised Richards's mother to have her son home by October; how he wanted Stanton to go back and explore the Grand River for him; how he could not in good conscience send a party back without the benefit of Pete's guidance. He said everything he meant to say, yet the men took the news differently than he expected. With all the grumbling, he supposed he would see relief on their faces. Instead he read shock, surprise, disappointment.

Richards had tears in his eyes. Stanton protested loudly. Even Pete asked over and over for the chance to go on, practically begged. "Seems like I take four men in bush, lose two. Very bad, that. Don't know how I see your sisters. I go home well. They ask me, 'Where my brother?' I don't know. I say nothing. Maybe you die in rapids. Maybe you starve. I don't know. Your sisters cry." But Wallace turned aside all arguments and pleas. He had spent long nights making his decision; there could be no changing it.

The plan was to divide the gear immediately, leaving everything in camp except what Wallace and Easton would take, plus a few bare essentials for the other men. Then everyone would proceed as far as Michikamau before parting. Richards, Stanton and Pete refused to take more than eight days' rations to carry them to the cache. That would be plenty, they said. Richards delved into his pack and insisted Wallace take his waterproof Pontiac shirt for the cold days ahead. He gave Easton a pair of moleskin trousers to replace his patchworn pair.

As they started across the final divide on September 1, the feel of the country changed. Low swampy lakes were replaced by rocky ponds with black, deep waters. On the third day of pond hopping, Wallace forged ahead with Pete.

"Now we make last portage and reach Michikamau," he said. He led the way down a steep defile, broke through the bush and—there was the lake.

They were in a deep bay, so the sheer expanse of it didn't overwhelm. But it was Michikamau, all right. What stirred Wallace was not the water itself so much as the memory of Hubbard: The look of joy as he came bounding over the hillside of blueberries.

"We've seen it, we've seen it!" Hubbard had given his life for a view of that lake, and finally Wallace was standing on its shores, after an eternity of toil and disappointment, watching the blue stretch out to the horizon.

The others had not caught up yet; Pete watched Wallace quietly, then fashioned his felt hat into a cup and dipped it into the water. Carefully he handed the hat to Wallace.

"Drink Michikamau waters before others come."

Wallace drank, almost reverently. Then he just stood and looked.

THERE WASN'T MUCH for Easton to do but write last letters home. He composed one to his folks, telling them not to worry. Then he walked the shore of their bay with Pete, who gave him a constant stream of advice. Never leave camp without taking bearings. Never cut across big water. Stay close to shore, away from the big waves, closer to the woods and good game. Even now, there were whitecaps toward the middle of the lake. When they got back to camp, Stanton had a fat duck roasting—one he'd shot on the wing.

Everybody was pretty quiet. Wallace read a chapter from the Bible. Pete played his harmonica one last time and sang a few songs. He did "Home Sweet Home," only sang it in Ojibway, and then a couple of hymns he knew. When the embers got low, Stanton poured out a little toddy for a good-bye cup, and then everyone went to bed.

September fourth was sunny. After breakfast Mr. Wallace made his good-bye address, and there wasn't anyone without tears in his eyes. Even Wallace had to clench his pipe between his teeth when he talked.

Richards helped Easton carry his gear down to the shore, then load it into the canoe. Easton had changed his mind about Richards. He was a good sort of fellow at heart, but, being so husky, he felt the pangs of hunger worse. The two of them talked about Easton's chances of getting through to Ungava: Richards had to admit he thought them pretty slim. Still, he didn't feel particularly happy to be heading home. It was as though he hadn't accomplished anything, he said.

Wallace climbed into the bow of the canoe and Easton took his place at the stern. The others watched as the boat headed out into the bay. The wind was fresh—getting fresher all the time.

Easton settled into the rhythm of the paddle. Hubbard had loved to quote Kipling, and so did Wallace. In *The Lure of the Labrador Wild* he had featured a verse from "The Explorer": "Something hidden. Go and find it. Go and look behind the Ranges—Something lost behind the ranges. Lost and waiting for you. Go!" Easton knew Kipling too, but it was another verse that kept echoing through his head. "Never allow God or man to go north of 53°." Already they were north of 54°.

Feeling the stiff breeze against his cheeks, watching the waves slap at the gunwales, Easton was sure that he would never see home again. But he dug into the water with quick, strong strokes, determined that no matter what, he would not let Mr. Wallace down.

35

Top of the World

August 8: First sunny and blue; then clouds and spats of rain, and a stiff wind to blow one chunk of weather after another right on through—blue chasing gray chasing blue. . . . Fish hawks loved to soar on those currents, spying out the land and lakes below. George wondered what a hawk would see now if he swept up and rode the wind, circling higher and higher until the two canoes were only tiny specks on Lake Michikamats, and the parade of squalls stretched all the way to Michikamau, blown along by the breeze.

A fish hawk could ride those currents south, beat with the wind across the wide waters, eyes open all the way. He could fly on and on until—somewhere down on the tableland—he would see a couple more canoes by the riverbank and a certain familiar, grizzled buzzard of forty-two. Wonder where Wallace really was?

But George wasn't any kind of hawk, and he didn't have much to do but watch the canoes bobbing in the waves and the wind herding its squalls along, first gray, then blue, then gray. That, and a little thinking.

She liked colors—every color of the rainbow. She was always noticing 'em, and when he looked, now, it got so he noticed more too. Not that he hadn't before; it was just that, with her along, he noticed differently. It had got so it was hard to keep walking if he saw violets alongside a pond, because he knew she'd like to see them and exclaim over the color. The other men noticed too—Bert had brought her dandelions.

The funny thing was, George didn't want only to please her; after a while he got to liking the flowers himself. He even picked a couple of pretty bluebells—the ones that lay along the bogs and smelled so sweet—and slipped them into the back of his diary for safekeeping. Pressed 'em, so they'd be nice to look at a long while after.

No, when a person who was different came into someone's life—especially if that someone was the sort who'd been just going along ordinary—the new person made *you* different. She made you see things you hadn't seen before and feel what you hadn't felt, in a way that did your heart good.

And when she did all that, it was hard not to notice things about her—the dear Lord knew it was hard. When he brought her those flowers, he couldn't help looking to see—just a little—how much she cared for them. He couldn't help noticing if she stayed up by the campfire liking to talk to him, the way he liked to stay up talking to her. He noticed little things, like her hands working the dough when she was making bannock or the way she lifted her eyebrow just before she was about to tease him or the curve of her sweater as she lay against the gear, tired after a portage.

Don't. Georgie, Georgie. . . . Don't think about it. Don't even say it in your head. Not being a half-breed, don't. It's one thing to bring to mind the flowers and the other things, one by one. But don't start putting 'em together and thinking *thoughts.* You don't want to think any thoughts at all, not even so a fish hawk, circling with sharp eyes, could see them deep inside.

Still, he couldn't deny she had made him see differently. And when George saw things, he saw them like pictures in his mind. Folks had always been impressed with how he could remember—like finding Hubbard's stuff in eight feet of snow. Well, he saw things somehow: he didn't know how he did it. He just looked at a place once, and all he had to do was call up in his head what was there. The picture jumped in front of his eyes.

That was the way things were, thinking of her. Suppose he remembered a time on the river—say, when they were looking for the ax at Donald's tilt. Instantly there's a picture. He can see himself sitting after lunch in the heat of the day, pipe lit up, leaning against the cabin. Donald's book of hymns lying on the duffel at an odd angle. Two old marten skeletons in the moss, from trapping. George is tired—didn't get much sleep the night before. He's nodding off when suddenly she laughs and makes him jump.

He says, "What's the matter?" He can see himself saying it.

And she says, "That's the first time I ever saw a man try to sleep and smoke a pipe all at the same time."

The picture just jumps to him, her laughing, what she said,

all of it. He can call these things back any time he wants to. Almost any campfire he cared to think about, he could remember her joking with him or talking or having some fun about something. When he put those pictures together, it seemed there was something special in the way she treated him. The way she felt about him, even? *Don't.* Georgie, don't.

Still, she treated him different than any white man or white woman ever had. She trusted him—and not just with things a guide was trusted with either, like hunting or portaging. She trusted him to take pictures with her camera. And she had plans for his stories and little books. He couldn't get over that. Nobody had ever asked him about those little boyhood books. Never, never. Hubbard hadn't asked, and if he had, he'd probably think they were kind of funny. A good story, maybe, for *Outing.*

But here she was not only interested but wanting to help him write. That wasn't how you trusted a guide—no sir, that was something different! She'd talked about the books with him only one time, but she meant it. Didn't she? He thought so. He believed it.

Talking together, sitting close and learning Cree. . . . That wasn't the kind of thing you did with a man you thought of only as a guide or a half-breed. Was it? Somewhere deep inside, George couldn't help wondering when she teased him with that light in her eye—not angry, but liking it so much—whether that liking wasn't something more than teasing.

Mightn't it be?

Georgie, don't think about it—not even so a hawk can see. Just pay attention to the everyday things. Watch the water swirl by your paddle and the clouds pass—blue, then gray, then blue. Don't try to figure which the last color's going to be.

There was plenty else to look for anyways—Indian sign, for one. He'd begun to see lots of old wigwam poles lying around, and this morning they'd found a burying ground along shore. One big grave and three little ones, each with a picket fence and a wooden cross at the head. One of the little ones was recent, with shavings nearby. It made George uneasy.

The country seemed full of game too. The day before, George had bagged a partridge, two young geese, and then, with Job's help, their second caribou. The packs were so heavy with meat, Mrs. Hubbard made Job forget fifteen or twenty ptarmigan he flushed near the Indian graves. And then, paddling along in the afternoon, Job called out "*Georgie!*" in that low voice of his. George looked, and up above the riverbank—deer! Ten or fifteen of 'em! The blood leapt through his veins.

He and the boys beached their canoes as fast as they could and skinned through the alderbushes. Mrs. Hubbard ran too, her camera catching in the bushes. And excited? Why, she was as flighty as the boys!

They stole over the top of the bank, and there they were! Maybe thirteen deer in all. Mrs. Hubbard was fumbling with her camera, trying to unfold the bellows, when suddenly the band got wind and turned tail. Not bolting or anything—just heading over the hill at a trot, like they weren't too scared.

"Did you get any pictures?" he asked.

"One or two." She looked disappointed. "They aren't likely to be any good."

"The deer are just over the ridge," he said promptly. "I could see how they were running. Why don't I take the camera and get some pictures for you?"

She looked at him suspiciously. "If you can go, why can't I?"

"Well—you can't run. We'll have to go quick, or they'll get away."

Job was on tenterhooks, wanting to get over the ridge. So was George. She didn't say anything for a minute, only studying the whole business grumpily; then handed the camera to George without a word. In a flash he and Job were off, while the other boys stayed with her.

Coming over the rise, they nearly had the breath knocked out of them. There were the thirteen deer, but now George and Job could see the valley and hillside beyond. And—

Caribou everywhere!

Hundreds of 'em, all over the hillside, down in the valley, stags, does, young ones, some with little stubs of antlers, some with full racks; some deer feeding, some trotting along, some lying down and not doing much of anything.

George forgot all about the camera. "We got to tell Mrs. Hubbard," he whispered.

"Yes," said Job, and turned around, and they ran like demons. Neither wanted those deer disappearing from the time they went over the rise to the time they got back. The deer wouldn't, of course, but that's what it felt like.

"Hundreds of 'em," said George between lopes.

"How I want to shoot one," said Job.

"We can't. Mrs. Hubbard won't have it. We got plenty of meat."

"I know," said Job. "I sure would like to shoot one."

Back over the hill, she was waiting.

"Hundreds of them," said George.

"Many, many," said Job. Bert and Joe were about wild, and she gave a little skip too.

"If we take the canoes, we can paddle around faster," said George. They all ran to the canoes.

When they reached the next bay, everyone jumped ashore. The herd was spread over the whole valley and up the hillside. Mrs. Hubbard got her camera from the boat and they went up the bank. Some of the herd noticed them, some didn't. Pretty soon twelve big stags, all with racks, came together and faced them like a guard. The stags tried to look fierce.

Mrs. Hubbard couldn't get over their antlers. "How can they walk around with such a heavy load on their heads?"

George smiled. The antlers were big, though. You had to wonder.

"Do you think I could get closer for a picture?"

"We can try," he said. He told the boys to wait by the boats; maybe two people alone wouldn't scare them off.

The stags were about four hundred yards away. They didn't move—just looked fierce. Mrs. Hubbard walked close to George. After about a hundred yards she said, "They seem much taller now. The antlers alone must be nearly as long as I am."

Another fifty yards and one of the stags gave a snort. Then all jumped in line and started walking straight at them.

The antlers *really* began to seem bigger.

"Maybe we'd better look from the canoe," George suggested. She thought so too. She could move quick when she had a mind.

The boys didn't say anything watching the retreat, only wore big smiles. They thought it was pretty funny someone being scared by a few caribou. But of course George couldn't use his rifle.

"You try it," he told the boys. "But remember—no shooting."

So they went, and the stags did charge, and the boys moved as fast as anybody back to the canoes. Pretty soon the herd started peeling off and running, half around one side of the hill, half around the other. The stags stayed guard.

The boys figured they'd paddle up to the next bay, and when they did, there was the herd swimming for an island halfway across the lake. The deer were so thick, it was like seeing one long bridge—you could walk nearly all the way across on top of their backs. Mrs. Hubbard wanted to try for another picture, so both canoes pulled in by the hill. Most of the herd had crossed the lake, but there were still bands of fifteen or twenty grazing everywhere, looking just like nothing had happened.

Job and Joe took off at a run—with the stags gone, they figured it was about time to have some fun. George and Mrs. Hubbard climbed the hill to get a better view, with Bert tagging along. Looking down from the top, they saw Job already over the next hill, running about like a happy drunk, waving his hands and hallooing and chasing deer just about everywhere. Oh, he loved it! He started a big bunch running toward the lake. Mrs. Hubbard figured it out about the same time George did—the way the deer were running, they were going to reach the water just at the foot of the hill.

"If we can get down in time, we can get good pictures!" she said.

He was doubtful. "You'd have to run pretty fast. . . ."

She gave him a fierce, funny look that made him laugh and tremble at the same time. "George Elson, don't tell *me* about running. Here!" And she handed him the Kodak and next thing he knew, she grabbed his other hand and was pulling him down the hill.

Dear Lord Jesus—it nearly took his breath away! Her holding his hand! He was half laughing and half running and going full tilt down the hill, and there she was smiling in that way of hers, and a white woman holding his hand! It nearly felt on fire, and he thought, *Georgie, Georgie don't.* But it was so much fun, and when she glanced at him with that smile of hers, he couldn't help laughing. She was going so fast he could hardly keep up, and she loved that too—loved to show him up. She was so quick—such a fine little woman!

At the bottom of the hill, they had to cross a bog. She held on and he loved it—didn't stop, just splashed right through with him. "There's a rock to hide behind!" she called, and pulled him over and crouched down behind it, and he was so close to her he could feel her breathing. He could hardly breathe himself.

"Quick! The camera!"

The camera—he had almost forgot his other hand. She took

the Kodak and swung it around; then exclaimed and pointed up the hill. Blamed if the herd hadn't changed course and gone right up where they'd been! She was looking pretty sorry, when suddenly she heard a noise just behind, and they both turned to see two does and a big stag not twenty feet away. She gave a little "Oh!" and then caught herself and snapped a picture—of three deer running a mile a minute up the hill.

They gave up trying to get pictures. There were plenty of deer around, and you could watch them all you wanted—just, they'd move away if you tried to get close. So they climbed the hill again, this time to get a look at the country. From the summit they could see the end of Michikamats, and to the north, some smaller lakes.

"Your river ought to start just past those," he said. "We'll scout tomorrow."

She nodded, and then looked over the country below, the lake spread out pretty and deer running this way and that. A couple of thunderheads were raining on the lower part of the lake, but he could see blue coming in again, and the sun breaking out all around. It was like being on top of the world: everything where it should be.

She said, "George, look—a rainbow!"

Sure enough: The sun was shining through the leftover rain, making the spray glow in one big bow, the colors shimmering brighter all the time. The end of the bow plunged right to the foot of the hill, not far from where the two of them had been hiding.

She loved colors. And there they were—every one of 'em sharp and sweet as could be. Then she looked at him with mischief in her eyes.

"Do you want to get rich?" she said.

It kinda stopped him.

"What?"

"I said, do you want to get rich?" And she laughed this time. "I can tell you how, you know."

Gilbert had been tagging along behind, and he popped up before George could even collect himself.

"*I* want to get rich, Mrs. Hubbard."

"How?" asked George quickly.

"That rainbow. Don't you know about rainbows and pots of gold?"

Well, George didn't—he'd never heard anything about it. Bert hadn't either.

"There's a pot of gold at the end of every rainbow," she said. "All rainbows have them. There's enough to make a man rich! All you have to do is go fetch it."

Gilbert pointed, kind of feeble. "Down . . . there?"

"That's where the rainbow ends, isn't it?"

"Yess'r."

"Right by that boulder. The gold must be under the rock. Go down and see for yourself—if you rolled it over, you'd find the gold right there, I'll bet." Her eyes were dancing—she looked first at George, then Bert.

Bert stared and stared as hard as he could, as if the gold were going to jump out from sheer squinting at it. George looked at her hard and she laughed.

"Hurry up! The rainbow might disappear!"

She was joking, of course—he was almost certain. Blame it all, it was so hard to tell sometimes! Those eyes would be sparkling and dancing—daring and teasing him—and he could look as deep as he wanted and never get to the bottom of them. What did she want with him anyway?

"Oh, you're joking," he said at last.

And she laughed again. "Really, George—if you don't believe me, go see for yourself."

That was enough for Gilbert. He went tearing down the hill.

"Underneath, Gil!" she called after him. "You have to be right at the foot of the rainbow!" Then she turned to George.

"You see? He'll be rich and you'll be poor."

"Mmmph," said George. If he went just to see, she'd be sure to laugh at him. She was laughing now anyways.

Georgie, Georgie—why do you like it so much?

He decided to stay with her. He could see the rainbow fine where he was.

36

A Touch of Anger

MINA AWOKE EARLY August tenth with a sense of anticipation. The men had become increasingly eager to find the headwaters of the George—"her" river, as George called it. Lake Michikamats was succeeded by a string of smaller lakes and ponds. On each, Job unfailingly navigated the bends and bays to discover yet another inlet, with a feeder brook flowing in. They were still proceeding upstream, higher and higher.

Finally they came to a pond less than a mile long, with no brook entering anywhere. Beyond lay flat fields, a bog, and another lake. Portaging to it, they paddled quickly to the far shore, where they found a stream. Job jumped out and ran along a short distance. Was it an inlet? No—it flowed out—and north! He called excitedly, his English mixing with Cree. "Hey! Hey! George's *sebo!* George's River as George's River, boys!"

The country seemed to fall away on all sides, with more than the usual sense of earth and sky. Mina had the feeling of standing at the summit of the world. She had come nearly 300 miles and climbed 1,600 feet across the Labrador plateau. In the arc of her expedition, this was the point of maximum isolation: sitting in the middle of a bog, miles from any genteel post, trusting her life to four swarthy men who jabbered in Cree, chased caribou, and lunched on meals of boiled intestine.

And she felt wonderful. Not the least bit alone, not the least deprived by the vast isolation. She was at home with these men—happy to learn Cree, happy to chase deer, happy to eat gut. At the same time, she recognized the unreality of the situation. It was an enchantment: the pain of the past suspended, the difficulties of the future postponed. Perhaps that was why the men were so comforting. Not only were they thoughtful and considerate, they were safe. They made no demands on her. Once home, she would face more empty evenings; then the first gentle hints from friends about "eligible" men, followed by polite social engagements—all forcing her to think about the future and a life without Laddie.

"I wish I need never go back," she wrote that evening.

Preoccupied with these thoughts, she did not at first notice how uneasy the men had become as they headed downstream on their new river. But shortly a heavy gale made travel impossible, leaving everyone to pass the time under the fire tarp. While the men sat and talked and stirred the stew pot Mina began to see that something was bothering them. They didn't voice their worries openly—only worked around them at a circumspect distance.

George had been reminiscing about his boyhood days at Rupert's House and the Indian game of football, played with a sealskin ball stuffed with moss. Then they talked of fights and pranks; and speaking of that, edged around to the Indians who came to trade at Rupert's House every summer. "Inlanders," they were called. The Inlanders hunted caribou and beaver all through the bush, and were different from "Coasters" like Job, who stayed close to James Bay. The two peoples had a good time whenever they got together, but each still felt a little different from the other. Inlanders wondered why anyone would want to hang around the Bay with white men instead of hunting where they pleased. Coasters regarded the bush people as superstitious and, because of that, maybe a bit dangerous. After all, Inlanders still had conjurers who performed magic against enemies.

The men shifted uneasily. Someone mentioned the trouble at "Hannah Bay" and there was silence.

"Hannah Bay?" asked Mina.

It was a Company trading station, George explained—near Rupert's House. Some Inlanders came down one time with a conjurer who dreamed he must take strong actions to keep the fur traders from starving his band. He lured the Coasters and half-breeds away from the fort with the excuse of showing them some sorcerer's dances. While they were gone the conjurer's people snuck into the fort and killed the whites. Then they came back and killed most of the Coasters and half-breeds too.

"Of course that was sixty or seventy years ago," George added.

The Inlanders weren't like that now. But it showed what might happen under—certain circumstances.

Finally he was out with it: "At least we know that the Hudson's Bay Indians aren't like that anymore. We should be sure of a welcome. But these Naskapis . . ."

Mina was taken aback. The past few days they had seen increasing signs of Indians. Each time the men had gotten out and looked around, debating how old the camp was, how many had stayed there. But she had been so eager to meet natives of any sort, the possibility of an unfriendly reception had never occurred to her. Surely George couldn't be serious! Yet the men were not joking. As the gale continued another day Mina found it hard not to think a little, at least, about the stories of Hannah Bay. Hesitantly she brought out her revolver after supper. It needed oiling, after all the rainy weather.

The men noticed immediately.

"You're giving that pistol a fine rubbing," said George.

"Yes," she said, laughing nervously. "I'm getting ready for the Naskapis."

Absolute silence. The men stared at the revolver as if in a trance.

"They would not shoot you," replied George at last. He was quite serious. "It would be us they killed if they took the notion. Whatever their conjurer tells them, they will do."

Gilbert spoke up. Being a half-breed Montagnais, he qualified as somewhat of an expert on Naskapis, even though he'd never met one. "No, they wouldn't hurt women, I don't think," he said reflectively. "They want the women for themselves. If they killed us, Mrs. Hubbard, it would be to keep you at their camp."

She had laughed a little at George's fear, but hearing Gilbert talk like that gave her a jolt. Gilbert never joked with her. And he was speaking quite matter-of-factly of her abduction, and worse.

She swallowed. She had not taken that aspect of the question into consideration.

The men wore the same pale look they had the day she ran away. It came to her again that they were dead men if anything happened to her. If not by Naskapi treachery, then by white justice once they ventured out of the bush.

She flushed and said, "Do you think I would stand there if the Naskapis started firing at you? Just because I don't shoot ptarmigan or caribou doesn't mean I'd have any objection to killing a Naskapi if it were necessary."

The remark didn't appear to reassure them.

EVERYWHERE GEORGE looked, he saw sign—most of them recent. Wigwam poles on either bank of the river. Drying stages along ridges. Campfires. He didn't like it a bit, but there was nothing to do but press on.

The morning of the seventeenth, he was up about half-past three, before first light. He knew Mrs. Hubbard was anxious to be off. A fog covered the lake when they started, but the water was still as glass, so sounds carried a good ways. He was listening to the rush of rapids beyond the end of the lake, when Job called to him. Not excited or loud—just trying to sound ordinary.

"*Chichiwayma kwayneekamos*," he said. Which meant: "Hark: I can hear someone singing with a loud voice for some distance."

Job had sharp ears; George couldn't hear a thing other than the rapids. Mrs. Hubbard didn't understand, of course; Job didn't mean her to.

They ran down the rapids and came out on a bigger lake. There were still wisps of fog, but it was clearing away. The boys decided to stop a minute on an island. Everyone had their ears open.

"Did you hear a dog bark?" asked Job. Still in Cree.

George thought he did. So did the other boys.

"I don't like it," said Job.

They went down the lake, and now the sun was bright and clear. About four miles away stood a high, barren point. George said nothing as he paddled, only stared at the point. There were dark patches that might be tents and some specks that might be people. It was hard to tell from so far away. He set himself to watch and see if the specks moved.

They moved all right. He told Job.

"I seen them some time ago," said Job quietly. He kept paddling. "I didn't want to tell you because I think we better not go near them. I think they are watching us. They might do something to us."

The men kept paddling, trying to decide what to do. George never took his eyes off the far shore. *She* said nothing; hadn't noticed yet.

"Did you see that?" asked Job.

"Yes." The flash of sunlight on metal.

Job said, "I think they have their rifles out. They're getting ready for us."

Then Mrs. Hubbard cut in. "Is that caribou, George? Something's moving on the point."

George cleared his throat. "They're Indians. I don't know if we better go too close."

A rifle shot rang out. For the first time, Job looked relieved. The canoes were too far away to make good targets: anyone unfriendly would wait.

Mrs. Hubbard fired her revolver into the air. Several shots came in quick reply.

"I think they want us to visit them," said George. He hesitated, then asked her if she wanted to go over.

"I most certainly do."

She had the same look as when she ran away. So they went, but paddled slowly all the same.

When they got near shore, the people on the hill began running back and forth waving kerchiefs and pans and screaming loudly. To George's surprise they were women and children.

"Go away, go away!" they shrieked. "We are afraid of you! Our husbands are all away!"

George shook his head and laughed. After all that worry.

The words were a little hard to catch but near enough to Cree to understand. He translated for Mrs. Hubbard and she laughed too. Then he sung out to the women, "Don't be afraid! We are only traveling about and we won't hurt you. We want you to tell us something about the river."

The women stopped their screaming and began to talk among themselves. Then they laughed and called out, "You had better put ashore at our landing place." Four of the older women ran down and pointed out the spot. After the boats had beached, everybody shook hands all around—some twice. They seemed to like saying hello. The younger women and children stayed on the hill at first, but, after a bit, they joined the crowd.

Well, these weren't Naskapi after all—they were Montagnais. Their hair was parted in the middle, Montagnais style, and rolled into a bun in front of each ear. The buns were held together with pretty beaded bands. The dresses were wool and all the women wore tuques for hats—black and red like the Montagnais women

George had seen around Northwest River. There were crosses around their necks too, even the youngest boys, so they must have gone to see priests from time to time.

The women were pretty glad to get over their fright. "Our men are all over at Davis Inlet," they said, "trading for winter supplies. We have no tea or sugar or tobacco." Davis Inlet was a village on the coast.

George asked if the Naskapis lived anywhere nearby.

"The Barren Ground people, yes. Down the river a little ways. You will sleep twice before coming to their camp."

"Are they friendly?"

"Yes, yes. We visit them sometimes. They talk much the way we do, only very fast."

George asked about the river, but the women seemed to know little about it, beyond the Naskapi camp. It kept going to another white man's post, they said. Many, many miles, many hard rapids. It was a long trip.

"How long?" asked George anxiously.

"Oh, many days. Two months perhaps."

His heart sank. Mrs. Hubbard was standing right there. He didn't even want to translate.

"Two months," he told her at last. "Or nearly that." And the smile on her face faded. Well, she knew, of course. They couldn't hope to catch the ship.

After that, she didn't seem to care what the Montagnais said. The Indians didn't notice. They were so glad just to have friendly visitors, they started right up the hill. "Come and talk with us for a while," they called. George didn't much care to, but Mrs. Hubbard had started up the hill alone, and he knew he'd better keep an eye on her. He let himself be led up to camp.

There were two wigwams on the hill, one round, one large and oblong. Both were covered with deerskin that was sooty at the top from so many fires. Inside, you could see white enamel dishes and teapots, a bit of china, and four rifles laid out neat on balsam boughs. Six or eight dogs growled about. Some of the little boys went back to playing.

A few women watched Mrs. Hubbard go her way along the hill, but most crowded around the men. They sure were interested in the men—young women as well as the old. Where had George and his friends come from? How long had they been traveling? What ıimals did they hunt in their own country? George answered as best he could, and even the other men did a little talking. In the middle of it all, the dogs jumped into a roaring fight, so everyone scrambled to keep 'em from chewing each other to pieces. Out of the corner of his eye, George watched Mrs. Hubbard. He didn't want her tangling with any dogs.

Finally he said it was time to be going.

"Oh no!" said the women. "You must stay and eat with us."

"We would like to," he said, "but we have many miles to travel. We must hurry."

"We will make a feast for you," they replied, "and cook very good things. Besides—except for the white lady, you are without women. Stay with us and you can have many good wives until you leave."

Blamed if Mrs. Hubbard didn't come back just then, so George had to translate. She thought it was time to be going, all right. The Indians didn't come down to say good-bye; only watched from the hill.

As the canoes floated away Job stood in the stern, took his hat off and made a low bow to the women. He called out in his best English, "Good-bye, good-bye, my lady!"

Job had gotten to feeling a lot better once he figured out the women wanted him to stay.

For the rest of the day they made pretty good time along the ponds and rapids of the upper river. George figured twenty-three miles in all, even though they'd spent nearly half the morning with the Montagnais. But how much sense was there to making good time? *He'd* seen her smile disappear when she heard about the two months—so she knew as well as he did that it made sense to turn back. Yet she said nothing all afternoon.

Toward evening he pulled in above a little gorge with three rapids. It was too much to carry the canoes around that night, and, anyway, he had to talk to her before they got any farther. Every rapid they passed meant a harder trip upstream if they turned back.

After getting the gear up, he looked around for her. Gone off, of course.

"She went toward the rapid," said Job, and added, "she had a good smile on her face." George shook his head and started after her. She was probably ready to jump into one of the falls, now that they were near gorges again.

She was by the river, all right, but not paying much attention to it. Just by herself thinking. See seemed to know what he came for.

"I suppose we have to turn back," she said.

George shrugged. Now that it came to it, he'd sort of lost his tongue. He knew how much she wanted to keep going.

"I don't see that we have any choice," she continued. "Even starting back now, at least half the return will be in winter. If we go on to Ungava, the whole trip would. I don't think I could manage that."

"It would be hard," he agreed. He hesitated. He had a feeling she was not going to like what was in his mind. The boys didn't want to winter over, but they didn't want to go back by the Naskapi either. That river spooked them. Maybe it was because they'd tipped over once. Or maybe because the current ran so fast, you could get sucked into bad falls before you knew it. Whatever—if the boys turned back, they wanted to go home by the Grand River. The Grand flowed out of the other side of Michikamau, and it led eventually to the post at Northwest River. There was a good map of the route, and a lot of trappers followed the lower part every autumn to lay out their traplines. In case of trouble, help would be a lot closer. George thought it was a pretty good idea.

But thinking those things wasn't quite the same as saying them, not straight out to her. Especially when she looked at him the way she was, half-pleading, half-fierce. It flustered him. So instead of all the things he was thinking, he only said, "I guess we could go back to Michikamau and find the Grand River. We could go out that way."

And the minute it was out, she shook her head. If they went back, they must go the way they came, she said. She didn't trust the sextant readings she'd taken on the Naskapi—hadn't gotten the proper hang of it then. And if she didn't come back with those latitudes right, and didn't go all the way down the George, what would she have done? The whole trip would be a failure.

He wanted to tell her that coming as far as she had, she'd done plenty enough to make any lady proud. But it wasn't easy to say that so it come out just right. Instead, he found himself saying, "All of us think the Naskapi River is too dangerous. Joe already told me that nobody could ever get him to go that way. So we can't do it."

"Well, I don't know about Joe," she said, "and I don't know about Job. But I'm sure Gilbert is perfectly willing. So the two of you can just take me back and let the others go their own way." And it stung him, the scorn in her voice. She was accusing the boys of being afraid. He'd never seen her so angry. And taunting him—daring him to come with her. How he wanted to! But it was their lives she was playing with. He couldn't do that.

"It's too dangerous," he repeated stubbornly. "If we go down that river, our lives will be in danger all the time."

"And yet you have always been quite willing to go down the George River, which you don't know at all!"

Where was his tongue? What she said—it was true enough. But the boys had bad feelings about the Naskapi, and so did he. And they knew what had happened on the trip with Hubbard—George better than any of them. Nobody wanted to go through that—especially not with her. But how could you say that right out?

So he said, "It's just—we think the river is dangerous. All those falls and the fast current. . . ."

It had begun to rain; she didn't seem to notice. "I want to go down the Naskapi," she said. "I've failed to get the observations I need, and if I go back at all, I want to go back by the river. Now, you may refuse to take me. I can't force you and I won't try. But you will record in my diary that I asked you to go and that you refused. You can state your reasons which you think are good."

And with just a touch of anger he said, "Yes, and I will be very willing to do that."

"All right. Talk it out with the men and make your decision. You can let me know what it is tonight." Then she turned and walked back to camp.

37

Whole World on a Tilt

WHEN GEORGE CAME out to the fire that night, Mina knew by the look on his face that the men had decided. "We're going to make a try for Ungava," he told her. "We've thought about it some, and those Montagnais women didn't talk like they knew too much about the country down river. Maybe the Indians living two sleeps beyond can tell us more."

So she went to bed relieved, and also convinced there would be no question now of enough "snap" in the men's game. They were up promptly the next morning, ready to travel.

The river's current proved an immense help. On the Naskapi they had battled upstream week after week, until Mina had nearly come to accept the struggle as a given of wilderness travel. Now, even seemingly calm stretches of the river pulled them along. Loading the boats one morning, Joe and Gilbert launched while George and Mina finished the last of their packing. Looking up only a moment later, she was astonished to see the other canoe several hundred yards downstream.

With every mile paddled, the tableland receded as the river cut its way into a valley. Tributaries swelled the river's volume, and along one stretch the course divided into numerous channels and falls, cascading around a multitude of pink-and-white islands.

Two sleeps and nearly fifty miles of paddling brought renewed signs of Indians but no camps. Then, on August 20, the river widened into a long, narrow lake that stretched north for miles. High on a sandy hill stood two wigwams.

This time there was no hesitation on the part of the men.

Rifle shots were exchanged, and about thirty Indians quickly appeared on the bank. Cautiously the menfolk approached the water's edge and stared at the canoes, talking rapidly among themselves.

"Who are they?"

"See—the man steering looks like an Indian."

"These are white men. This is a white man at the bow."

"Why, there is a white woman too!"

"Where have they come from?"

Mina, of course, couldn't understand a word, but George translated. As the canoes touched shore, the man in the group who was evidently their chief stepped forward to catch the bows. "Of course you have some tobacco," he said.

"Only a little," said George. "We have come far."

The men gathered around, eager to talk. They were Naskapis, all right. They wore deerskin breeches and moccasins, with scarlet leggings pulled over and held in place by straps fastened about the waist. The young men were tall and lithe, but the faces of the older men showed how harsh the country could be.

"Where did you come into the river?" asked the chief. When George told him, he was astonished. "Northwest River is a long way," he said. "I visited there, but only once."

"We are hoping to reach the post at Ungava," said George.

"Oh, you are near now," said the chief. "You will sleep only five times if you travel fast."

Mina saw the smile on George's face even before he translated. Five days! The news seemed almost incredible, for her sextant readings indicated they had nearly 200 miles yet to cover. Still, the Naskapis seemed well acquainted with the country. Other men were chiming in now, each explaining what to expect downstream. From their gestures, the river was obviously turbulent. Often an arm was held at an angle, indicating a steep slope, and more than once a sharp drop of the hand indicated rapids and falls. But the few portages, George told her, were not long. Furthermore, the Indians had just returned from Davis Inlet, where they said the Hudson's Bay supply ship had not yet arrived. That meant it probably hadn't reached Ungava either.

Mina wanted to spend a little time at the camp, but George refused to allow her more than about fifteen minutes. He was anxious to be off, pointing out that they still had no idea how accurate the Indians' information might be. Since she had pressed him so hard to continue, she hardly felt in a position to object. She walked around the wigwams and then spoke, mostly in gestures, with the women. They hung back until she turned to a young mother holding a baby wrapped in old cloths. The child wore an expression of utter wretchedness. But, when Mina gently touched him, the women gathered around and began speaking rapidly.

Before departing, she had George unload a forty-pound bag of flour, along with some rice, tea, and salt. With no supplies from Davis Inlet, the band faced a long winter. As the canoes slid away and turned down the lake Mina waved her handkerchief over her head. Instantly the shawls and kerchiefs on shore flew up in response.

Sitting in the canoe, Mina could hardly contain herself. Five days to Ungava! She had no doubt now that this was the "Indian House Lake" marked on A. P. Low's map, which meant she was farther along than she expected. The lake never widened to more than two miles, pointing like an arrow, always north. Hills rose on either side, barren of any trees and dotted with huge boulders. Only in the lake's sheltered valleys did spruce and tamarack persist—one reason the Naskapis chose the area for their winter camping grounds.

A favorable wind sprang up, and the men rigged the tarps for sails. Twenty-seven miles they made that day and twenty-four the next. The lake just kept going. But on the third day the hills crowded in again and current gripped the canoe.

It was remarkable. The water remained smooth as glass, but now there was a slope to it, as if all of Indian House Lake were draining inexorably off the plateau and the canoes were being sucked along. When the river bent around curves, the slope tilted, slipping from one side to the other. The whole world seemed on a tilt, with everything in motion.

And then the rapids began—running mile after mile. In magnitude and sheer velocity they were far beyond Mina's wildest imaginings. Thousands of boulders lined either bank, piled like huge cannonballs, and the riverbottom was covered with them too. As the canoe shot through rapids like a careening toboggan she watched the boulders rush by under the foaming water, seemingly inches below the hull and every moment threatening to upset the canoe and pitch them all into the river.

Standing astern, Job guided the craft, his eyes fairly blazing as he scanned the river. He shouted directions, first to George and then back to Gilbert and Joe as they followed behind. Most often the canoes hugged the shore, where the waves were not so large, but sometimes Job would swing the boat abruptly into the heavier swells, remaining standing for the longest time, until Mina felt him drop to his thwart as the canoe skinned past a difficult obstruction. Then George bent to his paddle, turning the bow toward shore, and Job was back on his feet, charting a new course.

The current carried them into one rapid, out another, down slopes and over cascade after cascade. Once, Job changed his mind about a course an instant too late, and the boat was swept onto a rock before being swirled free. But nothing seemed to stop them. Prominent peaks appeared, seemingly far in the distance; yet in an hour or two they had drawn even and were soon left behind. The landscape seemed to change before her eyes.

The pace was stressful as well as exhilarating. When she asked Job whether the rapids didn't tire him very much, he said yes, with a smile that showed surprise that she should understand such a thing. She couldn't help being nervous herself, trembling sometimes through the worst drops. In part, this was because she had not been getting much sleep; the mosquitos had become positively ferocious, both in the tents and out of them. George remarked that it was "like walking in a snowstorm" at times, and the men finally resorted to their veils.

By Friday, August 25, they had come approximately 150 miles—averaging nearly thirty a day—and the men were starting to drink periodically from their paddles to see if the water tasted of salt. For the first time, Mina began to think of success. To her surprise, she found herself almost regretting that the long journey was ending. What would she do when she got home?

> Though I dread going back, I think I should like to spend the summer like this always. . . . Was thinking today how strange it is. I have not wanted to see anyone, I have been lonely for no one, etc., have come these two months to this deserted wilderness and have never felt as if I were far from home, I suppose because no place can ever seem like home to me here. I think I have felt more at home here in this Labrador wilderness than I have ever done any place since I was in our home in Congers. But I mean to try to face the other life as bravely as I can and in a way that will honor the one I loved more than all the world and who loved me with such a beautiful generous love. Only what am I going to do? I don't know.

Of more immediate concern was the Hudson's Bay supply ship. Would it have made its trip through Ungava Bay already? She couldn't help fretting.

> If we should get the *Pelican* and get out soon I might possibly get back and get my story and some of my pictures in print before Wallace is even heard from, and that would be the thing for me. If I am to be successful, that would make it complete. Oh, if it might only come out that way how grateful I should be and how complete would be my victory and how completely it would make of no account Wallace's reflections. . . .

On the other hand, if the ship had come and gone, it would be a long winter in Ungava—utterly unbearable if Wallace ended by wintering over too.

On Saturday evening her sextant indicated that the post was only a half-dozen miles away. She wanted desperately to continue paddling in the dark, for she would never forgive herself if the ship turned out to have been waiting that very evening and then sailed before she arrived on the morrow. But with so many rapids, there was no taking chances with the river—not at night.

Sunday morning they were off at 7:30. It was a sunny day and the river broad and majestic. It stretched now more than two miles wide. Coming around a curve the men were surprised by yet another rapid, and both canoes were nearly sucked in unprepared. George and Job paddled furiously, barely reaching shore above the lip of the drop. After looking it over, Gilbert and Joe decided to carry around, but George and Job voted to chance it. The pitch was a short one, only several hundred yards, though it was steep.

Mina walked to the bay below, thinking of the notes and the chart of Ungava Bay she carried. As George was climbing into the boat she called, "When you get out beyond those points you should be able to see the island opposite the post."

"All right, I'll watch for it," he replied, smiling. The men had been a bit skeptical of her abilities with the sextant.

Pushing off, George and Job headed upstream, to give themselves enough room to line up their course. Evidently they underestimated the current, for the river pulled the canoe too quickly toward the drop, and it swept into the cascade broadside, without getting fully turned around. Job yelled something and George gave up trying to turn. Instead, the canoe shot down the curl stern first, with barely enough time for the men to pivot in their seats to face the oncoming waves.

Mina's heart stopped as the boat was swirled like an autumn leaf in the current—it was hard to know whether the craft was even under control. In an agony of suspense, she watched George and Job's paddles flail, until at last she heard a yell of triumph, and the canoe headed in to shore. George waved his cap and with a big grin shouted, "I saw the island!"

Sure enough, when they were underway again an island could be seen some miles in the distance. But there was no evidence of the post. As each new bay opened up Mina searched anxiously for signs of life. Presently she saw a few specks on a point and, drawing nearer, a boat. An Eskimo and his son stood at their nets, hauling in fish.

The man looked up, catching sight of her. He smiled broadly and walked to the end of his boat. It seemed he wanted to shake hands.

Mina's heart sank. From the gleam in his eyes, it was plain he was expecting them. That could mean only one thing. The *Pelican* had already arrived, bringing news of her attempted crossing.

"Good morning," called George. "Do you know how far it is to the post?" And the man smiled again, seeming to understand. But he replied only in Eskimo. George asked a few more questions, both in English and Cree, but each time looked at Mina and shook his head. He couldn't understand a word.

So they left the man to his nets, still smiling and waving. Mina was on pins and needles, but the men paddled along in leisurely fashion, chatting and laughing, seeming to have not a care in the world. She wanted to shake them by their collars, to speed them along. How could they not know their fate? But they continued calmly until George suddenly exclaimed, "There it is!"

Deep in a cove lay several tiny buildings, nestled at the foot of a huge mountain of rock. Other barren hills flanked the cove. The tide was evidently out, for a great mudflat stretched for half a mile between the post and the water. From the hills a little stream flowed, cutting a deeper channel to the river. The canoes turned up the stream, passing between the sloping mudbanks.

Suddenly, to Mina's astonishment, the men pulled out their poles and, pointing the bows in shore, poled right up the mudbanks. It was such a funny performance, she laughed along with them as the canoes slithered over the top and onto the flats.

In the distance she sighted a man making his way across the mud. He was followed by a retinue of Eskimos. As he approached she stood up and asked if he were Mr. Ford, whom she had been told was in charge of the post. He said yes, and she explained how she had come there. Then, nearly beside herself, she put the question to which she most feared an answer.

"Has the ship been here?"

"Why, yes," said Mr. Ford.

She swallowed. "And gone again?"

"Yes. That is—what ship do you mean? Is there any other ship expected here than the Company's ship?"

"No, I mean the Company's ship, the *Pelican*. Has she been here?"

"Yes," he said. "She was here last September. I expect her in September again, about the middle of the month or later."

And after that she remembered almost nothing of what happened. She was aware, only vaguely, of Mr. Ford offering his arm and asking her to come up to the house.

GEORGE WATCHED her go. She walked in small steps across the flats, choosing her way carefully, one hand steadying herself with a paddle, the other—the one without the glove—being held by Mr. Ford. She got to the post and disappeared inside.

She never looked back.

He heard the Eskimos talking—pointing—talking to him. Telling him and the boys to get back in the canoes. He did it. Then the Eskimos pulled them over the mud to a tiny brook, where the gravel made for better walking, and began ferrying gear up to the post. The boys were left sitting alone.

George looked up to the post. He felt empty. It didn't seem quite right to go up there. Not without being asked and not being white.

He turned to the bay. A nice breeze was blowing and the sun shining on the water. He'd made their crossing—gotten her almost six hundred miles from Northwest River, in good health and fine spirits. In a couple of weeks the ship would come and pick them up, they'd take a steamer to Halifax, and then he and the boys would board a train to Missanabie, and that would be the end of it.

Wouldn't it?

He looked at the post's blank windows and rather thought it would. He thought he'd better help the boys put up a tent.

Then he heard a voice calling—hers. She burst out the door at the front of the post. She was waving. Then running down the banks toward them and this time not so careful of the mud. George stood up—they all did—and ran to her. And when she got there, she took his hand and the hands of the other boys and thanked them all for what they'd done. She said they had brought her through an immensely difficult journey—and brought her through safely, with not a hair on her head harmed, and with greater courtesy and gentlemanliness than she ever could have hoped for. They had been at all times gentle to her and kind. She said she could never, never have done it without them.

Then she brought them up to the post and introduced them all around, and helped them to find a spot for their tent. They picked a fine place among the willows.

He set about cutting stakes.

They had two or three weeks until the ship came, Mr. Ford said. Two or three weeks with nothing to do. But it came into George's mind also—these were two or three weeks to think carefully and to plan.

38

Shepoo Matchi

D*o or die.*

That had been Hubbard's motto and Easton was determined to follow in his spirit. The leave-taking from Richards, Stanton, and Pete had been a high moment. The damp eyes of the others, hearty handshakes all around, and a high spirit of resolution all made it easy to wave farewell and paddle briskly into the bay. Heading deeper and deeper into the unknown, one day after another—that would be the real test. Easton was determined to measure up.

Separation Day continued blustery with whitecaps running not only on the open lake but also in the more sheltered bays. After only three miles, Wallace decided to pull into shore and wait for the wind to abate. Easton was just as glad; in rough water, Wallace seemed a little stiff in the bow.

The two of them spent the afternoon on a small barren hill, picking berries and basking in the sun. With Michikamau stretched out at their feet, they were able to spot their position pretty well on Low's map. Talking the situation over, they agreed that once they hit the river they need not worry. Wallace recounted some information he'd gotten from the Indians two years ago—all to the effect that the portage into the George would be a cakewalk. The only thing to worry about was getting off Michikamau before the winds had a chance to pin them down.

By 3:30, the breeze began to slacken and they went back into the boat. At first the lake was roily, but gradually the wind died down and they began to make good time. Easton was surprised—even a bit disheartened—to have Wallace call it a day with two hours of daylight remaining, but he bit his tongue. After all, Mr. Wallace was the leader.

That night, their first alone together, they served up boiled owl, stewed mossberries, a slice of pork smothered in grease, lots of coffee, and half a darn good. It was a fine meal except for Wallace forgetting to put baking powder in the darn good. Afterward, though, he shared his private stock of Gluck Durham and a plug of Lucky Strike. Puffing contentedly on his pipe, Easton figured the two of them would get on just fine.

The next day, September 5, brought perfect weather—blue sky, bright sun, and air that didn't even breathe. Michikamau looked like a millpond. They made a dozen miles before lunch, then another eleven in the afternoon before Wallace decided on another early camp. Easton was starting to get a sore tongue.

The thing was, Wallace seemed to need so much time to write in his diary. Every spare moment of the day the notebook seemed to be out. Only the other night, he'd confided to Easton that he'd written some "great touches" about their parting campfire, which would make a wonderful scene in the pages of *Outing*. That was all to the good, but the way things were going, Wallace was bringing home enough material to fill the Encyclopaedia Britannica.

The good weather held and they got off Michikamau all right. But that left the George to find, and where *that* will-of-the-wisp was, was anybody's guess. Everywhere, the countryside was flat as a pancake—Easton was lucky some days to find even a tree high enough to scout from. Day after day Wallace seemed to push along supremely confident, pleased with the weather, in no particular hurry; whereas Easton considered the situation much more chancy. "Sorry to say I worry a great deal," he wrote; "Wallace does not, not seeming to realize how difficult travel will be after the first snow, which may be expected any time now; this weather cannot last." Even worse, it appeared that Lake Michikamats did not end in a straightforward narrows, as Low's map had suggested, but with bays stretching this way and that—each one a potential portage route for the Montagnais. "From the numerous Indian signs, they must hunt here often and the portage once found should be very plain," Easton speculated, "but then there will be some 10 miles of shore to search, bays and inlets, and these beggars have no sign which may be seen from a canoe. It may take weeks."

Most often, Easton was sent out to "scout," and it was discouraging work—a combination of hot sun, cold mud, and swirling flies that even a week of frosts couldn't kill. Each time he would come back, his moccasins a little more decrepit, his pants a little more ragged, and his temper a little more frayed. He tried his level best to control his swearing, conjuring up his mother's reproachful smile every time he took a dive into the oozy mire. But that seemed to work only about two times out of five. The other three, he was likely to return completely frustrated, and loaded for bear. "Wallace breaks my heart at times," he noted:

> Returned to camp dead tired. He had not done a thing, tent still standing, everything scattered around, bluebottles on meat. Said, "he has been writing in his diary." Damn the diary until we are sure of George River. We are not sure of getting out and if not, his diary will do him little good.

After nearly a week of fruitless searching, the dead ends and false bays even began to irk Wallace. On September 11 a downpour with an icy tinge moved in, along with a wind that made for the worst kind of torment carrying the canoe. Wallace went sailing through the marshes like a windjammer on wheels, blown backward two steps for every one he took forward.

Around the fire that night, the two of them stared at the charts until they were dizzy. Low's map was back to dotted lines—he hadn't gotten this far north—and Ahsini's was worse than a Chinese puzzle. For the first time, Wallace mentioned the possibility of a "way out" if they couldn't find the George: going back to Northwest River Post by way of the Grand River. Well, that would never do. Wallace knew that and Easton knew it. They were committed, and the only course was to push on to the last ounce of grub. Easton lay awake that night resolving it would be "George River or Bust."

Then the weather cleared on September 13, and Easton awoke with an indescribable feeling. He told Wallace this would be their "lucky thirteenth." So, right off, the canoe hull got scraped half bare going over a shallows, the two of them missed a partridge with their pistols, and then they found a "river" which turned out to be nothing but a dead-end bay. Wonderful luck. Scouting ahead, Easton followed the bay to another mudhole, followed the mudhole to another swamp, and followed the swamp into brush so thick not even a waterhole could be raised.

He had never felt gloomier—never once on the entire trip. "Thinking it all over on the way back could see nothing but starvation at the end, knew Wallace would never turn back, sure I should not suggest it, would rather die in here than go back a failure." He thought of that sunny day in May, eons ago, when his family had come to see him off at the Brooklyn pier. His older brother, Rob, had taken Wallace off to the side for a talk; Easton overheard him saying, "Don't worry, the kid will be true blue." Even in this hellhole of a swamp, Easton was damned sure he was not going to quit.

Returning to the canoe, he tried not to let Wallace guess his feelings, but bad news was bad news. Wallace gave him a long look, thought a little, and said nothing.

They paddled to a point for lunch, and while Wallace boiled a kettle Easton climbed another tree. This time he spotted two narrow lakes—nothing great, but at least something to head for. Eating quickly, they portaged to the first and had almost begun their haul to the second, when Wallace decided to explore the far bay. It seemed to extend a good way and he even thought he detected a current. Easton couldn't, but Wallace was insistent. He thought he heard rapids ahead.

Easton listened hard and heard nothing. Paddling up the bay, Wallace kept staring into the water, trying to spot the faintest swirl. "This just might be it," he said. "Look at the water—it's clearer than the ponds we've been paddling."

"All right," said Easton grumpily, "but will you make me one promise?"

Wallace looked dubious. "Anything in my power to grant consistent with conditions."

"If we get to the George River, I would like one big darn good with lots of grease."

"Granted," said Wallace, but couldn't help adding, "if we have enough flour."

Easton kept his ears open. To his amazement, he did hear something. Then in the distance, he saw a white line across the water. Rapids! Wallace sent up a hurrah.

Easton wasn't satisfied until he climbed a tree, where he spied a ribbon of water stretching away to the northwest. Even so, he wouldn't rest until he ran along the bank to the rapid itself — not till he put his hand in the cold water and felt the current tumble by.

Wallace came up and slapped him on the back. "What do you think of that?"

Easton shook his head. "It's just the way Ahsini had it on his map. Running straight across our path."

"Low spent $10,000 on his expedition and never got this far!"

"That's right," said Easton. "Now, what about my darn good?"

The next morning Wallace decreed they could eat as much pemmican for breakfast as they wanted. Easton put away a pound of the stuff—three times the usual ration—and so did Wallace. *That* was a mistake. The two of them felt fine for about half an hour, and then—trouble. It began with vague gnawing pains in the stomach and from there wormed its way downward. Easton took to writing in his journal, in a wild effort to stave off the internal, or rather infernal, pains, but to no avail. He vowed it was the last time he'd experiment with condensed foods.

On the river the situation was hardly better. Crossing into the arctic watershed seemed to have ushered in a change of seasons. When they finally started downstream, the thermometer read 22° and a gale was howling. In the narrows the river funneled the wind right into their faces; and with such frosty temperatures, shooting rapids was no easy task—not with mitts on. Most chutes they played safe and lined the canoe around, but one they decided to run and, halfway down, struck a hidden rock, dipped, and shipped two or three gallons of water. Easton had to jump out and grapple the boat to safety. "Barometer falling, may have snowstorm any time now," he wrote worriedly, "must get . . . into lower river before freeze-up or we may croak even yet."

Almost every day they were finding Indian sign—teepee poles, paddles, piles of antlers, camp stuff. So it wasn't really surprising, on the eighteenth, to sight four or five Mountaineer Indians along the bank, out hunting. The Indians spotted the canoe almost immediately and started waving to beat the band. The minute Easton stepped ashore, they were smiling and shaking hands with him. He was grinning too; it was good to hear new voices after so many miles. Of course, everybody was jabbering in his own tongue, but the word *stemmo* came through loud and clear—tobacco. They wanted as much as they could lay their hands on.

With a little signing, Wallace made them understand he'd boil tea at their camp, so they led the way to the rest of the party, about three miles down river. Squaws, huskies, little kids wearing nothing but rags—everybody turned out. After Easton and Wallace set up their tent, eleven of the men wedged in somehow, cheek by jowl, while the women hung about the entrance. Wallace boiled up at least four gallons of tea and it was gone in minutes—they drank the stuff scalding hot. And did they ever crave Wallace's "stemmo!" The chief, a fellow named Toma, reciprocated with his own gifts: venison, smoked caribou tongue, and a bladder of fat so refined you could nearly see through it. The men stayed, signing and talking far into the evening, until finally Easton dropped off to sleep.

Next morning everybody was back for more tea, and Wallace tried to find out about the river. Toma drew a rough map and kept gesturing rapids, rapids—steep—plus a high falls. On his fingers, he counted fourteen days travel to the post, but it seemed he'd never actually been beyond Indian House Lake, where the river widened. Below that, he made numerous signs of trouble and repeated, "*Shepoo matchi, shepoo matchi*"—river bad.

Wallace wanted to take a few pictures before he left, but Toma suddenly turned canny, angling for a little pay. When Wallace pulled a wrinkled dollar from his dunnage, the chief turned the bill over and over, examining it closely; then gave it back with a shrug. "Stemmo," he said. Wallace reluctantly donated another plug and took his snaps. Then the entire village ran to the riverbank and waved farewell. The men picked up handfuls of small stones and threw them in the direction of the departing canoe, a Mountaineer custom something like throwing rice at a wedding. If a stone hit you, it meant good luck.

Naturally nary a stone found its mark. *Shepoo matchi.*

CONTINUING DOWNRIVER, Wallace pondered the expedition's prospects. He felt by turns confident and apprehensive. He was not worried about surviving, of course. Game seemed to be available, if not abundant, and he could even envision "wintering over" if need be. But September was drawing to a close and the weather did give one pause. It seemed to be progressing from good to indifferent to intolerable. Half a day's paddle brought them to a large lake expansion, full of many arms and bays, and before they could locate the outlet, a new gale roared in. They managed to shoot two caribou, but that proved almost more of a peril than a blessing, for he and Easton gorged on the meat so heavily, they were incapacitated by diarrhea for several days.

Even had they wished to make time, the winds would hardly let them. At night the tent billowed and flapped so badly, its stakes seemed on the verge of ripping out. Easton was up more than once chasing the stovepipe, and during the worst gusts they were forced to take it down altogether. Another night Wallace stoked the stove as full as he could before turning in, to ensure a warm night's sleep. He awoke in the wee hours choking, as if he were descending the last gloomy rungs of Hades. Through the thick smoke he could make out the stove, glowing red, and the ground beneath beginning to smolder. Frantically he heaved all their water on it, and the ensuing commotion convinced Easton, still dreaming, that he had been trapped in a steam bath.

For nearly a week they could do no more than camp and watch the whitecaps roll along the shores of Atuknipi—or Reindeer Lake, as Wallace dubbed it. Easton, his patience wearing thin, chose simply to refer to it as "Damned Lake." Finally, having at last located the outlet, they were checked by a new storm, which left half a foot of snow on the ground.

Suddenly the whole world was white. The spruce were weighed down with their winter coverings, and along shore rough boulders were encased in icy shells. The river sparkled in the sun. Back in the canoe, they found their old enemy, the wind, implacable as ever. To cross half a mile of flat water required more than an hour of hard paddling. Then came three rapids in succession, but even in the quickwater they had to stroke mightily just to stand still. The wind-driven chop made it impossible to see any lurking rocks, and, after receiving a hard dig on one boulder, they headed for shore and made camp.

The weather held them prisoners for three more days. Black, billowing clouds dropped huge quantities of snow, while winds of hurricane force sculpted shifting drifts. Wallace could hear the tent ropes singing, they were so taut from the wind and the strain. On September 29 he determined to press on, bitter headwind or no. By now he knew better than to hold out for truly fair weather.

They ran a few short rapids and the spray from the waves nearly paralyzed them, freezing almost on contact. Their packs quickly iced up, as did their mitts, their beards—even their paddles. Wallace didn't care. At least they were making progress.

Then the river entered a short steep rapid with a band of white at the bottom. It looked insignificant—certainly no rougher than the other drops they had run that morning. He and Easton didn't even bother to scout it. As the canoe headed into the V, rocks flying past on either side, Wallace was jolted as the hull snagged on a submerged boulder. He turned, started to climb amidships to push the boat off, when suddenly it lurched free of its own accord. The bow careened wildly, hitting the rock, while the stern spun into the main current, sweeping over Easton's paddle and jerking it from his hands before he could even pull it out of harm's way. Caught off balance, Wallace grabbed for a gunwale, but the canoe, fully broadside now, plunged into the bottom of the chute. With one last swirl it struck another rock and in an instant capsized, spilling the two of them into the river.

The shock of the frigid water jolted Wallace, numbed him, and took his breath away. Floundering, he managed to lift his head enough to see the boat sweeping along underwater and Easton being dragged with it, his trousers caught on a protruding bolt. He seemed to be struggling desperately for air. At last he managed to pull off a mitten, draw his sheath knife and, with a lunge, cut himself free.

Wallace flailed toward the bow, grabbed it, and tried to right the boat, but the inexorable current whirled it along. It was all he could do in his ice-laden clothes to hang on. The duffels and gear, which were not tied in, began to float downriver piece by piece; he could do nothing to stop them.

Somehow Easton hauled himself to the stern and grabbed the tracking line. Clenching it in his teeth, he hobbled and half-swam through the rapids to a rock island in midriver. With Wallace treading water and pushing, they at last succeeded in wrestling the boat into the shallows and emptying it. Gasping for air, shivering, dazed and numb, they splashed to shore and looked about.

The island was absolutely barren—not a stick of wood anywhere for a fire.

Wallace stared at the canoe—then the riverbank, which was perhaps an eighth of a mile away—then again at the canoe. Their paddles were nowhere to be seen. Almost without thinking, he stumbled back into the boat, Easton following. The two of them began to dog-paddle for shore, their hands chilled by the excruciating cold. The eighth of a mile seemed to take an eternity to cross.

Wallace beached the boat and shouted "Fire!" to Easton, but the word came out a croak. He could hardly speak. Gathering a bit of moss and spruce brush, he dropped to his knees. They were dead men if they could not raise some warmth. To his dismay, he discovered that his hands were almost wholly without feeling. He could not even maneuver the tips of his fingers into his pocket to reach his matchcase. Finally he thought to loosen his belt and lower his trousers, until the pocket was at an angle where he could push his hand in. Painstakingly he lifted the case out and unscrewed the top.

Easton was staggering badly; he appeared to be only half-conscious. He had retrieved his matchcase, but could remove the cap only by biting it off. He seemed to be intent, now, on trying to light the branches of a fair-sized, fully standing spruce.

Wallace concentrated on trying to make his own fingers work. Everything around him seemed wet or covered with snow. He tilted the matches out of his case; half fell into a drift, ruined at a shot.

He paused to collect himself. Then, ever so carefully, he held the case against a rock with one hand and with the other grasped a single match between thumb and forefinger. He was particular to select one of the wax-taper kind, doubting whether the old sulfur-heads would even light. Bending to his tinder, he struck the match against the case. The head buttered, soft and useless. He tried another and another, always with the same result.

The matches seemed hopeless. He glanced at Easton and was shocked: the boy had a wild bloodstain in his eyes and clearly was not comprehending what he was doing. He seemed only to clutch aimlessly at the trees.

"Run, Easton, run!" called Wallace. Somehow they had to build up their body heat. Wallace stood and tried to run himself, but his legs were so numb they wouldn't work properly. He lurched a few paces, only to pitch into the snow; he got up, tried again, and fell. Easton did as badly. The last time Wallace couldn't even stand, so he crawled on all fours back to his brush. Without a fire they were doomed.

There were three matches left, the old sulfur-heads. Taking the first, he made his fingers curl around it as best he could. At least the wind was drying out the box bottom. He steadied the case on a rock with one hand; then scratched the match against the case and—got a spark! The sulfur-head began to sputter! But his fingers failed him and the match dropped into the snow.

He took the second match—his next to last—and wedged it between his fingers, glaring at them to try and raise some feeling. They seemed like dead sticks. He moved his arm up, down, across the case. The match sputtered and caught.

God be merciful, he prayed.

He forced his fingers to remain stiff and moved his whole arm under the brush, watching the flame lick upward. He did not breathe. The flame curled around one twig, then another, sending up a whiff of vapor. Hardly daring to trust himself, he grasped several more twigs and lowered them gently onto the flame. It licked these too, spreading from one branch to another, to another. Wallace edged a thumb-sized stick over the flame. He watched it catch. Then moved another branch. He could not take his eyes from the fire. He began to feed larger pieces, one after another, shivering as he heard the wood crackle and spit. Still not satisfied, he staggered to a pile of driftwood, dragged back larger limbs, whole small trees, and threw them on, watching the flames wheel in the wind and throw sparks to the sky.

Easton was on his feet again, swaying and mumbling. "Thank God," he was saying, "thank God, thank God . . ."

"Stand close, b'y," called Wallace, and pulled him nearer to the blaze.

He threw on more wood and again more, until the blaze became a bonfire. A kind of joyful mania seized him and he laughed aloud. He began stripping off his clothes, which were already steaming from the heat of the fire. He wanted to dance a jig. Thanks to the old sulfur-head, they had triumphed over fate and the elements! For the moment he did not care that their rifles had sunk to the bottom of the river, that their extra clothing was lost, their axes, their stove, even their paddles. He and Easton were alive. And life, no matter how uncertain, was sweet! Wallace laughed with the very joy of living.

39

Snaring the Sun

A MONTH AT GEORGE River Post was about as close to rich man's heaven as Bert Blake ever expected to get. The last of the salmon was running, and if you got tired of eatin' salmon three times a day, you could spear trout. If you got tired of trout, you could try ptarmigan or get after a seal. On Sundays, there was plum duff from the post. And all through, Mrs. Hubbard was payin' a dollar a day. Who cared about gold under that rainbow! Bert figured by the time he got back to Northwest River, he'd have more than a hundred dollars to his name.

By Garge—a dollar a day! There wasn't anything to beat workin' for Mrs. Hubbard and George. The two of 'en was always makin' sure the boys was fixed with what they needed. Now and again Mrs. Hubbard baked up a little something—sweet doughnuts or such. Sundays she'd talk a while and read the Bible to them. The other days, you never knew. She and George had all kinds of ideas.

The two of 'en took Mrs. Ford for a ride, up seven miles to the last rapids on the river. Bert come along as a paddler. 'Twas a little picnic. Well, Mrs. Ford couldn't get over it. She'd been livin' at that post twenty-two years, and never been up the river so far. And once Mrs. Hubbard heard that, why it only made her want to take Mrs. Ford more places. Another day they sailed to the Narrows, where the salmon was gathered. After the first snow squall, they gave Mrs. Ford a ride in a dogsled. Mr. Will Ford, her son, had a forty-foot dog whip, and Mrs. Hubbard wanted to try it. She hauled way back for a snap and the dogs fair jumped. On the backlash, she nearly took off her own nose. Oh, Mrs. Ford loved it. She took such a shine to Mrs. Hubbard, she begun to treat her like her own daughter.

Another time George had the idea of makin' tightropes. He put two posts in the ground, then strung a rope about waist high. Pretty soon Mrs. Hubbard spied it and come down, but George wouldn't let on what was up. He only said 'twas for conjurin'—they was goin' to cast a spell and find out where Wallace was. That made her laugh. Well, that evening all the Eskimos and the Fords and Mrs. Hubbard come down and after everybody was ready, George called for a contest to see who could walk farthest across the rope. Most everybody fell who tried, but Bert got a good ways. George was the best of course. George could do about everything.

How he loved to joke Mrs. Hubbard! 'Twas a caution to see the two of 'en go. Gilbert—he'd never dare joke with a white woman like that. He mainly watched what George did and then did that. Like, he noticed George pickin' flowers for Mrs. Hubbard along the river—and how much she liked 'en. So Bert picked some dandelions too. He even tried his own joke once, when the flies and mosquitos was thick and crawlin'. "There's one!" he says, and she looks up. "One what, Gilbert?" "A fly!" he says. "If we had a little salt for his tail we'd catch him and be all right!" She laughed, though not quite like with George's jokes.

Then there was the Eskimo kayaks. These was little sealskin boats, slick and narrow, so only one person could fit in. You paddled with a two-bladed paddle—*dip, dip*—first one side, then the other. The Eskimos made it look easy as rollin' over a log, but the trick was *not* to roll over.

Anyway, Mr. Will Ford took out his kayak one day for anyone to try if they had a mind. There wasn't a wind and it looked safe. Joe and Job didn't want anything to do with Eskimo boats. But George got in, and once Mrs. Hubbard saw that, she was in for it too. Bert hardly figured she could fit her skirts in the hole, but she did, and then started off down the cove—pretty wobbly at first. Mr. Ford signed to one of the Eskimos to get a canoe ready in case, but by the time she reached the point and come back, the boat was slipping along straight and she was smiling. She liked it so much, 'twas a while before she'd get out.

"You're nearly an expert," called Will Ford. "You do a lot better than George."

Well—George wasn't goin' to stand for that. He got back in

and plowed to the point in no time. But he was so big for that boat, the faster he went the more his elbows flung one way and the next. He wasn't so smooth as she. "And I could beat you too," she told him, "if I were as strong." Oh, she fair loved it, to hear Mr. Will Ford say she was better than George!

What a pair! Back and forth at each other, and always teasin'. But you could see, really, they liked it. Both of 'en did.

FOR ALL GEORGE tried, he couldn't help keeping his eye on her.

Almost every day they'd do something together. She'd come by the tent and want to go walking, to measure how high the hill was behind the post. Or she'd give him lessons on how to use the sextant. Another time, she got him to help write down the Indian paddling song he and the boys liked to sing. What a clever lady! And going back like she did to finish high school in Williamstown. How many grown women—even white women—would do that? How many white women would ever want to learn Cree or teach a half-breed how to figure latitudes?

They never run out of things to tell one another. Yet they could walk along quiet too. Hiking up the hill, George would watch the wind in her hair, puffing at a strand just above her ear, eventually tugging it loose from her ribbon and blowing wildly about until she brought up a hand and tucked it back. Or he would watch the hem of her skirt swirling one way, then the other, over the moss, each swirl drawing the cloth over the curve of her.

He found himself telling her about the things he yearned after. How he missed not having tobacco for a good smoke; how he looked forward to some fresh fruit; how the boys needed baking powder for their bannock. Yet some things he couldn't bring himself to talk about—not to her and not to the other fellus either. And some things, well . . . some things he tried to put right out of his head. But they kept popping back in.

Now and then, he tried to have it out with himself. Something would set him off—maybe seeing her stockings hung out to dry on a bush, maybe the light of her lamp in her window at night—and he would give himself over to his thoughts. And then he would wonder—what *was* there to all of it anyway? Was she really taking an interest and caring about him, or was she only bein' good to the boys, like always?

Now the caribou skin and the water bottle—those meant

something maybe. You couldn't share them in quite the way you could sweet doughnuts. The other day he'd mentioned it was gettin' colder in the tent, and straightaway she gave him her hot water bottle. Also the caribou skin she'd gotten from the Naskapi Indians. Well, he could've done without, of course, but it sure was nice to be able to lie on that caribou skin on cold nights. And it was awfully fine to be able to boil a bit of water by the fire, and pour it careful into the hot water bottle, and then use it to keep his hands warm when sewing or writing in his journal before bed. And it was hard not to think about whose feet had hugged that bottle nights before.

The time they took Mrs. Ford up to the falls, they'd had to cross some mudflats. The mud was soft and you sank down pretty deep. Well, Mrs. Hubbard wasn't used to that kind of walking and she about walked right out of her sealskin boots. That's the kind of thing that got George's mind going. Thinkin' about if Mrs. Hubbard got stuck, then laughed, and got him to hold her arm until she just slipped out of her boots and skipped along, barefoot and free.

A few days later, on the trip down to the Narrows, she told him how she couldn't sleep all night. She'd had one cold foot. George couldn't help thinkin' about her awake inside her blankets. And all the ways to warm that foot, so white and slender.

One hand of hers was white too. The other she'd lost her glove to, and it had gotten browner in the sun like his. Not so different from his at all, only soft and finer.

But he kept coming back to something. Even if she learned Cree, would she ever understand it quite the way he did? What would she think of all those stories he had from his mother that were so deep in his heart? On his first trip with Hubbard, looking at the moon one night, he'd told the story of the Cree boy and girl who lived together in a wigwam by a great water. Their father and mother were dead, but the boy had learned to be a great hunter, for he had to hunt not only for himself but for his sister too. One day he found a tree that was very high and climbed it, and told his sister to climb it with him. As they climbed, the tree grew taller and taller and after a while they reached the moon. Then the boy and the girl laid down to sleep, and after a while they woke up with a bright light shinin' in their faces—it was the sun passing along that way. So the boy set a snare for the sun and caught it, and after that it was always bright on the moon.

Hubbard had wanted to hear more, but George always felt

uncomfortable about Indian stories around white men. He knew what ministers thought of superstitions. And now, when he looked at Mrs. Hubbard's white hand, or even the one that the sun had darkened—he wondered what she would think of those stories he loved. And then he would feel careful.

Yet even trying to be cautious about what things went where in his journal, his pencil sometimes run away with him. He tried to write a little something about the trip. But he got to putting down so much about how well Mrs. Hubbard "done in her traveling" and how "very good" she was to him, and how she'd done "what no other lady could do," that he kept right on going for a couple pages saying things that, another time when he wasn't feeling so bold—why, maybe he wouldn't have.

When he came to consider what lay in his future, he wasn't quite so free. "I have thought a great deal of what I ought to do this winter," he wrote.

> I would like to go to school, then in the summer I would go down to James Bay and start as fur trading and stay out there all winter. Besides I could catch lots of fur myself and maybe, or I am very sure, could write a nice little story. I am sure someone would be good enough to help me in doing so. Another thing is in my mind. I would like now to get married this fall if I was lucky enough. What if I could strak luck and could get a white girl that would marry me and especially if she was well learnt. We then could write some nice stories because she would know lots more than I would but not likely I would be so lucky. I think some way my chances are small in that way. But I know I would be very happy. I am very sure it is a happy life anyway. So many nice girls in the world and yet none for me or it looks very much like it.

All the same, he couldn't help letting his mind run when the two of them were together. Thoughts flew too swift, sometimes, to stop them.

She'd begun writing her own book there at the post, and when she finished a piece she had him read it and tell her what he thought. She didn't do this with Mr. Ford, nor Will Ford, nor anybody else. George was the one she trusted.

And then one day she had a talk that made him think maybe

he wasn't imagining the things that came into his head. The two of 'em were just passing the time, when she started to dream about what she would do after the *Pelican* came. She was thinking of going to England. People there might be interested in hearing about her trip, she said.

And then—George could hardly believe his ears—she wondered if he might like to come along with her. It about took his breath away. England! He could hardly get his lips around the words to say yes. But he did. Oh, yes—he'd like to go to England, he said. So she told him she'd see about it—her plans weren't fixed yet. And then she went back to talking more about what she'd written.

George's cheeks burned. England! That was a different thing entirely from going along in the bush. You got a half-breed to help you in the bush—there wasn't anything out of the ordinary in that. But traveling in England! She wouldn't do that unless she felt—well, easy with him.

That night, before he wrote his journal, he filled her hot water bottle to help keep his fingers warm. "Fine day . . ." he began. "Mrs. Hubbard and I working and too talking about something great important. Great afternoon. (See L)" He wrote a great deal more at "L," in his special place. Though it wasn't anything he'd ever actually send, what he wrote was sort of a letter. At the end he put, "If I was tould to go around the world and pick one out I would come back and still have you for sure." Even in the regular book, he couldn't hold back. "I could not sleep last night. Awake all night thinking lot of new plans was up 3 A.M. What a happy life if it would really happen. New plans. So good of her to think of so kind thoughts of me. She is more than good and kind to me."

Whenever he was with her now, he tried to please her. For instance, he knew how she loved to hear the men sing. So when the boys got together in Mr. Ford's kitchen and Mrs. Hubbard was there, George found himself leading the others in hymns and paddling songs. One morning, some Eskimos was there, too, and one of their little girls fainted. Well, her father came over and picked her up gentle as you might a little bird. What stuck to George, though, was the sweet look Mrs. Hubbard gave that man. It didn't seem to matter how dark he was or that he couldn't speak English good; she saw straight into his heart.

Other times, though, George figured he had to be careful how he acted. One thing the Eskimos did was hold dances in the evenings. Will Ford played the violin and the post got to jumpin' pretty good. All the boys joined in, Bert especially. He'd swing one girl across the room and then grab another till he had them all laughing and gaspin' for breath. George loved dances normally, but now he come to feel a little awkward and he hung back. Because *she* came along too, and the only people dancing were the Eskimos and the breeds. George didn't quite want to dance with any of them in front of her—it wouldn't seem natural. If he was going to dance, she was the one he ought to dance with. But she didn't look exactly like she was expecting that, and anyway his tongue had left him again. So he stood and watched.

A few nights later she came over to visit him and the boys at the tent. She'd learned the Indian paddling song by heart and wanted to sing it for them. She did—soft and quiet, the way it was supposed to be. The boys said her Cree was so good, you'd think she spoke the language. Then she sang some hymns, and her sweet voice just sent the shivers through him. He begun to think. It was two nights in a row, now, that she had visited them in their tent alone, and she hadn't ever done that before.

Maybe he wasn't imagining things. Maybe, after all, she did care about him.

After the hymns she fell silent. It seemed she had something on her mind. She looked from one to the other of the boys, and George felt a little uneasy; he didn't know why. The look in her eyes made him feel as if some of those things he'd been thinking—things that darted in and out of his head—were being gathered now in front of him, rising like a mist on an early summer morning. And like every summer morning's mist, thinning and vanishing before the light of the noonday sun.

She asked them if they would object to writing something in her diary. Or rather, she would write something in her diary and they would sign it if they wanted. What she would write was that she had always been treated by them "with respect." She would declare that their conduct had been proper at all times, and that no one had ever thought otherwise. She looked from one to the other and back, anxious a little. Would they mind signing a statement like that?

The boys looked at the floor, and George's throat went dry. Was she making a point not to look at him for some reason? Or was he imagining that? Finally he led off and said no, he wouldn't mind. What else could he say? The boys agreed to sign too.

She said that if they wished, she would be glad to write a statement in their diaries—"to the same effect." They said they would. Well, of course they would. There wasn't much else to say.

The statement read:

> George River Post, September 16th 1905
>
> We the undersigned do hereby declare each for himself that during the trip across Labrador with Mrs. Leonidas Hubbard, Jr., leaving Northwest River Post June 27, 1905, reaching George River Post August 27, 1905, we at all times treated Mrs. Hubbard with respect, and each also declares his belief that Mrs. Hubbard was always treated with respect by the other men of this party. Each also here records his promise that he will never by look or word or sign lead any human being to believe that during the trip there was anything in the conduct of Mrs. Hubbard and her party towards each other that was unbecoming honorable Christian men and women and also that he signs this statement entirely of his own free will and accord.

So he signed. Why shouldn't he? Hadn't his conduct been Christian in every way? He prayed to the Lord Jesus it had.

For a few days he didn't see so much of her. Then one afternoon he come back to the tent to find that the dogs had gotten in and tore the place up. Dogs was everywhere around the post, and always into everything. But his stomach sank when he saw what was gone—the caribou skin she gave him. It was the only thing she'd got as a gift from the Naskapis. The dogs had taken it, and, even if George managed to get it back, it would be torn and chewed so bad there wouldn't be anything left.

He told her, of course. There wasn't any choice. And the reproach in her eyes just seared him. It was the same as when she'd learned about the brandy they'd drunk along the river. It wasn't so much this mistake, or this time. It was just what he saw in her eyes and what it meant for his plans and hopes.

Outside the post it had begun to rain. He walked to the water's edge and looked over the bay, watching the wind push the waves along. He got awful wet. He prayed. Then he came away to his tent and wrote the words of a hymn; one he'd sung many times as a boy and a man. Its title was "Will Your Anchor Hold?"

Will your anchor hold in the storms of life?
When the clouds unfold their strings of strife
When the strong tides lift and the cables strain
Will your anchor drift or firm remain?

He wrote out all the verses—the ones about "the straits of fear," "the waters cold," "the floods of death." To sing them brought tears to his eyes, but there was a chorus too, and that comforted him.

We have an anchor that keeps the soul
Steadfast and sure while billows roll
Fastened to the rock which cannot move
Grounded firm and deep in the Saviour's love.

On his own he added one more line, "An anchor of the soul both sure and steadfast. (HEB.VI.19)"

And signed *that*. "Geo. Elson. September 21, 1905."

DILLON WALLACE pulled hard at his pipe, stared into the inky mist and shook his head. What a way to end the trip! Only half a mile away he could see the lights of George River Post flickering in the night. Almost within hailing distance. Yet he and Easton were apparently trapped, unable either to advance or retreat, climb up or down, send for help—or for that matter, even pitch their tent for the night.

"Hard luck," Easton remarked. "Good bread and molasses just across the way and we've got to sit here and freeze to death."

"Let's not give up yet," said Wallace.

Wallace had noticed, especially during the days and weeks which had followed their capsize, that Easton had become more pessimistic. With a certain amount of reason, to be sure. When the two of them had dried out and completed an inventory of the gear that remained, they discovered how much had been lost in the rapids. They had no ax, no tent, no stove, no rifles, no blankets, no extra clothing; not even paddles. Easton wanted to turn upriver and strike for the Indian camp. Wallace tried to buck him up; assured him he'd been in far worse straits with Hubbard and that they could fashion poles to work their way downriver somehow. All the same, success on those terms was an extremely tall order, as Wallace himself well knew.

Their big break had come when they walked below the site of the capsize and discovered much of their gear washed ashore. They recovered their paddles as well as blankets, clothing, tent and tent stove, and a good supply of dry matches, though not their cook set, the axes, or the rifles. Without a weapon to bring down caribou or other game, survival obviously lay with a dash to the post, subsisting along the way on their emergency pemmican, tea, and five or six pounds of caribou tallow. The odds were still inauspicious, but they had improved enough to make Easton game.

So the two men began a voyage almost as harrowing as Wallace's escape down the Susan two years earlier. Once again it was a race against starvation and cold, but the strain this time was of a different sort. On the earlier expedition, entire days had been given over to gaining a mile or two of ground, from one pond to the next. On the George, their progress was almost dizzying. They were making fifteen, twenty, even thirty miles a day. And that was the problem. Around each bend seemed to lie another rapid, each swifter and more violent than the previous. Ordinarily Wallace would have portaged—he and Easton were novices at river work. But with Ungava yet two or three hundred miles away and the season so far advanced, there was nothing for it but to throw caution to the winds. Delay meant death.

At the same time, their capsize left them with no illusions. If they tipped again, they could hardly expect to survive. Neither of them had entirely recovered full feeling in their legs and hands, and frostbite from the first capsize had left Easton with bones that continually ached. In the turbulent cascades, the canoe would be pulled into the maelstrom before either man could properly assess the difficulties. One morning, fog kept them from seeing more than fifty feet ahead, and still they plunged on, nearly coming to grief at an unexpected falls. More than once the canoe lodged on a rock, swung broadsides, and was saved from overturning only by the two of them hopping up to their waists in icy water. The canoe's hull had been scraped and wrenched so many times, it seemed a miracle the boat even remained afloat. Wallace tried patching the worst leaks with spruce gum, to little avail.

Silently, in the midst of a swirling snow, the two of them paddled down what they assumed to be Indian House Lake. Along one promontory, a wolf stood at water's edge and howled at the canoe. Wallace was strangely comforted by the company. Along shore were signs of Indian camps, but all were deserted. By the time they had covered half of the lake's fifty miles, it had snowed nearly a foot and the two of them were so benumbed, they could hardly walk to set up a tent. Without axes, hunting firewood in the snowdrifts was torture; had it not been for the warmth of their tent stove, they would have perished.

Each day became a mindless routine. Up in the morning, off paddling, pemmican three times a day, exhausted slumber at night. The two of them spoke little. Some days, Wallace guessed not more than a dozen words were exchanged. Easton, too, had become inordinately shy of water after the capsize. He would drink it, he said, but he'd had enough washing for a while. It seemed to them both they had been placed on a giant treadmill, always straining forward, never getting anywhere, doomed to go on with the grind forever.

Beyond Indian House Lake the rapids reappeared and the canoe careened along like an express train. The mental and physical strain of tempting fate one hour after another left them utterly exhausted. The drenchings from the waves and near-capsizes would surely have wicked away the last of their strength, except that the weather took a sudden turn for the better. It was the same kind of respite that had allowed Hubbard, two years earlier, to get as far as he did.

On October 14 they came at last to a large falls where signs of a portage gave Wallace hope that the post might be in reach. Another day of rapids followed, but then the second morning brought flatwater and unusually slow progress—as if actually paddling against the current. Sure enough, when they stopped for lunch they found that their canoe was shortly left high and dry on the rocks. They had reached tidewater, which was now turning on its way out. Eagerly they jumped in the canoe and began paddling, scanning each new bay until Easton cried out, "There it is! There it is!"—several buildings at the foot of a steep fjord.

Reaching the post proved difficult, however. With the tide at lowest ebb, more than a mile of mudflats intervened. Wallace decided to ferry the gear ashore instead of waiting for high water, but the work proved slow. Once on firm ground, the two of them had to pick their way up the face of a steep hill. As the footing grew trickier and trickier, the light became dimmer. Dusk caught them halfway up, with the holds so precarious they dared not move until dawn. Finding a niche in the cliff, they gathered what little brush was within reach for a signal fire. But no one stirred at the post, and with only enough tinder for a brief blaze, Wallace decided to wait until someone appeared outside.

A few minutes after settling down with their pipes, they saw a lantern emerge from the main house. Quickly, Wallace set his bonfire crackling, while Easton waved and danced and yelled himself hoarse. The lantern wended its way down to shore, and a boat started into the river's channel. But the craft headed downstream, away from the bay, and its light suddenly winked out.

"Someone's been waiting for the tide to turn and he's just going home," said Easton. "I'm afraid I began to taste bread and molasses when I saw that light."

But not long afterward an old Eskimo stepped suddenly into the glow of the fire, along with a young white boy of fifteen or sixteen.

"*Oksutingyae,*" said the Eskimo. And he proceeded to light his lantern at the fire, paying no more attention to Wallace. The boy introduced himself as the grandson of John Ford, the post agent. He explained that the Eskimo had spotted the spark of their matches when Wallace and Easton lit their pipes, but then, crossing the bay in the wind, their lantern had blown out.

With a light now to show the way, all four men scrambled down to the mudflats and rowed to the opposite shore. Mr. Ford was waiting there, a silhouette in the darkness. Two others were standing beside, and, for them, Wallace needed no introduction. George Elson and Gilbert Blake.

So any remaining uncertainty was gone. Beyond a doubt, Wallace knew now who was waiting at the post.

Making his way across the mud, it was a little hard to concentrate. Ford was being the consummate host, while Gilbert—obviously delighted to see Wallace—kept grabbing his hand, smiling and jabbering as they made their way up the path.

The door opened, flooding him with light and warmth. Mrs. Ford, a gentle older woman, hurried to greet him, while standing off to the side—stiff, eyes glaring—was Mrs. Hubbard. Mrs. Ford innocently ushered the two together for introductions, and Wallace managed to say something and bow. Mina Hubbard nodded, equally formally. Then George and Mr. Ford and the others swarmed about, wanting to know how things had gone, what perils had been endured, and so forth. Mrs. Ford prepared a supper of fried trout, white bread, mossberry jam, and tea. Wallace ate and ate, stopping only when he was ashamed to eat more. And then he learned that the *Pelican* had not yet arrived and probably would not, at this late date, until the following spring. The Fords had been too kind, prior to his feast, to tell him of the desperately low state of their provisions.

Finally he and Easton were escorted to their room for the night, complete with two featherbeds, thick blankets, and clean pillows. For Easton, the comfort of the snug house—its warmth, dryness, the pounding of sleet harmlessly against the window—was luxury beyond contemplation. Wallace, though, found it harder to relax. It was clear already, from Mrs. Hubbard's bearing, that she intended to claim pride of place around the post. The very thought of spending a winter cooped up with her filled him with gloom. And if the *Pelican* did make an appearance, it would be equally galling to have to return to civilization on the same ship, being constantly reminded that she had beaten him across Labrador by more than a month. Never mind that his was the more exciting story, that he was the one to finish the trip without benefit of Indian guides, and that he had explored the high country. He knew newspaper reporters and could well imagine them swarming the docks, wanting to know who had "won" the race. As for Mrs. Hubbard—who knew what wild charges she would lodge? The woman was unfathomable.

He sank into his feather bed, trying to appreciate the luxury of the post. But in his dreams he found himself back on the river, shooting rapid after rapid, plunging on and on, apparently without ceasing.

FOR MINA, DILLON Wallace's appearance put a sudden end to all peace. It was impossible to write now or even accomplish the simplest chore—not with that booming voice echoing its note of false cheer. She had to admit that Wallace looked remarkably fit for all he had gone through, but he was so vulgar and coarse as to be utterly repulsive. She attempted to do a little sewing in the parlor the morning following his arrival but finally gave it up and retreated to her room.

What had gone wrong? Far from enjoying her triumph, she felt absolutely despondent. Even her book, her ultimate gift to Laddie, was not going well. She would write a chapter, then cross out large chunks of it and start again, working and reworking, never sure she could produce anything of interest to the reading public. George liked what she wrote, of course—he praised it to the skies. But that was George. The one time she let him show something to Gil and Joe—her account of the caribou migration—they complained that she made too much of their wanting to shoot so many deer, which irked her immensely. "Ordinarily I should like to be considerate of their feelings," she wrote, "but such silliness makes me realize I might just as well pay no attention to them. How can people be so childish? All the world's queer. Am afraid I am too."

Was she? Perhaps a bit. Partly it was a case of nerves, she supposed—not really knowing what awaited her when she returned home. Not even knowing where "home" was, or what she would do with her life. Settle again in Williamstown? Lecture from city to city? Travel to England? The possibilities would bounce randomly in and out of her head. And then she would thrust them aside and take Mrs. Ford on an outing or go for a walk with George, to clear her mind completely.

Even then, though, she could not quite trust herself. She had begun to worry about George. His carelessness over the caribou skin upset her more than she cared to admit, perhaps because of other fears that were harder to put a name to. Little things in George's behavior; what he said or even how he looked at her. She almost didn't want to speculate about them. "Am beginning now to see through quite a few things I did not understand before," she wrote. "He has been contradicting himself lately in a way that makes me sick at heart. Makes me feel depressed and blue. Try to persuade myself that I am wrong in my thoughts but I always suffer for that kind of thing."

But surely she was imagining things! Other days he would be his usual sunny self, the two of them going along splendidly the way they had the entire trip. Only it was such a topsy-turvy world—that was all. And she knew that, at bottom, the source of her anguish was simply not being able to put aside what had happened two years ago. That was the undertone that would not go away.

In the evening she came down for supper and tried to be civil, but it was difficult. Wallace and Easton stayed at table longer than anyone else and devoured whatever was put in front of them. Then they went out to "help" with the dishes. So she retired to her room again, seeking comfort in solitude.

> This evening seemed as if I should go distracted with Wallace's claptrap in the kitchen. . . . Got out Laddie's little Testament and looked at his picture a long time. Then read about the Resurrection and about the coming of the Light. Tomorrow I mean to get up early and go away on the hills by myself and spend the day there.

His photograph had comforted her so often. Staring at it, she felt as if Laddie were almost within reach. And having crossed Labrador herself only heightened the sensation. Its barren emptiness was a kind of enchantment, brushing away time and making it almost possible to feel the wind flutter the balloon silk tent along Susan Brook and see the last fierce look in Laddie's eyes as he tried to write his "dearest, dearest girl." She was afraid that once she left this country the enchantment would pass, and her separation would be permanent.

Day by day, she marked the passing of time by the landmarks of his journey. "Today the last day he could walk," she wrote.

And then, hard on its heels, came the one day of the year that left her totally, dreadfully black. In her room, with night falling, she took pencil in hand and stared at the blank page in her journal:

> Wednesday, October 18
>
> Dea—
>
> Was just going to write Dearest Laddie. Did not go on the hills today. Blinding snowstorm. So stayed in my room. Wallace and Easton not gone to their tents yet. I shall go to mine tomorrow unless they do. The view threatens to take away my appetite, and the continual dropping of a not too melodious voice threatens to break up my nervous system. So for the sake of peace and quietness I shall slip away. Trying hard to get peace and strength. Sometimes seem to have attained it, then not sure.
>
> Mrs. Ford came in to see me this morning and petted me a little and tried to comfort me in such a beautiful way. I shall never forget her face as she bent over me. It was beautiful. She said, "I loves you because you are far away from your home and your dear father and mother." She stroked my hair and kissed me in such a beautiful tender way. It was really more like one of Laddie's caresses than anything I have known since, and again this afternoon she came in and stooped over

> me in the same way and said, "I misses you terrible out there today." Oh, I shall never forget it. She said, "Don't fret too much. The blessed Lord will take care of us and bring us safe through all our troubles. I have had my troubles and I just cast all my burdens on Him and He helped me through them all." I am ashamed of my poor weak faith and for my unrest. I think I must again take up my writing to Laddie. It makes me sadder, but I believe it makes me stronger too and it can't be wrong.
>
> Two years ago tonight the veil was drawn away and he stood before the Great Father.

And then she closed her journal, knowing that nothing in this world could give her solace.

SPIRITS AROUND the post were getting pretty low. Mrs. Hubbard was staying out of sight now that Wallace had pulled in. The Eskimos had given up on the H.B.C. ship and were off huntin' grub before winter settled in. Everybody was expecting hungry times.

Then, early the nineteenth, George heard the sweet sound of a fog horn down to the narrows—the *Pelican* after all! When the longboat came in and everybody had a chat, it turned out she'd had her hull stove in by a rock earlier that summer. Making the repairs set her back a couple months. The whole post turned out, of course, and she stayed a couple days—long enough to unload supplies, take on furs, and catch up on news. But by Sunday morning they were ready to hoist anchor.

The snow was coming down in spats, swirling here and there across the bay as George took a last look at the gear loaded in the longboat. He didn't want to forget anything.

Wallace and Easton were already aboard—they'd gone on the night before. Once the *Pelican* made it to open water, she was going to lower them in a leaky old boat along with some Eskimos who didn't even speak English. Wallace had decided to dogsled home—around the whole coast of Labrador. Well, that was one thing, but the only sleds to spare was in Fort Chimo, a hundred miles away. Mr. Ford had said wait until freeze-up and go by land, but Wallace wasn't takin' no for an answer. It was go, ice or no ice, fair weather or foul. George looked at the low clouds and the snow and shook his head. There was forty-foot tides in Ungava. What drove Wallace to do those things anyways?

Mrs. Hubbard made her way across the flats with Mr. and Mrs. Ford. The Eskimos turned out too. They told George they'd miss him and his tightropes, and the women told Mrs. Hubbard they'd miss her. She'd been such fun around the post. Then the boys got in and George gave Mrs. Hubbard a hand.

The two of 'em had made up some. Not that she ever said anything right out, or that he did. They just got on better in their walks and talks. She even told him one of her new ideas for the book. She'd been reading *Pilgrim's Progress* up at the post. It was the story of a man named Christian, who went on a journey. This was like anyone's life. He had good times, but often it was troubles. Sometimes his burdens seemed too much to bear. Along the way there was some people who helped him, and others who didn't. And each one had a name showing what he was like, deep down in his soul. Well, Mrs. Hubbard thought of giving names to the people in her own story.

She wanted to call Job *Eagle*—for his sharp eyes. George liked that. Then she said she wanted to call him *Great Heart;* and his chest swelled with pride to hear it. But some of the things he might have thought earlier, he didn't now. He just felt a little sad.

The longboat pushed off. He and Mrs. Hubbard watched the Fords wave good-bye, and then Mr. Ford gave his arm to his wife as they walked toward the post.

The tide was flowing out, taking him away from those many miles of river. The hard days of hauling in July, with bluebells fresh beside last winter's snow. And Lake Michikamau, as still as glass with the loons crying from far off. And the George River, with its rapids. So much to be proud of. And all now behind him.

But he had his little books. Was that why you wrote things to yourself? There were seasons in your life when things happened, and they never happened quite that way again. There was no way you could ever bring them back, not at least until the dear Lord came and called you home. But you couldn't help trying. You'd write things down or press bluebells in the leaves of your journal with colors so fresh. And you'd save things in your heart, even if they couldn't be written. The bluebells would fade, and the hand that held the pencil grow old and stiff, but you had what you could keep in your heart.

—from Elson's journal

Epilogue

SOME EIGHTY YEARS after the *Pelican* sailed off, we rode the ebb tide of the George River on a late summer's day: past the last rapids where Mina, George, and Job were nearly drawn in unprepared; past the steep bluffs facing John Ford's post, where Wallace and Easton found themselves in the falling darkness. The post is long gone, its settlement moved some years ago to a more sheltered bay downstream. We swept past too, our canoes firmly in the grip of the river and the tide.

It has been hard at times, as we worked to trace the strands of this tale, to know whether we were riding its currents or they riding us. At first we believed that we had chosen our story, just as we had been choosing wilderness rivers to canoe in our free time for a dozen years and more. But as we look back on our involvement with the Hubbard stories, we wonder whether the story did not choose us. The seeds of our encounter were sown three generations ago, when John Rugge's grandfather delivered himself of a modest discourse from behind a kitchen table in Ridgewood, New Jersey. Grandfather Rugge had long possessed an abiding interest in all matters remotely nautical, being a tugmaster in New York harbor. He was well acquainted with the Hubbard controversies and held strong opinions on the subject. Hubbard's fatal mistake, he once informed his young son across the breakfast table, lay in his failure to supplement the expedition's rifles with a shotgun, which would have allowed the party to bring down smaller game.

The younger Rugge devoured this bit of oral history—as of course he was meant to—and then went out and read Wallace's *Lure of the Labrador Wild*, which by 1930 had become a venerable war horse on the publishing scene, well into its twenty-third printing. The book and its youthful reader were a perfect match: Rugge loved the outdoors as Hubbard had, and even after he had grown up and moved to upstate New York, he spent his odd hours dreaming about traplines and concocting his own schemes to penetrate the Canadian North. During those years, he raised his own son, "Rug," in an old log cabin, where the Hubbard tales again were passed along over a kitchen table. Wallace's *Lure* was out of print by then, but Rug found a copy in a local library, together with Wallace's 1905 adventures, narrated in *The Long Labrador Trail,* and Mina Hubbard's *A Woman's Way Through Unknown Labrador*. There matters rested for about twenty years.

Rug returned to the Hubbard expeditions, briefly, when the two of us were completing a guidebook on wilderness canoeing. In our section on notable literature of the outdoors, he penned a single paragraph, noting that "when Wallace made it out, Mrs. Hubbard apparently blamed him for Leonidas' death and resolved to make the journey properly herself. Wallace retaliated with his own expedition and the race for the mouth of the George was on." Only after the book was published did his somewhat negligent co-author get around to reading the Hubbard literature. When he did, he became a bit uneasy. Where, Jim asked, had Rug gotten his information about Mrs. Hubbard blaming Wallace for her husband's death?

"Oh, it's all in the books," Rug replied.

But it wasn't. The casual reader who pulls *A Woman's Way Through Unknown Labrador* or *The Long Labrador Trail* off the library shelf will receive not the slightest intimation from either book that there was another canoeing party within hundreds of miles, much less parties well known to one another and embarked upon the same wilderness route. Neither author so much as acknowledges the existence of the other. When the two accounts are set side by side, it becomes obvious that hostility of a rare order must have prevailed between the two parties. But how had Rug leapt to the much more specific—and astonishing—conclusion that Mrs. Hubbard had blamed Wallace for her husband's death? After re-reading the books himself, he could only assume that this piece of news had been part of the lore passed down from grandfather to father to son.

Our curiosity piqued, we began looking up the New York newspapers of the day. On microfilm we found the headlines and stories that the books did not disclose (RIVAL LABRADOR EXPEDITIONS MEET . . . MRS. HUBBARD SUSPICIOUS . . . LABRADOR SENSATION). And in 1975, during the early stages of our research, we did as Hubbard did: booked passage with two other friends on a steamer heading up the north Atlantic coast. In Goose Bay and Northwest River, we found that the local trappers still remembered the Hubbard saga; they also remained as hospitable yet taciturn as in Hubbard's day, and still called each other "b'y." From Goose Bay we charted a route by canoe that took us through Lake Hope. Paddling to the end of its steep-walled shores, we beached our canoes, dug from our packs a copy of Wallace's book, and climbed the rise where the 1903 expedition had portaged into the lake. The sight gave us shivers. Before us spread the same vista Hubbard had recorded on film seventy years earlier. The scene had hardly changed at all: even the three stunted evergreens in the foreground stood in their places, the only difference being that the middle tree had surpassed its neighbor by a foot. From the stillness of the spruce forest, we half-expected to hear Hubbard below, launching his canoe.

We paddled down Hope, picked blueberries on a hill where Hubbard had done the same, and worked our way into Disappointment Lake, continuing north through a series of ponds and streams to the Red Wine River. The Red Wine is larger than Susan Brook—that is to say, it is actually canoeable—and we followed its course back toward Grand Lake. Along the river's lower stretches, we had penciled on our map a possible side trip: a dotted line leading overland about ten miles, to Hubbard's last campsite. The trek was to have taken about two days, beginning with a climb 1500 feet out of the river valley, and then proceeding through one bog after another to Susan Brook. Unfortunately, this was high summer and a year particularly horrendous for bugs: Rug's eyes had swollen shut from the bites at one point and another member of the party picked up a dose of black fly fever. In the end, we were not tempted even an instant; we just kept our paddles in the water and continued on toward civilization.

Quite understandable. At that point, we hadn't learned enough about Hubbard, nor of Labrador and its ways.

Back home, we kept returning to the story and our newspaper clippings. Comparing the version of Hubbard's diary published by Mina and the one appearing in *Outing*, we discovered discrepancies. Some passages in Mrs. Hubbard's version did not appear in *Outing;* many passages in *Outing* did not appear in Mrs. Hubbard's book. Where was the original diary? Had other journals from 1903 and 1905 been preserved by any of the families? Mina Hubbard's descendants, we were convinced, would be difficult to track down, for she had moved to England and remarried. As for Dillon Wallace, a 1939 obituary noted that he had been survived by a son and daughter living near Poughkeepsie. "Why don't you give them a call?" asked JoAnne, Rug's wife. The two of us—serious researchers by this time—had a fine laugh over the prospect. We didn't even know the son's first name; the daughter had no doubt married; both children had probably moved out of the area. For that matter, how could we even know if either were still alive? While we scoffed, JoAnne picked up the phone, reached directory assistance, and told the operator she was looking for a Wallace.

"First name?" asked the operator.

"I don't know," said JoAnne. "Dillon?"

"247-1298," replied the operator.

Not long afterward, Jim was invited to give a talk on wilderness canoeing at the Eastern Mountain Sports store, in Boston. Inevitably he mentioned the Hubbard expeditions. About a week later a young woman with an English accent and no interest in the wilderness whatsoever struck up a conversation with one of the store clerks. The talk, after a few twists and turns, turned to astrology, and the woman remarked that she was a Sagittarius. "Sagittarius," responded the clerk. "They're explorers." "Oh, really?" replied the young woman. "My grandmother was a real explorer." So it was that Jim received a call from a young woman with an English accent. "The bicycling chap at EMS tells me you've been giving speeches about my grandmother," she told him.

Gradually we assembled files on all three expeditions. When we visited Dillon Wallace III, he was most helpful but confessed that his father's Labrador diaries had been lost. "And we Wallaces are savers," he added with chagrin. "I don't know what happened to them." Mina Hubbard, it developed, had late in life allowed the Canadian Public Archives in Ottawa to microfilm not only her diary from 1905, but also Hubbard's 1903 journal and Elson's 1905 diary. A series of telephone calls yielded additional material. Clifford Easton's journal turned up in the Explorers Club of New York; William Cabot's had been tracked down by an anthropologist friend. And one June morning we received an excited phone call from Wallace's son. At the bottom of an old cardboard box in his attic, he had discovered three leather-bound volumes, his father's missing diaries. He had a collection of original negatives as well, from both 1903 and 1905. Bit by bit, the pieces were falling into place.

Newspapers provided unexpectedly valuable information, though the search was at times frustrating. Reporters of the day covered the story haphazardly. Hubbard, in various dispatches, was reported as making his way to "the Foerge River," or to "Lake Michikaman," while Wallace was said to be "an amateur photographer" who in 1905 was headed up the "Nascoutee River." George Elson was spoken of variously as "Frank Elson," "the famous guide George Gelson," the "half-breed guide," or simply "the Indian" in the party, who "soon afterward died from exposure," according to one newspaper in 1904. Yet by cross-checking stories, the narrative of events began to emerge. The New York *Daily Tribune*, for example, had Wallace making a trip in 1905 to recruit Elson along "the St. Lawrence coast." Elson, of course, did not live along the St. Lawrence coast, but the North Adams (Mass.) *Evening Transcript* corroborated Wallace's trip and indicated that Elson had told him "he did not intend to guide a party this summer." It was the earlier dispatch, however, from which we learned George's original excuse for not hiring on: he had "been smitten," the *Tribune* reported, "by a young Indian lass, and wrote to Wallace that since he contracted the new fever the old fever for the trail had left him." Finally Wallace's son discovered Elson's remarkable letter, written hastily to his father from a hotel in Montreal—asking him to "trust me"—which was the first indication in any surviving source that Mina Hubbard had summoned George to Williamstown late in 1904.

Scrawled letters, waterspotted journals, photographic negatives with black faces and white-coaled eyes . . . To us, these seemed ghosts—long dead, mostly forgotten, but not yet beyond reach. We had gathered enough material to trace the course of all three expeditions day by day; more than that—to know these people as individuals and to share in the events of their lives even to the point of overhearing their conversations. We came to regret not making our trek to Hubbard's last campsite. Some years later, we booked passage on another steamer (Reid-Newfoundland reigns no more) and, with two companions, set out to cover more of the country the earlier expeditions had crossed.

We again passed through Lake Hope, still empty and silent, and recalled how Hubbard had sat under a rainy-day fire tarp before making the rough portage into its waters, wondering how far beyond the mountains Michikamau lay. Why, we asked ourselves, *did* Hubbard keep pressing on, when he was hungry and already reduced to rags? Why, when the trail kept disappearing, did he seize on every trapper's blaze or rotten wigwam pole as a sign that he was back on the Indian trail?

There was, to be sure, the matter of inexperience. As William Cabot recognized on their trip up the coast together, Hubbard was not a seasoned traveler of the bush. More dangerous, he was a continual optimist. There was a bit of the "story-book" strain about him, as Cabot observed. And he shared with Caspar Whitney a taste for risk, pure and simple. "A sport must have its uncertainties or it is no sport at all," Hubbard proclaimed in the pages of *Outing*. Even more adamantly, he believed in the power of the human spirit. In the tradition of Rudyard Kipling's "The Explorer," the peaks blocking the way to Lake Hope lured him on as much as they discouraged him. More than once he recited Kipling's verses to Wallace and Elson by the evening campfire:

> *"There's no sense in going further—it's the edge of cultivation."*
> *So they said, and I believed it . . .*
> *Till a voice, as bad as Conscience, rang interminable changes*
> *On one everlasting Whisper day and night repeated—so:*
> *"Something hidden. Go and find it. Go and look behind the Ranges—*
> *Something lost behind the Ranges. Lost and waiting for you. Go!"*

Modern readers, uncomfortable with such unabashed oratory, may find Kipling's spell difficult to comprehend. But at the dawn of a new century, when the American frontier had only recently been proclaimed officially closed and President Teddy Roosevelt was setting the example of "the strenuous life," Hubbard had no doubts about the course that lay before him.

Nor should one underestimate the effect of the country itself. Labrador is a severe land. Hesketh Prichard, an Englishman who crossed its barrens several years after Hubbard, deftly characterized the country in the first sentence of his book: "The life of the Labrador is entirely predatory." Prichard was thinking, of course, of the black bear roaming the rock-strewn ravines; of the wolf pack cutting a yearling from the caribou herd; of the voracious pike devouring frogs, trout, mice, and ducklings; and not least, of the reigning mosquitoes, winged tormentors who inspired him to dub the high barrens the "kingdom of Beelzebub." Prichard did not mention, though well he might have, the unobtrusive *Sarracenia flava*. For even the plants in Labrador are predatory. Thousands of pitcher plants grow in the endless bogs and marshes, hugging the ground, their leaves cupped and bristled, gathering and collecting rainwater. And the bristles all point one way: downward. Insect after insect lands; and each one, try as it may, cannot turn around, but only creep onward to its doom.

As we stood at Lake Hope it was all too easy to see how Hubbard was brought to his own doom: working his way up the Beaver River, entering its expansions and steadies, always looking to go north and west toward Lake Michikamau. Just as his progress seemed thwarted, he broke through the ranges and saw water stretching serene and beautiful, directly to the west. Hope again! Labrador was Hubbard's pitcher plant. Ever restless, he pushed onward, full of energy and inner compulsions. But with every move, the bristles carried him in one direction, so arranged that with every step taken, he was allowed less room to move again. So arranged, they would not let him go.

At Windbound Lake, Hubbard admitted failure; and in an odd way, discovered the better part of his nature. As storms held the three men prisoners of the wind they lay tentbound, like wool-wound mummies in a canvas coffin, watching the walls billow and snap, seeing the balloon silk stretched to its limits. Those were the hours, if there were to be any, when the fabric of the expedition would be strained to the breaking point. On wilderness trips, forced idleness is as much a psychological danger as the more obvious physical hardships. We think, for example, of Henry Hudson trying to find the Northwest passage in 1610. Hudson pushed deeper and deeper into the recesses of a huge inland sea, hoping daily for open water, finding nothing but mud flats and picket fences of barren spruce. Day after day he beat back and forth, every bit as uncertainly as Hubbard in search of Michikamau. And then he watched the ice form in the shallow waters, trapping the ship for the winter. First mate Robert Juet tauntingly reminded Hudson of his boast that they would be in Java by February, and Hudson, flaring, stripped him of his rank. All winter, according to another crew member, the ex-mate "nursed his hatred like a red-eyed ferret in the hutch of his dark soul." And when the spring ice went out, Juet did not forget. When his mutiny was complete, the ship was headed home and Hudson was left adrift to die on the bay that now bears his name.

Or consider Charles Hall in 1871, icebound with his crew at

Thank God Harbor, in Greenland. While Hall led an exploring party onto the ice cap, it was one of the men left idle at the ship's base camp who brooded over past slights and then, upon Hall's return, laced the commander's coffee with a lethal dose of arsenic. Or there is the moody Thomas Simpson, who charted the coastline of the Arctic Ocean and, upon his return, killed two Indian companions and then shot himself, in an apparent melancholic rage. Given tales like these, it is worth noticing what did *not* happen on Windbound Lake. Lying in the tent, it would have been easy for Elson and Wallace to sour on their plight, to begin asking questions. Why had Hubbard insisted on pressing his luck? Why hadn't he brought a shotgun or thought to write ahead for a gill net? Not that such queries need even to be consciously asked. It is enough that they lie deep in the mind, unspoken yet troubling. Given strong enough undercurrents, almost any break in routine may bring matters to a boil.

Perhaps most remarkable was Hubbard's own equanimity in the face of adversity. His diary shows none of the irascibility evident, for example, in Captain Peary's "God damn K[oodlooktoo] to hell," written when one of the explorer's Inuit guides grew anxious over the shifting pack ice. And there was certainly no recourse to violence under Hubbard's leadership—nothing to resemble Caspar Whitney throttling one of his Indians and choking him "until he gave up a piece of musk-ox intestine he had stolen from me." Hubbard, of course, was subject to the same privations and anxieties as his companions, but it was also his expedition. He would be the one to inform Whitney he had neither reached the Naskapi Indians nor witnessed the caribou migration. And Whitney was the man who had hiked two thousand miles of Arctic barrens to bring back his vaunted hunting trophies, nearly killing himself and his guides to do it. Starvation first, failure second: that was Whitney's credo.

Yet despite the many pressures that goaded him to continue, Hubbard turned back. For all his exuberance, he lacked a certain ruthlessness—the monomaniacal will of the true explorer, that places success above all else. "What I've dared, I've willed; and what I've willed, I'll do!" cried Melville's Captain Ahab. "Swerve me? The path to my fixed purpose is laid with iron rails, whereon my soul is grooved to run." Explorers of the North were imbued with that fanaticism and a jealous zeal to be first in the field. "Fame I will have," wrote the melancholy Simpson, "but it must be *alone.* My whole soul is set on it." And Peary, commenting on why he did not take any white companions with him on his final dash for the Pole, explained, "Because after a lifetime of effort I dearly wanted the honor for myself . . . the only white man who has ever reached the North Pole."

Hubbard dreamed of being like Peary. Believing as he did in the power of the will, he applauded Peary's motto, "Find a way or make one." Yet having found himself at the far shores where the spikes of his pitcher plant drove him, Hubbard lacked the requisite ruthlessness. There would be no mutinies for him, no poisons, no melancholic rage. Only a retreat toward the familiar territory of humankind.

Throughout the expedition, only one disagreement threatened discord. That was the question of whether to retrace the route along Susan Brook or to continue by canoe down the Beaver. Wallace and Elson were convinced that their lives hung on the outcome of the decision. "Suicide" was how Wallace described the abandonment of their canoe, and Elson was so troubled by the prospect that the recurrence of his lumbago seems to have been a psychosomatic expression of his distress. Certainly his dream about the Lord speaking to him arose out of desperation. Yet such was Hubbard's influence that, by simple, quiet pronouncement, he was able to induce his companions to follow him.

To the end of their lives, both Elson and Wallace believed that if they had only stayed on the river, Hubbard too would have survived the ordeal. Robert Baikie, a trapper whose grounds were along the Beaver, assured them that only one bad rapids remained to be passed—and "from there smooth and deep water, no rapids, but swift current. Even if you didn't have the strength of paddling, the swift current would have brought you down, right down to my house." But modern topographic maps make it clear that the three men left the river much farther upstream than Baikie believed. The rapids that George and Wallace actually paddled drop at a gradient of 10 to 15 feet per mile: easy whitewater in a stream of that volume. One photo from 1903 shows them running such a rapids, George standing in the bow with a pole and Wallace seated in the stern. Downstream of their take-out point, however, the gradient increases to an average of 55 feet per mile, with some sections dropping as much as 100 feet—near-impossible canoeing in open boats, even for experienced and healthy whitewater paddlers. When we flew over this part of the Beaver in a float plane, it proved to be a solid ribbon of white. Ironically, then, Wallace and Elson never learned that Hubbard's decision to return along the original route saved their lives. As it was, the trio marched on, two men convinced they were walking to their deaths, one convinced that the trail offered the only remaining hope. All three were right, but for the wrong people.

The country around Goose Creek and the upper Susan is of a piece for miles in every direction. White meadows of caribou moss mixed with small bogs, ponds, and thickets of spruce. We followed our proposed route from our earlier trip, caching our canoes along the Red Wine and climbing out of the river valley, a cold rain falling. For a day and a half we bushwhacked from one pond to the next, until we struck the Susan a little way downstream from Hubbard's last camp. Our pace quickened, each of us hoping to be the first to find the old site.

In a small clearing Rug spied it. The rock was still there, where the tent had been pitched. And on the rock, securely pegged, was this bronze plaque:

LEONIDAS HUBBARD, JR.
INTREPID EXPLORER
AND
PRACTICAL CHRISTIAN
* * *
John XIV.IV: And Whither I go
Ye Know, And the Way Ye Know.

We had expected to find the plaque, for it has become part of the Hubbard legend. In 1913 Wallace made a return pilgrimage to the rock. He had commissioned a memorial marker but, to his bitter disappointment, lost it when his canoe overturned on the trip in. He pushed on anyway and, arriving at the old scene, found the boulder with the charred embers from Hubbard's last fire at its base. The boughs that Wallace had cut in 1903 to make a bed for his friend were still there, withered but undisturbed. Scattered about were some spoons, Hubbard's worn moccasins, and remnants of their tent. Before leaving, Wallace had taken hammer and chisel and cut a simple inscription into the rock, then filled the letters with white lead. Gilbert Blake, who accompanied him this time, supplied a tuft of his hair to make the paintbrush.

Many years later, in 1976, Wallace's son and a companion returned with a replica of the lost plaque. With drills and bolts they secured the new marker to the rock. Set firmly in place, it would withstand the elements far longer than the chiseled inscription. But we found ourselves running our fingers over the letters carved by his father, those faintly visible around the metal rectangle.

LEONIDA JR.
INTRE R

PRACTI AN

DIED

As we stood there the sun, which had appeared briefly for our arrival, disappeared under low clouds. The rain began anew. We snapped a few photographs and began our return, thinking how similar the day had been when Wallace and Elson had bade Hubbard their last farewell.

Setting our course overland, we knew that we would be making our way to this place another time. But the next trip would be through the written word: trying to chart the path that brought Hubbard to his death and led his companions to their even more remarkable journeys. The story's appeal to us was no longer just the lure of the Labrador wild. Like Wallace and George and Mina, we found ourselves drawn to Hubbard, and our own return to Labrador guided by his self-inflicted fate.

Hubbard's expedition, by most standards, was a failure—but a fascinating one, because of the yearnings and emotions that it called forth. Hubbard came to grief, no doubt, because he was rash, impulsive, and inexperienced. Those qualities cannot be denied—and were not, even by those closest to him. Mina, for all her fierce devotion, conceded that Laddie was "naturally sensitive" and "high strung." Wallace described Hubbard as being "stale" and "overtrained" at the start of their trip and admitted that they had "plunged into the interior of an unknown country" insufficiently provisioned. Yet so strong were his feelings that the dedication of the *Lure* bespoke the bonds of matrimony: "Here, b'y, is the issue of our plighted troth." George allowed in later years that Hubbard was not much of a woodsman; yet he could never forget "what a friend he was, and what a brave man. . . . Oh wasn't he a brave man! I have seen a good many fine people in my time; but I have never seen a man like Hubbard, and I never expect to see another." If ever there was a grace to failure, Hubbard captured it.

Yet as our telling of Hubbard's tale evolved, it spun out in ways we had not anticipated. We had begun our research, as historians inevitably do, with the gift of hindsight. We knew all too well how Hubbard met his end. We could jump from one diary to another at will; could draw upon outside observers like Cabot; could compare newspaper accounts side by side. In short, we could judge events from a perspective well above the fray, professing to see anywhere and everywhere at once.

Ultimately, we found this olympian perspective unsatisfying. Bonds of affection and loyalty, of rivalry and revenge, are not easily comprehended from too lofty a perch. So we chose to narrate the tale through the eyes of those who lived it, shifting our point of view from one participant to another and then back. We wanted readers to experience for themselves the agony of decision without hindsight: not to know in advance how Susan Brook came to be taken for the Naskapi River, or where the Beaver actually led. We hoped too that readers would appreciate motives without condemning out of hand: to feel Wallace's bewilderment when Mina attacked him for disloyalty; yet also to comprehend her own resentment upon learning that her husband's companions had survived when he had not. To share Elson's terror, riding the rails south in the winter of 1904, answering a summons whose meaning he could not divine.

Yet telling the story through the eyes of the participants introduced new problems. Even allowing for the detailed diaries and recollections, the innermost concerns of Mina and George, Hubbard and Wallace, often remained beyond reach of the written record. When, for example, we describe why Wallace opted for the Indian portage to Seal Lake, rather than staying with the Naskapi River, we necessarily make our own inferences. "My object was to trace the old Indian trail and explore as much of the country as possible, and not to hide myself in an enclosed river valley," he noted in *The Long Labrador Trail.* No doubt he sincerely believed that. Even so, his veiled criticism of Mina, who did "hide" herself in the river valley, makes it clear that Wallace harbored strong feelings beneath his gentlemanly prose. Certainly he must have been dismayed to discover the hobnail boot-tracks of his rivals along the Naskapi's bank. If he chose to follow the Naskapi as she had, he could regain the lead only by passing her, which would entail an unpleasant encounter along the riverbank. Wallace's unexpressed anxiety over that prospect surely pushed him to choose the Indian trail and, in that way, strongly shaped the outcome of his expedition.

For leaving the river forced Wallace into a laborious, time-consuming hunt for a little-used portage. It ensured that, far more than he could have wished, his party came uncomfortably close to duplicating the tragic end of the first expedition. Hubbard had turned back along the shores of Windbound, with Michikamau just beyond and his provisions virtually exhausted. Leading his own expedition—with winter approaching, supplies dangerously low, and Michikamau yet to be crossed—Wallace chose to split his party and press on. This time, he knew he would have no second chance if he failed. Whitney was waiting anxiously for a story; Mina had forged ahead, by all appearances making good progress toward the George. In terms of reputation and honor, Wallace had no choice but to continue. The anguish behind that choice would not have been so obvious, however, had not Easton's diary related the worries Wallace left unspoken in his own accounts.

An even more delicate matter for us as historians was the uneasy relationship between George Elson and Mina Hubbard. Canadian writer Pierre Berton was first to make the case that George had fallen in love. Having read Berton, we too examined Elson's diary in the Canadian Public Archives. In truth, the journal is full of hints and suggestions, but it lacks any kind of outright declaration, as Berton indeed made clear. On most days George's entries amount to a paragraph or two, and many confine themselves to matters of fact concerning the party's campsites or the game they bagged. When George did record his feelings, he was careful about the way he did it, sometimes placing passages at the back of his journal or in the "other book," to which he so often referred. To the best of our knowledge, that material has not survived.

See other book. How the phrase tantalized us! Perhaps the second journal contained only logistics or field notes, but that seems improbable, for Elson resorted to it only sporadically. Was it a devotional book of some sort? Possibly, for George was certainly a religious man. But it seems more likely to have been a place where he could record his most delicate and private feelings. Most often, "See other book" appears on days of particular moment, as when the expedition was launched from Northwest River or after the capsize on the Naskapi.

In any case, nowhere in the surviving records does George

explicitly confess to falling in love. The case must be drawn, to a great degree, by inference. Had we chosen to write an analytic essay, we would have been free to hedge our conclusions with qualifiers: a *perhaps* here, a *may have been* there. But having narrated the story from the perspectives of our protagonists, we were forced to weigh the evidence and make a choice. If George did not fall in love, then of course we would be materially distorting the record by suggesting otherwise. If he did, it would equally be a distortion to pass over his feelings in silence. There was no "safe" way out. Furthermore, if George did fall under Mina's spell, then to portray that process accurately, we had to show the gradual alteration of feelings that must inevitably have occurred—even though George's surviving entries maintain a discreet silence on his most personal thoughts.

We debated these matters often as we paddled the George River ourselves, several summers ago, pulling out transcripts of the journals, puzzling over published and unpublished accounts. Sweeping down the river gave the question a certain immediacy. Were we the victims of our own wishful thinking, disposed to interpret the documents in a way that would make the story most dramatic? Perhaps. In the end, though, we have come to believe that the evidence is persuasive beyond reasonable doubt: Day by day, George found his affections being captured by the woman he had sworn to protect; who bantered with him every night around the campfire; who trusted him; who fathomed his boyhood dreams as no white woman before ever had; and whose white skin was forbidden to him by the unwritten law of Hudson's Bay culture.

Put yourself in Elson's position that thundery day along the Naskapi, when Mina ran away from her guides. Losing track of her that afternoon must have been one of George's most harrowing experiences. The other men became so frightened, they couldn't stop trembling even hours later. Worse, Mina had relished her escapade, taunting George when he finally caught up with her. Given what he could expect from white society if he emerged from the bush without his charge, he had every reason to be angry. Yet his journal mentions the incident not at all, even though he describes in fair detail events earlier in the day. The entry breaks off with the telltale "See other book." Then, after a space of a few lines, comes the passage about how "brite and smart" Mrs. Hubbard was, and how George didn't "only want to say she is only a friend to me. . . ." Finally, for the second time in one day (the only time this happens), George again writes, "See other book."

It seems clear that Elson saved the story of Mina running away for his second journal; that he wrote it that evening in the tent; then returned to his regular diary to write the complimentary language about Mrs. Hubbard, before going back again to his second journal. Is it coincidence only that, having partaken of the brandy, George wrote his most admiring description of Mina? That he did so after a day when, by all rights, he should have been thoroughly angry with her? We think not.

Similarly, George's entry for August 8, written after he and Mina witnessed the caribou migration, is brief and perfunctory, even when describing the herd, a subject we know excited George. ("We seen lots of caribou in the afternoon," is all he records.) But he also wrote "See other book," suggesting sensitive material elsewhere. Again, we have no way of infallibly penetrating George's inner thoughts, but we have made our reconstruction as factually accurate as possible. Mina and George did stalk the caribou; did watch the rainbow from afar as Gilbert ran to fetch the gold; did run down the hill hand in hand. (Perhaps significantly, Mina omitted any reference in her published account of George holding her hand. That detail appears only in her diary.)

Most telling of all, when George finally brought the expedition safely to Ungava on August 27, he described the moment of triumph and then went on to write what appears to be a reflective summary of the whole journey. "Well, we got through our trip across country and I want to say our little lady Mrs. Hubbard has done very well. . . ." Just as this flattering entry is getting underway, however, four pages are cut from the journal, which resumes with the entry for August 30. On August 31 comes George's revealing plans about going back to school (note that Mina, too, had returned to school the previous year in Williamstown), as well as his hope of getting someone to help him write his books (Mina, of course, having been the only one to offer such assistance), and then the dream of getting a "white girl" to marry him.

The "great afternoon" when he talks with Mrs. Hubbard about "something great important" is September 7. His diary refers to a separate entry ("see L"), which we have been unable to locate. However, in the back of the journal, where George occasionally wrote additional material, several more pages have been cut out.

Where the diary resumes, two lines remain, evidently the conclusion of the missing entry. They read, "If *he* was tould to go around the world and pick one out *he* would come back and still have *them for sure.*" A close examination, however, indicates that the words we have italicized are alterations, written over the original ones, still faintly legible beneath. The entry originally read, "If *I* was tould to go around the world and pick one out, *I* would come back and still have *you.*" Following this entry are the moving verses of the hymn "Will Your Anchor Hold?"—dated September 21. This sequence indicates the probability, though not the certainty, that the excised passages were written before September 21.

How to interpret this suggestive material? A few additional entries from Mina's journal are revealing. In them, she notes her wish to have the men sign the statement about their behavior in her diary (September 15–16), as well as her disappointment with George when the dogs destroyed her caribou skin (September 21–22). The latter entries also make clear Mina's uneasiness that George might write his own account of the expedition. "Am wondering," she wrote, "whether or not I had better ask [George] to sign an agreement not to write anything about the trip without my written consent and approval. I almost think I had. There would be no questioning about the thing then."

As far as we know, Mina never did ask George to sign such a statement, as she made him sign the one regarding his personal conduct. But she seems to have taken another precaution. George's diary survives because it is with her papers in the Canadian Public Archives. At some point, she came into possession of it. George's last entry is November 18; the expedition arrived in Quebec City on November 20; and Mina wrote on November 19 a cryptic phrase, "Talking with George." Did she ask him then for his diary, ostensibly to help her write her account of the trip? If not, she must have later. Our guess is that George, unwilling to refuse her request, cut out certain sensitive passages. One, evidently, referred to the argument he had with her over whether to turn back on the George River. Others appear to have been his more intimate thoughts about her, given the material surrounding the missing pages.

If we are right in our reconstruction, the story of Mina and George has particular poignance because their relationship was played out along the boundary between white and Indian cultures. George, a man caught between, found it difficult to exist in both worlds. Many of his closest friends, like Job Chapies, were Cree who could still be moved by the legend of a young brave snaring the sun. Yet George was also a devout Christian, who hoped to marry a white woman and become a part of the world his Scotch father had bequeathed him. In a sense, Mina was, for George, like the gold of the rainbow that Gilbert chased along the shores of Lake Michikamats—ever receding, yet almost within one's grasp in a world where boundless blue horizons shrank distance, blurred boundaries, and made all dreams seem possible.

Coming down the George we too were graced by sunny days, crystalline skies, and a wind at our backs. Is our reconstruction of the time George and Mina spent on the river too great a leap of the imagination—a taste of our own boundless blue horizon? We sincerely hope not. If, as historians, we have on occasion been forced to play God, we have done so in the interest of resurrection, not creation. But we have to admit, the former enterprise is not a whit less audacious than the latter.

THERE REMAINS ONLY ebb tide: to trace out the fortunes of those who took their memories of Labrador with them.

Among Wallace's original party, George Richards, Leigh Stanton, and Pete Stevens watched Easton and Wallace head north across Lake Michikamau on September 4, and then retraced their route to Northwest River, scrambling across the barren countryside as fast as their legs would take them. Pete, fretting over the mournful cry of a loon ("very bad sign"), set such a rapid pace that Stanton had trouble keeping up, complaining of faintness. Richards nearly swamped the canoe in whitewater, but the party reached Northwest River intact on September 26, Richards and Pete proceeding on to New York in mid-November. Their arrival, along with the news that the party had split, caused some consternation in the public press. "When Wallace's friends saw the half-breed they threw up their hands," reported the *Tribune*. "They said things about 'bad judgment,' 'indiscretion.' . . . Richards' private opinions are not of a nature even to make one hope." Fortunately, a telegram announcing Wallace's arrival at Ungava Bay reached the outside world only a week later.

We know little of what happened to Richards, Stanton, and Stevens in later years. Pete returned to Minnesota and there continued to hunt and trap as well as raise a family. He has a daughter still living in Grand Portage. When Richards joined Wallace, he was an undergraduate pursuing geological studies at Columbia's School of Mines, but surviving records at the university contain no trace of him and we could unearth no further leads. Stanton wintered another season in Northwest River, then departed in the spring of '06, presumably to pick up his career as general factotum and knockabout.

Clifford Easton, upon leaving the relative comfort of George River Post, found himself hurtled into yet another harrowing ordeal. As soon as the *Pelican* reached the turbulent waters of Ungava Bay he, Wallace, and three Eskimos were lowered into a small boat in hopes of reaching Fort Chimo, over a hundred miles away. The venture met with disaster almost at once. Icy seas continuously drenched the party, and Easton and Wallace's ragged clothes were hardly suitable for winter travel. Outgoing forty-foot tides stranded the boat overnight on mudflats miles from shore. Finally winter gales blew in pack ice, forcing everyone hurriedly to abandon ship. The Eskimos then set out on an overland march so grueling that one night they refused even to stop, for fear of freezing. Easton thought every step would be his last, while Wallace continually lagged behind, on the brink of total collapse. Reaching a crude log tilt, the two men sought shelter while the Eskimos pressed on, promising to send help. As one day succeeded another, weakness from cold and starvation set it. "Realize now that we have staked all upon this last cast," Easton wrote grimly. "Hubbard was right. A man can live once, and if I ever pull out of this I shall live better, rest better, and enjoy what little I have as I go along." By November 6 he was reduced to gnawing scraps of deer hide, while Wallace chewed at the ashes from his last pipe. Another long arctic night had begun when Eskimo rescuers at last appeared out of the darkness.

The dogsled trek homeward was accomplished without mishap. Easton and Wallace started from Fort Chimo shortly after New Year's, proceeded around the coast to Northwest River by late February, and arrived in New York on April 30, 1906.

In the years that followed, Easton obeyed his injunction to "live and rest better," pursuing a life of moderation. He settled down, married, and worked as a landscape designer in Scarborough, New York. The near wilderness of Essex County, New York, along the shores of Lake Champlain, provided a summer home and vistas that no doubt reminded him from time to time of Grand Lake.

With pride, he also published, in 1908, an article on the Indians of Labrador in *The Canadian Magazine.* A long-time member of the Explorers Club of New York, Easton died at the age of seventy-five in 1958, after a long illness.

Gilbert Blake, Job Chapies, and Joe Iserhoff sailed for home with Mrs. Hubbard on the *Pelican,* around the coast of Labrador. At Rigolet, Mina paid Gilbert for his season's work—$55 in cash and a note for $65—and bid him farewell. The other men transferred with her to the *King Edward* and continued south. Late the afternoon of November 20, the steamer tied up to a wharf in Quebec City. From Mina's diary, we know that Job and Joe loaded their gear into the canoes one last time and paddled round to a steamer "anchored just near." With those strokes, they glide silently beyond our reach. We know nothing—save one detail—of their later lives.

Gilbert, on the other hand, we nearly met in the flesh. In 1976 he was still living in Goose Bay, thirty-five miles down the coast from Northwest River. He was in his nineties and no longer hail, but—whatever his infirmities—still the man who had helped rescue Wallace in '03 and accompanied Mrs. Hubbard in '05. The two of us knocked on his front door, only to find from his family that he was ill that day and indisposed. By the time of our next return, he was dead.

Bert's life spanned changes the likes of which few people experience. He was born into a wilderness populated by a few bands of Indians and a handful of trappers. The only flag belonged to the Hudson's Bay Company; the only currency was reckoned in "Made Beaver." There were no schools, no doctors, no policemen—no real government of any kind. Yet by the time of his death, the local marshes contained paved highways, a Mounties barracks, a hospital, a Chinese restaurant featuring excellent vanilla milkshakes, and an airbase for jet fighters and transcontinental bombers.

Bert lived through the changes and adapted. By the time a finance company opened its offices in Goose, he had pretty well caught on to things. There was a government, all right, and with it came a "Family Allowance," an "Old Age Pension," and even "Welfare" for those who didn't work. This threw him some—he'd never heard of being paid without doing work. But he figured if "Finance" was part of the system, he'd better come in for it. He was surprised later to find he was expected to pay the money back.

Whatever heavenly investments Bert Blake is now pursuing,

he—if anyone—is surely in a position to chase the length of that rainbow, which stretches now and again across Michikamats, and fetch the pot of gold at the end of its arch. May he rest in peace.

When Dillon Wallace reached Ungava Bay, he had the opportunity, as he had had at Northwest River in 1903, to return to New York before the winter ice closed in. As in 1903, he declined. John Ford, the Hudson's Bay man at George River Post, attempted to dissuade him from setting out for Fort Chimo, just as Mackenzie, at Northwest River, had tried to keep him from bringing Hubbard's body home by dogsled. But Wallace knew his own mind. In such matters his own sense of propriety had to be squared. His journal for October 18 noted that it was "the anniversary of the day I parted from Hubbard two years ago;" and, like Mina, he must have keenly felt the loss of his companion. Was the dangerous journey he undertook to Fort Chimo another attempt to live up to Hubbard's high standards—to finish the expedition properly? Mina, of course, would be returning on the *Pelican*, and Wallace already had a taste of what it might be like to spend several weeks aboard a small ship with her. A journey by dogsled around the Labrador coast would avoid her withering "stony stare," as well as provide a good story to round out the new book. Whatever his motives, Wallace set out for Fort Chimo and, having twice escaped death by the narrowest of margins, courted it yet a third time.

His persistence—and remarkable luck—held out. He returned to civilization preceded by headlines proclaiming his success as the FIRST WHITE MAN TO CROSS PENINSULA WITHOUT EITHER GUIDES OR INDIAN ASSISTANTS. He had the opportunity to resume his law practice with Alonzo McLaughlin but exercised it infrequently. "Just let him sit down in his office here for a day and he becomes restless," McLaughlin admitted. Wallace continued to travel on assignment for *Outing* and other magazines, publishing such books as *Beyond the Mexican Sierras* and *Saddle and Camp in the Rockies*. In 1908 he was selected by the Arctic and Explorers clubs to lead a rescue expedition for Frederick Cook, the adventurer still missing in his attempt on the North Pole. Cook reappeared, however, before the expedition could get underway.

In 1917 Wallace remarried. He made his home near Poughkeepsie, New York, and brought up a son and daughter, both alive and well at this writing. When the Depression struck, he contributed to the Federal Writers' Project guidebook series, writing about the

Dutchess County region. Over the years his activities turned increasingly toward youth. Of his twenty-six books, most were adventure novels for boys and girls, including *Ungava Bob*, *The Gaunt Gray Wolf*, and *The Fur Traders of Kettle Harbor*. Wallace helped found the Boy Scouts of America and spent many summers teaching woodcraft at camps in the United States and Canada. His devotion to young people came, perhaps, from having had so little chance to live a carefree childhood of his own, during the hard years of the 1870s and '80s. Having discovered at age forty that sense of comradeship and high adventure that comes to relatively few in life, he delighted in re-creating the wonder and marvel of it for a new generation of youngsters. He died in 1939, at the age of seventy-six.

Mina Hubbard's journey home was a voyage of triumph tinged with sadness. Some who met her expressed admiration for her feat; others, amazement bordering on skepticism. At Rigolet a "big burly Irishman" named O'Sullivan could hardly believe "that I had made the trip across Labrador," Mina recorded. "Mr. O'Sullivan keeps exclaiming every once in a while . . . 'Well, you are the brave woman!' 'Well, when I look at you I can hardly believe you made that trip.' 'I can't believe it.' etc., etc." Her first telegram announcing success was greeted with some skepticism by the outside world. "According to those in Williamstown who are familiar with her plans," reported the North Adams *Evening Transcript*, "she cannot have carried out her original intentions. She was to have proceeded to Ungava, which would take her on a much longer journey than she has apparently made." At Quebec City a journalist noted that Mrs. Hubbard looked "so frail in appearance, that it is scarcely possible to credit the 550 miles of the canoe and portage journey which she has just completed. . . ." Mina found, however, that the public had fewer reservations. "When we arrived, a lot of people came on board. Many came to shake hands with me, apologizing for doing so but anxious to say an appreciative word and looked at me with genuine admiration and appreciation shining in their faces. . . ."

Starting life anew proved difficult. The attention and admiration that were now hers gave a good deal of satisfaction but such times were also the most treacherous. "Had to laugh a good many times and very heartily, but when laughing hardest was hardest to keep from crying. . . ." In Williamstown, the Reverend Sawyer arranged her first public talks about the trip, and, when these went well, she felt glad and grateful to have "something to do." Inevitably, though, the sadness and the longing still pierced her. On Christmas eve, returning home from church on a cold, clear night, she wrote perhaps the most poignant entry in her diary: "Stars so beautiful. Heart so hungry, so hungry, oh so hungry. How his eyes would shine if he could stand by me now to tell me how proud he was of my success. Oh Laddie, dear precious beautiful Laddie, I want you, oh I want you this beautiful Christmas eve. I love you."

In 1908 her speaking engagements took her to England. There, one of the listeners in the audience was Harold Ellis, a coal magnate and son of a member of Parliament. Charmed by her talk, he pursued her acquaintance; within the year the two were married. Settling in England, she raised three children, although the marriage eventually ended in divorce in the 1920s. Always restless, Mina became a committed world traveler.

In 1936 she returned to America, with her Labrador adventures much on her mind. In addition to dedicating a plaque in Hubbard's memory at the University of Michigan, she stirred controversy in Haverstraw, where Hubbard was buried. Ordering the coffin to be disinterred, she took it back to England, where it was buried close to her new home. At Haverstraw, she left tablets memorializing the exploits of her husband as well as the heroism of George Elson. But still not a word of sympathy for Wallace.

To the end of her days, she remained a woman of captivating charm and pertinacious will. One acquaintance recalled her "intrepid, dauntless courage," concluding: "There was no fear in her heart." Mina's granddaughter remembers sitting at the feet of a *grande dame* who presided over the household and whose affectionate nature—sometimes hidden behind a lofty dignity—could be glimpsed much as her "shocking pink" bloomers could: just a hint visible beneath a grandmother's sober skirts.

Mina was accustomed to having her way. In later years, when she crossed any intersection, she would plunge into the street heedless of crosswalks or onrushing autos, extending her arms to halt all traffic. In a small English town not unaccustomed to eccentricities, this accomodation to a faster world sufficed. In 1953, however, on the last day of her life, she sallied forth across the local railroad tracks, heedless of the locomotive, and indomitable to the end.

George Elson accompanied Mrs. Hubbard all the way to Williamstown before returning home to Ontario. This time, no letter came down the tracks summoning him.

The Hubbard expeditions left their mark, of course. George became known as someone who would never throw away small fish or even the wing of a partridge. He always remembered the hard times.

And the memories did not fade. Almost thirty years later, during the winter of 1932–33, he befriended one W. G. Brittain, an agent for the Temiskaming and Northern Ontario Railway. Brittain found he could set his watch by Elson's visits to the station house. George would walk in, say hello, and launch into his tale—not the trip with Mina (those memories he kept to himself)—but the earlier, fatal expedition. Invariably, on reaching the part about kissing Hubbard's cheek and leaving to get help, tears came to his eyes and rolled down his cheeks.

George spent at least one more season as a guide. In 1906 he hired out to Mr. and Mrs. Stephen Tasker of Philadelphia for an expedition up the Clearwater River along the east coast of Hudson Bay, taking with him the ever-reliable Job Chapies. Later, he entered into service for Revillon and Frères, rivals to the Hudson's Bay Company and the company with whom he and Mina had stayed at Northwest River.

For reasons we find not hard to imagine, he married late, to a Cree woman from Mistassini, Quebec. Eventually he moved to Moose Factory at the southern tip of Hudson Bay, where he lived out his days. So far as we know, he saw Mina Hubbard again only once. On her tour of North America, during the summer of 1936—at the age of sixty-six—she made a side trip to Moosonee. George rounded up a canoe and the two of them set out on a paddle up the Moose River.

We have canoed the Moose ourselves. It is a broad, blustery stretch of water whose shifting current is subject to the tides of the Bay. It does not, to be honest, evoke quite the majesty of another river farther to the east and north. At least not for us. In any case, whatever words or memories may have come to Mina and George that day, they have long ago been carried high by the wind and scattered—beyond recovery now and forever.

Afterword to the 1996 Edition

It is remarkable the degree to which a single life, lived across its span of a relatively few years, can etch so many traces in the historical record: broad strokes and fine, to say nothing of the random nicks and scuffs. By the time we first sent *Great Heart* to press, we had become intimately familiar with the expedition diaries of the Hubbards, Dillon Wallace, and their companions. We had sifted through contemporary newspaper accounts, from New York, Halifax, St. John's, and North Adams; read letters, magazine articles, spoken with descendants; we had even canoed much of the expedition route ourselves. We believed, with some justice, that in certain ways we knew more about the lives of these people than they had known about themselves.

Still, we underestimated the nicks and scuffs. Soon after *Great Heart* was published, the letters began to arrive. A historian in Rockland County, New York, sent information about the house (still standing) where Leonidas and Mina Hubbard had lived in Congers, New York. Another New Yorker provided photographs of himself with George Elson, taken during a visit to Hudson Bay during the 1930s. From Labrador came word of previously undiscovered letters preserved in the archives of a Nova Scotia lumber company; from Ireland, news of a grandson of Mina Hubbard whose existence was entirely unknown to us. With chagrin, we began to recognize the impossibility of ever putting a final period to the tale. Human lives are finite; the stories of human lives refract infinitely.

For those who wish to pursue those refractions, there is now an essential place to begin any investigation of the Hubbard and Wallace expeditions: Memorial University in St. John's, Newfoundland. Thanks to the energy and dedication of Anne Hart and her staff, the Centre for Newfoundland Studies at the Queen Elizabeth II Library has amassed the most significant collection of primary materials on the subject. That includes the original diaries of the Hubbards and Dillon Wallace, from 1903 and 1905 respectively, and George Elson's journal of 1905. (Indeed, the whereabouts of the original Hubbard and Elson diaries were completely unknown until 1993. Before Hart's discovery, researchers were forced to content themselves with microfilm copies, made during the 1950s by the London branch of the Canadian Public Archives, to which Mina briefly loaned the manuscripts.) In addition, many valuable newspaper clippings and letters have been passed on to the collection from Dillon Wallace III, as well as photographs and information from the descendants of Mina Hubbard.

The retrieval of these documents, as well as the appearance of *Great Heart* in a new edition, affords us the opportunity to correct several errors. Mina Hubbard was married to Harold Ellis in Toronto, not England, and she died in 1956, not 1953. During the winter of 1904–1905, Mina summoned George Elson in order to learn more about Laddie's expedition. According to an interview Mina later gave to the *New York World,* George stayed in Williamstown at least through January, when Mina first decided to mount her own expedition, and he agreed to be part of the trip then, and not, as we suggested, through any correspondence that passed between them that spring. We were also mistaken in supposing that George, Job Chapies, and Joe Iserhoff traveled to Bewdley, Ontario, in order to depart with Mina for Labrador. Susan Felsberg of Mud Lake, Labrador, has discovered that Mina arranged (by way of a coded telegram, safe from the prying eyes of the public) to meet George and his comrades in Halifax. Finally, our epilogue reports that Mina, during a return to America in 1936, ordered that Hubbard's coffin be disinterred and taken to England, there to be reburied. Anne Hart has established that, in fact, Hubbard's grave remained undisturbed. In 1904 it had been marked solely with a birch tree planted in his memory; only during her visit to America in 1936 did Mina finally revisit Mount Repose Cemetery in Haverstraw, New York, to install the three memorial plaques that now commemorate the expeditions.

Are the nicks and scuffs numerous enough to merit changing the portrait in material ways? Perhaps not. Yet the person we still know least about is the figure who gives our book its title: Elson himself. Undoubtedly there is a good deal more information to be gleaned about him and the career he had both before and after his years with Hubbard. Clayton Klein, an outdoorsman and writer, visited the Hudson Bay region and spoke with a number of people about George's history. But Klein's novelized retelling of Elson's life, *Challenge the Wilderness* (1988), mixes a large dollop of fiction with fact, including invented letters, names, and dates that stand cheek by jowl with authentic diary entries, and in the end proves so inventive that there is no way for readers to sort out the real from the feverishly imagined.

The documents at Memorial University, on the other hand, contain fascinating hints of George's complex and conflicting emotions. On November 22, 1905, Wallace's sister Annie wrote her brother that "the general opinion of people seems to be that Mrs. H. & Geo. will get married. Whatever she may think, I feel sure that is what Geo has had in mind. He broke his engagement some time before he went, with the Indian girl . . ." In our own telling of the story, we had assumed that the engagement was a white lie George told as a way to avoid Wallace's recruitment in 1905. But perhaps George was indeed engaged. Wallace, visiting Missanabie, surely could have confirmed the claim there. Did George's visit to Williamstown leave him enamored of Mina even before the expedition began in 1905?

See other book. To this day, Elson's second journal, in which he confided frequently during the 1905 expedition, remains missing. There are traces—certainly fine and perhaps even broad—still to be teased from the historical record. We look forward eagerly to the discoveries of others, and would be glad to hear from anyone who finds additional information.

J. W. D. and J. R.
Rhinebeck, New York, and Glens Falls, New York
May 1996

FREQUENTLY USED ABBREVIATIONS

CE Ms. diary of Clifford Easton, 1905. Explorers Club, New York.

DW 1903 Ms. diary of Dillon Wallace, 1903. Collection of Dillon Wallace III, Beacon, NY.

DW 1905 Ms. diary of Dillon Wallace, 1905. Collection of Dillon Wallace III, Beacon, NY.

GE 1903 "Narrative by George Elson." Reprinted in Mrs. Leonidas Hubbard, *A Woman's Way Through Unknown Labrador*. London: John Murray, 1908.

GE 1905 Ms. diary of George Elson, 1905. Microfilm copy in the Public Archives Canada, Ottawa.

HH Halifax [Nova Scotia] *Herald*.

LH Ms. diary of Leonidas Hubbard, Jr., 1903. Microfilm copy in Public Archives Canada, Ottawa. Incomplete published editions also appear in WW, 239–85 and *Outing* 45:648–89.

LLT Dillon Wallace. *The Long Labrador Trail*. New York: Outing Publishing Company, 1907.

LLW Dillon Wallace. *The Lure of the Labrador Wild*. New York: Fleming Revell, 1905. A more recent edition published by Breakwater Books (Portugal Cove, Nfld., [1978]) includes Wallace's prefaces to the sixth and eleventh printings (1906 and 1918).

MBH Ms. diary of Mina Benson Hubbard, 1905. Microfilm copy in the Public Archives Canada, Ottawa.

NAT North Adams [Massachusetts] *Transcript*.

NH New York *Herald*.

NYS New York *Sun*.

NYT *New York Times*.

NYTrib New York *Tribune*.

NYW New York *World*.

WBC 1903 Ms. journal of William Brooks Cabot, 1903. National Anthropological Archives, Smithsonian Institution, Washington, DC.

WBC 1908 William Brooks Cabot. Captions for photographic slides, 1908. Typescript. National Anthropological Archives, Smithsonian Institution, Washington, DC.

WBC 1909 William Brooks Cabot. Ms. lecture notes, 1909. National Anthropological Archives, Smithsonian Institution, Washington, DC.

WW Mrs. Leonidas Hubbard. *A Woman's Way Through Unknown Labrador*. London: John Murray, 1908. An American edition was also published, without the introduction by William Cabot. New York: McClure Company, 1908.

Notes

PROLOGUE: THE LAST BLANK SPOT ON THE MAP OF NORTH AMERICA

Since the events related in the Prologue are told in more detail in the body of the book, the references are included in the corresponding chapters below. The opening entry, of course, is from Hubbard's diary, October 18, 1903.

1: TOO SOON TO DIE

George Elson's thousand-mile railroad odyssey is briefly traced in LLW, 26–28. There, Dillon Wallace relates the story of Jerry not wanting "to die so soon." The other version of Jerry's travels, to our knowledge, survives only in a curious piece of graffiti found in the margins of one copy of LLW in Harvard University's Widener Library. Either the volume's original owner or a later borrower had evidently talked with a few old hands around Missanabie. Opposite Wallace's sentence that "Hubbard . . . engaged through the kind offices of Mr. S. A. King . . . the services of a Cree Indian named Jerry," the anonymous scribe carefully recorded the following note:

> First tried to get Antoine Soulière but he was off packing a cache of grub into the bush down the Missanabie for the G.T.R.R. [Grand Trunk Railroad] and did not get the letter. Jerry got as far as Chapleau, bought a new suit, got *very* drunk and never turned up!

For Hubbard's impressions of Jerry in 1902, see LH, "Off Days on Superior's North Shore," *Outing*, 43:650–51.

According to the June 1903 railroad timetables, available in such compendiums as *The Traveler's Ready-Reference Guide* (New York, 1903), the daily Canadian Pacific train passed eastward through Missanabie at 5:35 P.M. and arrived at Montreal twenty-five hours later. The Montreal Express left for New York every evening at 7:10. Details of the buffet menu are in LLW, 198–99. For George's love of bird calls, see MBH (August 7). We have found little scholarship available on the problems of half-breed sons of Hudson's Bay Company employees, but some inkling of the social pressures and anomalies can be seen in Sylvia Van Kirk's perceptive "Women and the Fur Trade," *The Beaver* (Winter, 1972), 4–21, as well as in her book-length study, *Many Tender Ties: Women in Fur Trade Society, 1670–1870* (Winnipeg, 1981). See also Jennifer S. H. Brown, *Strangers in Blood: Fur Trade Company Families in Indian Country* (Vancouver, 1980) and Gary David Sealey, "History of the Hudson's Bay Company, 1870–1900," (unpublished Master's thesis, University of Western Ontario, 1969), 75–76.

Details of the approach to Manhattan by rail can be found in Moses King, *King's Handbook of New York City* (Boston, 1893), 115, 193, 196, 231; and Edward Hungerford, *Men and Iron: A History of the New York Central* (New York, 1938). Views of the old Grand Central Station before it was replaced by the modern terminal in 1913 can be found in many sources; ours included Roger Whitehouse, *New York: Sunshine and Shadow* (New York, 1974); John A. Kouwenhouven, *The Columbia Historical Portrait of New York* (Garden City, 1953).

We should also, at the outset, say a few words about spelling. In charting northern waters, early mapmakers settled on the term "Hudson's Bay," using the possessive, and the Hudson's Bay Company followed suit when it was chartered in 1670. By Hubbard's day, geographers had adopted the simpler "Hudson Bay," although the company, even now, preserves its possessive. In addition, locals like George Elson continued to refer to the body of water itself as "Hudson's Bay." Hence the varying usages in this book. Hubbard also referred to the "Nascaupee" Indians, although we have followed the modern usage—Naskapi—except when quoting directly from his journal. To confuse matters further, Canadian maps refer to the river as the Naskaupi. Finally, the Montagnais Indians, so named by the French, were sometimes called Mountaineer Indians by the English.

2: EVERYTHING ON THE LINE

Caspar Whitney relates his own wilderness adventures in *On Snow-shoes to the Barren Grounds* (New York, 1896), a remarkable tale of endurance, starvation, sportsmanship and plain cussedness. For the story of his ravenous dogs, see 199–200 and 290; for the mutinous Indians and Whitney's holding them at knifepoint, 190–92, including the quotation about starvation and failure.

Whitney was never a man to hold back an opinion. Each issue of *Outing* contained his column, "The Sportsman's Viewpoint," a series of brusque obiter dicta issued on every conceivable sporting subject. The bulleted paragraphs were highlighted with boldface heads that set the tone of the commentary: "An Insult to American Rowing," "Hoodlum Hockey," "Mediocre Polo Prevailed," "Chicago, As Usual, Is an Offender," "Strained at the Mountain, Brought Forth a Mouse," "Ducking Stool Needed," "Come Out of the Glass House, Friend," "Look to the Beam in Thine Own Eye, Friend," and "No Back Talk." To Whitney's credit, much of this asperity was directed toward the widespread corruption and over-professionalization of the era's amateur athletics, but he could be forthright in less admirable ways. Whitney did not bother to hide his contempt for both full-blood and half-breed Indians. His attitude is reflected in *On Snow-shoes*, 153, as well as 88–89 and all of Chapter 8.

For Hubbard's salary, see LH, "January—Cash"; and his proposal to Whitney, LH (February 24) as well as *Outing* 44:241 and 45:643. Like most New York journalists, Hubbard earned a salary well above the national average, and his was relatively generous even by New York standards. See Ted C. Smythe, "The Reporter, 1880–1900," *Journalism History* (Spring, 1980), 1–10, and Allen Churchill, *Park Row* (New York, 1958), 54–55. For additional information on *Outing*, see Frank Luther Mott, *A History of American Magazines* (New York, 1930–1968), 4:633–38.

Wallace's account of missing Elson at Grand Central (LLW, 28) is silent about Hubbard's reaction to not finding George; our reconstruction is conjecture. Yet given the previous missed connection with Jerry, the tremendous stake Hubbard had riding on his expedition, and his general nervousness throughout the final preparations, that reaction can hardly be doubted. For Hubbard's nervousness, see NYTrib, May 28, 1904: 7; WBC 1903, July 8; and even the admission of his adoring wife, Mina, that Hubbard was naturally "high strung and sensitive" (WW, 45). For the story of his starving in New York, see LH (October 15); LLW, 211, and WW,

42–43; for the sale of his Congers home in 1903, LLW, 195; his loss of the *Daily News* job because of typhoid, WW, 43.

Hubbard's earlier camping experience was remarkably slim. In addition to the Missanabie trip, see *Outing* 41:529–40 and 39:634–41 for an excursion to Lac St. Jean ("north of Montreal"); for another to Quebec after moose, *Outing* 44:78–86. William Cabot tells the story of meeting Hubbard in the Canadian woods, in a personal notebook, WBC 1909, 3–4. Albert P. Low, *Report on Explorations in the Labrador Peninsula* (Ottawa, 1896), 8–19, has an incisive chronology of the many attempts to penetrate Labrador's interior. Hubbard corresponded with Low about his plans, LH (February 24). For a first-hand account of a Hudson's Bay trader who crossed Labrador on snowshoes in 1838, see W. S. Wallace, ed., *John McLean's Notes of a Twenty-five Year's Service in the Hudson's Bay Territory* (Toronto, 1932).

Wallace describes his recruitment in the Shawangunks, about November 1901, in LLW, 13–17. He gives the impression that Hubbard had already made his camping trips to Quebec and Ontario at that time. In fact, they took place after the recruitment, Lac St. Jean the following February and March, and Missanabie (what Wallace—generously—refers to as "the Hudson Bay region") in August and September 1902. A biographical sketch of Wallace may be found in *National Cyclopedia of American Biography*, 34:293–94, and NYT, September 29, 1939: 23.

3: FOREBODINGS

Mina Hubbard's devotion to Laddie runs through her writings like an unbroken thread. For a particularly poignant expression of her admiration, see WW, 234–235. For the eating habits of George Elson and Dillon Wallace at the farewell dinner, see LH (September 23). More material about the 1902 trip to Missanabie, including the stories about John and Tom, Mina's rejoinder about the "soft" rain, and the bushwhack after trout, are found in LH, "Off Days on Superior's North Shore," *Outing* 43:649–59. (In visiting Missanabie, the Hubbards were only following the footsteps of other similarly inclined outdoor enthusiasts. As early as 1886, the Canadian Pacific's General Passenger Department, in Montreal, issued *Fishing and Shooting*, an annually revised tourist guide to the outdoor opportunities along its lines. The 1896 edition notes that "By writing to the Hudson's Bay officer at Missanabie, guides and canoes can be secured without any difficulty." [42])

For background on Mina's engagement and wedding, see WW, 45. The voyage north is covered amply in the diaries of Hubbard and Wallace, as well as Wallace's LLW, 29–35 and William Brooks Cabot, *Labrador* (Boston, 1920), 16–28. While Hubbard was surprised to see Cabot, the two men had been "in occasional touch" (WBC, 1909) over the winter, and Cabot knew Hubbard was coming on the *Sylvia*. The huckstering of free passes by the Reid-Newfoundland Company is the subject of considerable indignation for Wallace in LLW, 33, while his success in obtaining the steward's berth is told with equal satisfaction. As for Mina's feelings toward the "mongrels" of Reid-Newfoundland, see NYH 1904, January 24:8.

Cabot confesses his unconventional curiosity about Captain Parsons' navigation in *Labrador*, 27. The rough weather experienced by the *Virginia Lake* was not uncommon on voyages across the Strait of Belle Isle. *Sailing Directions: Labrador and Hudson Bay* (Ottawa, 1974), a Canadian government publication full of helpful statistics, notes both the number of days with gales at Belle Isle in an average July—five—and the number of icebergs passing the island in an average year—one thousand. For the dangers of icebergs and growlers in fog, see page 55. (Cabot's private assessment of Parsons [WBC 1908, slide captions B-31 and B-32] is graphic and perceptive: the captain "is rather often scared, sometimes beyond need, but only half collapses; then bites on again and always makes good. . . . With 100 stops to make, fog and ice and an ill-charted coast, he brings [his boat] in trip after trip with whole bones.")

Mina Hubbard left no detailed account of her own anguish during the last hours before the parting, but other sources provide the framework for our reconstruction. The best diary description of Battle Harbor belongs to Wallace, in DW 1903, July 5. Mina's conviction that Laddie would never return is relayed by Cabot, both in WBC 1903 (July 6) and in *Labrador*, 28. Hubbard's "Will you miss me?" is from Mina's own recollection of that dismal night, recorded in her diary exactly two years later, MBH (July 5).

4: "GOOD-BYE AND GODSPEED"

Every historian dreams of finding an insightful, pithy diarist to accompany his protagonists during crucial moments of the story. William Brooks Cabot is our dream come true. *Labrador* (Boston, 1920) is his own book of northern travels, originally issued in less-detailed form under the title *In Northern Labrador* (Boston, 1912). It is full of vivid descriptions of the land, perceptive vignettes of his beloved Naskapi, deep appreciation for the Labrador settlers, and more than enough harrowing adventures for one who was so unpretentious about his ambitions as an explorer. The book tells in some detail of Cabot joining Hubbard's party at Halifax and accompanying it as far as Indian Harbor, Labrador. In this published work, Cabot speaks in flattering terms of Hubbard and indicates a high regard for the quality of his preparations.

The research for our book was well under way before we discovered a good deal more about the complexity of Cabot's feelings, in a phone conversation with Stephen Loring, an anthropologist with his own abiding interest in Cabot and the Naskapi Indians. The reader may imagine our delight upon hearing from Loring that he had managed to track down Cabot's private papers on behalf of the Smithsonian Institution's National Anthropological Archives. The papers, he told us, were in temporary storage while waiting to be sorted and catalogued—the storage facilities being an old trunk under Loring's bed. Our delight turned to astonishment upon learning that Cabot's 1903 diary, as well as additional slide and lecture notes, painted a significantly different picture of his feelings about Hubbard. Cabot was unflinchingly frank about the shortcomings of the outfit and the inexperience of Hubbard's party in WBC 1903 (July 6 and 8), with additional detail in the slide captions, WBC 1908, B-29. He also noted the high state of Hubbard's nerves and his conversation about "making a reputation in some northern exploit."

Hubbard's journey to Rigolet and Northwest River is told in LH and DW, July 10–15, and LLW, 38–54, with additional material on Thomas Mackenzie and Lillie Blake in LLW, 301–302. We have fleshed out these accounts by drawing on the memories of some Labrador old-timers as they appear in *Them Days*, a quarterly journal published in Labrador since 1975. (For subscription information, write *Them Days*, Box 939, Station B, Happy Valley, Labrador, Canada AOP 1EO.) Under the energetic editorial direction of Doris Saunders, *Them Days* has collected source material invaluable to any Labrador historian: old diaries and letters, early photographs, and, most of all, the reminiscences of an aging generation that have been taped, edited and collated by the journal's staff. *Them Days* is oral history at its colorful best.

The story of Mr. Low hearing the Indian maidens living and speaking under the falls of the Grand River (later known as Churchill Falls, and now dammed to a trickle to generate hydroelectric power) appears in the 1893 diary of Lydia Campbell, published by *Them Days*, under separate cover, as *Sketches of Labrador Life* (Goose Bay, 1980), 19–20. *Them Days* has supplied us with additional details—for example, the practice of wearing flour-bag aprons. As Elizabeth Coombs points out (2:2, 40), "Flour bags wears everlastin'."

Wallace briefly notes the viciousness of some of the dogs, recording that only a few days earlier, "a little Eskimo boy who stumbled and fell was set upon by a pack and all but killed before the brutes were driven off." (LLW, 47) For our description, we have also borrowed from "Uncle" Tommy Davis, who recounts the mauling of his little brother, Willie, in *Them Days* 6:4, 24–25. Willie's particular attack occurred about 1915, but all these incidents were tragically similar to one another; see *Them Days* 2:3, 46–47; 3:1, 10; 4:3, 56–58 for variations on the theme. William Cabot provides further detail in his essay entitled "Dogs," in Wilfred Grenfell, ed., *Labrador: The Country and the People* (New York, 1909), especially page 272.

Labrador is, we might add, still a land where the old folk are addressed as "Aunt" and "Uncle" and the truly exceptional fellow is bestowed the honorific "Skipper." These are a vanishing people, who dress up as "jannies" (roguish spirits), believe in "smokers" (ghosts), and know how to make sealskin gloves so they won't get "starky" (stiff); people who, falling in love, "ate the foolish apple,"who still worry over "getting square" with the H.B.C. and who, for as long as their time shall last, will fondly mind them days.

5: MARCH TO YOUR FRONT LIKE A SOLDIER

The first days of the expedition are related in LH and DW 1903 (July 15–21) and LLW, 55–67.

For the record (and since it later became a matter of controversy), we list the provisions Hubbard recorded as having set out with at the start of the expedition: "four 45-lb. sacks of flour; 30 lbs. bacon; 20 lbs. lard; 30 lbs. sugar; 14 salt; 3 or 4 lbs. dried apples from home; 10 lbs. rice; 20 lbs. erbswurst [peameal]; 10 lbs. pea-flour in tins; 10 lbs. tea; 5 coffee; 6 chocolate; 10 hardtack; 10 lbs. dried milk." (LH, July 7.) Wallace notes, however, that Hubbard had given 60 pounds of flour to the pilot of the *Julia Sheridan* (the boat which ferried them to Northwest River), leaving 120 pounds. Wallace also estimates only 13 pounds of lard and 25 pounds of bacon. (LLW, 51.)

Grand Lake is indeed grand. We have canoed it twice, though both times from west to east, the opposite of Hubbard's direction. The prevailing westerlies being with us, we yoked two canoes together catamaran-style, hoisted a makeshift sail, dropped a couple paddles astern for rudders and a couple more amidships for lee-boards, then sat back and enjoyed the ride. As in 1903, no one lives there permanently, although a few more trapper's cabins—"tilts," they are called—appear here and there along the shore.

About the insect peril. Some readers might suspect us of exaggerating their numbers and their ferocity, but anyone who has ventured into the North during the summer months will recognize our actual frustration: that the human mind is not built to conceive such numbers and written words do not exist to convey the torment they inflict. Furthermore, the farther north one proceeds, the worse the menace becomes. Both mosquitoes and flies breed in water—black flies in swiftly flowing streams, mosquitoes in stillwater—and large areas of the Canadian shield lie under water. In the permafrost of the tundra, frozen ground only inches below the surface prevents meltwater from freely draining, and so in addition to the numberless ponds and lakes, breeding mosquitoes may select from an infinity of puddles and marshes. As for the black flies, several hardy entomologists once made a formal estimate of the number of black fly eggs on a single fifteen-foot stretch of rock beside a northern waterfall. The total? Sixteen billion. (See Robert Stewart, *Labrador* [Time-Life, 1977], page 111.)

Given the importance of Leonidas Hubbard's journal, it may be helpful to provide a bit of information about it. In early 1903 Hubbard purchased an appointment diary that he converted during the expedition into his personal journal. Entries are brief at first, but they expand as the trip progresses. Often Hubbard did not have enough space allotted under a particular date, so he continued his notes on an earlier, unused page.

Outing originally published the diary in 1905 (45:648–89), and Mina Hubbard also included it in her own book, WW, 239–85. Readers who compare the two versions will discover that Mina Hubbard's text is significantly shorter, omitting many passages that *Outing* includes, although *Outing*, too, is selective. Examining the microfilm copy of the original manuscript in Ottawa's Canadian Public Archives, we found that both published versions omitted significant material. We have deposited in the archives a typed transcript of the full diary, indicating which passages appear in which versions.

To give an example of the kind of editing that has been done, Hubbard's entry for July 17 is printed below. The letters in brackets indicate that the material following [P] appears in *both* published versions; [M], is published only in Mina Hubbard's version; [O], is published only in *Outing*; and [D], appears only in the manuscript diary.

> [P] Rain and clouds. Rained hard in the night. Awoke, dreading to start out in it. [M] Got breakfast to let George sleep. [P] Water so shoal and swift that we would take part of outfit and return for the rest. Most places had to track. I pulling rope while Wallace and George waded and pushed and dragged the canoe. [O] We are eating four meals a day. Eat our second meal about 10, third about 3; sometimes a snack when noon observation is made. [D] Pancakes are great staple. Eat 'em with hot syrup (melted sugar) and bacon, have plenty sugar and it sweetens us up and keeps us in good spirits. At night—hot bread—and pea soup or stewed dried apples. Have a bunch of latter they are a bully corrective for bacon and tea. Homesick. How the longing for home grips me. Am wondering about the old folk and about M. No one depressed. Will get there. Low and Indian say chain of lakes up here some place. That will help us. Left can of lard and spruce clothes at morning camp. Flies have not troubled me so much today. All of us blotched and swollen at face and hands—but don't mind it as at first. Did not wash face. Kept dope on, and it helped. Made portage of 1/4 mile through cut-off in stream—over boulders. Camped on fine wooded bluff. 20 feet above river. Moss and spruce.

As can be seen, Mina Hubbard's version omits the material fact that Hubbard was drawing heavily on the expedition's provisions. *Outing* includes that fact, but Caspar Whitney's blue pencil struck the additional revealing details about Hubbard's carefree attitude toward using up the food. Both published versions also tactfully omit Hubbard's keen homesickness. Evidently Kipling helped him as much as it was meant to help Wallace. (The "spruce clothes," incidentally, refer apparently to the more formal "spruced-up" clothes the men wore on the steamer during the trip up.)

In matters of portaging, the expedition introduced Dillon Wallace to many a lesson in the outdoor school of hard knocks—so much so that in later years, when *Outing* put together a series on camping and hiking techniques, Wallace wrote the volume entitled *Packing and Portaging* (New York, 1912). For a description of the tumpline, as well as other packing techniques, see especially his Chapter 6.

6: THOROUGHLY LOST

By the time Dillon Wallace finally came to write *The Lure of the Labrador Wild*, he had survived many remarkable adventures, all within the space of a few months. Perhaps for this reason, the relevant portions of LLW for these early days (59–78) do not make clear just how hellish those first days were for Wallace, a man who had begun the expedition with virtually no wilderness experience.

As several unpublished passages in his and Hubbard's diary suggest, however, Wallace was having no easy time of it. LH, July 20 and 25, note Wallace's meager eating habits and his particularly severe torment from the flies. ("Complains constantly of flies. Says they poison him and make him sick.") On this point, Wallace was probably right. Certain individuals are particularly susceptible to fly bites, and overexposure can result in nausea and fever. Wallace's own diary also records his exhaustion. (July 25: "It seems to me I have exerted myself to the limit of endurance today.")

Dillon Wallace's dogged pursuit of a career, from farming to telegraphy and on into the law, is outlined in the *National Cyclopedia of American Biography* 34:293–94. But the biography does not reveal Wallace's alienation from his work, which can be deduced from a few remarks, one in LH (September 19) where Wallace mentions the "lethargy" that had beset him, and elsewhere in comments offered by Wallace's friend and business partner, Alonzo McLaughlin (NYTrib 1905, Nov. 22:7). McLaughlin makes clear how much Wallace's loss of Jennie Currie affected his outlook. Confirmation appears in DW 1903 (October 18).

George's jest about Wallace being seasick is in LH (July 22). Wallace himself mentions his own adjustment to the rigorous routine in LLW, 78, while Hubbard notes the improvement in LH (July 30).

Upon being asked whether he had ever gotten lost, Daniel Boone is said to have remarked, "No, but I was *bewildered* once for three days." Nobody out in the woods likes to admit to such predicaments, but when it happens, that initial realization almost inevitably brings with it a wave of fear—especially in a country whose features are so monotonous. Both of us confess to being bewildered in Labrador on one or two scouting expeditions, and it is to Wallace's credit that he slept through the night, made the necessary adjustments to his compass and thought to head south for his river. Many neophytes have done worse.

Hubbard's discovery of low food supplies (LH, July 29) makes a dramatic contrast with his earlier diary entries. Up until only a few days previous, the diary had continued to record heavy meals and such after-dinner luxuries as chocolate-in-sugar. Hubbard, to all appearances, succeeded in lightening his outfit faster than he realized.

7: GOOSE IS BETTER THAN ANYTHING

The relevant portions of LH and DW are July 31–August 5; see also LLW, 78–92. Hubbard's Mountaineer Lake, incidentally, uses the English version of the more common French name for the Indians, Montagnais.

George's twine-and-twirl method of roasting goose made a profound impression on his two hungry friends. When we visited Dillon Wallace III, he told us that he had one roll of 16mm film of his father, taken on a Memorial Day picnic in 1927. Eagerly we set up a projector and screened the three-minute movie. At age sixty-three, looking hale and hearty, Dillon Wallace was presiding over a bed of coals. It was lamb he was roasting, but the poles and the twine were all properly in place, and Wallace was happily demonstrating to friends the method of browning meat on all sides.

It may be worth noting here that "living off the country" is a difficult business in Labrador. We have noted, in the text, that it took forty-five fish a day to satisfy the three men's appetites—a quantity that would keep even a good angler busy. For the record, Hubbard and Wallace's diary show that for the entire trip the group caught 1 caribou, 12 geese, 6 duck, 21 partridge, 13 ptarmigan, 8 namaycush, 2 whiskey jacks, 1 squirrel, 1 plover, 1 rabbit and a "yellowlegs." The party also ate blueberries, mossberries and currants, and landed over a thousand trout. This, plus the provisions they brought, still was not enough to prevent starvation from setting in.

8: ALONE

The relevant sources for this portion of the trip are LH and DW (August 5–15) and LLW, 93–110.

Hubbard's diary is not clear about his wanderings during the night out alone. Our description is based on the facts he gives about the bluffs and our own study of the 1:50,000-scale topographic map of that area, 13F/11 Mountaineer Lake. It is not entirely clear, either, what Hubbard made of the "Big River" into which the expedition portaged. Nowhere in the diary does he indicate that he suspects his original river might not be Low's "Northwest"; and Wallace's book explicitly states that all three men always assumed it was. On the other hand, Hubbard noted on August 12 that his new river "runs north apparently; it must therefore be Low's Northwest River I think." As he continued through the country, he referred to other rivers as possible candidates for Low's "Northwest" River.

Wallace makes clear (LLW, 109) that Hubbard keenly felt his isolation during the time his companions were out overnight. Hubbard's own August 15 entry portrays him feeling "depressed and useless"—and Hubbard did not easily admit his fears, even to his diary. Perhaps some measure of his loneliness may be gauged, however, by the fact that after this separation, he never went out scouting alone again—nor even, with one or two exceptions lasting a few hours, did he remain alone in camp.

9: MICHIKAMAU OR BUST

The progress of the expedition up the "Big River," over the mountains, and across the long portage is related in LH and DW (August 16–September 8), and LLW, 110–45. The route can be followed on modern topographical maps with a fair degree of accuracy, the longest stretch of water between Disappointment Lake and Windbound Lake being Mary Lake.

We have noted Wallace's naming of lakes Hope and Disappointment, which appear on the modern topographical maps, as do so many other of his names. (The survey has placed one, however—Mountaineer Lake—incorrectly, six miles to the west of the actual lake the party traveled through.) From Hubbard's diary, it appears that most of these lakes received their names only after the trip was over; but in order to prevent readers from becoming hopelessly confused by the succession of nameless lakes, we have adopted Wallace's names in our text.

The outlet-hunting in Disappointment Lake was "hell on nerves," as Hubbard remarked in his diary. To the armchair explorer with map in hand, a route to Michikamau from Lake Hope could have been traced easily enough. But the experienced northern traveler A. P. Low, Hubbard's own guiding light, made abundantly clear the difficulties of exploring such lakes on the Labrador plateau. "All the rivers in central Labrador flow almost on the surface of the country, and are broken into chains of lakes often formed by dams of glacial drift, which in other places form low ridges that divide the streams into different channels. These channels wander about on the lower levels of the interior country in a most bewildering manner, and render travel without a guide excessively difficult." (*Report on Explorations in the Labrador Peninsula* [Ottawa, 1896], 27.)

With typical acerbity, Caspar Whitney tells the story of his encounter with the tyro in *Outing* 41:253–54. Whitney's indirect influence can also be seen in Hubbard's resolve to sleep without his socks or sweater to inure himself to the cold (LH, Sept 9): Whitney describes similar disciplinary measures in *On Snow-shoes to the Barren Grounds* (New York, 1896), 65.

10: LIMITS

The relevant portions of the narrative can be found in LH and DW (September 9–15) and LLW, 146–61.

For obvious reasons, Wallace called the large body of water they had reached Windbound Lake. As the topographical maps make clear, navigating its bays and islands was not easy. Hubbard was right in thinking it possible to reach Michikamau by heading northeast and then cutting west. There is also a passage more directly to the northwest. Neither route, however, is obvious without benefit of a map when making a search from the seat of a canoe. Even the map, with all its bays and islands, is not likely to convey a sufficient idea of the navigating difficulties for those who have not tried to chart their own course through a big lake. For a concrete demonstration of some of the problems of route-finding, see our discussion of the subject in *The Complete Wilderness Paddler*, 94–104, where the body of water in question is Labrador's Ashuanipi Lake.

The original sources make clear that the three men's obsession with food had become acute by this point. In fact, Wallace notes (LLW, 159) that although harder times lay ahead, these days were the ones where the craving for food became most intense. He reports many of these conversations, and Hubbard's list of restaurants may be found in the back leaf of his diary. Hubbard's discussion of supplies needed for a "Hard Trip" (which leads into a fantasy about "easy trip" foods) is found in the unpublished version of LH, September 14.

George Elson's conflicting feelings and his crucial role in the decision to turn back must be derived from the discussions in Wallace and Hubbard. Wallace (LLW, 155–56) recounts in outline Elson's conversations, "when George and I were alone," about "Indians that had starved to death, or had barely escaped starvation," as well as the Indian beliefs about loons and calamity. Hubbard's unpublished diary for September 12 indicates that Wallace relayed these stories, but that Hubbard expressed skepticism about their import. On September 14, the day before he decided to turn back, Hubbard notes, "George and I have decided that we must not start this way home before freezing-up time. Might get caught again by bad winds. Better freeze on the George River with the Indians . . . then snowshoe clear out." But Hubbard had not yet heard George's starving stories firsthand; and knowing as we do George's persistent concern, it seems that his assent to Hubbard's freeze-up plans must have been half-hearted at best, and that Hubbard's lying awake for so long that night was a result, in part, of his own growing recognition of George's true feelings.

11: UP AGAINST IT FOR SURE

See LH and DW (September 15–20) and LLW, 162–78.

Wallace's published account of the decision to turn back and the frustrating period of waiting on Windbound Lake is particularly full. He records in detail many of the conversations that passed between the men, and speaks with conviction of the growing bonds of friendship, especially between himself and Hubbard.

12: GEORGE'S SECRET

For the return march from Windbound to Disappointment, see LH and DW (September 20–October 6) and LLW, 178–206.

George's fear of starvation began to grow before either Hubbard or Wallace fully comprehended the possibility. That was perhaps only natural, for Elson had lived close to the country for many years, and knew far better than they the difficulties of living off the land. For his saving the caribou hoof, see LLW, 110; for Hubbard and Wallace laughing over the caribou skin, LLW, 125. Although Elson, by nature, would not have spoken easily about the reticence of all three men to discuss the threat of starvation, he was quite aware of the dynamics. Our treatment of them here derives in part from his account of the last portion of the trip, where he remembers telling the boys "it was no use trying to keep it [the threat of death] to ourselves any longer." (GE 1903, 292–93, 294–95) Wallace, too, describes the same dynamic of being willing to admit the dangers only after they had passed—specifically, after Hubbard caught so many fish at Lake Mary on the way home. (LLW, 189)

Wallace notes Hubbard's despair at not being able to remember Mrs. Cruikshank's first name in LLW, 203; Hubbard's unpublished diary also mentions it (October 4). Interestingly, the diary also substantiates Wallace's contention that the men's hunger pangs were at their height during the earlier stages of starvation, subsiding as the situation became worse. Hubbard's most obsessive entries appear in mid-September, on Windbound Lake; they subside along the return trip until he makes his big catch of fish and is eating again. Then the diary returns to the subject, as in the September 28 outfit list for a "nice easy trip" with Mina:

> Flour, hard tack, baking powder, salt, sugar, molasses, syrup, pickles, onion, potatoes, raisins, currants, figs, chocolate, coffee, tea—dried milk, evaporated cream, rice oatmeal, corn crisp, apples, prunes, baked beans, canned pudding, canned white label soup, red pepper, jam marmalade, lard, fat pork, bacon, pea meal, etc. I'll cook such dinners as 1) a chicken boiled with rice, thickened with flour to make gravy, biscuit dropped into batter. Serve boiled sweet potatoes and bannock. Follow with, say, canned plum pudding and hard sauce, coffee, cheese, toast, eggs (scrambled), bacon, chocolate. Rainy night dinner—cooked in tent on primus—can white label soup—canned salmon warmed with cream and butter, biscuits, cheese, bannock, marmalade, coffee. Another dinner of fish chowder and George's Indian pudding.

13: CHOOSE

Wallace tells the story of the flight from Disappointment Lake through the mountain pass and down the "Big River," in LLW, 206–26. See also LH and DW (October 6–14).

At this point in the expedition, an additional source becomes available, the "Narrative by George Elson: Last Days Together," published in WW, 286–333. While presented in journal format (the first entry is dated October 9), the account is not actually a diary, but rather a compilation of sorts. From the style of composition, some of the later entries were apparently written on the day being described, but the October entries are written in past tense, a reconstruction that Elson seems to have assembled at some unspecified time after the event. Conceivably the account is based on a diary kept during the expedition, but if so, we have been unable to discover its whereabouts.

On certain points, Elson's recollections vary from Wallace's account, but by and large they jibe. As it happens, the most fascinating discrepancy among the several accounts arises not between Wallace and Elson but Wallace and Hubbard. The discrepancy is a simple one and it speaks volumes: Hubbard never once mentioned that he, Wallace, and George debated whether or not to stay on the "Big River." Yet both Wallace and Elson's accounts make clear how important that question was. Wallace (LLW, 199) places the first debate as early as October 2, even before the men finished the portage back to Disappointment Lake.

Evidently the issue troubled Hubbard so much, he could not bear to write about it in his diary. (A similar pattern occurs in other entries, where he takes note of his depression—"feeling blue"—only when his optimism had returned, a day or two later.) The most striking example of his determination simply to will the disagreement out of conscious existence appears in the entry for October 12. On that day—the very day Wallace told Hubbard it would be suicide to return to their original valley (LLW, 221)—Hubbard wrote: "Made about nine miles today. . . . Hope to leave stream tomorrow, and that makes us happy."

Elson indicates that while he sided with Wallace to the end, he still saw the merits of Hubbard's reasoning: "And the reason why I did not try and persuade [Hubbard] more than I did for us not to leave the Big River was, we thought perhaps there would be lots of places where we could not run our canoe in some wild rapids, and would have to carry our canoe. I knew the last two days how we were when trying to carry our canoe—also as we only know the river above there, of course, we did not know where the river ran to." (GE 1903, October 14) This passage may owe more to hindsight, however, and consideration for Mina Hubbard. Certainly George's dream sufficiently indicates his own worries. (Incidentally, we deduce George's worry about what whites might think of the Lord speaking to half-breeds from his omission of that point in his own report of the dream. There, he speaks only of "a man" who came to him.)

Hubbard and Wallace's idea of buying a farm together is indicated only by a single cryptic remark in Hubbard's unpublished entry of October 13: "Wallace suggests Orange Co. [County] as place for our farm. Good idea." Our conjecture that Hubbard was willing even to give up his full-time job with *Outing* is suggested by his earlier entries of September 19 and 28, where he complains of his career taking too much time from the important things in life, and notes that he has been reevaluating not only his past but his future relations with *Outing*.

14: "I'M BUSTED"

The march overland from the big river to Hubbard's breakdown is told in LLW, 227–42, and in LH, DW and GE (October 13–18).

George's recollections about the berries in his bowel movement come from perhaps the most unusual source available to us, an oral history by one John Blackned, a Cree Indian on Hudson Bay who knew George in later years. The history—recorded in 1965 by anthropologist Richard Preston of McMaster University and translated from the Cree by Anderson Jolly, whose wife's sister had married George—is garbled in many ways but convincingly vivid on certain points, including this one.

Wallace's published account makes it appear that Hubbard was the one who suggested he stay behind while Elson and Wallace made a dash for the flour and outside help. But in his unpublished diary, he refers to the idea as "my suggestion." To top matters off, George's account states that it was he who first came up with the plan, after deciding to "tell them what was in my mind (not about restaurants this time) but before it was too late. Seeing that death was just near . . ." (GE, October 17). Hubbard first opposed George's plan ("at first said it was no use of trying"), but then agreed it would be for the best.

The account of Wallace's all-night vigil (LLW, 241–42) ranks among his most vivid passages. We have relied on it heavily in re-creating the scene ourselves.

15: THE LOONS HAD A CALL LIKE THIS

Wallace describes the parting movingly in LLW, 243–248. His diary makes clear that all of them knew the chances of survival were touch-and-go: "It is a lost, forlorn hope. Whether we ever get through or not is a question and we may not find the flour. My only thought is for my dear sisters. . . . should I not return I now say to my dear Annie and Jessie, good-bye dear sisters and God be with you and prosper you. No man ever had truer or more loving sisters. I have neglected you sadly in the last few years and my only excuse is that I have taken little interest in anything since the death of my dear wife. . . . Remember me as the old brother of years ago who loved you."

George provides additional material in GE (October 17–18). His account is especially helpful in substantiating Wallace's claim that Hubbard charged him with writing the expedition account. George also adds the tantalizing detail that Hubbard told Wallace to do so "for Mrs. Hubbard."

Hubbard's own final entry is the man at his best. It is witness to patient suffering and reveals the generous spirit capable of inspiring tremendous exertions on the part of those who knew and loved him—Wallace, George and Mina.

Hubbard's short letter to Mina and his letter to Mr. King are included in the back pages of his journal, as noted. His letter to his mother and his failed attempt at writing a "long, long letter" to Mina have been removed from the diary, presumably by Mina herself. Wallace mentions the letter to Hubbard's mother as well as his friend's "evident attempt to write again to his wife" in LLW, 290.

Death can be described only in anticipation. Our account is drawn from Hubbard's own journal and from the likelihood of cardiac arrhythmias in the terminal stage of starvation.

16: HOW FAR TO THE FLOUR?

Wallace and George's journey to their own parting is told in LLW, 248–57 and in GE (October 18–20). The only material discrepancy between the two accounts concerns what George read out of his Book of Common Prayer when they parted. Wallace remembers vividly the ninety-first psalm; George, the sixty-seventh ("God be merciful unto us and bless us, and cause his face to shine on us. . . .") and a Thanksgiving prayer.

17: MAN PROPOSES

Wallace gives his agonizing account of wandering alone in LLW, 258–70, and, more briefly, in his letter to his sister as published in NYT 1904, Mar. 24:1–2.

Wallace's description of turning homeward was to have a significant impact on his own future. In a letter, written in December 1903, he explicitly states that "after walking up and down several times where I thought the camp must be I was at length compelled to give up the search [for Hubbard] and headed toward Grand Lake." As we shall see, because of the unexpected turn of events in the winter of 1904–05, Wallace's description of the ordeal, written at that time for LLW, is much more circumspect. There, he is careful to emphasize the possibility that he had passed beyond Hubbard's camp in his wandering, leaving it ambiguous as to whether he turned back in order to continue his search for Hubbard or to flee for his own life. George's account (GE, October 31), based on what he was told by the guides, indicates that Wallace never got beyond the brook just below Hubbard's tent before turning back.

18: YOU CAN'T LOSE ME

George's recollection (GE 1903, October 20–27) supplies the backbone of our narrative. He is most eloquent about getting across his unexpected river, not to mention monumentally understated about the effort involved: "Oh! but I was so proud of that raft, and talking to myself all the time, and telling myself what a fine raft it was. . . . I got across safe and without much trouble at me." No—hardly any trouble at all!

Wallace includes a number of valuable details, in LLW, 271–77, which George omitted. These include George's wrenching discovery that he was following his own tracks in a circle, as well as his wonderfully defiant remark to Grand Lake—"You can't lose me."

19: FAIR STARVED

Principal sources are LLW, 277–90 and GE (October 27–November 5).

Information about Harriet Goudie Blake's lineage is given by her son, Robert, in *Them Days* 2:2, 12–13. In the same volume, Wallace McLean writes about Donald. Now, we should note that "Uncle" Wallace, still alive at this writing, has a reputation around Northwest River for sparing no labor when it comes to providing the most vivid of colors for his stories—always, of course, in the interest of painting the true picture. Anyway, this is what Wallace McLean has to say about going trapping with Donald Blake in 1920:

> He was a strong man. . . . Uncle Donald could put a stove like that in his game bag. He put in two bags of flour, that's forty pounds each. He put in the rest of his supplies. There was his tent, stove, snowshoes, gun, axe, and whatever else he had. Now, t'was too heavy. He couldn't put it up on his back. He had to put it on something and get under it. He walked 50 or 60 miles around the river side like that. Some places over pumbly rock, in the muck, through woods and over fallen sticks. He mucked that from a place we calls Agru Lake to Seal Lake. He was out of practice, he said. Not as good as he used to be. Ten years out of practice, so he said he couldn't carry as much as he used to. His load was about 230 pounds.

None of the men who rescued Wallace left an account of their trip up the Susan, so we have relied primarily on those relayed by Wallace and Elson. Young Gilbert Blake does play an important role in the 1905 expeditions, however, where his wide-eyed youthfulness is made evident.

20: BITTERBERRIES

For George's recovery and journey to New York, see GE (October 28, 1903–May 28, 1904). For his worries, as well as his remark about Hubbard's bravery, see October 28 and 30. For Baikie's beliefs, see November 5.

Wallace details his struggle to bring Hubbard's body home in LLW, 295–336. His diary does not continue beyond October 18, but on November 7 he began a second journal, back at Northwest River. Both the new journal and LLW demonstrate how much his life revolved around recovering Hubbard's body. Wallace himself admitted that the concern became "almost an obsession." (LLW, 303)

It may be worth noting that the treatment given Wallace's frostbitten feet after his rescue is, to modern physicians and first-aiders, a medical horror. Once a body part is frozen, all effort must be made not to subject it to physical trauma after thawing and, above all, not to allow it to refreeze. Wallace, of course, warmed his feet at his rescuers' camp and then undoubtedly refroze them on his long march out to Grand Lake. That Wallace survived without losing his feet is a marvel; how he managed to do so is anybody's guess.

As for George Elson's ability to find gear under eight feet of snow, it was a truly remarkable accomplishment. Apparently he had an almost photographic memory for locations. It was certainly not ordinary woodcraft, for both Blake and McLean, veterans of the bush, were astounded by the demonstrations. On the dogsled trip home, George found to his surprise that his reputation had preceded him along the coast, word having been passed from settlement to settlement.

Wallace did not get word of Hubbard's death to the *Virginia Lake* for its last trip to Newfoundland in 1903. As a result, the New York papers speculated from time to time about Hubbard's whereabouts. Caspar Whitney, in his usual blunt manner, discounted the rumors of trouble. Hubbard was "no tenderfoot," he remarked, "but a man of experience and resource . . . [who] had carte blanche as to his route and itinerary, and I should not be greatly disturbed if I did not hear from him until the beginning of next year." (See NYTrib 1903, Oct. 23:9 and Nov. 14:9 and 25:3; also NYT, Nov. 1:4; Nov. 14:9.) A condescending letter offering assistance, written by the self-promoting explorer Willard Glazier, appears in NYTrib, Dec. 25:10. This evidently inspired Whitney to announce in the February 1904 issue of *Outing* (43:599) that Hubbard was surely "all safe and sound," and in no need of assistance from any "professional and unemployed 'explorers.' "

Unfortunately for Whitney, it was only days after the *Outing* went to press that Wallace's first telegrams appeared on the front pages of the January 23 papers. For the exact texts, see NYS 1904, Jan. 24:1. Since these brief messages were relayed by dogsled courier to the telegraph station at Chateau Bay, and then wired to Quebec City, there was some confusion over their authenticity. One of Hubbard's personal friends, D. J. O'Keefe, even publicly questioned both the telegrams and Caspar Whitney's intention of ever sending a rescue expedition (NYH, Jan. 24:8). O'Keefe and Mina Hubbard had been organizing their own trip, to be led by William Binion, a physician familiar with the Labrador coast. Whitney's response to O'Keefe is in NYH, Jan. 26:5.

On March 19 a few papers printed a more detailed (but still garbled) version of the tragedy, cabled from Quebec. It was not until March 24 that a long letter from Wallace appeared, again on the front pages, which provided the first detailed accounts of events. The most complete version may be found in NYT, Mar. 24:1–2.

For Wallace and Elson's arrival in New York City, see the New York papers of May 17 and May 28, including NYT 1904, May 17:2 and 28:5; NYTrib, 17:7 and 28:7; NYH, 17:8 and 28:14; NYS, 17:1 and 28:8; NYW, 17:7 and 28:14. It is the *New York Times* that notes Wallace's remarks about the lack of a shotgun and Hubbard being overtrained, and specifically that they were made "just before he left the pier."

Our reconstruction of the memorial service at Mount Repose is partly conjectural. The local newspaper, the *Rockland County Times*, has only a brief paragraph (1904, June 4:1), noting that the ceremony was brief, and that Hubbard's grave was located "in the new part of the cemetery, high up on the hillside." We assume, but do not know, that Whitney was among the "several personal friends" at the service; we assume, also, that Mina Hubbard was there, although women of the era did not always accompany the casket to its interment. That she did, however, seems to us highly likely because no other service was held at a church or residence, and because, as subsequent events demonstrated, she was extremely reluctant to part with her husband—even with his mortal remains.

High Tor still overlooks the Hudson, and the interested reader who visits it on a fine summer afternoon, as we did, will see the river flowing majestically in the distance, and will discover under the shade of a cedar tree three plaques commemorating the remarkable events—both of 1903 and 1905—that were set in motion by a man with a boyish grin and boundless dreams.

21: TRUST ME

Only George's remarkable letter survives (in the collection of Dillon Wallace III) to tell of the train ride south in December 1904. Its hasty scrawl and breakneck composition clearly indicate Elson's anguish. For more on the art of pulling fox hearts, and a wealth of other trapping lore, see Martin Hunter, *Canadian Wilds* (Columbus, 1907), 195–98.

22: THE PURPLE VALLEY

The period between expeditions, from May 1904 to June 1905, remains the most mysterious and least explored of the Hubbard saga. The few historians recounting the tale invariably devote only a paragraph or two to the events of these crucial months. Our own search has turned up little more than scraps of information; and acquiring even these has required techniques akin to what cod fishermen on the Labrador refer to as "jigging": dropping an unbaited barb into the dark waters and then jerking it up and down on the chance of hooking some passing quarry. Yet the scraps do make the outline of the story clear.

Searching the North Adams, Massachusetts, Public Library for information on Mina Hubbard's friend and counselor, the Reverend James E. C. Sawyer, we were astonished to learn that Mina herself had spent the fall of 1904 attending high school in Williamstown (NAT 1905, Jul. 6:2, Nov. 10:8, 15:8). The vivid colors of the surrounding countryside evidently impressed her (MBH, July 19). The intensity of her adoration for Laddie and her grief over his death are recurring themes of her diary. Her response to Wallace's January 1904 telegram from Labrador is mentioned in a contemporaneous letter of James Compton, Hubbard's cousin, written to Annie Wallace (collection of Dillon Wallace III); see also NYW 1904, May 28:14. For Mina's habit of praying to Laddie, see her letter to Wilfred Grenfell, March 22, 1907 (Grenfell Papers, Box 7, Yale University Archives, Sterling Memorial Library); for her writing letters to Laddie as a form of therapy, MBH, October 18. Mourning dress and etiquette for widows is described in such contemporary guides as Mrs. Burton Kingsland, *Correct Social Usage* (New York, 1903), 146–48; and Abby Buchanan Longstreet, *Social Etiquette of New York* (New York, 1887), 258–68. That Mina strictly observed such customs is clear from HH 1905, June 13:2, which refers to her as wearing "deep mourning."

Casual readers of Wallace's *Lure of the Labrador Wild* will no doubt find his account quite admiring of Hubbard. While no direct record survives of Mina's reaction upon first reading the manuscript, later reports make clear she was upset by it: "Mrs. Hubbard did not like some statements in Wallace's book" (NYTrib 1905, June 13:1); "she has not been satisfied with the apparent variance in the diaries of the two men" (NYW 1905, June 13:3). Wallace's friend Alonzo McLaughlin is specifically quoted as saying that her displeasure arose from Wallace's questioning Hubbard's "judgment when he [Wallace] said that the party had plunged into the region without any definite knowledge of how or where they were going, and that 'without provisions.' " (NYTrib, June 13:1). In fact, these opinions were expressed not in the *Lure,* but in Wallace's earlier letter to his sisters, printed in the first news accounts of 1904 (NYT, Mar. 24:1–2). Prostrated as she was by grief at that time, Mina apparently did not take notice of Wallace's comments, for in October 1904 she amicably signed the contract with Wallace for the manuscript. (The contract survives in the collection of Dillon Wallace III, although we do not know whether Mina demanded that Wallace return her $250 advance.) Once embittered, however, she presumably returned to the earlier letter, where she found even more to disturb her. By June 1905 the enmity was so great that she could refer to Wallace as "infinitely my husband's inferior in every way." (Letter to William Cabot, June 2, 1905, Cabot Collection, National Anthropological Archives, Smithsonian Institution, Washington, D.C.)

23: HARD CHOICE

Dillon Wallace III recalls his father telling him he wrote the *Lure* while staying at a cousin's farm near Adams, Massachusetts. Wallace and his collaborator, Frank Barkham Copley, apparently worked off steam between writing sessions by going out to chop wood. For Wallace's acknowledgment of Copley's help, see the front matter of LLW.

In our reconstruction of events, we have assumed that the manuscript Wallace showed to Mina was virtually identical to the one finally published. That assumption deserves a little qualification. Although Wallace would not have had enough time to make substantial changes, he may have added a few glosses. The passage near the book's end, where he talks about how "only men that have camped together . . . can in any degree comprehend the bond of affection and love" (LLW, 339), strikes us as an addition that may well have been written after the falling out with Mina. It is also interesting, as a measure of Wallace's restraint and diplomacy, to compare the letter he first wrote to his sisters ("We plunged madly into the interior of an unknown country . . . with almost no provisions") with his concluding defense of Hubbard in the *Lure:* "The critics have said that Hubbard was foolhardy, and without proper preparation he plunged blindly into an unknown wilderness. I believe the early chapters of this narrative show that these criticisms are unfounded. . . ." (LLW, 337) There were, of course, vocal critics of the expedition (see, for example, *Forest and Stream*, April 2 and 9, 1904); but given the bitter dispute that Mina began and the remarkable hold Leonidas Hubbard exerted on both Mina and Wallace, even from beyond the grave, it seems reasonable to suppose that the critic Wallace felt most sensitive about, consciously or not, was himself.

It may be worth noting, too, William Cabot's response to critics of the Hubbard expedition, which he published in WW, 22–26. While Cabot indeed had harbored his own private doubts about the party, he pointed out, accurately enough, that even Indians and professional trappers who were at home in the bush faced starvation from time to time. "Few are the travellers of the north who have not chanced upon the day when a 'trivial happening' would have led to a tragic end, and they who have known the northern way can best understand how unkind were the happenings which bore against unflinching Hubbard and his companions from the time they resolved to retreat."

The larger public received *The Lure of the Labrador Wild* enthusiastically. The *New York Times* noted that Wallace had "told the story simply and without unnecessarily harrowing details, its mistakes not glossed over, and its actual heroisms not painted too vividly." (1905, Feb. 18:98) In the first year of publication, the book went through six printings.

As for George's encounter with Mina, there is a great deal we simply do not know. George must have arrived in Williamstown on December 13 or 14, but there is no record of how long he stayed or where he lodged. (Our guess is with Dr. Sawyer—see NAT 1905, Nov. 24:5.) More important, did George ever meet with Wallace during his stay? Did he have the chance to read Wallace's manuscript? Did the two of them ever discuss Mina's antagonism? The answer may have been no on all three counts, but that again is speculation. We base our account of George's encounter with Mina on what, in light of subsequent events, must have passed between them, and from bits of evidence in other documents. For George's need—even compulsion—to retell the story of the 1903 trip, see Pierre Berton, *The Wild Frontier* (Toronto, 1978), 188–89. For Mina's tendency to blush easily when upset, see MBH, Nov. 13. George's published narrative makes it clear that he supported Wallace in the debate with Hubbard on whether to stay with the Beaver River. His account also makes clear that he passed along to Mina the conclusions of Allen Goudie and Duncan McLean (gleaned from tracks in the snow) that Wallace never passed beyond the brook near Hubbard's tent on the Susan (GE 1903, Oct. 31).

As her letter of June 2 to William Cabot indicates, Mina had the idea of writing a book about her husband's expedition before she thought of undertaking a trip of her own. It was not until January 1905 that she decided to return to Labrador herself (WW, 50). Other historians have assumed that she made her plans public, but the New York newspapers of June 1905 show clearly that Wallace left for the north completely unaware of her intentions. For Wallace's trip to Missanabie (after George wrote that he had matrimonial plans), see the somewhat garbled account in NYTrib, Apr. 25:3, as well as NAT, July 6:2. Newspaper accounts, as well as Wallace's 1905 diary, make it clear that while George admitted to Wallace in Missanabie that he was not getting married, he remained silent about teaming up with Mrs. Hubbard. (HH 1905, June 2:1, and DW 1905, June 1.)

24: HEADED NORTH

For Dillon Wallace's preparations in 1905, see NYTrib, Feb. 26:6 and Apr. 25:3; NYW, Apr. 26:16, and the editorial page of the Brooklyn *Daily Eagle*, April 25. These mention Wallace's interest in mineral riches as well as his recruitment of Richards and Easton. Wallace, in joking about his age, was taking note of a controversy begun by Dr. William Osler of the Johns Hopkins University, who had announced his belief that "a man can accomplish nothing material after he is forty." (NYTrib, Feb. 25:6) The press had been gleefully quoting the outraged reactions of older doctors, senators and other noteworthies. For Peter Stevens' arrival in New

York, see LLT, 5, 37. As for the expedition outfit, Wallace generally followed Hubbard's lead, but he took care to purchase a good gill net in New York. In addition to rifles and pistols, he also included a double-barreled 12-gauge shotgun. As for food, he ordered substantially larger amounts of flour (300 pounds compared with Hubbard's 120), salt pork (298 pounds versus 30), and cornmeal, as well as an emergency supply of pemmican, an Indian concoction made of dried beef, sugar, and raisins, all suspended in tallow.

For Mina's travel from Williamstown to Bewdley to Halifax, see her letters to William Cabot, May 8 and June 2, 1905, with the Cabot papers. The importance Mina placed on keeping her plans a secret is made clear by her good friend James Sawyer, in NAT 1905, July 6:2. That she had to proceed carefully is further made clear from NYTrib 1905, June 13:1, which notes that she obtained funds for the trip from Alonzo McLaughlin, Wallace's attorney friend and also executor of Hubbard's estate. Apparently she may have told McLaughlin she was going to Labrador, but only for the purpose of gathering information about her husband's 1903 expedition. Mina's first impressions of Job Chapies and Joe Iserhoff appear in WW, 51–52, as does a description of her outfit, 53–54.

25: BRICKS WITHOUT STRAW

This chapter marks the appearance of a new primary source: the vivid diary of Clifford Easton. The diary is rich in detail and fresh-faced innocence. For more on the Wallace party's trip north, see HH 1905, June 2:1 and NAT, June 7:6.

Paradoxically Easton's remarkable encounter in St. John's harbor receives only one line in his diary: "Richards and I had serious adventure with iceberg." Evidently he was too embarrassed to record the details there. Wallace gives a slightly longer account, noting that a large section of the berg broke off and almost swamped Richards' boat, leaving both boys "much scared, particularly Richards." (DW, June 11) Easton did write his parents about the adventure, however, and a garbled account in the newspapers supplies additional details, which we have drawn upon to round out our reconstruction. (NYTrib 1905, Nov. 16:16)

Mina Hubbard's "interviews" with the Halifax press created a notable stir, both in that city and in New York. Caspar Whitney, writing in the August 1905 issue of *Outing* (46:620), informed readers that "a sensational dispatch from Halifax has been going the rounds of the press, quoting Mrs. Hubbard . . . as charging Mr. Wallace with practically causing the death of her husband. . . . [U]ntil I hear the infamous charge from her own lips I cannot bring myself to believe that Mrs. Hubbard could harbor, much less make public, such outrageously cruel and false accusations." Harbor—yes. Make public—not that we can find. Whitney's impressions to the contrary, Mina seems never actually to have disclosed to any newspaper her fiercely held suspicions. Nonetheless, many of her friends and Wallace's associates were aware of them, and when reporters discovered Mrs. Hubbard's presence in Halifax, her hostile silence about Wallace and the admission that she was leading an expedition to Labrador, this information relayed along the wires to New York goaded enterprising reporters there to tease fuller details from Edgar Briggs, Wallace's editor for *The Lure of the Labrador Wild*, and from Alonzo McLaughlin. Ironically, then, it was Wallace's own friends who supplied most of the details about the rivalry, believing that Mrs. Hubbard had already given out her version of the story. Eventually even Hubbard's family was drawn into the argument, taking Wallace's side. (See *Outing*, 46:759 and NYTrib 1905, July 22:11.) The succession of stories can be found in HH, June 2:2; 13:1; 15:8; 17:1; NYTrib, June 11:1; 13:1; NYS, June 11:1; NYW, June 13:3; New York *Evening Journal*, June 13:3; St. John's (Newfoundland) *Evening Herald*, June 19, unpaged.

Wallace, in St. John's when the story broke, had to piece it together primarily from a few one-paragraph dispatches in the *Evening Herald*, a fairly primitive tabloid in St. John's, consisting primarily of advertisements for patent medicines. According to the *Herald*, Wallace's friends in New York had declared "that the widow's suspicions that Hubbard's chum is responsible for his death are absolutely groundless." The (false) impression that Mina had publicly accused Wallace left him to vent his wrath in his diary (June 14), noting his intention to have Mina arrested for criminal slander. Annie Wallace, passing through Halifax on her way home, also forwarded clippings to Wallace from the Halifax papers.

In the midst of this high suspense, comedy intervened—as it inevitably must have, once the *Virginia Lake* and the Reid-Newfoundland Company entered the scene. The hundred or so fishermen who overloaded the steamship at Brigus were there due to another Reid-Newfoundland promotional scheme. At the next stop, in Harbor Grace, a *second* crowd lined the wharf, bags packed and ready to go. Captain Parsons angrily informed the local ticket agent that the ship was already filled to the rails. To compound the confusion, His Excellency the Governor of Newfoundland chose that moment to appear at the wharf on an inspection tour, at which he blithely greeted the crowd and praised the conditions of the local harbor as being second to none, "in certain respects." The governor having departed, however, the fishermen on shore waxed unruly, hanging on to the *Virginia Lake*'s mooring lines and refusing to let it depart. The b'ys had *bought* their tickets and they wanted aboard—that's what! Matters seemed at an impasse until Richards, among others, pulled out his trusty "little hatchet" (CE, June 11 ff), which he used to help cut the hawsers, allowing the *Virginia Lake* to steam out to sea. For details, see the St. John's *Evening Telegram*, June 17, headlined THE GOVERNOR AT HARBOR GRACE/LABRADOR BUNGLE, and concluding, with perhaps some hyperbole, that the ensuing imbroglio had been "the greatest bungle of the century." (The century, of course, was only five years old.) For H. A. Morine's beleaguered rejoinder, see June 19.

26: CHRIST SHALL GIVE THE LIGHT

The relevant journal entries are from June 21–27; see also LLT, 9–17, and WW, 50–55.

While the two expeditions traveled together from Rigolet to Northwest River, the participants wrote diary entries that reveal not only their own doings but their attitudes toward their rival adventurers. Readers who consult the official accounts, however, will discover none of this: Neither Dillon Wallace's *Long Labrador Trail* nor Mina Hubbard's *A Woman's Way Through Unknown Labrador* ever once mention their respective rivals.

Indeed, such were Wallace's feelings that his daughter Ann never had any idea when growing up in the 1920s and '30s that her father had a competitor in 1905. In 1941 she spent Thanksgiving with the family of Leonidas Hubbard's sister, Daisy Williams; there she first learned that the Hubbard clan thought Mrs. Hubbard a bit eccentric, to say the least. But the topic of Mina's expedition never came up, and it was only years later that Ann Wallace came upon *A Woman's Way* and discovered that Mina Hubbard had been in Labrador in 1905! In fact, Daisy had publicly defended Wallace at the time, in a letter to the newspapers. For the text, see *Outing* 46:759–60, or NYTrib, July 22:11.

As might be expected, the diaries and letters written in 1905 are more candid. Mina Hubbard's entries (MBH, June 21–27) are vivid and full, although apparently she could not bear to write about her brief encounter with Wallace aboard the *Harlow*. She did make clear her anxiety, on the voyage up from Halifax, about Wallace's whereabouts, and recorded George's late-evening knock, his subsequent news, and the fact that she "trembled like [a] leaf for an hour or more. . . ." (MBH) June 21 contains her somewhat curious comparison of Stuart Fraser with Laddie ("none so beautiful as my Laddie, none so loved as he").

The diary also has one puzzling reference to a conversation or communication that Mina apparently had in April with Wallace. "When I got up about six they and their outfit all on board," she reported June 22. "Disgusted at first and mad remembering promise of April 3rd, but after reflected that one cannot always have the earth and one cannot always have people stand fast at the critical moment. Only a few, a very few will do that." What Wallace may have promised—or what Mina thought he had promised—remains a mystery.

Determined to prove her suspicions about the 1903 expedition, Mina sought out Allen Goudie, Donald Blake and Duncan McLean (the men who had rescued Wallace), once she arrived in Kenemish. "Talked with Allen a little tonight," she reported (June 23), "and asked him about their finding Wallace. He says, as did George, that they found Wallace by tracking him in the snow. He had, Allen says, a good fire and a good bed of boughs, and was quite able to walk. They also tracked him to within 200 yards of the tent. There was no trace of his having wandered about looking for the tent. He simply turned round and went back. He had never left the river. Allen said he and Donald said to each other when they saw it that it just looked as if he did not want to get to the tent. He still had some of the flour when they found him. He was not at all in the condition he describes."

Letters home, digests of which found their way into newspapers, supply additional details of the rival expeditions. Wallace tells of meeting George, and of Mrs. Hubbard's "stony stare, which, of course, was terrible to bear," in NYTrib, July 26:11. See also the valuable material in NAT, July 6:2, 7:6, 15:6, 24:8. For Mr. Gillis trying to scare George and his friends into taking care of Mina, see MBH, June 17.

27: TRAIL OR RIVER?

Relevant diary entries run from June 27 to June 29; see also LLT, 17–28, and WW, 55–63.

By tracing the path of the two expeditions on a topographical map, it becomes evident that on the night of June 27 they camped opposite each other on Grand Lake. Although Wallace expressly notes that he looked across the lake, just discerning "the dim outlines" of the far shore, Elson's campfire was not visible. The three-mile distance, with the night mist gathering, was enough to obscure the view.

For Richards' geological reports, see LLT, 289–308. It may be worth noting that, while George warned Mina that porcupine was no good cooked at that time of year, he and the other men ate their quarry. Wallace records Easton's skepticism about porcupine both for supper and again for breakfast, although for some reason Easton's journal indicates he found the breakfast specimen "very good." A letter to Caspar Whitney from Wallace puts the best face on his being passed by Mrs. Hubbard, reporting that "we permitted George and other Indians and Mrs. Hubbard to pass us on the Nascaupee. They stopped at portage, but evidently could not find trail and went on straight. We landed, and Pete found trail at once, and we are on it. They will evidently try another route. We are on the right one." (NYS, Aug. 23:2)

28: CLIMBING HILLS OF WATER

The relevant dates are June 29–July 3; see also WW, 63–81. The material and its treatment are straightforward.

29: THE WAY SHE WAS

The relevant dates are July 4–16; in WW see 82–106.

On most days, George's entry in his journal amounted to a paragraph or two, though occasionally he wrote at greater length. Mina, on the other hand, had plenty of time for writing, as she generally did not paddle. Often her entries tell us more about what George was doing than his own. They could not, of course, penetrate his innermost thoughts, which we must deduce by inference, as in his reaction to her "All aboard" summons (July 6). But deeper issues arise in our attempting to uncover George's inner emotions, which we have discussed at length in the epilogue.

Trail etiquette would have suggested that the party swap an item in return for the ax taken from Duncan McLean's tilt, but Gilbert Blake expected to be back before trapping season to tell Duncan of the borrowing.

30: SWEAT, GROAN, AND STRAIN

The journal dates are July 1–August 4. See also LLT, 29–83.

Easton's diary provides many of the details for this chapter's narrative. For his problems with laxative tablets, see July 1, 18 (Pete's balsam gum), 29, and August 2 ("nothing short of dynamite"). Stanton's "ant"-ics are noted on July 3; the crayon drawings July 16; Pete's ideas on the fox barking, July 29. For Wallace's brief loss of temper, see July 27; for the caribou chases, July 27 and 28.

Easton is a particularly valuable observer because, while he never wavers in his loyalty to Wallace, neither is he afraid to be critical. More than once he remarks that a faster pace by the group would be preferable (July 7, 9, 10, 15, 16). During the long rainy spell (July 20), he notes, "Again I wish to state that I do not wish to criticize Mr. Wallace for he is a much older man than I and has had the experience of his former trip, but were I leader of this party we should utilize every moment now wet or dry, and make very early starts, this would allow us to make camp early and would give the men something to look forward to during the day. . . ." Yet despite the slow progress, on August 2, Easton noted "that I like and respect Mr. Wallace more every day. He is a man of rare personality and I count myself lucky in being under him."

For Wallace's estimate of how the men were working out, see his letter of July 23 to Whitney, NYS 1905, Aug. 23:2. Among his recruits, only Richards, apparently, had any experience running rapids (LLT, 112–13). Even Pete was used to portaging around such cascades (CE, July 13). For Elson's message on the sled runner, see CE (August 4). From the signs at the tilt—broken branches, footprints—Pete estimated that the Hubbard party had a lead of about ten days on Wallace; in fact, the advantage was about three weeks.

31: "YOU HAVE JUST ABOUT HAD US CRAZY"

See GE and MBH (July 15–28); also WW 108–32.

Mina's talk with George about his boyhood and the habit of keeping a diary took place July 20 and is noted in both journals. (For Mina losing her glove, see MBH, June 29.) George could be quite careful about how he recorded material: In his account of the caribou chase that so strongly affected Mina, he crossed out his having "killed" the caribou, replacing it with the less emotional "shot." We have already called attention to his evasion, "tremble about so and so" (July 26).

32: THE VERGE OF SUCCESS

The relevant journal entries are July 30–August 6; also WW, 133–57.

Pierre Berton, in *The Wild Frontier*, 203, was the first to point out Mina's ambivalence about her expedition—wanting to succeed, yet also feeling that it might be better *not* to, since her husband had not. The ambivalence is much more clearly stated in her journal than in the published narrative. Climbing the hill to see Michikamau, her book says only that the heat was "stifling"; in the diary she says that she "should strangle on the way up with heat and flies and effort and most of all thoughts." Earlier that day (August 1), she included a revealing passage about fishing:

> While men were portaging, fixed up my fishing rod, feeling ashamed that I had not yet used it. Was a little afraid I had my reel on upside down, or something like that. This one thing about me my husband could not understand, that I did not love fishing. He tried to teach me, but though I loved to be with him on lakes and streams, I could not care so very much for fishing. Made a few casts while men were away but somehow, though I have felt so often what a shame it is that I have not fished, I almost hated that rod and my own attempts at using it; in my heart grew heavy all the time with the thoughts that came. We were nearing Michikamau now, too, and instead of feeling most glad about it, I was growing more and more to dread the thought of seeing it.

For Mina's dream, which reflects similar ambivalence, see MBH (July 23); for her reflections about the male ptarmigan who might wish to join his loved ones in death (August 5).

Similarly Mina underplays the emotion involved for both her and for George in the matter of the missing brandy. The book makes a humorous joke out of it—the men were so shocked by her escapade that they supposedly drank the entire bottle (132). The journal (August 1) makes it clear that a few ounces were left, and that George somewhat uncomfortably made the suggestion of saving the remnant for medicine.

We use George's spelling of "hep-hep-oh-ray" (GE, August 2); for the conversations and Indian lessons on August 6, we depend on Mina's full account (August 6) and on the vocabulary of Cree terms Mina lists at the end of her journal. The account of her imitating George's *"Nekupetan anganscen"* is in MBH (July 14).

33: REGULAR CONSPIRATORS

The relevant dates are August 4–20. See also LLT, 84–100.

Wallace's decision to split the party was perhaps the hardest of the expedition. Because it involved an evaluation of his companions' relative strengths and weaknesses, and because it eventually created temporary controversy in the newspapers, his public account in LLT does not provide many of the details found in Easton's private journal. When Richards returned to New York, some press reports claimed that Wallace had sent back the "dead wood" in his party; no doubt Wallace, wishing to be diplomatic, did not later dwell on the problems that he and Easton often discussed.

More specifically, LLT places the first discussion about splitting the expedition as being on August 12. In fact, Wallace had been considering the option even before he began the trip. In his letter of June 26 to Whitney (NYTrib, July 26:3), he noted, "I may not be able to get out until winter with dogs. In fact, that is what I believe I shall do. However, Richards will come out with one of the men in October and report." (LLT, 113, indicates that Wallace had promised Richards' mother that her son would return by October.) But these plans were not announced to the party, even on August 12; that day Easton reports only that Wallace told him personally that the two of them, in dire straits, might "take the 18' canoe with a little grub and push on at top speed. . . . This would leave the others to come on more slowly, hope it does not come to this but we must succeed somehow." Four days later Easton had a similar "confidential talk" with Wallace.

But it is only August 20 that Easton reports, "Mr. Wallace told me while we were alone this morning the time must come when the party must separate as he could not take five men on to Ungava. . . ." Later in the day he notes, "Mr. Wallace brought up the subject of separating party, all the men said they wished to go on. Decision to be left until we reach Michikamau." But on August 22, Easton noted, "Mr. Wallace and I had a long talk last night after others had turned in. . . . Mr.

Wallace has determined finally to send back three men should we be short of grub when we reach the river."

Easton was most sorry to be leaving behind Pete Stevens, with whom he had increasingly grown close. After the ax injury, Easton wrote, "Pete, that good friend of mine, confided to me upon reaching camp that he had been thinking of the results should I be laid up; and after relating several bloodcurdling stories of the dire results of axe cuts received by his friends, tried to persuade me to lay up for two days offering to carry my share. A fine fellow Pete." (August 14.) Upon parting at Michikamau, Stevens invited Easton to visit him in Minnesota.

Karl Friedrich Hieronymus von Münchausen served (according to *Brewer's Dictionary of Phrase and Fable*) "in the Russian army against the Turks, and after his retirement told extraordinary stories of his war adventures." For Easton's knowledge of the baron, see CE, August 2.

34: LONG CHANCES

The relevant dates are August 21–September 4. See also LLT, 101–120.

Again, Easton's diary proves invaluable for crucial details. As the other members of the party became more worried about their situation, they were more likely to confide in him than Wallace. For Pete's worries, see August 21–24; Richard's gloomy journal entry is noted on August 22; see also August 26. Easton also regularly recorded his late-night conferences with Wallace; on August 31 he noted, "Wallace and I waited up last night after the others had turned in and reviewed the situation fully. Arranged a plan which Wallace unfolded after breakfast this morning."

Pete Stevens' graphic account of seeing Michikamau is in LLT, 111–12. Wallace also makes clear how bad Stevens felt at not being able to go on. Easton's reference to his own version of Kipling may be found in CE, September 4.

35: TOP OF THE WORLD

The events of August 8 are described in MBH and GE, and in WW, 158–66.

George Elson's feelings toward Mina Hubbard constitute one of the most elusive, yet pivotal, elements of this narrative. Precisely because deeply felt emotions are at issue, Elson's own journal is of little help. We have discussed the larger issues of our reconstruction in the epilogue. As to the details, for Mina's love of color (and of flowers), see MBH (July 10, 11, 19, 25, and especially July 9). George and the other men not only brought her flowers, but George himself kept his own blooms pressed between the leaves of his journal. For the example of his being able to remember much later the day Mina laughed when he fell asleep smoking, see MBH (October 7). He records taking her picture, in GE (August 6).

36: A TOUCH OF ANGER

The relevant entries in GE and MBH are August 9–17; see also WW, 166–97.

Both Mina and George provide full accounts of their meeting with the Montagnais. George's entry, in fact, is one of his longest. For more information on the Coasters and Inlanders of the Hudson Bay region, see Richard J. Preston, "East Main Cree," in the Smithsonian Institution's *Handbook of North American Indians*, June Helm, ed. (Washington, 1981), 6: 196–207. John McLean has a brief account of the Hannah Bay Massacre in W. S. Wallace, ed., *John McLean's Notes of a Twenty-five Year's Service in the Hudson's Bay Territory* (Toronto, 1932), 99–101. For a more balanced discussion of the incident, see Richard Preston, "Eastern Cree Community in Relation to Fur Trade Post in the 1830s," *National Museum of Man, Mercury Papers in Ethnology* (1975), 324–35. For information on football customs, see Lucien M. Turner, *Indians and Eskimos in the Quebec–Labrador Peninsula* (Quebec, 1979), 90–93.

Further indication of George's sensitivity to controversial material can be seen in his argument with Mina Hubbard over the route to be taken if the expedition turned back. Mina details the confrontation in her own diary, but George's long entry stops at just the point where he goes to the river to talk with her. Or more precisely, the journal itself does not stop, but the next several pages have been cut or torn out. The journal resumes again with the entry for the next day, August 18.

As we indicate in the epilogue, we believe George cut this and other passages from his journal when he turned it over to Mina Hubbard after the conclusion of their trip. Evidently he felt that she ought not to read his discussion of the controversy; certainly this was the one time on the trip when the two disagreed openly. For an entirely different account of the difficulties half-breeds have experienced trying to stand up to whites in a white society, see the autobiography of Maria Campbell, *Halfbreed* (Toronto, 1973), a moving account of her youth during the mid-twentieth century.

37: WHOLE WORLD ON A TILT

The relevant entries are MBH and GE, August 18–27, and WW 198–235.

The George remains an impressive wilderness river, though these days dotted with the occasional fly-in fishing and hunting camp and less formidable to canoeists versed in modern whitewater techniques. George Elson, certainly, was struck by the fast current and turbulent waters:

> We run some wild rapids today. Some nearly too rough for such small canoes but those canoes surprised me what heavy swell they can stand. They are really good canoes and fast canoes to travel in, what makes me so scared of the rapids is on account of having a woman in the canoe and running the rapids because I don't want to get Mrs. Hubbard in any trouble if I can help it. Such a dear little lady and a sister to me. [August 23]

38: SHEPOO MATCHI

The relevant entries are DW and CE, September 4–29, and LLT, 121–45.

The chemistry between two people traveling together alone can, over the lengthening journey, become both symbiotic and quirky. Such was the case with Easton and Wallace. In some ways, they were a perfectly matched pair: each determined to push on—Easton content to be the subordinate, Wallace to lead. On the other hand, their respective diaries clearly reflect temperamental differences. Easton, the youth, tended to swing abruptly from high hope to abysmal despair. Wallace, ever the stoic, seemed to forge ahead unaware, often, of just how dicey his chances actually were. While Easton was fretting, as we have seen, about Wallace's diary-keeping and the wind on Michikamau, Wallace was cheerfully brushing up his literary techniques. "Next to a Labrador sunset," he wrote on September 5,

> What is more beautiful than a Labrador sunrise? The gorgeous colorings of morning melting away from orange to cream, then the sun in all his glory bursting upon the world beyond, over the waters of a placid lake, lighting the dark fir trees on the other shore, making silver of the lake that, since moonset, has been so dark and bottomless. And the crisp moss crackles under your feet—crisp where it is hoarfrost—and you take lung-deep breaths that you may inhale your full share of the clear bracing atmosphere that acts as a tonic to you as you come from your blanket and the tent.

(Somewhat anticlimactically, he ends by noting, ". . . but late hours by the cheerful evening coals entices one to the dissipation of sitting cozy and talking . . . so as usual I overslept.") Despite the two men's differences, they fell into a compatible rhythm pushing along the trail.

The horrendous capsize on September 29 followed the classic form for whitewater novices: The boat snags a rock, is turned broadside to the current and then has its upstream gunwale dragged under. What makes Wallace and Easton's mishap remarkable is the severity of the weather and the time the two men spent in the frigid water (Wallace estimates about half an hour). Easton, with the slenderer physique, was quite overcome by hypothermia. In such situations, when the body's core temperature drops below 95 degrees, shivering—the usual warming mechanism—begins actually to *decrease*, while both activity and thinking become sluggish. Below 90 degrees, muscular incoordination causes jerky movements and general comprehension declines, as indeed happened in Easton's case. Only Wallace's iron constitution got them through their scrape. The tale, which rivals Jack London's fictional "To Build a Fire," is rivetingly told in LLT, from which, in particular, we have borrowed Wallace's classic finale, including his laughing "with the very joy of living." For a more detailed version of the episode, see Wallace's account in Frederick A. Blossom, ed., *Told at the Explorers Club* (New York, 1935), 351–63.

39: SNARING THE SUN

The relevant entries are GE and MBH, August 27–October 22; DW and CE (September 29–October 22); LLT, 146–72.

To our knowledge, Bert Blake kept no journal during his trip with Mina Hubbard. We have drawn the materials used in his narrative from Mina and George's diaries. For his pay, see MBH (November 3); George also wrote with amusement (August 31) of Gilbert "having a great time in his sleep, bought a pair of boots, 4 forks, pork and tea." For Mina's dogsled adventures, see MBH (September 18 and 27); for the kayaks (September 30 and October 2); the tightrope (September 2); Gilbert's joke to Mrs. Hubbard about the black flies (July 24).

Our interpretation of George's behavior and feelings is spelled out in more detail in the epilogue. If his "Other Book" or these excerpts had survived, we might know a great deal more about his feelings. But even without them, the contours of his affections and conflicting feelings seem clear. For Mina's stockings spread out to dry, see MBH (August 28 and September 26); for her nearly walking out of her boots in the mudflats (September 1); the loan of the water bottle and caribou skin (August 30 and September 21); George and the Eskimo dances (September 9–10). The myth of the Indian boy snaring the sun is told in LLW, 139–40. "Will Your Anchor Hold?" by Priscilla Jane Owens, appears in more than one hymnal of the day; George wrote all four verses from memory, with only minor slips. We are by no means sure that the "new plans" Mina hatched with George on September 7 centered on a trip to England with her; this is only our best guess, based on a cryptic entry in MBH (November 1). It is perhaps ironic, and indicative of the misperceptions of both George and Mina, that on the day George noted with excitement the "great afternoon" he had spent with her and the late hours he had kept staying up thinking about it, Mina wrote perhaps the briefest entry of her entire diary: "Tried to write. Didn't do much. Couldn't work. Day very fine."

The journey of Wallace and Easton down the George River was filled with one harrowing episode after another, as even random excerpts from Easton's journal make clear: "Tracked one rapid and shot six, three of which I never expected to come out of alive. . . . Feet especially trouble me, have turned almost black in places. . . . these rapids cannot go on forever or they will let us through to China. . . . Both so benumbed we could hardly walk at camping time. . . . canoe leaks. . . . got worse and worse ending up in a howler with big rocks. . . . plunged over two [rapids], going in head first Wallace in bow of canoe lost in foam and spray and we barely got through without swamping, had it been a hundred yards longer would not have been here to write. . . . can't say I enjoy this work. . . . going like an express train. . . . This uncertainty to our position being very trying and going on mile after mile without seeming to get anywhere is enough to send a man crazy. . . ." The two men actually might have perished from the cold, had they not chanced upon an abandoned stovepipe lying along the upper George River; their own pipe had been washed away in the capsize, leaving their stove useless until they found the replacement. With their tent often frozen "stiff as a board," it was sorely needed. As for their welcome at the post, the Eskimo greeting *oks-utingyae,* means "You two be well." (In later years, Wallace used this greeting when he autographed copies of his book.)

All of the diaries provide accounts of the few days the rival parties spent together. Easton, least involved in the rivalry, provides an interesting commentary. "George came in and we talked over the trip," he notes (October 16); "seems like a nice fellow and glad to see us, never expected us to get through, even he and the other men who have shot rapids all their lives say the George is the worst river they were ever on. . . . Mrs. Hubbard very pleasant to me, talked a good deal over the trip." Mina, for her part, noted that "Easton said 'good-bye' in a very friendly way and said he was glad to have met me. I wonder why. Said it as if he meant it but not especially as if it were any compliment to me. It was rather funny. Some sort of curiosity I suppose."

Mina's moving entry for October 18—the anniversary of Laddie's death—speaks for itself, as do the pressed flowers that still remain in the final pages of George Elson's diary. And the name "Great Heart," which never did appear in Mina's published account was bestowed in her diary on October 7.

KODANSHA GLOBE

International in scope, this series offers distinguished books that explore the lives, customs, and mindsets of peoples and cultures around the world.